Hildebrand's Travel Guide

INDONESIA

Bhinneka tunggal ika

Diversity yet Unity – One People

HIPPOCRENE BOOKS INC., NEW YORK/N.Y.

ROGER LASCELLES, CARTOGRAPHIC AND TRAVEL PUBLISHER,
47 YORK ROAD, BRENTFORD, MIDDLESEX TW8 0QP. TEL.: 01-847 0935

Publisher
K+G, KARTO+GRAFIK Verlagsges. mbH

Schönberger Weg 15
6000 Frankfurt/Main 90
1. Edition 1985
Printed in West Germany
ISBN 3-88989-036-9

Distributed in the English Market by
Roger Lascelles, Cartographic and Travel Publisher,
47 York Road, Brentford, Middlesex TW8 0QP
ISBN 0-903909-37-5

Distributed in USA by
Hippocrene Books,
171 Madison Avenue/New York/N.Y. 10016
ISBN 0-07052-020-2

Author
Kurt G. Huehn

Photo Credits
Kurt G. Huehn,
Mauritius

Illustrations
Eckart Müller, Peter Rank, Manfred Rup

Maps
K+G, KARTO+GRAFIK Verlagsgesellschaft mbH

Translation
Jacqueline Baroncini

Lithography
Haußmann-Repro, 6100 Darmstadt

Type Setting
LibroSatz, 6239 Kriftel

Printed by
Schmitt+Läufer, 6300 Gießen

Contents

2

3

4

6

7

8

9

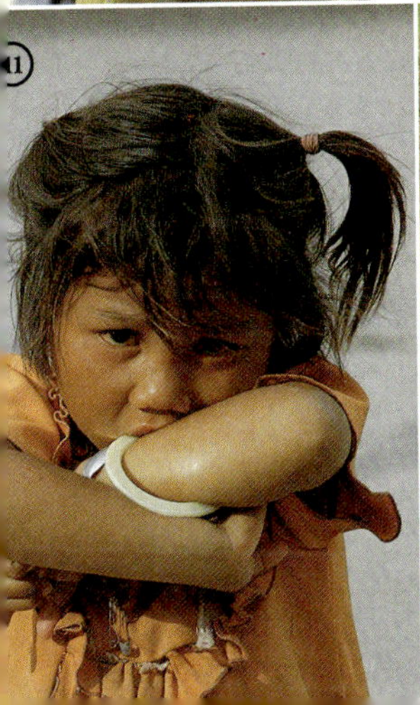

12

13

14

15

17

19

20

21

22

3

24

25

6

27

29

30

1

32

3

4

35

36

37

38

39

40

Captions

1. Delicious refreshment to some... hard work to others. Javanese market-women carry their heavy loads as far as 60 km (37 miles) from their villages to the markets. Profits are minimal and barely cover costs. The most they can earn in a day is between 1,500 and 2,000 rupiahs.
2. A girl of the Toba Batak tribe of Samosir Island in North Sumatra. Her jewellery for her wedding ceremony is provided by the bridgeroom and has often been in his family for generations.
3. There is always a great deal of curiosity on both sides when tourists meet the Papuan people who live in remote areas of Irian. The tribes are renowned for their hospitality. If ever a tourist gets the chance to return this friendliness he should definitely do so. It makes a change to be taking the initiative!
4. Most of the Batak people are Christians. All around Lake Toba in N. Sumatra people dress up in their "Sunday best" to go to church and on other special occasions. The Batak people in the South, however, are Moslem – less colourful clothes are worn to go to the mosque.
5. Central Java. Palace guards in the "kratons" (palace complexes) of Yogyakarta and Surakarta (Solo) are themselves of noble blood. They often act as guides and amaze many a tourist with 2 or more foreign languages. Slightly different versions of the "blankon" (the turban-like head covering) are found in the two towns.
6. South Nias. An old man of the Niah tribe in war dress. Around his neck he is wearing a "kalabubu" – a ring which is the sign of the successful head-hunter. For more than 30 years, however, there has been no head-hunting on Nias. Festivals and dances in South Nias have retained much of their old splendour.
7. The Danis of Irian Jaya live in and around the Baliem Valley. It's always a pleasure to meet these people who are of a calm and friendly disposition. To use the word "primitive" to describe the Danies seems very presumptious and misplaced when we consider their self-sufficient lifestyle and the way in which they have adapted to their surroundings. Especially in these days of mass technology it is worth bearing in mind that most tourists would be at a complete loss in the rainforests of Irian. How many would be capable of even a "primitive" existence?
8. Dayak tribes live in Kalimanton's interior. The blow pipe is used even today as a hunting weapon. The pipes are made out of a piece of hard wood, the centre of which is hollowed out with an iron rod. Normally, there is an iron spearhead at the end of the tube. Poison for the arrows comes from the "bohon Ipon" (a tree) and effects the nervous system.
9. Children are precious to the Dayak people – as they are to everyone in Indonesia. They are not only the pride of their parents but also their security in old age. Most children living on navigable stretches of Kali-

mantan's rivers attend school nowadays. In school they learn that their futures are in the towns. Sooner or later they make their way there, looking for well-paid jobs. Life in the towns is expensive, however, and there's usually very little money left over to send home to parents.

10. Water buffaloes are the "faithful friends" of the children of Toraja land in South Sulawesi. The children often see their "karbau" (Indonesian name for buffalo) being slaughtered as part of a festival for the dead. Besides sadness the children also show signs of pride that it's their bull which is to accompany the deceased into the next world.

11. Children's reactions to foreigners are a mixture of curiosity, embarrassment and fear.

12. Children – Indonesia's future. More than half the population is under the age of 15. Although most children now attend school, the chances of their finding work later are very slight.

13. West Java. The rice is usually planted by the women. Thanks to the fertile, volcanic soil of Java, rice can be harvested 2 or 3 times a year.

14. Java. Batik patterns, whether they're traditional or modern designs, are always done by hand. In contrast to "batik cap" (hand-stamped technique), true batik work, "batik tulis", involves applying wax by hand, using a special implement, a "canting".

15. Central Java. Patience is the name of the game when selling souvenirs. The souvenir-sellers rarely make their own wares – instead, they have them on commission.

16. Arts and crafts have always been based near the royal courts. In Kota Gede, south of Yogyakarta, the silversmiths produce articles for the tourists rather than the Sultan nowadays. Purchasers should bear in mind that the relatively low prices reflect the low wages of the smiths.

17. Tea growing in Indonesia has not been developed to the same extent as in Sri Lanka or India. Whole families work in the rural tea gardens, cultivating and picking. The green teas which are popular in Indonesia are the main product. Processing the leaves is, however, a co-operative concern. This system works – efficiency of the existing land available has increased. Consumption of tea has also increased: from 7,000 metric tons in 1972 to over 30,000 metric tons at present.

18. Rice terraces with their complicated system of irrigation have been in existence for over 1,000 years. Modern-day experts could only achieve the same effect with the aid of pumps, pipes and some form of energy.

19. The Borobudur was built in the 8th century A.D. It is the largest, most impressive manifestation of Buddhist faith in the world today. Several villages which had for years lived off the stream of visitors to the monastery on the hill were re-settled elsewhere when the Borobudur was included in plans for a monument park. The restoration of the Borobudur was completed on February 23rd, 1983 after 10 years work.

20. The temples of Prambanan apparently date back to the 9th century A.D. The central temple, Lara-Jonggrang, is 46 m (150 ft) high and is dedicated to the Hindu god, Shiva. Four staircases have been built pointing North, South, East and West. At the top of these staircases are four inner rooms each containing a statue. These statues represent Shiva, Shiva's wife Durga, his son Ganescha (the god with an elephant's head) and Shiva himself as a teacher.

21. South Sulawesi. Torajan Cult of the Dead – A different world.
The first graves to be formed in the rocks were built in Lemo in the 17th century.

22. The Tau-Tau embody the dead ancestors of Toraja nobility (makada). They watch over the graves and are seen as the second abode of the dead man's soul. Tau-Tau do not watch over the caves where the ordinary people are buried.
In the caste system which formerly existed in the Toraja land, society was made up of the higher nobility (tana bassi), the normal nobility (tana karurang), the ordinary people (bulo diappa) and slaves (tane kua kua). There were normally no caves for the bodies of dead slaves.

23. The mosque is the social centre of Muslim villages, towns and. Islam first arrived in the Malayan Archipelago in the 13th century as a result of the mainly friendly mediation of Arabic, Indian and Persian traders.

24. South Nias. Villagers perform a traditional war dance. Colonialists had a great deal of trouble and needed several attempts in order to overcome the resistance of these small valiant people.

25. North Sumatra. The wind instrument being played here produces a sound rather like that of bagpipes. It is one of the instruments in a "Gondang Band" – otherwise the band consists of several gongs, 1 or 2 lutes and a series of drums which harmonize. The Batak people are, however, best known for their tuneful singing.

26. Bali. On the day after the cremation the ashes of the deceased are carried in procession to the shore and delivered into the sea. The number of roofs which the tower contains indicates the rank of the dead man. Brahmans are given as many as 11 roofs while lower ranking people have to make do with 3 to 9. These rules also apply to the construction of the cremation towers which are similar in appearance.

27. North Bali. The Pura Beji (pura = temple) at Sangsit is typical of North Balinese "baroque". The temple is dedicated to the goddess of rice Dewi Sri. "Merus" (pagoda-like roofs) and shrines are usually not found in the temples of North Bali. The Pura Jagaraga in Sawan and the Pura Medruwe Karang in Kubutambahan are not far from the Pura Beji. They are, however, well-known for their representations (in relief) of cars, planes, bicycles etc.

28. The Ramayana is a Balinese dance drama. Usually what people see is the version of the dance developed for tourists. The origin of the dance is a Hindu epic which dates back to the 3rd century A. D. and India.

29. The Indonesian Tiger – approx. 300 still live on Sumatra, a maximum of 3 on Java and on Bali the species is extinct. In 1973 it was estimated that the Sumatran tigers numbered some 800. According to the World Wildlife Fund, 70% of all the Sumatran tigers have died out within the last eleven years. There is no hope now of saving the Javanese tiger – its fate will be the same as that of the subspecies which used to be found on Bali.

30. The paradoxure – a notorious chicken thief and feared as such by the people. Occupants of houses with corrugated iron roofs are often disturbed at night by the paradoxure scurrying across the roof.

31. The only kind of rhinosceros bird to be found in Irian is the Burang Tahun. The rhinosceros birds in Kalimantan, Sumatra, Siberut and on the other Indonesian islands often play a central role in the mythology of the local people.

32. Nowadays orang-utans are rarely found in the wild in Sumatra and Kalimantan. In the so-called rehabilitation centres orang-utans are prepared for a life in the wild. There are now four such centres in Sumatra.

33. The komodo lizard (Varanus komodoensis) is both a scavenger and a skilful hunter. They are thought to number over 2,000 at present.

34. Indonesia boasts more than 2,000 different types of orchid. Exportation takes this flowers all over the world.

35. Bali. The beaches at Sanur are safe for everyone (including non-swimmers) since the coral reef protects the bay from the dangers of the sea. The outrigger boats on the beach can be hired for excursions.

36./37. The underwater world is no less colourful than the beaches. A dive in and among Indonesia's coral gardens is sure to be an unforgettable experience.

38. Kalimantan's rainforest – 59% of Indonesian soil is covered by primeval forests. In Borneo's virgin forests there are still twice as many species of tree as in the whole of Africa. The wood industry is only allowed to fell trees which have a diameter of more than 60 cm (about 24 ins.). The felling of the trees is disrupting the natural formation of the rainforests. As a result of this many trees and plants which have only recently been re-cognised are dying out. The effect that the rainforests have upon the climate means that they are vitally important – not only to Indonesia but also to the whole world.

39. Indonesia has 300 volcanoes and of these some 125 are active. Apart from the destruction they cause, the volcanoes also make for fertile soil. The photo shows the Bromo in East Java. On the 14th and 15th days of the Kasada month the Tengger people make sacrifices to the god of the mountain, Dewa Kusuma. In the background the Batuk is easily recognis-able because of the markings made by erosion. The Batuk is often mistakenly called Bromo.

40. Sunset at Krakatau Beach near Carita, Java. What remains of the volcanic island. Krakatau, is visible on the horizon – the island can be reached in about 4 hours.

Selamat Datang – Welcome!

Coming in to land at Jakarta's airport, we can see the Pulau Seribu (Thousand Islands) sparkling like emeralds in the turquoise sea, their glistening white beaches merging with lush palm groves, where we can just make out some tiny fishermen's cottages. The surf is breaking on the reef beyond – a ring of foam-crested waves separating the blue of the reef from the darkness of the sea around it. In the distance, the northern coast of Java seems to draw a greyish-brown line against the misty horizon.

We are now at 4,000 feet and our plane is continuing its descent. Below us, heavily laden Bugis schooners, their masts billowing in the wind, are slowly making their way to the port of Sunda Kelapa near Jakarta. Here on board, the excitement of the Indonesian passengers seems to be giving way to increasing restlessness. Some of them are obviously returning after a long absence to this, their homeland – or as they call it, Tanah Air Kita (Our Land and Water). In the distance, the volcanoes of the Bandung Plateau are now discernable and below us, the sediment-rich rivers emptying into the sea have turned the water along the coast a greyish-brown.

A moment later, land, red from the lateritic soil common in many regions of Indonesia, is below us. Coconut groves alternate with the varied patterns made by the rice fields before eventually giving way to kampungs and industrial parks.

At length, we are flying over the virtually boundless sea of houses that makes up the six-million-strong city of Jakarta. Here and there, the seemingly unbroken mass of brick-red roofs is intersected by wide streets and canals teeming with intense and exotic life. These dust-filled traffic arteries contain more people than one can imagine. From the air, Jakarta might well be a colourful village were it not for the distant, phantome-like skyscrapers on Jalan Thamrin, the eight-lane boulevard in the heart of the city. We are now at 200 feet. Bicycle-taxis, the famous "becaks", oxcarts, street vendors, cars, houses, gardens, people and more people pass by in quick succession making it impossible for us to absorb these strange, penetrating images one at a time.

A muffled screech and the roar of the jets in reverse thrust signal the landing at Jakarta's Halim Airport. As we taxi along the runway, the glittering tarmac warns of the oppressive heat outside, and indeed, as soon as the doors are opened, there is a blast of hot air and tropical humidity. The initial sensation of being taken by the throat, however, gives way to a euphoric feeling as soon as we step off the gangway. Our long journey is now over; we have reached our destination: Jakarta, capital of the Indonesian Islands.

"Selamat datang": these words spoken by the pretty ground hostess make us aware of where we are. The air is filled with familiar and unusual odours: outside, the smell of kerosene mingles with the aromatic fragrance of the tropical vegetation which forms the backdrop for the airport. In the airport lounge the pleasant smell of "kretek" pervades – these clove-flavoured cigarettes are popular with many Indonesians. Within this sober, western-style interior, the distinctive aroma creates the almost mystic atmosphere of a Hindu temple, heavy with incense.

Standing in the queue slowly making its way toward passport control, we feel our patience being put to its first hard test. The immigration officer with his affable smile and practised hand is slowly making entries in the visas placed before him and illustrating for the visitor a characteristic of the Indonesian people. In such close and humid quarters as these, it is only through poised and courteous behaviour towards others that life can bring pleasures and rewards.

"Sabar" – patience – is the magic word that will open almost any door in Indonesia. After having gained insight into this behavioural particularity, the visitor may like to show off his experience in Indonesian ways by keeping at a distance from those travellers impatiently waiting for their luggage.

Later, outside the arrival building, the energy that pervades Indonesia becomes apparent. This is where the drivers from the numerous cab companies struggle for daily survival. "Hallo mister, where you go?" is the battle cry heard from all sides. In no time at all we find ourselves sitting in an ancient taxi moving in the direction of the city. The driver's face radiates triumph as he tells us that today he was able to beat the competition from the blue and yellow taxis which are preferred by the locals. Sitompul is his name and he belongs to the Batak tribe whose territory covers the land around Lake Toba in North Sumatra. At 36, he already has a family of five to feed, which he only just manages on his fourteen hours of work a day. Five years ago, he took over from his brother who had been injured in accident. Sitompul now supports his disabled brother as well as his own family but, in spite of many difficulties, is a happy and cheerful man. While speaking in glowing terms of the songs and vocal talents of his people, he drops a tape into the cassette player, and the cab, working its way through the ever-increasing traffic, resounds with music that could have originated in the Polynesian Islands of the South Pacific.

Around us, the becaks, helicaks, bemos, bajais and oplets, all looking even more exotic than their names, fill the air with an ear-splitting din. A myriad of pedlars, including pre-school children, dominate the street scene. Their attempts to sell newspapers and sweets to the passengers of the passing cars, seem only seldom to be rewarded with success, however. Now on a four-lane highway, we are progressing steadily towards Jalan Thamrin, Jakarta's wide main thoroughfare. There, where wooden huts once crowded the roadside, giant hotels and administration buildings now rise to score the reddening sky.

After the brief twilight, typical of equatorial regions, the tropical night descends upon the city. Driving past well-kept squares with imposing monuments to Indonesia's long struggle for independence against the Dutch, we approach our hotel.

In the evening, a light breeze from the coast blows through the garden of our small colonial-style hotel providing welcome relief from the heat of the day. A heavy cast-iron petroleum lamp throws quivering shadows on the walls and ceiling as if wanting to conjure up the spirits of bygone days. The sweet and intoxicating fragrance of a kambodja tree renders us insensitive to the now distant clamour of the traffic. It is gradually becoming evident that in this bustling city of six million, the past still lives on into the present. The fascination of Jakarta (a city which has not, as yet, gained total acceptance as a tourist centre) certainly lies in the intermingling of the traditional with the modern. The friendliness and candour of its people enhances the city's attractiveness and serves to bridge the gap between the past and the present.

Deep in thought, we glance at the map spread before us. The jungle islands of Irian and Kalimantan are the second and third largest islands in the world. Their interiors are inhabited by tribes of remarkable native people whose lives as hunters and gatherers are, even today, closely bound with nature. For them, the mountains, rivers and forests embody an eternal natural law that is as constant as the sky and the stars. Aboriginal tribes also inhabit the island of Sumatra, where the tiger, the rhinoceros, the elephant and the orang-utan have found their last sanctuary. One already suspects that Indonesia must be a land of untold scope and diversity. Besides century-old temples, a multitude of different cultures, snow-covered volcanoes and a fabulous flora and fauna, there is an underwater world which has barely been explored. It is clear to us as we refold our map that this visit can only be a beginning.

At the Beach

Along the eastern horizon, the darkness of night gives way to the brilliant red of dawn. On Pulau Dewata, or Island of Light, as Bali was once known, a new day is dawning. Accompanied by the sound of cocks crowing in the surrounding villages, we make our way towards the beach through terraced rice paddies. Care is called for when crossing the embankments, as just one step in the wrong place would allow water to seep through, ruining an entire day's work. The light of dawn is now spreading over the shimmering irrigated sawahs mirroring the fronds of the coconut palms as they fan gently in the cool morning breeze. A narrow stream, whose task it is to feed the many irrigation canals, gurgles and splashes its way through this idyllic scene. Women and children dressed in sarongs are already busy carrying water home in long, hollowed-out bamboo stems. Meeting them on the narrow embankment, we step off and walk a few steps over unplanted soil, and are met by their smiles as they do the same. Here, courtesy is half the battle. A dark palm grove, not yet penetrated by the sunlight, is murky from the smoke that curls out from the palm-covered roofs of the neighbouring cottages. From where we are standing, we can already hear the muffled roar of the surf which, on the south-western coast of Bali, offers varying conditions for swimming and water sports. Mike, a lanky Australian, assures us "Today it's really great". He is taking his surfboard to the beach on a rented bicycle. As we come out from under the coconut palms, we see the sea, which yesterday was smooth as glass, now coming in in tall waves which pound against the shore. For the time being, inexperienced swimmers are better off using their hotel pool or swimming at Sanur, where a coral reef holds back the fury of the sea.

The white-green coastline stretches out before us from the mountainous isthmus of Nusa Dua, past the runway that extends into the sea, then past Kuta Beach and beyond, before it merges into the horizon to the west. Depending on weather conditions, there is something for everyone on this immensely long coastline. Venturing out too far can be dangerous, however, because of strong cross-currents which give even experienced swimmers trouble. No-one need worry about barracudas, sharks or sea snakes here, but children and occasional swimmers would do well to use the supervised beach near Kuta. On Indonesia's less-frequented beaches, it is always a good idea to ask the advice of the local population as to the dangers that could be encountered. The beaches on the southern coast of Java which do not lie in sheltered bays are notorious for their undertow and tend to attract sharks.

As the first early-risers romp in the surf before us, the beach slowly comes to life. "Do you want massage?", an elderly Balinese woman in "sarong kebaya" calls out to the sunbathers lolling about on the sand. This is not the dubious proposition of a woman of ill-repute, but rather the straightforward offer made by a masseuse who practises her craft as generations before her have done. She has already made many a tourist forget the ill-effects of sunburn or of a long night on the town. As the temperature rises, the wind and the waves begin to subside.

Onlay a few die-hard sunshippers can withstand the heat of the midday sun but at other times the beach is alive with a multitude of roving merchants peddling everything from sun-ripened pineapples to beautifully decorated chessboards. By selling their wares rather than begging, these people make a worthy attempt at wresting a living from the tourist industry, the birth of which has inevitably increased prices for them. Balancing a tower of straw hats on his head, little Djandra strolls over the hot sand. He has travelled a long way from his home near Mount Batur where this typical peasant headgear is made by young and old. An elderly couple purchases several of the hand-woven hats at once, seeing them as ideal presents for friends at home, With this sale, Djandra has paid off his fare to Kuta.

In the distance, the wind surfers with their brightly-coloured sails plough furrows through the blue waves. They have recently become part of everyday life on Bali's beaches, often executing daring jumps over the waves. Like dolphins, they leap out of the foaming waves only to dive right back after a short time in the air.

Absorbed in the fantasy world of children playing, we watch three tanned Balinese boys as they chase about on the white sand with kites on long strings hovering over their heads. Along with dolls they make themselves, and a toy consisting of a pole with wheels attached, these paper kites, called "layang layang", are the only playthings most Indonesian children know – but this does not detract from their hours of enjoyment.

By late afternoon, the sea is totally calm. We stroll along the shore-line with the surf breaking gently and rhythmically at our feet. Ebbing water collects in tracks left here and there in the sand and looks silvery in the oblique sunlight. In an instant, however, the trail is washed away by the returning tide. On the horizon, the sea and the sky slowly unite in an indescribable explosion of colour. Beyond Legian, illuminated outriggers sail out to the incoming tide, the dark silhouettes of the characteristic sails clearly visible against the blazing sun. A light breath of wind carries the scent of drying coconuts from the palm groves and the staccato chirp of the cicadas seems to accompany the descending twilight. Many people would travel to the ends of the earth for scenes like this.

Selamat Makan – Enjoy Your Meal

After carefully placing the last bowls and platters on the already crowded table, Amir, our waiter, wishes us, "Selamat makan". Spread out before us is a complete Indonesian "rijsttafel" composed of a wide selection of Javanese and Sumatran dishes. Several bottles of good, locally-brewed beer form the centrepiece of the feast. From amongst these freshly prepared and attractive-looking dishes, there is something to suit every palate: grilled king crab, spicy beef coated with grated coconut, baked bananas wrapped in dough, mackerel marinated in a red chilli sauce, jackfruit and chicken in coconut milk, a large serving of rice and many other delicacies.

These steaming, savoury dishes are accompanied by a battery of condiments, the most important being "sambal" and "kecap". "Kecap" (pronounced like "ketchup") is actually soya sauce, but the word gained distinction through its use by the British in neighbouring Malaysia to refer to a seasoned tomato puree that is now commonly known as tomato ketchup. At least in the beginning, one should be careful with "sambal", a hot sauce of which there are many variations, but whose basic ingredients include grated chillis, tomatos and salt. After becoming familiar with its effects, however, the advanced "rijsttafel" connoisseur uses it to spur the taste buds on to new levels of refinement.

As one can guess from the spelling, the "rijsttafel" is a creation of the colonists of the former Dutch East Indies. They put together a collection of those Indonesian dishes that came closest to their own tastes – and that was no small number. A normal Indonesian meal was and is much less sumptuous. The addition of meat or fish to the staple diet of rice, vegetables and sauces (called "nasi campur") is not a matter of course. Many Indonesians are even happy with just a bowl of plain rice.

In order to experience the versatility of Indonesian cooking, one should plan to enjoy a "rijsttafel" at least once during one's stay. The large number of Indonesian restaurants in the Netherlands (which always feature a "rijsttafel" on their menu) proves how habit-forming and even addictive Indonesian food can be. Here at the source, however, where fresh ingredients and seasonings are in abundance, authenticity is ensured. Garlic, shunned by some foreign visitors, is used sparingly here and lends a pleasant flavour to many dishes. Although hardly detectable, its absence is easily felt if ever it is left out of a recipe.

"Tuan sudah selesai?" – Amir asks us after a while if we have finished our meal and, with a broad grin that sets the beautiful snow-white teeth in his bronze-coloured face aglow, he clears away the empty bowls and plates. We are sorry that we have to answer his question with yes. We would love to go on enjoying these delicacies, but as we have another culinary adventure planned for the evening, we try to curb our appetites a little.

Those who believe that to know the "rijsttafel" is to know Indonesia's entire bill of fare are far off target. In place of rice (of which there are many varieties), sago or yams form the staple diet in many regions of the country. The cooking of West Sumatra, which boasts the spiciest dishes in the land, can be sampled in "Padang" restaurants found all over the country. In this type of restaurant, no orders are taken; instead, the guest takes a seat and the waiter then places several dishes in front of him. No need to worry, though: you only pay for what you eat. In spite of the fact that this hot, spicy fare quickly brings tears to the eyes, many holidaymakers come to develop a liking for it.

Javanese dishes, as well as those of the eastern islands, are usually milder and may even have a somewhat sweet flavour to them. Although every region of the country can boast of culinary specialities, the cooking of Java and Sumatra is generally considered to be the best.

The numerous Chinese restaurants also offer the gourmet many authentic and novel dishes. Here, fish and crustaceans are prepared in especially delicious ways. The Sundanese people of West Java raise goldfish in fishponds until they reach imposing sizes. Then they are grilled to become "ikan mas bakar".

As a hearty alternative to the usual American breakfast, an Indonesian-style breakfast can be ordered. "Oh no, not rice again", many will lament when the waiter appears with "nasi goreng" (fried rice), but for those who want to banish their hunger for the rest of the morning, this is the right choice. In addition, this breakfast is light on a digestive system that is still suffering from jet-lag and the excitement and confusion of the first days.

In the evening, we take a taxi to the Pecenongan, a street in the northern part of Jakarta, and are struck by the number of street vendors there. At the so-called "kaki lima" (the foodstalls along the street) they prepare a variety of small snacks using cooking utensils which they carry around on their shoulders or on two-wheeled carts. "Martabak" (a type of pancake), "saté" (skewered meat) and "bami" (noodles) are among the items offered in this way. When the "tukang bami" comes into the neighbourhood, joy abounds, especially among the young – noodle soup from the "bami-man" is always a treat. As our taxi turns into the Pecenongan, the wet and shiny asphalt appears from a distance to be in flames. As we get closer, we notice a mass of foodstalls of all sizes with counters and benches and canopies over them. Tasty dishes are being prepared here in large crescent-shaped pans which are bathed in the red glow of the darting flames. A plump Chinese cook, dressed in only a vest and shorts on account of the heat, impresses us as particularly masterful at his craft. Enveloped in flame and smoke, he flips over sputtering frogs' legs with a quick flick of the wrist. Just another dash of oil – it ignites immediatly, the flames dancing under the canopy – and they are ready to be served. While he prepares another serving of broccoli, the waiter rushes the steaming frogs' legs to the waiting guests. The place is buzzing with activity. Brightly-dressed street musicians strolling from stall to stall provide entertainment for the guests. In spite of the fact that the benches are uncomfortable and the street noise inescapable, this type of food and the quality of it, as well as the lively atmosphere, attracts many guests night after night. Even a considerable portion of Jakarta's foreign community comes here to enjoy fish, crustaceans and frogs' legs. It is here that many have been won over by this exotic fare. After watching our cook in the vain hope of picking up a few tricks of his trade, we add an Indonesian cookbook to our list of souvenirs.

The Underwater World

Our boat, the outrigger Aquanaut I, sways in the blue sea off the island of Bunaken. Sloping under us in the crystal-clear water, the yellow-green contours of the reef are clearly visible. Adjacent to the reef, a dark blue glow shows us the way to a steep trench 90 metres/295′ deep. This is North Sulawesi's underwater nature reserve, the object of our diving expedition. Loky Herlambang, who is sitting next to me on the boat's side, had applied in good time for all the necessary permits for this dive through his diving centre in Mandado. Fortunately, measures have been taken to check the advancing destruction of the reefs. Coral collecting and harpooning are now illegal. As a means of exercising control, all divers must be escorted by a licensed guide.

While Loky checks our scuba gear one more time to see that it is properly secured, we take a last look at the scene before us. The palm trees on the beach seem to be sweeping out to touch the turquoise sea. Not far from us, the landscape is dominated by the immense cone of a dead volcano towering up from out of the sea, its flanks covered with lush tropical vegetation. At first, the decision to trade in a sun-swept paradise for the obscurity of the undersea world is not an easy one to make!

Loky, having concluded all the preparations, gives the signal for the

dive to begin. Holding our diving masks in place, we drop backwards from the shipboard. The steel blue sky falls away as we plunge among thousands of silvery air bubbles into an iridescent-blue world. After the beads of air finally reach the surface, a fantastic realm opens up before us: the virtually untouched coral reef. Fish of all sizes, frightened away by our impromptu invasion, now swim back full of curiosity. The multi-coloured beauty of these creatures is indescribable; their lavishly radiant scales seem to be a thing of fancy. You forget all too easily that in the serious business of day-to-day life in the reef, this colouration is necessary for territorial defense and for mating.

Carried by a slight current, we glide past a group of brain coral upon which the play of waves is reflected from above. In the diverse structures of the reef, we can recognize countless animal species that have found an ideal environment here. Over thousands of years, they have developed through adaptation and mutation into highly specialized forms of life which, be they predatory or peaceable, share shelter and hunting grounds here.

The edge of the reef is slowly approaching. Beyond it, the dark blue seems to continue on endlessly. My diving partner disappears headlong into the deep where the colour spectrum gradually reduces itself to blue-grey hues. In the beam of light from our lantern, however, life shines forth in the most fantastic colour combinations. Accompanied by a triggerfish intently watching us, we follow the downward current. A school of flagfish passes ahead of us. Here, where the verticle reef affords only minimal shelter, they swim together for protection. A hawksbill turtle, overcome by panic at seeing us, makes a hasty retreat, leaving its meal behind. Gliding rather than swimming, we move through a forest of leaf, fan and pipe coral whose colouration and design resemble the surrealistic backdrop of a science-fiction film. Swimming at a depth of 40 metres/131′ in this unusually clear water, we can see the outlines of the Aquanaut on the surface as it follows the trail of our air bubbles. Colourful sponges and sea lillies, looking more like plants than corals, make us forget that we are surrounded by water.

We begin thinking about returning to the surface. The silvery, shining bodies of almaco mackerels glide past in the light of our lanterns. Following in their wake is a dark shadow displaying the characteristic lines of long pectoral fins. With short, hard flaps of the tail, a large white shark swims against the current that is carrying us. Fortunately, the motionless eye, that does not escape our attention, hardly takes notice of us at all. Before this eerie encounter has a chance to really sink in, it is already over. The behaviour of sharks is usually not as bad as it is purported to be; however, the warm-blooded mackerel shark of the open sea should be avoided at all costs. One should bear in mind that diving in tropical waters becomes riskier when, through the harpooning of fish, bait tracks are inadvertently laid.

On our last decompression stop at 5 metres, the sun-sparkled undersea world has regained some of its colour – even if only in pastel hues. A young crew member equipped with a diving mask swims towards us drawing our attention to a porcupine fish which has just inflated itself to a ball in order to appear less appetizing to its predators. In addition to our little spiny friend, many other underwater creatures have come to say good-bye. Our oxygen is running low, forcing us to discontinue this fascinating voyage of discovery.

As I surface right next to the boat, I am met by the beaming faces of the crew members: the temperature has reached 40 °C/104 °F in the shade and they are more than glad to see us. Not until the outboard motor has provided fair wind, however, are we able to breathe properly again. Behind us lies an enchanting island realm whose extraordinary beauty above as well as below water will not, we hope, prove its undoing.

People

Outside on the tarmac, our plane's engines are warming up. Here inside, flights to Tokyo, Manila, Sydney and Amsterdam are being announced. The odour of kerosene underscores the mood of departure that prevails here in Jakarta's international airport. It is now time to leave. Sitting around me are tanned holidaymakers and pale, weary-looking businessmen. The tourists, in particular, seem to be lingering among the rustling palms of their holiday islands – if only in their minds.

Was it all just a dream? – all that passed before my eyes during the last weeks: the graceful ancient dances, the temples that inspire even non-believers with a sense of the div-

ine, the huge unexplored rainforests where the evolution of life goes on undisturbed...

While thinking back on the events of my holiday, I sense that the tranquillity and harmony that has enveloped me since the day I arrived is in danger of slipping away in the hectic atmosphere of the airport.

More images appear before my mind's eye: images of the Indonesian people. I see once again the fishermen of Java whose lives still follow the rhythm of the sea and the tides. In the light of the setting sun, they gently and expertly launch their boats into the surf; then, as the message of the Koran is sounded from a nearby mosque, they sail out in the falling darkness to put their lives in danger once again. I recall the dance they performed following a large catch: how much grace and agility these small, solid men were suddenly able to display. I can still see their thick, course hands casting out and drawing in invisible nets while contentment and serenity shone from their faces.

Then there was the encounter with the amazing Papuas in the mountains and jungles of Western New Guinea, who, despite my strange appearance and language, showed me untiring hospitality: they fed me and sheltered me and introduced me to their fascinating culture. Together, we crossed many a torrential river, and, whenever the going got rough, one of the many dark-skinned hands was there to lend assistance. The steaming jungle paths and the weight of our gear took a lot out of each and every one of us, but in spite of this, we sang cheerful songs together around the campfire every night. While in repose, their broad-nosed faces showed an expression of serenity even though their bare feet were certainly suffering from the daily marches.

It was through the hardships of this expedition that I came to fully comprehend the magic of their nature-bound existence. The notion of responsibility toward one's fellow man, notwithstanding who he is or from where he comes, does not only exist in the codes of law, but is alive and well and living in the souls of these people who were at one time considered "primitive". While saying good-bye to these kind people, I realized that tourism could indeed be instrumental in furthering the goal of better understanding among peoples. In areas where aboriginal peoples have had only minimal contact with "civilisation", and thus have not yet had the usual bad experiences, they can still be found living in self-sufficient and peace-loving communities. The question is: Should their last remaining sanctuaries necessarily be infringed upon?

In the cities, on the other hand, I met people who repudiated their village origins in order not to appear backward to the visitors. Machmut was one of these. "Batik is something for old people", he told me. "When you come back, bring me a pair of jeans." While lighting up an expensive brand-name cigarette, he mimicked the facial expression of a western film star and proudly pointed out that money was no problem.

Machmut's father, on the other hand, is a modest and unassuming man who, like his ancestors before him, makes his living on a smallholding. Using the water buffalo which belongs to his more prosperous neighbour, he ploughs, like most Javanese rice farmers, less than 2½ acres of land. The little he has asked of life so far, has been granted him. His son, Machmut, however, for whom Allah's teachings no longer play a central role, is a cause of worry. "Allah, forgive him his inexperience", he prays, and his face, which at first showed apprehension, beams in a way that is typical of Indonesians.

Children are the greatest possessions that a person could have: for their parents, they are not only a source of pride and joy, but also a source of security in their old age. In Indonesia, one encounters children everywhere: at present, over 50% of the population is under 15 years of age. (The increase in the birthrate will, however, cause the country many problems in future.) I can still hear the cheerful shouts and laughter of these children and recall how these "good spirits" often led me to hidden temples or found things I had lost, or pointed out the way (sometimes the wrong one).

Children are privileged individuals in Indonesia – particularly on Bali, where they are considered full members of village society. Here, they are born into a sympathetic environment in which everything revolves around the growing child. The soul of a newborn baby is believed to be close to God and therefore they are treated as sacred. Their thoughts and actions are considered to be pure and innocent, and for this reason, they must be kept from touching the "impure" ground. As a result, they are constantly held and carried by their relatives, thus becoming well-anchored in the family and in the community from the very beginning. As soon as they can walk, however, their days of being waited on hand and foot are over. At an early age, Indonesian boys and girls are given their first responsible tasks. Fetching water, leading the buffalo to its bath, looking after younger brothers and sisters and helping with the rice harvest are just a few of these. Indonesian children are not expected to enter adulthood at a certain age, however – perhaps this explains the even-tempered nature of these people. Like everyone else, though, Indonesians oviously do have their faults, but they consider criticism of others worthless when one's own faults are ignored.

With the announcement of my flight number, I am suddenly pulled out of my reverie. Soon our plane will be departing in a wide loop over Jakarta, from where my journey through the archipelago once began. All the people I met here, from the short, stocky Batak people and the tanned and wavy-haired Moluccans, through the slender and fairer-skinned Javanese and Sundanese, to the dark and often extremely tall Papuan people – whether they were rice farmers or businessmen – all had one thing in common: the candid and sincere smile of Indonesia.

The Magic of the Jungle

Unburdened by civilization, the muddy jungle river flows silently into the bay before us. Behind the tall bushes on the opposite bank, the wide tree tops of the tropical rainforest that tower up in the pale morning sky are still heavily swathed in fog. Moving slowly from the forest floor through the separate layers of jungle life, the rising damp penetrates the verdant canopy. Scattered banks of fog hover over the river. From our vantage point on a hill, we have a sweeping view of this primeval landscape. Only the occasional barking call of the hornbill disturbs the peace and quiet that lies over it.

Kalimantan, this little-known jungle island, spreads out before us. Explorers and adventurers were once hired under the utterly endless leafy canopy of this so-called green inferno. Inexperienced and poorly equipped, they succumbed under the many privations that a several-week-long journey in this region entailed. Their disappearance was often erroneously attributed to the tribes who live in the island's interior, some of whom once engaged in head-hunting. Coastlines overgrown with mangroves once formed ideal hideouts for pirates such as Sandokan of the Makassar Strait. Borneo, as the island (the third-largest in the world) is also called, still possesses vast tracts of virgin forest, which are, however, increasingly falling victim to the electric saws of the logging companies.

After packing our tents and backpacks together, we set out for the river. Stepping over roots and stones, we head down the hill by way of a small path that soon disappears among the pillar-like trunks of the giant jungle trees. Here, we are received by a stifling, putrid odour as well as the seeming cacophony produced by the creatures here. Above the din, however, the cicadas can be distinctly heard. Only after close observation does one discover the many animals that crawl, leap, climb, fly and glide in this environment, extending from the jungle floor through the separate layers of growth and up to the 60–70 metre/ 197–230′ high crown.

A tapang tree, one of the tallest in the rainforest, blocks the way with its huge buttress roots. Since the sharp hooks on the fronds of the rotang palms on either side of this giant prevent us from making headway, we decide to scale this hurdle of roots covered with the droppings of the animals that make their home in, and on, this colossus of a tree. The beos that live high up in its crown announce our arrival to the other forest inhabitants through loud crowing and whistling. Further below hangs one of the large bees' nests that are frequently found on tapangs.

Here, near the jungle floor, humidity is well over 90%. This, together with the high temperature (around 32 °C/89 °F in the shade), means that you sweat profusely at the slightest exertion. In surroundings brimming with so many beautiful and exotic life forms, however, such bothersome "side effects" are of little importance.

Two metallic-green butterflies (troides brookiana) dance around a pond in the light of a sunbeam that has reached us through the foliage. They are named after the Englishman, James Brooke, who once ruled as a white rajah over Sarawak in the north of Borneo, now part of Malaysia. The hundreds of species of tortoise and metallic beetles also add splashes of colour to the rainforest.

While crossing a clearing, we hear the distinctive call of the gibbon, and soon we see the herd swinging past us overhead. Seeing us, they pause for a moment and their leader swings forward and hangs upside down by one foot in order to observe us better. Obviously his appraisal does not turn out well for us, for after letting out a charge of scornful laughter, he leads his group onward, swinging from branch to branch in the direction of the river.

On a fallen tree in the clearing, we see an orchid, a flower which normally only unfurls its colourful splendour in the upper "storeys" of the rainforest where the correct amounts of light, air and nourishment are available. A few steps further on, we see a pitcher plant. Contrary to popular belief, the soil on the jungle floor is poor in nutrients and must nevertheless provide for a multitude of consumers. Because of this, the pitcher plant has developed its own method of gaining sustenance. In its pitcher-shaped leaf, this epiphyte catches insects which furnish vital nitrates and other substances.

Sibuling, our guide and local expert, suddenly calls to us excitedly. He has discovered a clump of reddish-brown hairs caught on a fallen tree limb. This is the first sign of an orang-utan we have seen in the two weeks we have been here. The inhabitants of the Indonesian archipelago gave it this name because they took it for a man who had fled to the forest to escape the trials and tribulations of life. The orang-utan, or man-of-the-forest, is one of the most endangered species of apes. As early as the 18th century, they fell victim to the European intruders who trapped and killed them for scientific experiments and zoological collections. Today, the orang-utan is rigorously protected. Outside their designated reserves, such as Bohoruk in North Sumatra or on Borneo, however, these apes are rarely seen. That is why we are especially pleased to have found an obvious sign of this rare animal on this, the last day of our jungle expedition.

After having heard rumblings in the distance for quite some time, we notice now that the leaves overhead are beginning to rustle. A large stilt-root tree, whose free-standing roots look like the arms of an octopus, is even beginning to groan menacingly. As we reach the bank of the river, lightening flashes down from the dark storm front and illuminates the swaying tree-tops. Shortly afterwards, thunder rips the air and heavy raindrops begin to splatter down on the muddy riverbanks. At first, there are only a few drops, but soon it is clear that we are in for a rainstorm of the kind only seen in the tropics. The pouring rain conceals the surrounding scenery like a heavy, grey curtain. Soaked to the skin, we cross a plank and reach the boat which is waiting for us at the mouth of the river. After loosening the ropes, we find ourselves taking leave of these magnificent surroundings with mixed feelings.
Those who have experienced the unique atmosphere that prevails in the cathedral-like gloominess of a tropical rainforest will be forever fascinated by this living natural monument.

The Fascination of an Ancient Legacy

Crowded together with men, women and children, I am sitting on the hard bench of a "bemo", racing at full speed down the precipitous slope of the Gunung Agung. A few passengers are even riding outside on the running-boards, their hair windswept. A pot-bellied hog lying in a basket on the floor of the vehicle is grunting contentedly. I have just spent some eventful, strenuous days on Mt. Batur. Now, after visiting the Besakih Temple, I find myself drawn once again down to the coast, which, on clear days, can be seen from Bali's mountains.

The toils of the day are clearly visible on the faces of the market women who are dressed in traditional sarongs and have large baskets in which to transport their wares. They apparently did good business today, for nothing but a few scraps remain in the vegetable baskets. As our glances meet, their mouths, red from betel, form sly grins. Embarrassed, a small boy hides behind a fold of his mother's sarong. Suddenly we all burst out laughing: this passenger from a strange and distant land is after all made of flesh and blood.

Shaking and rattling, our small vehicle continues on its way into the twilight – but then suddenly, the ride is over. Most likely, the "levaks", evil spirits of the island of Nusa Penida, have been up to their mischief again. The heavy knocking sound coming from the engine tells us, that for the moment, there is no hope. Together we push the vehicle off the road – the handbrake will hold it in place until morning. Theft is nonexistent among the deeply religious Balinese, and the lower elements from the cities tend to make for the tourist centres where the money is.

I am about to collect my belongings and look for another car, when I hear the familiar "Hallo, Mister" behind me. "You want to see Odalon?", one of the passengers of the unfortunate "bemo" asks. "Odalon" is a celebration held on the anniversary (in the 210-day Balinese year) of the consecration of a temple. Although there are thousands of temples on Bali and the chain of Odalon-celebrations never breaks, I have not as yet had the good fortune to attend one – so I gladly accept the kind invitation. My host, I Gusti Ketut, carries my bags as he walks beside me on the asphalt still radiating the daytime heat. The smell of burning wood coming from the surrounding yards is typical for this time of day – the evening meal is being prepared.

We turn off the road and onto a small sandy path skirted by palms and bushes that leads us away from the world of cars and buses. In the distance we can hear the music of a Gamelan orchestra – it lends the stillness a touch of solemnity.

"Disana ada pesta odalon", Gusti Ketut says, pointing to where the celebration is taking place and the whites of his eyes glow with expectation. A dog on top of a wall is barking at the silvery full moon that is slowly rising between the trunks of the palm trees. "We believe that bad people are reborn as dogs", my companion tells me. "At night, we don't feel comfortable around them." Indeed, the doleful howling makes even my flesh creep.

The belief in rebirth is prevalent on Bali. Everyone strives, however, to escape the cycle of life on earth by becoming divine through a flawless religious life. The ancient animistic belief that rocks, plants, mountains and lakes are inhabited by the souls of gods and demons is still in existence too. Those who wish to understand Bali must open their minds to the mysterious.

Ahead of us to the right, we see the outlines of a "Pura Dalem" (temple of the dead), where cremations take place. We sense the air of enchantment that lies over the moss-covered walls and shrines. Bali's religious inspiration can be plainly felt here. Even though death is something positive and natural for the Balinese, the proximity of this temple makes Ketut ill at ease. From out of the darkness, more and more people appear. I see the slender silhouettes of women balancing offerings on their heads as they walk with measured steps to the top of the hill. The black, towerlike "merus" of the temple ahead of us seems to pierce the silvery, limitless vault of the sky. The metallic strains of the Gamelan-orchestra seem to cover the whole

area in a blanket of sound. This is no longer the tourists' Bali, but rather the Bali of the Balinese.

Ketut tugs at my sleeve and points out a spot from where I can watch the goings-on without being in the way; then, summonded by religious duty, he disappears into the crowd. So as not to disturb the air of devotion that prevails, I keep camera and flash in their cases. An endless procession of wonderfully decorated sacrificial trays holding colourful rice adorned with flowers and stacks of fruit appears from out of the void. The bearers – embodying fertility bestowed by Shiva – are dressed in multi-coloured "sarong kebayas". These Odalon-celebrations unite people from all walks of life who adhere to the tenets of Dharma Hindu-Bali.

The long line of worshippers now files past the shrines before kneeling down in the inner courtyard of the temple. The temple priests (Pemangkus) accept the offerings from the faithful; then, together with the high priest (Padanda), they offer them to the divine forebears. Offerings are an essential part of every ritual on Bali. Incense, blessings and incantations are used to carry the essence of the offerings up to the deified ancestors. After the celebration, these offerings of food will be eaten by the family members. The priest blesses the group of worshippers with holy water, which they then use to cleanse their mouths and hands. The hands are then folded for prayer in the Hindu manner and a flower is placed over them. Once again, the priest steps before the seated worshippers with holy water, which they then drink and dab on their foreheads.

At the close of the ceremony, the head of each participant is adorned with a consecrated flower and rice is sprinkled on his forehead to symbolize contact with the divine. The faithful carry out this religious observance conscientiously but without indulging in rigid solemnity.

More and more people are now gathering around. The Gamelan orchestra strikes up again with a stirring beat. Small hammers set the bronze bars of the xylophone in motion – but in the next moment, these same hands dampen the reverberating sound. As if obeying a call from the next world, young girls clad in magnificent brocade robes suddenly drift out through the highly decorated temple gate. Like goddesses, they move about gracefully, the highly stylized steps of the dance giving the impression that their tiny feet are hardly touching the ground. Their soft silhouettes are the embodiment of femininity and grace. In classical "Legong", now being performed, the hands, feet and eyes speak in esoteric symbols, their message remaining mostly obscure to the "down-to-earth" westerner.

Everyone, from infants to white-haired old men, is enchanted by this fascinating play of gestures that, in earlier times, was mainly performed at the courts of Balinese princes, and today, is performed for the entertainment and goodwill of the temple deities. For the mortal admirer, it is an exercise in devotion as well. The fluttering of the fingers, the controlled play of the eyes, the probing movements of the feet all show that the dancers have traded their beings for those of the figures represented. They move in unison – each dancer a mirror-image of the others – only to go back to dancing independently in the next moment.

Because this is the most beautiful of the classical Balinese dances, girls start dreaming of becoming Legong-dancers even before they reach school-age. Training often begins when they are five and ends at the onset of puberty.

The 50 or more dances still in existence on Bali today vary greatly both in the way they are performed and in the feelings they express. The "Barong", depicting the benevolent Barong and the evil witch Rangda, and the "Kecak", are two of the wildest and most impressive dances. In the "Kecak", a choir of over one hundred men all wearing black-and-white-checked sarongs and seated in a circle intones the wild staccato-sounding ke-cak-ke-cak-ke-cak so that it swells and levels off in turns. Sometimes visitors imagine that they see vestiges of "primitive cult rituals" in the wild confusion – especially when entranced "Barong" dancers suddenly turn the "kris" (ceremonial dagger) against themselves while under the witch's spell. Many a shocked tourist has been known to walk out of a performance, not understanding that a dance of this kind seeks to banish evil from the community, strengthen social ties and eliminate worries and fears from the lives of the people. Self-inflicted pain and the belief in invulnerability are not feigned, but rather come from the depths of the soul. This dance, however, is often purged of its more gory elements for tourist consumption. The trance section, which has profound religious connotations, is also performed in a simulated and shortened version. In this form, however, the "Barong" can hardly be recognized for what it is: a drama of a magical reality that even today exerts great influence over the lives of the Balinese people.

The Legong-dance now slowly coming to an end illustrates the smooth transition from fable to reality. Gusti Ketut tugs once again at my sleeve – he has brought me a few rice cakes from his family's offerings, which now, at the close of the ceremony, may be eaten. Bali is the land of share and share alike, but on Java too the sharing of joy and sorrow, of good and bad fortune, is deep-seated in the character of the people. With a stranger, of course, they prefer to share happy events and so it was that while visiting Yogyakarta, I was invited to a presentation of a shadow-play which was to take place in the courtyard of a private home. Even as a stranger, I was allowed to attend the performance, which was part of a wedding celebration.

Here too, the night was an arena of human emotions, all of which were focused on a screen illuminated from behind by a single oil lamp. By the flickering light of a lamp shaped like the bird-god, Garuda, the ghostlike shadows of princes, demons, princesses and gods flitted back and forth across the screen. Guided by the almost invisible hand of the **Dalang,** the figures of the **Ramayana** and **Mahabaratha** epics came to life. It may seem odd to us to watch the same story being performed night after night, but for the Indonesians who are captivated by the play of shadows, it is a perpetually fascinating encounter with their heritage. On studying the faces of these people, it is clear that, caught up in the realm of the shadows and at one with themselves and their surroundings, they do gaze into their past. Only seldom do the spectators leave before dawn.

With my host's permission, I took a look behind the screen. Together with a few Gamelan-musicians, the "Dalang" sat here on a podium built against the high, white wall of the Sultan's palace. The cast of gods and demons fashioned from leather parchment lay stored in two large wooden boxes, impatiently awaiting their entrances. Following a prayer and an offering of flowers and rice, the "Dalang" began the play with a description of the princes and their realm. The point of the story became evident in the dialogue between sovereign and subject: the abduction of a princess, the warding off of a demon and his cohorts, love and hate. Then it was the adversary's turn to enter and offer his side of the story. Villainous characters appeared from the left; the heroes, from the right. As usual, the intensely-awaited entrance of the main character occurred around midnight, when it was finally time for him to hold his own in combat and to prevail against the plots of his enemies. Good eventually triumphed over evil in a huge battle that took place at dawn. The **kayan,** or tree of life, was used to indicate the end of each act, to illustrate the elements air, earth, fire and water and to represent a palace.

The "Dalang" is thoroughly familiar with the set dialogues of approximately 300 figures out of the Java-

Shadow play

nese **Wayang Kulit** (wayang=shadow, kulit=leather) and is able to modify his voice to suit each one. The Wayang-puppets are held by rods made of horn which are attached to their backs like a spine. When not in use, the figures are placed in a container fashioned out of a banana trunk stripped of leaves and branches. During the performance, they can be seen there in the lamplight – sometimes one hundred or more for a single play. The background accompaniment provided by the Gamelan players accentuates the mood and underscores the action. The Dalang gives them the beat using small bells (campala) that are attached to his hands and feet. To suggest a raging battle, he shakes sheets of metal and bangs together slabs of wood. His art, which takes eight years to learn and demands patience, perseverence and endurance, is slowly dying out despite popular interest.

"Wayang kulit" performances are now often aired on television and even on radio. Although only the dialogues can be broadcast by radio, the imagination of the listeners makes it possible for them to envisage the world of shadows before them. And even for me, surrounded as I was by children intently following the Dalang's presentation, the play seemed to become reality.

From out of the crowd of spectators, the bridal couple appeared dressed in beautiful batik-sarongs and gold-embroidered robes. With fragrant jasmine blossoms in her hair, the young woman looked like a princess out of the Ramayana epic come to life. The bridegroom, wearing a fez-like velvet hat, appeared, on the other hand, to be an incarnation of Vishnu. On his sarong, I recognized the same batik design that I had just discovered on one of the intricately carved and inventively painted wayang figures in the Dalang's wooden box. On Java, in particular, the glorious past is often resurrected at weddings and on other festive occasions. On this particular occasion the Dalang's screen appeared to be an imaginary dividing-line between past and present which melted into one before my eyes.

Indonesia: Yesterday and Today

In the course of their history, the Indonesian islands have gone by many different names.

The Portuguese, the first western traders who appeared here, called them the Spice Islands because of the abundance of pepper and other spices. The Dutch, who forcibly enlarged their territorial holdings in this area at the beginning of the 19th century, made their position clear by calling them the Dutch East Indies, and the "Emerald Belt" was the name given to them by those Europeans who not only appreciated the islands' economic significance, but also recognized the beauty and charm of the land and its people. When independence was declared in 1945, however, the name adopted was the one coined by the ethnologists Bastian and Logan in the mid 19th century. "Indonesia" comes from the Greek indo + nesoi (Indian Islands).

Until just a few decades ago, Indonesia's prehistory and ancient history were still "hidden in the past". The birth of scientific research came about when the Dutch physician, Eugène Dubois, started searching for traces of early human forms in the then Dutch East Indies with which to support his studies on the role of man in the zoological system. While examining a deposit of volcanic rock near Trinil on Java in 1891, he discovered the skullcap and wisdom tooth of a prehistoric humanoid who must have lived approx. 500,000 years ago. When, in 1931, further excavations uncovered more skeletal remains of this primitive man (Pithecanthropus erectus), Java became known as the cradle of mankind – a

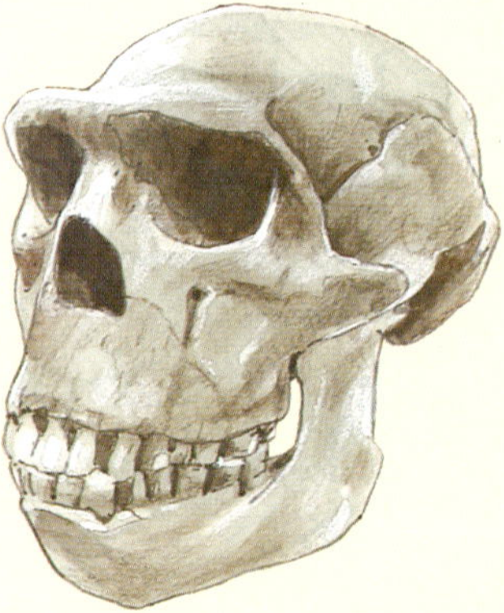

status it held until the 1960's, when traces of an even older prehistoric human were discovered in East Africa.

The first artifacts found were paleolithic tools, uncovered in several regions of Indonesia. From 3000 to 300 B.C., two great immigration waves took place, bringing the proto-Malayans, and later, the deutero-Malayans, to Indonesia. Only with the appearance of the deutero-Malayans, does the history of Indonesia become reconstructible. These newly-immigrated peoples were, moreover, excellent navigators and also settled on Madagascar and in the Pacific, thus spreading the Malay language, the influence of which is apparent today in many Madagascan and Pacific tongues. They also brought with them their knowledge of rice cultivation and bronze-working.

The islands first came under the sway of Indian civilization through their trading contacts with that land. Through the influence and support of learned Brahmans, powerful empires began to emerge in Indonesia, which, until then, had only known feudal principalities. The **Sriviyaya** was one of the Buddhist empires that sprang from this development and controlled sea-going traffic in the archipelago from the 7th to the 13th centuries. **Palembang** in southern Sumatra was the centre of power and culture at this time but unfortunately very little of it remains today.

The first Javanese empire, the **Mataram,** was, however, Hindu. The country's oldest temple ruins, located on the Dieng Plateau and surrounded by high volcanoes, date from this period. As so often occurs in history, Hinduism then temporarily died out in Indonesia as the result of a change of dynasty. Under the Buddhist Shailendra princes who followed, Indonesian architecture was brought to new heights. The **Borobudur,** the largest Buddhist shrine in the world, whose construction began at the close of the 8th century, stands today as evidence of this. The Mataram Empire, when it flourished again, also furnished proof of the architectural expertise of the time with the Hindu temple-complex of **Prambanan,** which was completed around 1000 A.D. Although each religion had greater influence at different times in the course of Indonesia's history, **Hinduism** and **Buddhism** were always able to exist side by side in peace and harmony. Together with animism and the worship of the spirits of ancestors, they formed the typical Indonesian synthesis of religions, to which **Islam** was later added. Elements of Buddhist and Hindu belief still live on. Seen politically, religious tolerance made possible the continuity of the empires and the expansion of their territories all the way to the Mekong Delta and southern China.

When **Marco Polo** first set foot on Indonesian soil in the 13th century, the East Javanese empire of **Majapahit** was already prospering, its domain roughly corresponding to the territory that comprises Indonesia today. Internal disorder and the rise of Islam led to its fall in the 14th century with the last of the Hindu priests migrating to Bali. The Islamic religion was brought to Indonesia by Arab and Persian traders on their voyages East. At court, the new beliefs were quickly accepted, but the rural population held on to its Hindu-Javanese traditions until well into the 18th century.

Jan Pieterszoon Coen

After the discovery of the sea route around the southern tip of Africa, European merchant fleets started arriving in Indonesia. The **Portuguese** for example succeeded in establishing themselves in many areas of the islands. The Dutch, enticed by the enormous profits to be made in the spice trade, followed in 1596. In order to put an end to existent and future competition between rival Dutch trading companies, the Dutch East India Company was founded. The acquisition of further territorial land was written into the statutes and after eliminating the Portuguese and driving back the approaching British, the Dutch were able to establish trading centres on even more of the islands. In areas where the populace resisted foreign rule, ruthless measures were taken and at the beginning of the 17th century, the Banda Islands were virtually depopulated in this manner. In 1618 the governor-general of the Dutch territories, **Jan Pieterszoon Coen** (who was responsible for the harsh treatment of dissenting native) founded the city of **Batavia** – present-day Jakarta.

In the 18th century, the Dutch East India Company expanded its domain far beyond its initial trading posts. Greater territories of land came under Dutch rule and a colonial empire was in the making. If ever ruling princes showed disloyalty to the Dutch, dynastic succession was redetermined by violent means. This was the case in 1755, when the Javanese Mataram Dynasty was split into the sultanates of **Yogyakarta** and **Solo (Surakarta),** the latter remaining under the direct authority of the Dutch.

At the beginning of the 19th century, and following the bancrupty of the Dutch East India Company, the Dutch crown took over the overseas colonies, only to be driven out shortly afterwards by the **British** who used Napoleon's occupation of the Netherlands in 1811 to claim the East Indies for themselves. The British governor, **Sir Stamford Raffles,** carried out social reforms and introduced a liberal trading system which, however, met with the opposition of the local princes. He immersed himself in the study of Indonesian civilisation and geography and was instrumental in the rediscovery of many of Java's cultural monuments (among them, the Borobudur).

Prince Diponegoro

After the fall of Napoleon, the Dutch returned to the archipelago and the remainder of the 19th century was characterized by armed conflict and rebellion.

From 1825 to 1830, the Javanese, under the leadership of **Prince Diponegoro,** waged their first great offensive against the colonial forces, laying waste vast areas of Java. To compensate for their losses, the Dutch instituted a system of compulsory contribution, which became known as the "kultuurstelsel". Farmers had to make one fifth of their land available for the production of coffee, sugar, indigo, spices and tobacco for the European market. These products were then bought up at the lowest prices.

In 1878, the Dutch staged large-scale campaigns against the rebellious **Aceh** sultanate and this finally brought an end to the bitter fighting that had been going on for 200 years.

In the 20th century, resistance groups began organizing themselves nationally. The members of **Budi-Utomo** (Noble Endeavour), a movement founded in 1908, formulated the principles of Indonesian nationalism. Growing pressure from the population brought about some improvements socially, but they were as nothing compared with the wealth and privileges enjoyed by the Dutch colonial masters.

In 1918, **Sarekat Islam** brought about the formation of a people's council through adept negotiating tactics. Under the subsequent Indonesian president, **Sukarno,** a national mass movement based on Hindu-Javanese principles came into being and in 1927 this evolved into the **Partei Nasional Indonesia.** Along with the nationalist, **Hatta,** Sukarno was arrested and exiled as an agitator, but during the **Japanese occupation** in World War II, the two were able to further the idea of independence. Before their surrender, the Japanese transfered power to the new national government under

Sukarno, and he proclaimed Indonesia a republic on August 17, 1945. The Dutch, who were not willing to recognize Indonesia's independence, dispatched troops who battled against the nationalists in a new three-year colonial war. But, with world opinion against them and the United Nations applying pressure, the Dutch finally recognized Indonesia's sovereignty in 1949. The Ambonese, who refused to join this new political alliance, proclaimed the Republic of South Moluccas. Under President Sumohil, they fought until 1950 for their autonomy. Following defeat, many South Moluccans went into exile in the Netherlands. Sukarno also insisted on the inclusion of Dutch New Guinea in the Republic. The Hague's argument against this – that the island belonged neither racially nor culturally to Indonesia – led to fresh altercations. Through the intervention of the U.N., however, Sukarno got his way on the New Guinea question. After Indonesia became the U.N. custodian of the region in 1963, a "referendum" was held on Irian in which only a portion of the population was allowed to vote. In 1969, the territory was annexed. Sukarno, following a leftist-nationalist policy, strove for an alliance of nationalist, religious and communist movements. He obviously lost control of the spirit he had evoked, however, for, on September 30, 1965, the Communists attempted to seize complete control of the government. Major-General **Suharto** intervened in the disturbances, but the retaliatory attack came, in part, from a purely unpolitical source. In many areas of Indonesia, bloody battles were fought in which the people released their fury against the atheistic Communists. After having received limited authority in 1966, Suharto was elected President by the Peoples's Assembly in 1968. In 1971, the first general election in 17 years took place.

In 1977, a new People's Assembly was formed. It is responsible for drawing up the government's programme (five-year plan) and for electing the president.

In 1975, Portugal's last colonial possession, East Timor, was granted independence and a civil war, fanned by the Portuguese themselves, broke out. Indonesian troops

Sukarno

occupied the island which was subsequently proclaimed Indonesia's 27th province.

Since 1967, Indonesia has been a member of the Alliance of Southeast Asian Nations (ASEAN). In addition to embracing the alliance's goal of coordinated regional policies, the country also adheres to the principles of non-alignment.

Structure and Competence of Regional Administration

Anyone who leaves the path usually "beaten" by tourists in Indonesia, will at some time or other come into contact with a Bupati or Camat. Perhaps you simply want some information, or you need to apply for a permit at the governor's office. The following information is designed to give a clear explanation of how the regional system of administration operates:

The President embodies the highest executive power in the State. He elects the regional parliamant on the recommendation of the governor. This regional parliament draws up a budget, which is however, not entirely based on their own fiscal income. On the contrary, the budget is largely financed by the Central government.

The autonomous regional governments are made up of the Kabupaten (rural districts) and the Kotamadyas (independent towns). A Bupati is the head of a Kabupaten, and a Walikota heads the Kotamadyas. Both men are elected by the Minister of the Interior. Depending on its size, each province can be divided up into as many as 10 Kabupaten, which are regional bodies on the so-called 2nd level. Though they do not have their own parliament, they are empowered to draw up a budget. Each Kabupaten is then further divided into several administrative units, called Kecamatan (3rd level). There are no clear cut divisions in spheres of responsibility between the regional and central government.

Within a town or village, several families will join together to form a neighbours' association (RW). Several of these associations grouped together are referred to as a citizen's association. Both appelations are used to assist with the delivery of post, and the RW's and RT's are often responsible for setting up and running public services and voluntary organisations.

Structure of Administration

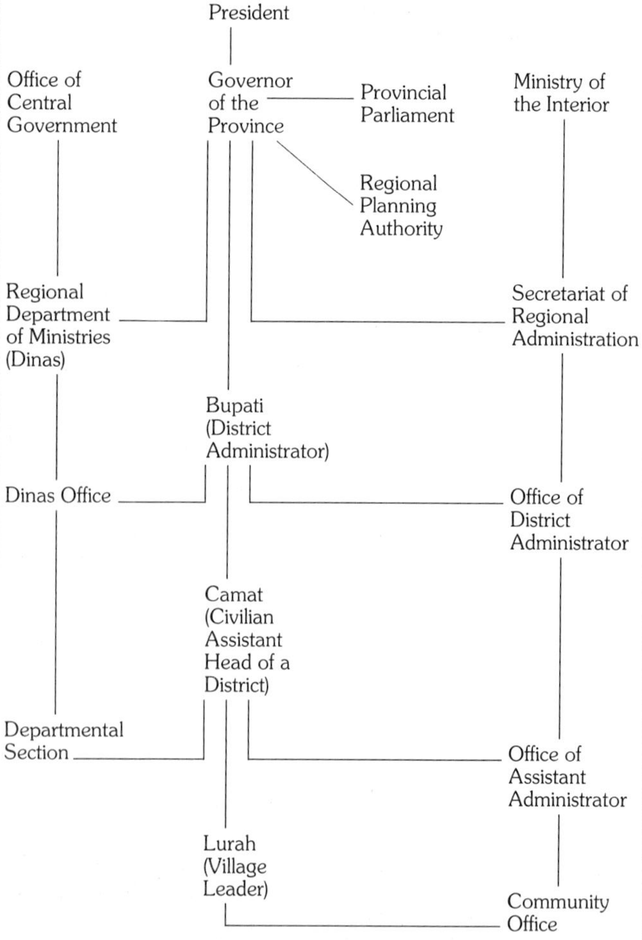

The Land

Indonesia's diversity is rooted, to a large extent, in the fragmentation of its territory. With its **13,677** islands, it is the largest island-nation on the globe. Large areas of the second- and third-largest islands in the world, New Guinea and Borneo, are part of its territory and, at the other end of the scale, the tiniest islets and atolls are also to be found. More than half of all the islands are uninhabited. It would take a good 38 years of uninterrupted island-hopping to visit and spend one day on each of the 13,677 islands. Even the most remote areas can be reached – given enough time. Indonesia has a land area of 1.9 million sq. km (734,000 sq. miles) plus 3.3 million sq. km (1.3 million sq. miles) of territorial waters that border on the Indian and Pacific Oceans. In an area covering more than one eighth of the earth's surface, Indonesia displays a host of fascinating and diverse geographic features – from coral islands surrounded by swaying palms to undisturbed rice fields; from dry savannahs to West Irian's snow- and ice-covered mountains – practically every type of scenery is represented. And as Indonesia, with its 300 volcanoes, is part of the Pacific "Ring of Fire", it is no wonder that much of the landscape has volcanic features.

The Malay Peninsula (including the Philippines) has only been in existence since the late Miocene Epoch, about 15 million years ago, when it began to rise up out of the sea as the result of tectonic activity.

(The ice age also contributed to the rising and falling of the ocean level.) The islands belonging to the **Sunda** and **Sahul Shelves** probably formed land-bridges to the continents of Southeast Asia and Australia. These earlier links explain the present-day distribution of Eurasian and Australasian plant and animal life in the area. The so-called **Wallace Line** is the natural boundary between the two realms (see "Flora and Fauna"). Formed by a shelf which extends from the Macassar to the Lombok Straits, it remained underwater even during the ice ages, thus keeping plant and animal species isolated.

The Indonesian archipelago is formed by two parallel mountain chains – extensions of the Indo-Chinese mountain ranges. The outer (and older) system of mountains lies, for the most part, under water. It first emerges in the Bay of Bengal in the

The Volcanoes

Indonesia's volcanoes are both a curse and a blessing. Composite-cone volcanoes rise up into Java's tropical blue sky between rice terraces and bamboo groves, their steep slopes supporting dense settlements even at high altitudes. Despite the danger to life and limb in the event of an eruption, Javanese and Sumatran farmers take advantage of the calc-alkali soil of the volcanoes up to altitudes of about 1,400 metres/4,593′. Regular showers of fine ash effectively promote the continuous high yield of their tilled lands. The moment sometimes comes, however, when the benevolent mountain turns vicious. In 1922 and 1930, entire villages in central Java were razed to the ground and thousands of people lost their lives when **Mount Merapi** erupted. Although the people had been warned of the danger and told to evacuate the area in 1930, no one did so because it was thought that the warning was a plan devised by the colonial administration to enable them to take over the region. The people couldn't believe that men could foresee the moment when the gods would unleash the primeval forces of the earth. Further eruptions of the volcano led to the destruction of vast tracts of cultivated land in 1961 and 1967. The sudden fall of the Mataram Empire in the 11th century is attributed to a violent eruption of Merapi as well.

Bali experienced its last great volcanic disaster as late as 1963, when the eruption of **Gunung Agung** claimed 2,500 lives. Wide lava streams which flowed into the sea east of Padangbai destroyed 30 sq. km of rice fields; in addition, 120 sq. km of tilled land was rendered useless. Even today, the story of the eruption of **Krakatoa,** a volcano which rose out of the Sunda Strait between Java and Sumatra, does not cease to horrify its listeners. In August 1883, after internal pressure had caused the mountain to increase in size by 150 metres/492′ in the course of a few days, the greatest eruption in the memory of mankind sent more than two-thirds of the 33-sq.-km/12.8-sq.-mile-large island tumbling into a gigantic undersea crater. The blast generated tidal waves of up to 30 metres in height which inundated the coasts of Java and Sumatra and cost 25,000 people their lives. Coastal ships were recovered 20 km/12 miles inland. The volcano ejected about 18 cu. km/23 cu. yds of hot ash and lava, covering the surrounding land with a 50–100 metre/164–328′ deep layer of pumice and ash which caused an additional 12,000 deaths. The effects of the eruption of Krakatoa, however, were not only felt in Indonesia. The blast was heard all the way to Sri Lanka and Australia. The tidal wave generated rolled twice around the earth. Volcanic debris that was ejected up to 27 km/16.8 miles into the stratosphere created blazing-red sunsets around the globe through the reflection of the sunlight. Where Krakatoa once stood, **Anak Krakatau** (Son of Krakatoa) now stands. Since it first appeared in 1928, it has already reached a height of 500 metres. The craters of Mts. **Batur, Tengger** (Bromo) and **Tambora,** as well as **Lake Toba,** are evidence today of similar if lesser eruptions. In addition to the damage caused by flows of molten lava, so-called **Lahars,** formed when newly-deposited ash is washed into the valley by rain, can bury fields and villages under their huge masses of sludge. Of the more than 300 volcanoes in Indonesia, only 71 show signs of activity at the present time and 49 are in a fumarolic stage, that is, they emit hot gases and vapour. The fact that between 500 and 1,000 small-to-minute earth tremors are registered here yearly, clearly shows that the country is situated on a young and unstable part of the earth's crust. The mountains of West Irian increase in height by 4–5 cm annually.

form of the Andaman and Nicobar Islands. The range carries on to form the islands lying just off the coast of Sumatra before coming to an end, for the time being, near Enggano. From Sumbawa, it then extends in a wide arch over Timor, Tanimbar and Ceram (Seram) to Buru.

Opposite this non-volcanic range lie the 300 volcanoes belonging to the inner mountain range that begins in Sumatra, runs virtually parallel to the outer belt, and ends in north-east Sulawesi.

Whereas the lowlands covered with silt and volcanic debris provide highly-productive soil for farming, the picturesque karst regions with their characteristic mogotes (cockpit karst) are mostly very dry. This is particularly evident on the islands of Sumba, Flores and Timor, as these lie in a dry climatic zone.

Laterite Soil, the reddish or yellowish colour of which comes from its high iron-oxide content, is often found in hilly country. This type of soil allows for only limited farming. Among the agriculturally productive regions, the volcanic zones play a dominant role. Only 12% of the total area of Indonesia is inhabited or cultivated. Vast areas (59%) are still covered with tropical rainforests. These so-called primary forests took root for the most part in the country's poorest soil and obtain most of the nutrients needed for growth from their own decayed organic matter.

The second largest kind of vegetation now covers more then 28% of the country and came about as a result of the massive felling of trees carried out by the timber industry and by migrant farmers. The need to protect the natural environment was, however, recognized, with the result that Indonesia now has over 55 nature reserves, comprising many different types of landscape.

A portion of the expansive **Mangrove Jungles** of south-eastern Sumatra and southern Kalimantan, periodically inundated by the sea, has also been made into a reserve.

Climate and Weather

Indonesia has a predominantly tropical climate due to its equatorial position with variations from region to region. Those who travel to Indonesia to escape the inhospitable winters of the temperate zones will find themselves confronted with the rainy season – especially if the trip falls in the months of December, January or February. During this period, downpours will occur at specific times of the day, but there is no need to worry about missing the proverbial blue skies of the tropics. The cloudbursts are generally heavy but of short duration and they provide welcome relief from the heat without spoiling the holiday mood. The Lesser Sunda Islands, in particular, experience heavy rainfall at this time, even though they lie in an arid zone which shares the Australian climate. A brief tropical deluge can be attractive in its own way and need not put an end to all activity – many an amateur photographer has taken his best holiday pictures in the rain. The reason for the heavy precipitation during this period lies with the so-called western monsoon. Winds which are generated by atmospheric currents also sweep over the equatorial islands from a northerly direction.

Those who want to be sure of having plentiful sunshine, however, ought to travel during the period of the southern monsoon. Blowing in

Months	1	2	3	4	5	6	7	8	9	10	11	12
Jakarta/W.-Java												
Av. Daily Temp.	26	26	26	27	27	26	26	26	27	27	27	26
(in °C and °F)	79	79	79	81	81	79	79	79	81	81	81	79
No. of days rain.	19	17	16	12	10	8	6	4	8	10	13	16
Medan/N.-Sumatra												
Av. Daily Temp.	25	26	26	27	26	26	26	26	25	25	25	25
(in °C and °F)	77	79	79	81	79	79	79	79	77	77	77	77
No. of days rain.	17	14	16	16	15	12	12	11	15	17	18	19
Denpasar/Bali												
Av. Daily Temp.	27	27	27	26	26	26	25	26	26	27	28	28
(in °C and °F)	81	81	81	79	79	79	77	79	79	81	82	82
No. of days rain.	16	13	10	6	5	5	4	3	3	5	8	13
Makassar/S.-Sulawesi												
Av. Daily Temp.	26	26	26	27	27	26	25	26	26	27	27	26
(in °C and °F)	79	79	79	81	81	79	77	79	79	81	81	81
No. of days rain.	25	20	18	11	8	6	4	2	2	5	12	22

from Australia, it brings relatively dry air to the archipelago from May to October. This season also has its share of tropical storms, but they are mostly short and insignificant. In the coastal lowlands, humidity levels are on average 83%, but on the Sunda Islands, humidity is considerably lower from May to October, hardly going above 65%. Most hours of sunshine are recorded in the coastal plains, where the mean temperature of 26.5 °C/80 °F varies only slightly from month to month. This average yearly temperature falls, however, by 1 °C/34 °F for every 190 metres/624′ of elevation. Hours of sunshine also decrease with elevation and distance from the coast – but always enough to get a sunburn. At elevations of over 1,500 metres/4,921′, it can get quite cool, especially at night. A warm sleeping-bag is indispensable on mountain hikes.

As will be evident Indonesia offers many contrasts and climate is no exception. During the day, the weather in North Java's coastal resorts can be roasting hot, and in the evening, on the Dieng Plateau, freezing cold. The persistantly hot and humid weather in the western part of the country stands in distinct contrast to the sharply defined wet and dry seasons of Central and East Java and the Lesser Sunda Islands. Generally, after a short period of acclimatization, many find Indonesia's warm, tropical climate quite pleasant and discover that they miss it after their return to the colder temperate climes.

Flora and Fauna

Flora

No region on this earth has been so well provided for by nature than the brilliant-green, Southeast-Asian islands of Malaysia, Indonesia and Papua New Guinea. In addition to a multitude of animal species, this region contains plants matchless in colour and form. The natural abundance of the archipelago has often been recognized – most notably by the field biologist, Alfred Russel Wallace. The Wallace Line, the natural boundary between the Oriental and Australian plant and animal worlds, was named after this man, who studied the distribution of plant and animal species.

With its abundant vegetation Indonesia's tropical rainforest is in no way as uniform as Africa's or South America's. In some areas, up to 100 different types of trees can be found on a single hectare of land, roughly 2½ acres. In Borneo's jungle alone, there are twice as many species as in all of Africa. While the forests of Sumatra and Kalimantan have Asian features and contain trees of the **Dipterocarp** family, the Moluccan Islands, West Irian and others exhibit Australian characteristics with trees such as the **Eucalyptus** and the **Casuarina.** As its name suggests, the rainforest is dependent on high precipitation and the humid climate of the tropics. In areas with less than 2,000 mm/80″ of rainfall annually, one finds only sparse monsoon forests which turn into savannahs or grassland if annual precipitation falls below 1,000 mm/40″. Today, up to 75% of the surface area of Kalimantan and West Irian is still covered by primary forests. In densely populated Java, however, they can only be found in the nature reserve of **Ujung Kulon,** as well as near the summits of volcanoes. In addition to the **Ironwood,** which has such a high specific gravity that it cannot float, many other interesting and unusual examples of plant-life are encountered in Indonesia. The rare **rafflesia** (named after the Englishman, Raffles), found on Sumatra and Borneo, boasts the largest flower in the world (1 metre in diameter – about 39″). Like the **amorphophallus** (the stem of which can grow to more than 3 metres/39″ in length) it lures the insects necessary for pollination by means of its putrid stench. Many botanists have never seen the rafflesia arnoldi despite long years searching in the Sumatran jungles.

Those who are more interested in fragrant plants can admire the countless wild species as well as the fantastic newly-cultivated species of **orchids** in the botanical gardens of Jakarta and Bogor. Owing to their pleasant scent and beautiful blossoms, **frangipani** (Kamboja), **jasmine** (Melati) and **bougainvillea** (imported from Brazil) are also widely cultivated in Indonesia.

Not only do fascinating and beautiful ornamental plants grow in this country, but also plants that fulfil vitally important functions. One of the most important is the fast-growing **bamboo,** of which there are 250 species in the archipelago. Deft and skilful, the Indonesians use the bamboo in a variety of ways. Carrying-poles, drinking-vessels, dwellings and bridges are only a few examples of "bamboo technology". The fact that Jakarta's skyscrapers are built using bamboo scaffolding shows that this plant has a place in the 20th century and perhaps even beyond. Besides, the bamboo is beautiful – and this holds true for the useful varieties as well as the ornamental ones.

Palm trees generally stand as a symbol of the tropics, of the exotic, and of the longing to visit far-away places. There are over 150 species in Indonesia. The most well-known must be the **coconut palm** which grows in profusion in the coastal lowlands.

For the inhabitants of smaller islands and atolls, **copra** (dried kernel of the coconut) is the main source of income besides fishing. Palm wine, coconut fibre and oil are just a few of the other products that can be obtained from this plant. **Sago, betel, rotang and nipa** are other useful varieties of palm.

The many so-called "carnivorous" plants are not, however, of great economic significance. Whereas most insects are dissolved by pepsins secreted by the pitcher plant, there is a certain species of mosquito that spends its larval stage in these juices.

The Coconut Palm . . .
The End of an Era

Talk about a change of scenery, and anyone who loves the tropics will automatically think of sandy beaches and coconut trees.

For the majority of us, coconut palms symbolise distant places, and the exotic in general. Yet for those people living in coastal areas of the tropics, this ancient tree – cocos nucifera, to give it its Latin name – often represents their second major source of nutrition after fish. In fact the tree can be put to a variety of different uses – it provides building and weaving material, for example.

When the terrible news became known that cocos nucifera had fallen victim to a deadly disease, the people who sat up and took notice were largely plantation owners and tourist organisations.

And indeed more and more trees all over the world are developing yellow and brown leaves. In many places a solitary stump, devoid of leaves, is all that stands out against the tropical blue sky.

Is the tree which fantasies are made of destined to the same fate as the forests of Europe and the Amazon? A few people who have so far stood idly by and done nothing for the cause of Europe's trees, will doubtless protest, "Don't let my palm tree be destroyed as well!" What's to be done? Once the dominant feature of the tropical landscape, the coconut palm presents a very dismal picture of itself today. Some of the regions now affected, include whole areas of Africa, India and Borneo. The first signs of the disease have also been detected in areas of Indonesia. "Can we still save some of these trees?"

Scientists have already pinpointed the culprits; they are micro organisms carried by cicadas. The damage begins when the cicadas pierce the bark of the tree, enabling these tiny organisms to work their way into the trunk's vascular bundle. Here, they multiply rapidly. This has 2 consequences: the tree's water supply is cut off, and its pattern of metabolism altered.

"So, it's nothing to do with acid rain," you say, and sigh with relief. Don't! After all, the tremendous increase in the number of cicadas is also due to environmental factors. How can we combat this?

At present, experiments are being carried out to develop both resistant strains of coconut tree and an effective insecticide. The cicadas, however, seem to be resistant to all existing insecticides, and who is to say whether these weren't responsible for destroying the enemies of the cicadas in the first place?

Should the trees continue to wither and die, there may come a point when cartoons about islands won't be able to feature the coconut palm any more, without risking giving a false impression of reality.

Fauna

Just as Indonesia's plant kingdom harbours many as yet unknown species, the animal kingdom too, contains species which have yet to be discovered or studied. Biologists guess that there must still be thousands of unknown species of **insects** in the Indonesian rainforest whose identification will probably never take place – the radical clearing of forests in recent years has severely threatened many of them. Although every tree shelters an army of especially adapted insects to live off its roots, its bark or its leaves, hardly any damage is done at all. Only when the symbiosis between insect and tree is thrown off balance through the intervention of man, does it come to uncontrolled insect damage.

Many of these chitin-clad creatures have adapted themselves splendidly to their surroundings. The family of stick insects to which the **praying mantis** belongs, distinguishes itself in the art of camouflage. Some resemble sticks, twigs or leaves. The many species of **termites,** on the other hand, excel in the building of nests of all shapes and sizes. While the spherical nests of some species hang from the tops of trees, others look like fortresses with high towers.

Since there are only a few carrion-eating animals in Indonesia, this task has fallen primarily to the **ants,** who perform an important function in the life cycle of the rainforest. Because most of them react with a stinging bite when danger is sensed, they ought to be observed from a distance only. Actually, the only tropical insect with which one really comes into contact is the **mosquito,** which, however, tends to avoid air-conditioned rooms. Only a few species of the **genus anopheles** are malaria-carrying, but because the disease is prevalent in the swampy coastal lowlands of Sumatra, Kalimantan and Irian Jaya, a malaria prophylaxis and the use of a mosquito net at night are recommended.

Apart from the magnificent beetles and spiders, which despite their multi-coloured raiment, rarely seem to find favour with the visitor, some of the most splendid members of the insect world, belong to the large family of butterflies. With a wingspan of 25 cm – about 11", the **attocas atlas** is the largest butterfly in Southeast Asia. The rainy season is the time when most species emerge. During this time, they are also larger and more beautiful than at other times.

The most celebrated representatives of the Indonesian animal kingdom are the **orang-utan** and the **komodo lizard.**

Today, the orang-utan can only be found on Sumatra and Borneo, although at one time, it was prevalent on the mainland too. Though this primate has never posed a threat to man, it was avidly hunted by the early European settlers, who gave themselves over to speculations about the animal's origin owing to its natural intelligence and manlike appearance. Its friendly and curious nature could not save it from being pursued, but today, thanks to vigorous protective measures, a few thousand orang-utans still live in their natural habitat. In **Bohorok** (North Sumatra) and in the **Tanjung Puting Reserve** (South Kalimantan), young orang-utans that have been rescued from the black market are rehabilitated for life in the jungle.

With its dark leathery skin and its long, forked, yellow-orange tongue, the **komodo lizard** seems to be the embodiment of a prehistoric monster. With its 4-metre-long – about 13′ body, it is the largest living reptile, and can reach a weight of 180 kg/ 397 lbs. It was first discovered in 1912 on the Lesser Sunda island of Komodo, as well as on the neighbouring islands of Padar and Rinca. Smaller versions of this species are also found in the western part of Flores. Not only does the komodo have a mysterious air about it, but the island of Komodo is rather forbidding with its rugged mountain peaks and primordial palm groves. These huge lizards supplement their diet of carrion by hunting wild pigs and deer and on hot days, they can be seen fishing in the sea.

As has been mentioned already, the distribution of animal species can be explained by the shifts in the earth's crust which occurred during the Pleistocene period. Brought about by the ice age, this tectonic activity caused land bridges to form between the continents, allowing the **elephant** and the **rhinoceros** to migrate to Sumatra and Kalimantan. In western Java, there are about 25

Javanese armoured rhinos left. Because pulverized rhino horn is believed by the Chinese to have aphrodisiac effects, the two-horned rhino of Sumatra is still hunted illegally and is in danger of becoming extinct.

The **tiger,** which in the course of time extended its habitat from Sumatra and Java to Bali, became extinct on that island in the early 1970's. It was the smallest of its species. Today, about 600 tigers live on Java and Sumatra. When population pressure forces man to encroach upon the tiger's territory, deadly encounters sometimes occur – especially in the vicinity of reservations, and especially when prey is scarce. The **leopard,** however, can be found in great numbers on overpopulated Java – generally in wooded volcanic areas – because it has learned to side-step human expansion. The **tapir,** hardly noticeable because of its black and white camouflage, is another rare species. It roams through Sumatra's rainforests grazing with its trunklike snout as it goes. The **banteng** is a species of wild cattle living on Java and Kalimantan, of which there are also domesticated forms (particularly on Bali). Along with the water buffalo (kerbau) and the zebu, these are the most important draught animals.

The islands east of the **Wallace Line** are home to an array of magnificent birds, as well as to marsupials such as the **kuskus** and the **tree kangaroo.** The unique **bird of paradise,** the ostrich-like **cassowary** and the **blue-crowned pigeon** are indigenous to New Guinea and its adjacent islands. The coat-of-arms of West Irian, the part of the island that belongs to Indonesia, is even adorned by a bird of paradise. Some birds are renowned for their ability to imitate sounds and voices: the black-feathered **beo** and the **cockatoo** are the uncrowned champions in this field. Those that live in Jakarta's zoo specialize in imitating their two- and four-legged neighbours.

With its more than 55 nature reserves, Indonesia is a true paradise for animals – including snakes! Although holidaymakers fear them more than any other creature, expecting them to slither out from behind every rock and bush, it is possible to spend weeks in the jungle without coming face-to-face with a single one of these reptiles. Most species of snakes will avoid an encounter with man but, as they are nocturnal animals, sturdy footwear should be worn in the bush at night. It's better to be sure! Among the more than 200 species on the archipelago, the **taipan** and the **banded krait** are the most venomous; the reticulated **python,** which can reach up to 11 metres/36′ in length, is the world's longest snake. There is even one that can fly through the air – not really a flying snake, but the **chrysopolea,** a snake that can push itself off a limb of a tree and glide to the earth with its body flattened-out. There are also other reptiles and amphibians which take daring leaps from trees and effortlessly glide through the air. The many species of **bats,** which swarm out in their thousands at dusk, are, however, true acrobatic flyers.

The Indonesian **crocodiles,** on the other hand, are terrestrial and aquatic creatures. Those that live in brackish and salt water can reach the awesome length of 7 to 8 metres/23–26′. They prefer mangrove swamps and muddy coastal waters which are rich in fish. Significantly smaller but just as successful at hunting are the **geckos** (cicaks), which inhabit the tallest skyscrapers and the tiniest huts as the "good spirits" of man. A source of light, near which they can lie in wait for the pests that fly and bite in the night, is all that is needed to assure their services. The somewhat larger **toké,** whose call gives it its name, is considered to bring good luck to the person who hears it sound its call seven times in a row. If this does not occur, everything just stays the same.

Those who are concerned about the preservation of nature should especially avoid buying souvenirs made from the skins, hides or horns of protected species. Tortoiseshell, reptilian leather, ivory and coral are some of these.

As an alternative to the rewarding but tedious search for animals in their natural habitat, a visit to **Ranguan Zoo** near Jakarta is highly recommended. In this zoo, which once won first prize in an international contest, many species can be observed in environments quite similar to their own natural habitats.

The People

The task which fell to the first president of the Republic – that of establishing political unity in an area inhabited by over 300 ethnic groups – was no easy one. Then as now, the most important link between the many dissimilar cultures was the national language, Bahasa Indonesia, developed from the Melayu language spoken in the Riau archipelago and showing strong similarities to Malaysian. The Islamic faith, making up over 80% of the population at the time, also contributed much to the idea of national unity. Today, the government endeavours to do justice to Indonesia's motto, **"Unity in Diversity"** (Bhinneka Tunggal Ika) – a motto which is the nation's coat-of-arms. The rapid development of transportation links and communications has helped in bringing the different cultures closer and closer together.

As already mentioned, Indonesia's ethnic diversity is the result of the mass migration of various peoples. The **Proto-Malayan Dayaks, Bataks** and **Torajas** came to the archipelago between 2000 and 3000 B.C., forcing the indigenous **Austronesian** people (**Atoni** and **Alfoeren**) into the remote mountain regions. With the appearance of the **Deutero-Malayans,** which include the **Javanese, Sundanese** and **Balinese,** the Proto-Malayans suffered the same fate. In their inaccessible homelands, however, they were little affected by the arrival of the Hindu and Islamic faiths. Only in the mid-19th century, when the Christian church carried out missionary work tailor-made for the people, did their cult of ancestor worship begin to become affected. Many of these tribes – the **Dayaks, Torajas, Tukudils, Kubus** and **Papuans,** to name a few – have succeeded in preserving their original beliefs to this day, thus making an important contribution to Indonesia's cultural diversity. Along with the glorious spiritual and artistic expressions of deutero-Malayan culture, as reflected in their fascinating folklore and beautiful temples, recognition is now being given to the unique cultural achievements of Indonesia's aboriginal peoples, who, up until recently, were considered "primitive" and thus unworthy of attention.

With more than **160 million** inhabitants (and the figure is growing at a rate of 2.2% annually), Indonesia is the fourth most-populated nation in the world. There are 95 million people on Java alone, a population density of 1,000/sq. km or 2,580/sq. mi. Bali and Lombok also lead in population density. On the other hand, islands such as Kalimantan and Sumatra with 8 and 50 people per square kilometre respectively – 28 and 129 per sq. mi., are greatly underpopulated.

The problems caused by high concentrations of population have hindered the social and economic development of the affected areas. Therefore large portions of the population of Java, Bali and Sulawesi have been resettled in less-populated areas through so-called Transmigrasi projects.

Family planning (keluarga berencana) has also proven effective in the battle against overpopulation. By this means, it has actually been possible to lower the rate of growth by 0.5% over a period of a few years.

Although more than 90% of the population professes to the Islamic faith, Islam is not a state religion. In the constitution, in which the **Panca Sila** (see "Appendix") plays a central role, freedom of religion is guaranteed. The largest concentrations of Christians are to be found on the Moluccas, on Flores and Timor, in Irian and among the Batak people of Sumatra. They account for only 6% of Indonesia's total population, but in spite of this small percentage, there is a relatively high number of Christians in the upper political echelons. Their strong position can be traced back to their loyalty during Indonesia's struggle for independence. Christian **schools** and hospitals, some of which have been taken over by the state in recent years, are among the best in the country. The respect enjoyed by most Christians in Indonesia is not accorded to the Protestant Fundamentalists, however. Blind to other religions, their missionaries became over zealous in their work for small American and English sects and got themselves a bad name. **Hindus, Buddhists and Animists** make up the remaining 4% of the population. Like Islam, these religions are partly influenced by the beliefs and concepts of Hindu-Javanese tradition.

Despite the many social problems that affect their lives, Indonesians are a friendly and cheerful people who approach visitors with curiosity and interest. Sometimes, however, their behaviour reflects the conflict between traditional values and the modern world: urban youngsters, in particular, are drifting further away from the fascinating legacy of the past. Tourism, which today has even penetrated into remote areas, also contributes to this cultural clash. Ethnic groups like the Toraja, who can scarcely identify with western philosophies and life-styles, have reverted back to old beliefs such as Aluk Tudolo.

The Indonesian **Educational System** is presently undergoing expansion. The village schools set up by the Dutch from 1907 onwards, as well as the institutions of higher learning which followed on a small scale, served primarily to satisfy the needs of the colonial administration and to train a limited number of Indonesians for subordinate administrative functions. In 1945, 93% of the population of 72 million was illiterate. In that same year, the number of university graduates stood at 480. In no other colonialized country was the native population kept at such a disadvantage as in the then Dutch East Indies. Because of this, the newly independent nation initially lacked the brain potential it needed for development. Only when this historical situation is taken into account, can the present achievements be properly appreciated. In 1963, already 45% of the population could read and write. While only 21,000 schools existed in 1938, this number was increased to 143,000 by 1971. Further education has not been neglected either. Today, more than 500,000 students study at state-run and private universities. This list of achievements should not lead one to

Islam

Islam is more that just a religion – it is a way of life and a social system; it is philosophy, law and science all at the same time. The word Islam means "submission" – but not to a hierarchical system. Analogous to Christianity in the West, the humanitarian preachings of Islam gave a sense of self-worth to the common people of Indonesia. The notion of religious solidarity, which developed within large portions of the population, was equally instrumental in bringing about a religious stimulus.

Every day at sunrise and sunset, the voice of the muezzin that pours out of the loudspeakers of the mosques summons over 140 million Indonesian Moslems to prayer. Dressed for worship in a sarong and with the black velvet peci on their heads, the men pour into the mosques on Fridays to proclaim their submission to Allah. Women generally pray at home wearing a rukuh – a white cloak that leaves only the face exposed. Despite their devoutness, the orthodox aspects of the religion are more wishful thinking than reality to the Indonesians. Their form of Islam requires neither the passivity and fervour typical of Asiatic religions, nor does it require one to follow the strict rules of conduct that are customary in Arab countries. This liberal interpretation of Islam is especially manifest in the social position of Indonesian women. Although in some regions women keep their head and face veiled, their total concealment and seclusion is, in general, not customary.

Islam came to the Malayan archipelago in the 13th century (600 years after its inception) through the peaceful intervention of Arab, Persian and Indian traders. Its diffusion occurred, as a rule, without force. The new faith gradually permeated the Buddhistic-Hinduistic belief systems and was absorbed into a synthesis of Hindu mysticism and traditional animism. The sultanate of Aceh, which converted to Islam in the 15th century, was, at that time, the only power in the country that tried by means of a holy war to force the spread of Islam on Sumatra. They were mostly unsuccessful, however, for they had not taken into consideration the power of adat.

After World War II, the islands became acquainted with a militant Moslem movement, the Dar-ul-Islam. Their aim was to establish a fundamentalist Islamic state based on the laws of the Koran. By means of a guerilla war, they first tried to eliminate the Dutch colonial authority, and later, even the central government of the Republic. Since 1966, however, the movement has lost most of its influence.

Like Christianity, Islam is a religion convinced of the universal truth of its teachings, which, consequently are actively propagated.

overlook the remaining deficiencies in the Indonesian educational system. Owing to the relatively high tuition fees, lower and middle-income earners are at a disadvantage.

Despite general advances in the Public Health System, the state of health of the Indonesian people still leaves much to be desired. The ratio of 45 sick patients (including many children under five) for every 1,000 inhabitants clearly shows the necessity for further measures. In 1980, there were approximately 740 hospitals with roughly 14,000 beds – that amounts to one bed for every 1,100 people. The majority of hospitals, however, are not filled to capacity, owing in part, to a lack of medical personnel. While in 1945 there was only one doctor for every 60,000 inhabitants, in 1978, this ratio decreased to 1/20,000. In remote areas of the South Moluccas, the actual ratio can even reach 1/180,000 – while most doctors establish their practice on the main island of Ambon. Statistically speaking, they serve the entire southern region.

Although in Indonesia food is available in adequate quantities, the lack of a well-balanced diet in many areas is the source of numerous health problems. In the last two five-year plans, however, attention has been devoted to public health and nutrition.

Economy and Transportation

During the Dutch colonial period, concentration was placed on exports, thus bringing about the exhaustion of Indonesia's natural resources. Improvements in transportation, communication and services were aimed, at the time, at increasing export profits from mining and plantation farming. The areas of production important for Indonesia, such as rural farming, crafts and small industries, were severely neglected. It often happened that Chinese middlemen supplied the products from these branches of industry to colonial entrepreneurs, who then exported them for a profit. This colonial economic system caused an economic dependence on affluent nations, the after effects of which were especially noticeable under the Sukarno government (inflation rate 65%). Under the Suharto government, the emphasis has been placed on a uniform economic development which includes small-scale farming and industry. The G. N. P., based on 1966 prices, grew from RP 412 billion in 1967 to RP 865 billion in 1976. In 1981, the inflation rate stood at a relatively low 15%. The **average per-capita income,** which stood at 143 US$ in 1975, is expected to increase to 245 US$ by 1985.

Indonesia's largest source of income is **Petroleum:** the net profits from the export of this resource amounts to more than 50% of the country's gross revenue from exports. Nearly 1.9 million barrels (1 barrel = 159 litres) of high-grade, almost sulphur-free oil are produced yearly. Until recently, however, the crude oil had to be refined abroad, as the necessary technology was not yet available. Processed petroleum products then had to be bought back using valuable foreign currency. As a member of **opec,** Indonesia's share in the organization's gross production stood at 5–6% in recent years. The country's largest oil field is on Sumatra, where the first exploratory drillings took place. At present, the wells near Palembang yield more than two-thirds of Indonesia's total petroleum output. Offshore drilling began on the shelf off the northern coast of Java in 1971 and already accounts for 20% of the country's production. Further drilling areas are located in North and South Sumatra, South and East Kalimantan, on Ceram and in Irian Jaya. These only account for a small percentage of the entire production of oil, however. On Indonesia's 80 oil fields, there are approximately 2,720 oil-drilling rigs in operation. At present, 46 drilling concessions are held by foreign (primarily American) oil companies. Crude oil is processed in domestic refineries and petro-chemical plants by Pertamina, Indonesia's state-run oil company. In future, **Natural Gas** deposits are to be further exploited and are expected to yield revenues that should eventually surpass those from petroleum. The technology needed for liquefication and transportation, however, requires capital which can only be procured through co-operation with foreign investors.

Indonesia has large deposits of **bauxite** and **copper** that should gain in importance in the near future. As the world's third-largest producer of tin, the country finds many markets for this metal. In many areas, probings for further mineral deposits have turned up traces of **uranium** and **iron ore.**

In the early 1970's, **Timber** exports jumped considerably. After petroleum, forestry is Indonesia's next largest source of income and accounted for 9.1% of total exports in 1977. The main market for Indonesian timber is Japan. No new logging licences are to be issued in future, however, because the exportation of raw timber has become economically untenable. Through the establishment of domestic timber processing plants, not only would many much-needed jobs be created, but valuable foreign currency would remain in the country. The fact that these domestic plants will probably

Rice

To the Indonesians, the green panacle grass that grows on terraced slopes or in irrigated fields is not merely a plant – rice is life, rice has a soul!

Harvest-time, which can occur two to three times a year depending on the soil's fertility, requires careful and attentive work. A few days before it begins, ceremonies, which vary from island to island, are performed to appease the gods, the demons and the soul of the rice. On Java and Bali, the goddess, Sri Dewi, whose cult is part of pre-Hindu animist rites, is honoured as the patroness of rice. As a sign of gratitude to her, a small spoonful of rice is left on each of the millions of plates of this grain, eaten daily on Java and Bali. Those who eat their plates clean are considered greedy and gluttonous. This may seem irrational to the visitor accustomed to abundance at the table, but for the many Indonesians who do not take their daily portion of rice for granted, it is considered fitting to show appreciation to Sri Dewi by sharing the last spoonful of rice with her. Since approximately 70 percent of the Indonesian people work the soil, many know through their own experience how toilsome the growing of rice is. In view of this fact, it is easy to see why rice is held in such reverence.

Depending on the location, rice can be grown at altitudes of up to 1,400–1,600 metres/4,600–5,250′ above sea level; however, the maximum elevation possible is not determined by climatic conditions, but rather by the water supply. Mountain slopes that are heavily furrowed as a result of erosion can only be irrigated up to an elevation of 900 metres. To prepare for a new crop, the rice field is first inundated to soften the soil; then, the farmer goes to work with his plough, which is almost always pulled by a water buffalo. The idyllic picture that most of us cherish of the rice farmer only seldom reveals the back-breaking work that lies behind it. The iridescent-green seedlings that are planted 10 cm/4″ apart in the muddy earth will mature in 4–6 months owing to continuous irrigation. A few weeks before harvesting, the field is then drained. When the time comes, the tops of the stalks will be cut – but not with a sickle. In many areas of the Greater Sundas, they are cut one by one with a small knife called the ani ani, so as not to frighten the soul of the plant and possibly jeopardize the coming harvest.

In most areas of Indonesia, rice is the main source of nourishment. Although huge tracts of land (ca. 850,000 sq. km/328,185 sq. miles) are set aside for its cultivation, Indonesia is also the world's largest importer of this grain today. From the point of view of production, the land available for cultivation is, for the most part, exhausted, and can no longer meet the demand for rice – which is increasing along with the population. The effectiveness of the traditional Javanese wet-rice method of cultivation has so far been able to prevent a socio-economic crisis. Sawah cultivation is a lesson in farming efficiency and yields harvests which were, until now, considered impossible. The present government has pledged itself to increasing production and keeping prices stable. At present, approx. 17 million tons of rice are produced annually and a growth rate of over 5% has been achieved. In Kalimantan and on Sumatra and Sulawesi, further regions are to be developed for wet-rice farming, for without rice, there can be no future for the country.

In the Indonesian language, rice is not merely rice. As a plant, it is called padi, the hulled grain is called beras, and after cooking, it becomes the everyday but highly treasured bowl of nasi.

not be able to work to the same capacity as the foreign plants gives rise to the hope that they will contribute to curbing the uncontrolled clearing of the rainforest, which threatens the habitat of native peoples, animals and plants. Cattle breeding and irrigation are to undergo improvements, and it is hoped that **Agriculture** will be given a boost by modern methods of marketing and transport. The demand for palm oil, copra and rubber that began building up in Europe in the latter part of the 19th century has since fallen off. The initially high price of latex rubber fell after it became possible to manufacture synthetic rubber from petroleum. Later, when the price of oil increased, the production of natural rubber re-gained some of its significance. Since 1970, the **Industrialization** of the country has been in full swing. In order to put the army of the unemployed back to work, the country needs, above all, labour-intensive industries. In view of the fact that arable land will sooner or later become scarce, agriculture is not in a position to accommodate the growing number of jobless people. The economic future of the country, and its social development, are, thus very dependent on continued industrialization. The government intends to move large and medium-sized industries to the outer islands as an incentive to people from overpopulated Java to settle in these lesser-developed areas. Cilegon, Jakarta, Surabaya, Medan, Palembang and the oil centres of Kalimantan and Irian Jaya, are at present still the industrial centres of Indonesia. The decentralization of industry, however, will certainly be impeded by a non-existent infrastructure and an inadequate **Transport System.** In regions where economic necessity did not call for it, some roads have never been asphalted. However, the highways of Java and Bali are, for the most part, in good condition, and in 1980, the first segment of the nation's first motorway (joining Jakarta and Bogor) was opened. With respect to the development of the country's traffic routes, navigable rivers represent the least expensive option, whereas the construction of roads and railways poses great financial problems.

Becak – bicycle trishaw

Modernization measures have done much to improve Indonesia's **railway network,** especially on Java's long distance routes, as anyone who has travelled to Surabaya on the Bima Night Express can confirm. To get somewhere fast, however, the **aeroplane** is the best option. In addition to the national airlines, Garuda and Merpati, there are many small private companies which provide a regular service to small, out-of-the-way airports and airstrips. Indonesia's 400 take-off and landing-facilities range in size from 200-metre-long grass-covered tracks to paved runways of several thousand metres in length. The direct services offered by Garuda and Merpati are quite extensive, and if one wishes to stop off in the bush of Kalimantan or on one of Irian's mountains, the many charter airlines (for example Air Indonesia and Airfast) will be glad to be of assistance. Those who love the sea – and have time on their hands – can travel to the island of their dreams by **boat.** In addition to the more than 90 ports, there are very many smaller landing-piers served by the state-owned Pelni Lines, whose ships range in capacity from 10 to 175 gross register tons. On the (larger) islands themselves, the best way to get about is by Colt bus. A good service is also offered by the larger Mercedes buses and the old Chevrolets, as well as by the army of two-, three- and four-wheeled short-distance vehicles.

Food and Drink

Rich in variety, Indonesia's cuisine has something for everyone's palate. Those not interested in such culinary expeditions, however, can find western dishes in the larger hotels, restaurants and coffee shops; but be forewarned: if you order Spaghetti Bolognese, expecting it to taste like the original, bear in mind that the term "al dente" is not known here, and go instead for the Indonesian dish Bambi rebus. Owing to the lack of the necessary ingredients, European dishes often take on new and not always pleasant forms. Besides, it would be a shame to leave the country without having enjoyed a **rijsttafel**. Though it isn't exactly cheap, the **Oasis,** Jl. Raden Saleh 47, can be recommended for its continental cuisine and its rijsttafel. The rijsttafel served at the **Rice Bowl** in the Nusantara Building near Hotel President on Jalan Thamrin is also much acclaimed – and fairly priced. Do not expect to find a complete set of utensils on the table: Indonesian food is eaten with the fork in the left hand and the spoon in the right. A knife is never needed as the food is always served in bite-sized pieces.

The traditional cooking of Java, which usually dominates Indonesian menus, makes use of beef, chicken and seafood, as well as an array of vegetables and condiments which are then served with rice or krupuk (shrimp or fish crisps). Those who hope to be served the snake meat and monkey's brain they have heard about will have to repair to the hunters and gatherers of the rainforest: as Islam wields great influence over the eating habits of its faithful, such so-called "unclean" foods – foods which are not halal – may not be eaten by the majority of the population. In addition to pork, delicacies such as frogs' legs and snails are also taboo. If you want a complete change, there are also many Chinese restaurants to choose from. Enterprising diners will find the night markets to be veritable treasure troves, selling food at reasonable prices. Those who cannot do without sweet pastries, can pay a visit to one of the many, mostly Chinese-run bakeries, for example, the **International Bakery** on Jl. Haji Agus Salim in Jakarta.

Special attention should be devoted to the many tropical fruits. In addition to **Mangos, Pineapples** and an endless variety of large and small, green, yellow and red bananas, of which the green **Pisang Ambon** and the small **Pisang Mas** are especially worth trying, there are also many lesser known exotic fruits. Besides the controversial **Durian** (stink-fruit), which has found many fans among visitors to Indonesia, there are also many other delicious-tasting fruits. In order to try **Papayas, Rambutans, Mangosteens** (manggis), salak, jambu and all the other colourful varieties of fruit, several months would have to be spent on the island, because they all ripen in different seasons – but because these seasons vary from island to is-

Sambal Goreng (serves 2)

½ lb. green beans, sliced
½ lb. beef, finely diced
1 cup coconut milk
1 tbs. sambal
1 thumb-size laos root
1 large onion, finely chopped
3 cloves garlic, finely chopped
1 tsp. shrimp paste (trassie)
3–4 bay leaves
2 tsp. sugar
3 tbs. cooking oil
salt

Heat the oil and fry the onion and garlic together with the sambal and the shrimp paste. Add the laos and the bay leaves and continue frying over a high heat for 3–5 minutes. Add the beef and continue frying for another 3 minutes, then add the beans. Allow to cook for another 5–10 minutes. Season with coconut milk and salt.

Nasi Goreng (serves 4)

1 large onion, finely chopped
2 cups rice
3–4 cloves garlic, finely chopped
1–2 tbs. sambal
1 tsp. shrimp paste
3 tbs. cooking oil
¼ head of Chinese or white cabbage, sliced
1 leek, sliced
3 sticks celery, sliced
½ lb. meat
salt

Heat the oil and fry the onion and garlic together with the sambal and the shrimp paste. Add the meat and continue frying; then add the vegetables. Finally, stir in the rice (cooked) and allow to fry for another few minutes. Salt to taste. Garnish with an omelette cut into strips and with slices of cucumber and lettuce. Serve with krupuk (shrimp crisps).

land, with a little bit of luck, one could get hold of some imported fruit. The quality of the fruit depends heavily on its island of origin. Especially tasty is salak, a fruit with scaly, reddish-brown, reptilian-like skin, to be found on Bali and in North Sumatra. Palembang in South Sumatra is known for its small but very aromatic pineapples, and the delicious belimbing grows in Central Java. The maracuja or passion fruit can be found at markets at higher elevations. Markisa, as it is called, is used in North Sumatra and on Sulawesi to make a high-quality syrup, which is then used as the basis for delicious-tasting soft drinks.

Among the traditional beverages enjoyed by the Indonesians, coconut milk is a particular favourite – it is cheap, refreshing, hygienically packaged and obtainable almost everywhere. Those who prefer to quench their thirst with cola or similar drinks can find them everywhere, too, though not always chilled. Sweetened black tea, which can even be bought by the bottle, is however cheaper and more effective. Besides exotic fruit juices, the bars of the international hotels also offer an array of tropical cocktails and long drinks, which can be very tempting. Those who would rather not see the sun go down in broad daylight, however, should wait until dark to enjoy alcoholic beverages. This applies to the many brands of beer which can be had in Indonesia as well.

As generally much care and attention is devoted to the preparation of food and drink in Indonesia, one can stop at even the smallest restaurant or foodstall along the road without a second thought about quality. Here, the guest can be sure of sampling a typical Indonesian meal as well as getting a first-hand look at everyday life.

A Guide to Conduct in Indonesia

Despite the processes of cultural and social change, the everyday life of the Indonesians is still very much governed by adat, a system of values based on religious beliefs and common law, which determines how one should think and act. By leading a life bound by adat law, even the most humble of individuals acquires an air of dignity (the few exceptions in the cities proves the rule here too). In large hotels, where the personnel are in daily contact with insensitive and superficial western visitors, one's search for what is typical and appealing about the national character will usually be in vain. Where courtesy and modesty have given way to obtrusiveness and greediness, one can be sure that tourism has had its hand in the affair. Therefore, it depends on us whether the people of the lands we visit, will pass on their traditional values to the coming generations. Those who think they can make an impression by showing off or taking a know-it-all attitude will be sorely disappointed. Technical advisers and consultants who have come to Indonesia as representatives of the larger industrialized nations, often return home in the knowledge that the humble man has a wisdom of his own and that these people set other goals in their lives than mere material ones. Those who have ever got to know the Indonesians and their lavish and untiring hospitality will have realized what is lacking in our society. Although the various ethnic groups all have their own characteristic attitudes, customs and ways, there are a number of fundamental rules which apply throughout the entire archipelago.

Exchanges: When Indonesians greet each other, they do so in a way that often seems timorous and restrained to us. The ritual varies greatly from region to region. When two West Javanese meet, each will place his palms together and raise his hands to his forehead; then both will bow slightly so that their fingertips touch. Among some West Irianese tribes, the ritual of greeting involves the linking of fingers. A vigorous handshake or a pat on the shoulders is generally met with cool reserve on the part of the Indonesians, because in their eyes, these forms of greeting have little to do with courtesy and respect. It should be kept in mind that many Indonesians, in particular the Sundanese, Javanese and the Balinese, regard the head as the seat of the soul and that it should therefore never be touched. Even a pat on a child's head could be regarded as an affront. The thoughtless offering of the left hand in greeting is likewise considered to be grossly offensive. But do not worry – allowances are made for the ignorance of foreigners.

Eating Etiquette: For the same reason, one should never accept or offer food with the left (unclean) hand. In general, it is best to accept food and drink (and gifts) with both hands outstretched – this way one does not convey the impression of taking courtesy for granted. As it is considered good manners to have a second helping of food, and the host will certainly encourage this, it is best to eat with moderation. Never turn down an offer to taste something else; instead, take a token helping and decline with thanks. When food and drink is placed on the table, the polite guest waits to be invited by his host to partake – as difficult as this may be sometimes.

Dress: Never enter banks or government buildings in shorts or beachwear – it could mean that the effort was made in vain. An Indonesian judges whether or not a person is worthy of his attention and respect, by the way he is dressed. A tourist in expensive, fashionable clothing, however, will not find it easier to meet Indonesians: best-dressed competitions are largely unknown here. Modesty and good grooming make the difference. Shoes should always be removed before entering someone's home.

Taking Photos: Being photographed in poverty and filth can certainly be humiliating – therefore you should always ask permission first. Often the person will agree to pose after having glanced in the mirror – vanity is not unknown here. Children, on the other hand, usually enjoy being photographed. Never make promises to send people pictures unless you are absolutely sure you can keep them.

Temples and Mosques: Please bear in mind that these are houses of worship and that visitors are expected to behave in a quiet and dignified manner. Similar conduct is also in order when visiting ancient religious edifices such as the Borobudur, which still today draws Buddhist pilgrims from all over Asia. When entering a mosque (as far as this is permitted), shoes should be removed. Smoking is prohibited. Neat and decent attire is a must (for women this means that the arms and legs are to be covered). In order to enter a Balinese temple, the visitor must wear a sash – usually available at the entrance. Shorts and beachwear are out of place here. Women undergoing menstruation are forbidden to enter Bali's temples. This rule should be respected, for nothing gives us the right to disregard practices which are deeply rooted in the Balinese Hindu faith. When participating in religious ceremonies on Bali, the spectator should take care not to stand in an elevated position as this right is reserved for the priests.

Time: The fact that our conception of time differs from that of the Indonesians does not necessarily mean that ours is better. In Indonesia, punctuality is not a sign of good breeding – those who allow their host more time to prepare for their visit by arriving up to one hour late are showing perfectly good manners. Always allow plenty of time for paying calls – a guest in a hurry makes a very bad impression. Visits between the hours of 12:30 and 3:30 in the afternoon are considered impolite.

N.B.: If you want your chips or your nasi goreng to taste like they do at home, then it might be better to stay at home!

A First Lesson in Indonesian

On their voyages in the Indonesian archipelago, where today, more than 250 languages are still spoken, the early Asian traders used Malay, or Bahasa Malayu, as a lingua franca. Natively spoken in some parts of Sumatra, this tongue later served as the basis for Bahasa Indonesia, a modern, dynamic language which is still developing and changing. Many of its words are of Arab origin, contributed by the same traders who brought over the Islamic religion. The Portuguese and Dutch colonial periods left their marks on the Indonesian language as well. Although poets and philosophers at one time used the extremely diversified languages of Java and Bali as their medium of expression, Bahase Indonesia has gradually taken over the function of the upholder of culture. Each ethnic group speaks it in its own way. The language may sound harsh and monotonous at first, but you will soon discover how delightfully onomatopoeic and descriptive it is. Mata hari, for example, means "sun" or literally, "the eye of the day". The North American Indians were not the only ones who called the locomotive a "carriage of fire" – in Indonesian it is called kereta api, which means just the same thing.

Grammar: In Indonesian there are no articles, genders or cases; conjugations and declinations are likewise unknown. The plural is formed by merely doubling the noun (kursi – chair, kursi kursi – chairs). The adjective is always placed after the noun (spicy hot food – makanan pedas).

Orthography: Indonesian is written in Latin characters, using 21 letters of the alphabet.

Pronunciation: Indonesian is a highly phonetic language. The following deviations from English pronounciation should be noted, however:
"u" = "oo", "c" = "ch", "a" = "ah", "e" = long "a", "w" = "v".

Courtesy

Welcome – Selamat datang
Have a nice trip – Selamat jalan
Good morning – Selamat pagi
Good day – Selamat siang
Good afternoon – Selamat sore
Good evening – Selamat malam
Good night – Selamat tidur
Enjoy your meal – Selamat makan
Thank-you – Terima kasih
Thank-you very much – Terima kasih banyak
You're welcome – Terima kasih kembali
Excuse me – Ma'af permisi
It's alright – Tidak apa apa
How do you do? – Apa kabar?
I'm fine – Kabar baik
Good-bye – Sampai bertemu lagi

Common Words and Phrases

yes – ya
no – tidak
this – ini
I – saya
he, she, it – dia
you (plural) – kalian
good – bagus
small – kecil
big – besar
that – itu
you – kamu
we – kita, kami
they – mereka
none – bukan
What is that? – Apakah itu?
Do you speak English? – Saudara bicara bahasa Inggris?
I don't understand – Saya tidak mengerti
I would like – Saya minta

Finding your way:

Where – dimana
Where to – kemana
here – disini
there – disana
to – ke
in – di
straight ahead – terus
stop – berhenti
left – kiri
right – kanan
down – bawah
up – atas
south – selatan
north – utara
east – timur
west – barat
street – jalan
mountain – gunung
village – kampung
beach – pantai
far – jauh
near – dekat
back – kembali
to here – kesini
to there – kesana
direction – jurusan

city – kota
train station – stasiun
lake – danau
Is there here...? – Apakah disini ada

Numbers and Money:

0 – nol, 1 – satu, 2 – dua, 3 – tiga, 4 – empat, 5 – lima, 6 – enam, 7 – tujuh, 8 – delapan, 9 – sembilan, 10 – sepuluh, 11 – sebelas, 12 – duabelas, 13 – tigabelas, etc. 20 – dua puluh, 30 – tiga puluh, etc. 100 – seratus, 200 – duaratus, etc. 1,000 – seribu, 2,000 – duaribu, etc. 10,000 – sepuluh ribu, 100,000 – seratus ribu, 500,000 – lima ratus ribu, one million – satu juta or sejuta
cheap – murah
expensive – mahal
buy – beli
lend – sewa
pay – bayar
paper money – uang kertas
change – uang kecil
to change money – tukar uang
for sale – untuk dijual

Time and the Calendar:

Monday – senen
Tuesday – selasa
Wednesday – rabu
Thursday – kamis
Friday – jumat
Saturday – sabtu
Sunday – minggu
yesterday – kemarin
today – kari ini
tomorrow – besok
fast – cepat
slow – pelan
late – terlambat
later – nanti
now – sekarang
day – hari
week – minggu
month – bulan
year – tahun
hour – jam
time – waktu
when – kapan
one o'clock – jam satu
twelve o'clock – jam duabelas
What time is it now? – Jam berapa sekarang?

Food and Drink:

I'm hungry – saya lapar
I'm thirsty – saya haus
Not so spicy for me, please – ma'af untuk saya jangan terlalu pedas
to eat – makan
to drink – minum
table – meja
plate – piring
fork – garpu
knife – pisau
food – makanan
drink – minuman
chair – kursi
glass – gelas
spoon – sendok

Breakfast – Makanan pagi:

bread – roti
coffee – kopi
tea – teh
sugar – gula
milk – susu
butter – mentega
salt – garam
cheese – keju

egg – telur
jam – selai
cooked – rebus
fried – goreng

Lunch – Makan siang:
Dinner – Makan malam:

hot – panas
a little – sedikit
spicy – pedas
cold – dingin
a lot – banyak
sweet – manis
boiled rice – nasi
fried rice – nasi goreng
pork – daging babi
beef – daging sapi
chicken – ajam
mutton – daging kambing
shrimps, prawns – udang
crayfish – udang besar
fish – ikan
vegetable – sayuran
potato – kentang
duck – bebek
soup – soep
salad – selada
fruits – buah buahan
pineapple – nanas
banana – pisang
mango – mangga
coconut – kelapa
mangosteen – manggis
grapes – anggur
citrus fruits – jeruk

The items of food and drink listed here are by no means representative of the whole range of Indonesian fare. There are many, many more traditional Indonesian products which have no English equivalent.

Beverages – Minuman:

sodawater – air soda
orange juice – air jeruk
rice spirits – arak
water – air
iced tea – tehes
beer – bir

Emergency – keadaan kritis:

Where is there a hospital? – Dimana rumah sakit?
I'm sick – Saya sakit
Where is there a doctor? – Dimana ada dokter?
Please call an ambulance – Tolong panggil mobil ambulans
Chemist – apotik
Medicine – obat
I would like to make a telephone call – Saya mau tilpon

Hotel – hotel

Where is the toilet? – Dimana kamar kecil?
Where is the dining room? – Dimana kamar makan?
Guesthouse – losmen
Restaurant – restoran
Towel – anduk
Soap – sabun
Bill – bon
Have you any rooms free? – Masih ada kamar kassong?

Regional Section

Java

Area: 129,000 sq. km/49,800 sq. miles – 1,060 km/659 miles long and between 60 and 200 km/37–124 miles wide.

Although this green island south of the Equator, which was once the "Centraalland" of the Dutch colonial holdings, is only the fifth-largest of the archipelago, it contains two-thirds of Indonesia's 160 million people. The capital city of Jakarta, with its skyscrapers, its monuments and the Presidential Palace, is the city with the most drawing-power in the country. For many Indonesians, however, the dream of seeing Jakarta just once in their lifetime will always remain just that. At present, the city already has roughly 6 million inhabitants and gains approximately 160,000 yearly.

In Java's coastal lowlands, the climate is tropical, while in elevated areas it is subtropical. The eastern portions of the island experience a pronounced dry season, while western Java has one of the highest levels of precipitation in the country. A chain of 112 volcanoes extends the entire length of the island, giving it its characteristic appearance. Java is the nation's most agriculturally developed island, whose high productivity is due to intensive cultivation of the rich volcanic soil.

The island's most important cities are Jakarta, Bandung, Semarang and Surabaya. They lie in the provinces of West, Central and East Java and are all connected by a dense railway network. Because of its many points of interest, Yogyakarta is Java's tourist-centre, but in other parts of the island, there are interesting attractions as well – specialties that only Java has to offer. Brilliant-green rice fields, steep volcanoes topped by clouds of smoke, colourful villages, mysterious temple ruins and gentle and courteous people with fascinating customs make up the exotic beauty for which Java is famous.

West Java

West Java extends from the peninsula and nature reserve of **Ujung Kulon** in the West to the city of Cirebon in the East. Aside from the cultural points of interest of the city of **Banten,** west of Jakarta, most of West Java's attractions are primarily of an outdoor nature. The white, sandy beaches of the **West coast** with their Badui-style bungalow hotels, and the **Pulau Seribu** (Thousand Islands), northwest of Jakarta, attract the most bathers in this region. A visit to the volcanic island of **Anak Krakatoa** can be easily organized from the **Krakatoa Beach Hotel** near Labuan, as can trips to Ujung Kulon. The Badui style hotel can be reached by bemo or taxi from Labuan. Its simple but inviting wooden bungalows stand on the sandy beach at Carita. Tourists often stay here longer than they intended.

Very few tourists visit South-West Java, an area with a spectacular and lush landscape cut by deep river valleys, cheerful Sundanese villages accentuated by red brick roofs – and bad roads. This is the home of the isolated **Badui People,** who strictly shun the use of all modern implements from the wheel to the radio. They fiercely guard their customs against outside influences and have a strong dislike of the curious eyes of onlookers. As a result, they do their best to avoid contact with strangers – be they Indonesians or foreigners. Eighty km/50 miles east of Jakarta lies the artificial lake of **Jati Luhur** which offers reasonably-priced accomodation, splendid scenery and many opportunities for watersports. **Bogor,** whose botanical gardens attract many visitors all year round, can be reached in no time via a new motorway. "**Buitenzorg**", located on the periphery of the gardens, was once the residence of the Dutch governors; now it is the summer residence of the Indonesian president. From Bogor, the road to Bandung continues via the **Puncak Pass** (elevation 1,200 metres/ 3,937′), whose pleasant high-altitude climate encourages an extended stay at the hotels and restaurants there. Here, on seemingly endless plantations, grows the treasured Javanese tea. **Bandung,** the provincial capital of West Java, is situated on an 800 metre/2,625′-high plateau that is surrounded by volcanoes. In addition to its Institute of Technology which is famous throughout Asia, and an atomic research centre, the city hosts an aviation industry that operates under European licences. This city has made a name for itself as a centre of contemporary art, but has little else to offer the tourist who visits it. Coming from Jakarta, however, one should not miss the scenic train journey to Bandung which passes through one of Java's most beautiful agricultural zones. This city can also be reached by air. Just outside Bandung lies **Lambang,** which for most people is no more than the starting-point for a visit to the **Tangkuban Prahu volcano.** This city does have more to offer, though: it houses the Boscha Observatory as well as an SOS Children's Village which is worth visiting for a look at the work of this relief organization. The vol-

Tea-picking on Java.

cano, which can be reached from Lembang by car in half-an-hour, is dormant – sulphur fumes emanate only sporadically from its three craters. The trip through this magnificent volcanic landscape is a unique experience in itself.

Central Java

Since the middle of the last century, this area has drawn visitors from all over. They come to see the spectacular cultural landmarks that are the legacy of its Buddhistic-Hinduistic past. From Jakarta or Surabaya, the cities of Semarang, Surakarta and Yogyakarta can be reached by air, and there are comfortable rail connections (night trains) as well – in particular, the Bima and the Mutiara Expresses. Those who wish to enjoy the beautiful scenery on either side of the tracks should ride the Bandung-Tasikmalaya-Banyumas-Magelang-Yogyakarta-Solo route during the day – extending over deep gorges and on past a wild, vocanic landscape which rises above terraced rice fields. This is one of the most beautiful stretches of railway in the world. Central Java lies on the edge of the arid zone influenced by the climate of Australia – which is especially noticeable during the south-eastern monsoon. The intensively farmed land of this region, which is owned mostly by smallholders, is planted with rice, soja, vegetables, taro and singkong. The southern coast is especially arid and has often had to be declared a disaster area.

Semarang, with its approx. 1 million inhabitants, is the administrative capital of Central Java and has long been included in industrialization schemes. Its port is one of the most important in the country, even though its shallowness forces ships to be unloaded at sea. The older quarters of the city, as well as its colourful markets, are located near the coast. On the hills overlooking the harbour lies an exclusive residential area with an outstanding view of the city and the sea. Other places of interest include the Snake Garden in **Taman Hiburan Rakyat** and the Chinese temple **Sam Po Kong.**

Ninety kilometres south-east of Semarang lies **Solo,** which can be reached via a good network of roads. This city, which was earlier called Surakarta, boasts two **kratons** or palaces (the royal house divided into 2 as a result of colonial influence), and an interesting museum, the **Rajapusaka.** In Solo, the unique atmosphere of Central Java and its Hindu-Javanese past is strongly evident, particularly because this city with comparatively little traffic conveys more of a mood of peace and tranquility than, say, Yogya does. The small things that give Solo its distinctive character, however, will only be apparent to the observant visitor. The profound wisdom of its people – manifested in their thoughts and feelings and expressed through their speech and gestures – reveals itself only to those who are patient. Although there is no nightlife in Solo, in the evening the city is filled with lively activity. The **Sriwedari Amusement Park,** with its theatre and dance performances, always attracts many people. Those interested in traditional Javanese court dances can visit the **Sasono Mulyo Dance Academy** where day-time classes can be attended free of charge. North of Solo lies **Sangiran,** where, in 1936, the paleontologist, von Königswald, found the remains of what later became known as Java Man. Near the site of the discovery is a small museum containing bones and stone artifacts dating from prehistoric times. The artisans at Solo's many **batik factories** are always glad to offer interested visitors a look at their craftsmanship – it is best to make an appointment, however. The most renowned manufacturers are **Batik Kris, Batik Semar** and **Dana Hadi.**

On the slopes of the Gunung Lawu, 35 km from Solo, stands the 15th-century Hindu temple, **Candi Sukuh,** which resembles the step pyramids of the Central American Mayas. The temple is a peculiarity in itself – both in style and in the subject matter of its reliefs, it is a contrast to all of Java's other temples. On a clear day, one has a magnificent view of the Central Javanese plains. In the evening, when the blazing sun sinks into a veil of mist and the damp fog rising from the forest begins to enshroud the Candi Sukuh, it almost seems as if the temple is trying to reveal some of the mystery that surrounds it.

Yogyakarta should be seen by biciycle. Anyone travelling with more horsepower risks missing the city. The contemplative life of the Javanese, however, is faster-paced in Yogya than in Solo, which is known for its tranquility and the serene nature of its people.

Tourism has turned this city of 3 million into the focal point of Central Java. Its attractions include the palace of Sultan Hamengku Buwono (Guardian of the World), the Borobu-

Batik work in Java is always done by hand.

dur, the Prambanan and the many craft shops in the vicinity. Owing to its former opposition to Dutch colonial rule, the sultanate of Yogyakarta is now a province in its own right (Special District) – Solo was denied this status because of its support of the Dutch. For a few years after Sukarno declared Indonesia independent, Yogyakarta was even capital of the young republic, which was, at the time, not yet recognized by the Dutch. Construction of the **Kraton,** was begun in 1755. It is an immense, rambling palace, but well worth seeing. Like the Borobudur, it is a three-dimensional model of the Buddhist cosmogram and depicts the Buddhist account of the creation. It consists of many courtyards with high white walls of more than one kilometre in length (5⁄8 mile). A portion of the kraton is open daily until noon. Shady pavilions whose roofs are supported by ornately decorated columns serve as the place where guests are received and ceremonies and celebrations are held. Old gamelan instruments lying in the shade waiting to be used, evoke scenes of lavish festivals, at which fascinating court customs spring to new life through their mysterious, metallic sound. Sarongclad palace guards with a specially folded batik cloth around their heads, the blankon, serve as multilingual guides, recounting the palace's past and present history and the deeds of its princely occupants. The gifts brought by the representatives of European governments and crowned heads in the 19th and early 20th centuries are kept in a small pavilion as documents of the scornful attitude the Europeans had toward the Asian royal houses at one time. On Sunday mornings, traditional court dances are performed by young princesses to the accompaniment of a gamelan orchestra. After leaving the kraton and venturing back to the bustling streets of Yogyakarta, one has the feeling of having returned from a journey back into time. Here, however, past and present form a fascinating unity that affects the daily lives of the city's inhabitants. West of the kraton stand the ruins of the former moated castle, **Taman Sari,** where the royal family and its household once strolled and bathed. Along its crumbling walls is a collection of batik studios – at least half-a-day is needed to see them all. Those who are interested in learning more about batik should visit the **Batik Research Centre,** Jl. Kusumanegara 2, where batik is exhibited, manufactured and batik techniques taught. The **Sono-Budoyo** Museum north-west of the kraton offers a comprehensive survey of Java's cultural heritage.

Jl. Malioboro is Yogyakarta's main thoroughfare. In the afternoon and evening, people come here to see and be seen, to shop and to bargain, and just to be part of the activity. Only after 9 pm does the flood of people begin to ebb. The covered market here is a treasure trove of interesting items, but, sadly, very few visitors know of its existence.

In **Kota Gede,** Indonesia's silver working centre located 6 km/about 4 miles south of Yogya, valuable jewelry and silverware are expertly fashioned out of this precious metal.

The **Borobudur,** which reigns over the countryside 45 km/28 miles north-west of Yogyakarta, has unfortunately been marketed for tourists. Now free of cranes and builders' sheds, it rises up out of the fertile rice fields of Magelang in all its grandeur, ostensibly offering peace and enlightenment to all. The **Candi Mendug** and the **Candi Pawon,** both located near the Borobudur, also share its square-shaped foundations. Of the stupas that once

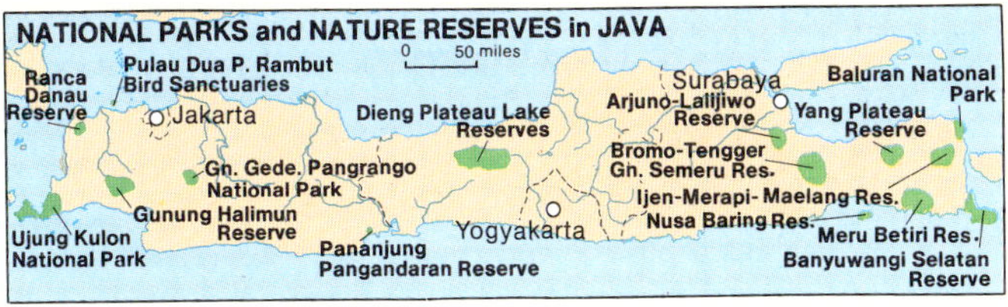

crowned both temples, however, only those of the smaller Pawon have been preserved. On the road between Yogya and Solo lies the **Prambanan** Temple. Those who initially decide not to devote time to visiting this temple will reconsider their decision, at the latest, when they see it. When crossing the bridge over the Opak River just before the village of Prambanan, one sees the 46-metre-high/151′ Loro Jongg-grang Temple clad in lush green vegetation overlooking the river.

The Prambanan Temple Complex, which dates from the 9th century, also has a square-shaped layout. The largest of the temples here is the afore-mentioned Loro Jonggrang, dedicated to the god Shiva. An urn containing the ashes of this temple's builder lies under its east staircase. Two more temples located to the north and south of this immense building are devoted to Vishnu and Brahma. Opposite these, there are three more temples dedicated to the same gods. The great temple in the middle contains an image of Shiva's mount, the zebu, **nandi.** By going slowly from left to right, one can follow the Ramayana story as it is portrayed in the reliefs, and on an open-air stage located in front of the Prambanan, the gods and mythical creatures that play a part in this epic come to life on each night of the full moon from June to October. Those who wish to acquaint themselves with the mystical beliefs of the Javanese today, ought to attend one of these performances.

The **sewu-complex,** which probably dates from the 8th century, lies 2 km/1¼ miles north of the Prambanan. The 246 individual temples of this, the largest temple complex on Java (59 acres), are surrounded by a large temple wall. Like the Sewu Complex, the **Plaosan** Temple (850 A.D.), which lies 1 km/⅝ mile to the east, is rather run-down, having been badly damaged by an earthquake in the 1860's. An excursion to the **Dieng Plateau** requires at least one whole day, but it is well worth the time. It is situated 135 km/84 miles north-west of Yogyakarta, in a 2,100-metre-high/6,890′ volcanic crater. The road to the plateau leads through impressive mountainous countryside sometimes blanketed by low-lying clouds. Tobacco is grown in this region where it ages to a mellow ripeness, full of flavour. Those who decide to stay the night on the Dieng Plateau will have to make do with the simple accommodation of

Borobudur

In the middle of the 8th century, Buddhism experienced a golden age under the dynasty of the Sailendra (Lords of the Mountains) – it was during this period that Borobudur was built. The structure was once the most important Buddhist sanctuary in South-east Asia, and is still valued today as a symbol of the Buddhist concept of "nirvana".

A hill serves as the foundation of this man-made mountain constructed from 55,000 cubic metres of stone (72,000 cu. yds). The temple design is based on a quadrate mandala, and symbolizes the Mahayana-Buddhist universe with the main portal facing east. Originally, the temple complex was painted white, but its colour faded in the course of time. Shortly after completion, the hill began to give way under the sheer weight of the construction, so the foundation and its 160 reliefs were reinforced with a broad layer of stones. In 1890, this encasement was temporarily removed to allow the panels, that had been hidden from view for 1,000 years, to be photographed.

In the four square galleries above the base, each connected to the other by gates, the life and teaching of Buddha are depicted in more than 1,300 bas-reliefs. In addition, there are more than 1,200 panels on the inside walls which provide a rare glimpse into the daily life of the Indonesians 1,000 years ago. The uppermost gallery serves as the base for the three circular terraces supporting the orderly rows of 72 stupas of stone lattice-work resting on stylized lotus blossoms. Each of these bell-shaped enclosures shelters a Buddha figure in silent meditation. Of the more than 500 Buddha statues in Borobudur, 92 are housed in niches in the first four galleries. An 8-metre-high (26 feet) empty stupa crowns the upper terrace. Whether it once contained a Buddha figure or not will probably never be known.

The walled-in base symbolizes the World of Desire (Kamakhatu). Above this lies the World of Form (Rupadhatu) with its four galleries. The circular terraces with their stupas belong to the World of Formlessness (Arupadhatu). The giant crowning stupa symbolizes the enlightened Buddha, the attainment of nirvana – Nothingness and All.

It has been estimated that as many as 10,000 people must have worked on the construction of the Borobudur 1,100 years ago. Incredibly large amounts of andesite stone had to be cut, transported and hewn. By the year 1000 A.D., the monument was already buried under volcanic debris and rampant tropic vegetation. After having lain abandoned and forgotten for centuries, it was rediscovered by Raffles in 1814, and partly dug out. In the following decades, the first documents (drawings and photographs) were prepared. In 1882, the reliefs and statues were to be removed for exhibition in a special museum – fortunately, this was never done. In 1907, the restoration of the circular terraces and their 72 stupas was carried out under Theodor van Erp. Van Erp's photographs were invaluable during the extensive restoration work carried out from 1973 to 1983. Because the drainage system had been clogged for centuries, heavy tropical rains had caused sand and earth to seep into the temple's core. The effects of chemical decomposition and mould had also taken their devastating toll on the andesite stones. Many of them had even been removed for use as construction material in the neighbouring villages, and some of the heads of the stupa-covered Buddhas had been sold to museums throughout the world. That the colonial administration failed to recognize the significance of this magnificent temple is proven by the fact that in 1873, the King of Thailand was sent off with several oxcarts full of reliefs and statues after a state visit. That was how cultural treasures were taken care of in those days!

Before the monument could be restored, the individual galleries had to be dismantled piece by piece. After the foundation had been stabilized and a modern drainage system had been installed, the stones were precisely reset. According to an estimate made by the Indonesian government, the cost of this project, which was partly financed by the member nations of UNESCO, amounted to US$ 60 million.

As of early 1983, the "Mountain of Enlightenment" once again presides over the lush rice fields of the Kedu Plain in its original splendour.

the mountain people, whose Asiatic features and dark, wooden houses call to mind the valleys of the Himalayas. In addition to the magnificent mountain landscape with its forests, lakes and hot sulphur springs, the ruins of 40 temples, probably dating from the Mataram Empire, lie here scattered over a large area. Eight of them have been restored.

East Java

This region with its almost 30 million inhabitants, one of the most densely populated of Indonesia's provinces, possesses, in addition to large tracts of farmland and a few wildlife reserves, many relics of past civilizations. High stratum volcanoes dominate the landscape particularly in the regions to the east. The **Semeru** and the **Arjuna,** which, for the traveller approaching them, seem to rise up suddenly from the surrounding plains, are among the most beautiful and impressive volcanoes in the archipelago. In addition to large sugar and tobacco plantations, 54 per cent of Java's teak forests are here.

Surabaya, the city known far and wide for its melodious name, has very little to offer its visitors. Its airport, however, forms an important link in domestic air traffic, and helps to draw people to the city – particularly those on their way to the bull-races held on the island of **Madura** regularly from April to August. With 3.5 million people, Surabaya is Indonesia's second-largest city. Owing to its important port, industrialization has developed considerably here within the last few years. The restoration of the city is also in full swing. A **zoo** with **aquarium** and a **recreation-park** make up its chief attractions.

Many of East Java's temples have fallen into ruin over the centuries, and the elaborate decorations of Central Java's temples are not found here. The remains of the ancient capital of the Majapahit Empire, which can be found near Trowulan, are not very extensive. The small museum nearby, however, gives an impression of how this former centre of political power looked in its hey-day. North of Blitar, on the slopes of Mt. Kelud, lies the **Panataran** Temple Group, which dates from the 13th century. Now partly restored, it is Java's second-largest sacred edifice after Borobudur. The original construction took place over a period of 250 years and ended during the Majapahit Empire. Many of the buildings are decorated with mythical animals and motifs from the Ramayana epic. Between **Gempol** and **Pandaan** lies the **Candi Jawi,** built in the 13th century in honour of the Singasari king, Kertanegara. In Pandaan, classical dances and dramas are performed in the amphitheatre, Candra Wilwatika, from May to October during the period of the full moon. Those who wish to see other temples dating from this period should not miss the **Candi Singasari,** the **Candi Jago** and the **Candi Kidal.** All three are temples of death. The last two are located near Tumpang; the first one is located near the village of the same name, south of Mt. Arjuna, and is said to contain some of the ashes of King Kertanegara, revered in the Majapahit Empire as an avatar of the god Shiva. On close observation, much of this temple's masonry proves to be incomplete. As the crowning event of a visit to Java, the sunrise over **Mt. Bromo** should be included. To get there, travel by Colt bus (usually twice as full as it should be) from Probolingo past breathtaking mountainous countryside to Ngadisari. From there, the journey to the "moon", which is what the inside of the giant crater looks like, must be made on foot or on horseback. On the ascent the panorama of lush vegetable gardens gradually loses its splendour as the blanket of volcanic ash becomes more and more visible. Suddenly, the vegetation disappears save for some sparse brush. One has a clear view of the Tengger caldera and the many conical volcanoes rising out of its immense sandsea. The Batuk, with its furrowed, eroded slopes, is a good illustration of the effects of opposing forces of nature. In a small losmen on the crater's edge, one can prepare for the early-morning ascent to the summit of Mt. Bromo. At 3.30 am the journey continues down into the crater's sea of sand (a guide can be taken along). On starry nights, this can become quite an unforgettable adventure – with the glittering night sky above, it is easy to imagine oneself transported to a far planet.

Shortly before dawn, the summit of the smoking mountain should be reached, from where the sun's appearance can be awaited. Little by little, the silvery light of the stars makes way for the first light of day which slowly creeps over the edge of the crater. Soon, the rugged, barren landscape is plunged into a reddish light which penetrates deep into the crater. This, too, is Java. Those who travel on from here to **Banyuwangi** to catch the ferry to Bali, will do so with reluctance, finding it hard to turn their backs on this fascinating island.

Madura

In contrast to the volcanic plains of Java, the permeable soil of Madura does not lend itself to the cultivation of rice. With its large areas of grassland, the island is, however, ideally suited to animal husbandry. Salt production, the cultivation of tobacco and fishing also form the cornerstones of the island's economy.

Pamekasan is the capital of the 150 km/93 mile long, 30 km/18.6 mile wide island. **Sumenep,** which lies 55 km/34 miles north-east of the capital, was once the centre of a kingdom which was influential even in parts of Java. Steeped in history, Sumenep has a mosque which dates back to the 18th century. For people who like **fine china,** there is an extensive collection in the museum opposite the mosque – sculptures and weapons are also on show here. 15 km/9.3 miles north of Sumenep lies the picturesque coastal town of **Ambunten.** You'll come away from Ambunten with more than just the pleasant memory of swimming in the sea.

The many hot springs found on Madaru are an indication of the **volcanic** nature of the island. At **Api Abadi** near Pamekasan the ground is like a mass of embers, even at the surface. Wood or paper left in the sand will catch fire immediately.

It isn't only the earth of Madura which is fiery – its people too are renowned throughout Indonesia for their fiery temperaments.

The island's **Kerapan Sapi** (bull races) are very well-known and the temperamental nature of the people really comes to light during them.

Two bulls are harnessed to a wooden frame resembling a plough. The rider takes his place on this frame and drives the bulls using their tails to control and direct them.

The races take place over as much as 140 metres/153 yds and the first team to cross the finishing line is the winner. On the whole they take place during the dry season, and at harvest time, and serve not only as entertainment but also as a means of selecting bulls for breeding purposes. Races first take place at village level but then competition increases when they progress to the sub-districts, districts and "Kabupaten" (rural districts). In the finals in Pamekasan and Ambunten the competitors are spurred on with music and daring wagers. The owners of prize-winning bulls are highly respected in their own villages.

Jakarta – Gateway to the Indonesian Archipelago

Jakarta, the capital of Indonesia, is affectionately known there as "Ibu Kota" – Mother town.

Over the years the town has been at the centre of political and cultural revolutions. Originally a small trading-post, the settlement was known as **Sunda Kelapa** and lay at the mouth of the Ciliwung River – today a leisure harbour of the same name is located on the original site and reminds all of Jakarta's origins. By the end of the 15th century, the small trading town was the main port of the Pajajoran Kingdom. Close trading links existed between the Pajajoran and the **Portuguese** in Melaka but, when the latter tried to stake out a claim in Sunda Kelapa, there was a confrontation. In June 1527 Prince Fatahillah was able to drive out the Portuguese fleet after only a short battle. To mark the town's triumph, its name was changed to Jakarta or Jayakarta (Town of Victory).

As the years went by, **Dutch** and **British** traders established bases in the town and soon there was no longer any doubt about Jakarta's commercial importance. In 1619 the town was attacked and captured by the Dutch, under Jan Pieterszoon Coen. Soon afterwards its name was changed to **Batavia.** It was under this name that the small town was to develop during the 17th and 18th centuries into a renowned **trading centre.**

The **Japanese,** who occupied the Dutch East Indies during the 2nd World War, introduced a kind of nationalism into the land as a whole and, in accordance with this, readopted the town's original name. Batavia became Tokubebushi Jakarta.

After independence was declared, the Indonesians also opted for the old name, Djakarta (now Jakarta).

Today Jakarta covers an area of nearly 700 sq km/270 sq miles, is home to around 7 million people and is one of South-East Asia's fastest developing cities. Many parts of the town bear a stronger resemblance to rural Java than to any city, however. Sanitation is, for example, very poor in the "Kampongs" – slum settlements which have sprung up in the city and continue to do so in spite of moves by the authorities to control their spread.

It is here that the "orang gelandangan" live. These are people from all parts of the Republic who have left their homelands in order to seek their fortune in the metropolis of Jakarta. Television has now reached even the furthest corners of the archipelago and pictures of modern life in Jakarta (buildings reaching up into the heavens, cars for everyone) guarantee the flow of people hoping to settle there – illegally.

In addition, there is the problem of the ever-growing population of Jakarta – even with birth control, this problem has not yet been resolved. It is hoped, however, that, by creating jobs in other parts of the country, people will be encouraged to stay away from the overcrowded capital – no-one can realistically hope for an exodus of those people already settled there.

In Search of Batavia

Twentieth-century Jakarta seems to deny any links between its own past and present. Those tourists who knew the old town of Batavia will probably search for it in vain today. It is sometimes possible to find emotional links with the past among the older generation of Jakartans. These people, provided they belonged to the privileged classes, would have enjoyed a good life under the **Dutch.** Indonesia's struggle for independence, when it came, claimed many victims and demanded much of the people and it is, therefore, hard for some to sing in praise of the changes wrought in this former capital of the Dutch East Indies.

Anyone who wanders through the dark and musty corridors and halls of buildings erected by the Dutch (some of which are now museums) will perhaps be able to feel something of the atmosphere of the old town. Treading the creaking floorboards of the **Stadhuys** (Government House, built in 1625) you cannot escape the gaze of faces from the town's past. Portraits of former rulers hang in heavy, and sometimes gilded, wooden frames – kings, governor-generals and their wives, trading magnates and native princes. The stern, effeminate or overbearing expressions on those pale, lean or swollen faces are somehow oppressive. The portraits are typical of the period in which they were painted. This style of painting, combined with the garments worn by those portrayed – the stiff hats, cloaks and large ruffs – makes them look like lifeless puppets. At times, however, the play of light and shadow from the huge windows of the venerable hall suddenly brings life to the inanimate faces. Although thousands of miles separated these people from their Dutch homeland (those making the journey would have been at sea for more than a year), they apparently managed, in time, to comply with every change in European fashions. It is clear from their heavy, black woolen garments that there was never any question of their changing their customary dress to suit the tropical climate. It wasn't up to them to adapt... no, they seemed to expect the colony itself to change for them.

As they made no effort in this direction, many of the European faces soon began to show signs of **chronic suffering** and symptoms of fast-approaching death. The canals, which the Dutch themselves had built in the town, proved to be the harbourers of disease. Water for the canal system had been channelled from the Krokot and Ciliwung rivers, but tides along the coast were not particularly strong and the water lay stagnant and became pestilent. It was no longer unusual for men to die before they reached forty. The Dutch strove to make their mark on their new territory with brick buildings, windmills and forts but in fact it was **cholera** and **malaria** which had the greater hold on the town.

Pictures of past battles prove, however, that the foreign despots did have strength enough to bring **war, oppression** and **misery** to their newly acquired territories. Jan Pieterszoon Coen left a trail of blood on many of the archipelago's islands. His portrait does indeed convey the far from glowing reputation he had everywhere – he stands as the overbearing lord and master. His predecessor, Laurenz Real (whose portrait also hangs in the Stadhuys) – was a more humane man who showed understanding and tolerance in his dealings with the native people. He was, however, never able to satisfy the Dutch traders' cravings for more power and profit, and was soon obliged to make way for the hard-hearted, hard-headed Coen.

So it was here in the former Dutch "Stadhuys" that decisions were made and resolutions passed by governors, regents and administrators. Some of these men went down in history, others were soon forgotten. Some of the changes they made were to the advantage of the native people, others exploited and oppressed them. And this was the scheme of things until the Dutch finally left Indonesia.

For a small amount of money ("uang sakku") you can climb to the dome of the **Stadhuys.** The wonderful view from here not only includes the **town hall square** and the old **colonial buildings** but also the distant **coastline.** Nowadays, however, you'd wait in vain for the sight of a heavy-bellied sailing-ship, its red, white and blue flag revealing the origin of the long-awaited cargo. (The goods which would disappear into the hold for the return journey were usually the product of backbreaking labour carried out by the natives.)

There are still some wonderful sailing vessels to be seen today, however. The **Sunda Kelapa** is a harbour for sailing boats near the **Pasar Ikan** (the fish market). Here you can still see the cargo boats used by the **Bugis** tribe from South Sulawesi. These boats haven't changed much over the years and they still carry out a large part of goods transportation within the archipelago. Captains usually have nothing against tourists – the latter should, however, be willing and able to adapt to the way things are done on the boats and should have plenty of time at their disposal.

Remnants of **colonial history** are to be found all around the Pasar Ikan. With the backing of Unesco warehouses and an old fort have been restored. The fortified warehouse, which was built in 1718 and is today a marine museum, still dominates the area around the fish market.

Hobby photographers can, by the way, get a good close-up shot of the harbour from the look-out tower of the small fort, which is still armed with canons. (Don't forget that you will pay an "uang sakku".)

Anyone interested in seeing the fish market in action should be here as early as possible. The main market for fish is in Muara Amco incidentally – 3 km/1.86 miles west of Jakarta.

Lots of old **businesses** and **warehouses** stand along the "Kali Besar", the landmark of which is the Dutch drawbridge (called the Chicken Market Bridge). This bridge is at the northern end of the canal right next to an ugly steel bridge.

The centre of what used to be Batavia offers many other examples of impressive colonial architecture besides that of the Stadhuys. The former **Club Harmonie,** now called Wisma Nusntara, was once the refined meeting-place of Dutch merchants, officials and plantation owners. At one time, it was also a monument to apartheid with its sign on the door warning: "Dogs and Natives not Allowed". Today, finally, it is open to all who want to see it. The small restaurant inside, however, is hardly representative of the club's former glory. The canals in this part of Jakarta – built in the 17th century for use as transport routes – bear witness to colonial city planning.

The well-known **Hotel des Indes** – the "Ritz" of South-East Asia up until the outbreak of World War II – fell victim to city planning in 1972 – to the regret of many. The residence of former **Governor-General de Klerk,** built in 1755 and located on Jl. Gayah Madah 11, now houses a collection of archives documenting the history of the city. An insight into the life of the Chinese in Jakarta can be gained by visiting one of their temples. The largest one, the **Klenteng Vihara Dharma Bhakti,** is located on Jl. Naga. The **City Museum,** which dominates Fatahillah Square, offers a glimpse at the city's pioneer days, and in the **Wayang Museum** on Jl. Pintu Besar Utara, exhibits and performances of "wayang kulit" and its Sundanese variation, "wayang golek" (see "Appendix"), can be seen and enjoyed. The 17th-century **Portuguese church,** located on Jl. Pangerang, is also worth seeing. Jakarta possesses an array of contemporary monuments which also stand as memorials to the past. The most impressive of these is the **Monument Nasional** (MONAS) located on Freedom Square. This 130-metre/426′ obelisk is topped by an "eternal flame" made of 35 kg of gold. A breathtaking view of the city can be had from its upper platform, which is served by a lift. This monument to Indonesian independence can be seen from many parts of the city as well.

Modern Jakarta

There are a great many things to see in Jakarta quite apart from those which are of historical interest. People who stay for only two or three days, however, will hardly have the chance to get to know the town properly.

Anyone who is sceptical about the merits of Jakarta would learn a lot from people who have lived in the city for a number of years. There's bound to be some criticism but they'd also hear lots of favourable reports.

Most people who visit Indonesia do so in search of the exotic and in order to experience the many cultures which are represented within the archipelago. This being the case, they more often than not only spend one or two days in any city – after all, a city is something you find everywhere. Historical buildings most often head the list of priorities. However, for those people who'd like to visit the other Jakarta, a few suggestions…

The **Pusat Museum,** or **National Museum,** stands on the boundary of the old Jakarta and the new. The museum was established in 1778 by the Dutch philanthropist, J.M. Rademacher, under the patronage of Batavia's "Society of Sciences and Arts". Nowadays the museum is like a peaceful enclave in the otherwise buzzing city and it does full justice to the land's **culture.** Unique collections of prehistoric, historic and ethnographic articles make a visit to this venerable building an essential part of any itinerary.

Like most of Jakarta's museums, the Pusat Museum is closed on Mondays. The museum is open: Tues., Wed., Thurs., Sat., Sun. 9 am–2.30 pm; Friday 9 am–11 am. The treasure chamber is only open on Sundays or upon special request.

Anyone interested in traditional Indonesian textiles shouldn't miss the **Textile museum** on the Jl. Satsuit Tubun in South-West Jakarta. Apart from about 400 different **Batik** articles (some are already more than 100 years old), visitors can also admire **Ikat** work from all over the archipelago. The museum also has examples of raffia clothing. Opening hours: Tues., Wed., Thurs., Sun., 9 am–3 pm; Friday 9 am–11 am; Saturday 9 am–1 pm.

People, who have only a limited amount of time on their hands but who would like a comprehensive, though inevitably superficial impression of Indonesian culture should go to the **Taman Mini Indonesia,** in the far south of the city. The park, which covers an area of more than 100 hectares/247 acres, contains examples of building styles from all parts of the Republic. In addition, the **folklore** of the islands is presented here in performances which take place mainly on Sundays. Besides an **orchid garden** and **aviary** the park has its own **museum** which exhibits traditional costumes, household objects, arts and crafts, weapons and many other items.

Taman Mini Indonesia is open daily from 9 am until 6 pm.

The focus of all cultural events is the **Taman Ismail Marzuki Art Centre.** The centre's programme of events changes every month and features performances of traditional or modern music and dance, folklore theatre and exhibitions. The centre contains theatres, exhibition halls and galleries as well as a planetarium and an art academy!

The Taman Impian Jaya Ancol Park is of less cultural interest but is more relaxing – both mentally and physically. Open 24 hours a day, the park could well be described as a town within a town and is a great attraction for well-to-do Jakartans. The park covers an area of some 140 hectares/345 acres and contains a modern **hotel,** the Horizon, as well as the Gelanggang Renang **swimming pool** (complete with streams, waves, a waterfall and a 10 m/33 ft long slide). The Gelanggang Renang pool is only open from 9 am to 6 pm. Other features of the park include a ten-pin **bowling alley,** drive-in **cinema, oceanarium** with penguin and dolphin shows, **beach, tennis-courts, golf course** and lots more.

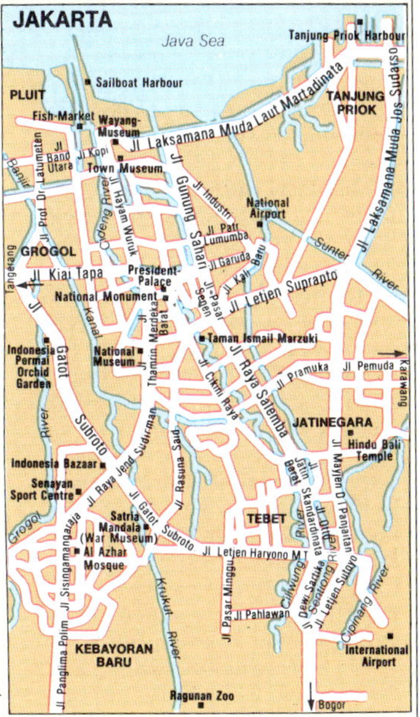

Jakarta Fair is due to be moved to the area between Ancol and the Tanjung Priok harbour. At the moment, however, it occupies a site near the National Monument. From time to time large national and international exhibitions of major importance are held here.

The **Ragunan Zoo** (full name, the Taman Margasatwa Ragunan Zoo) is a former winner of an international zoo contest. The zoo provides many rare Indonesian animals with adequate living conditions.

To get to the zoo, catch the No. 108 bus from Stand B in South Jakarta. At weekends the zoo is packed.

Lovers of orchids should find something to suit them in Jakarta's three orchid gardens. Not far from the centre of Slipi (an area of Jakarta) there is a unique selection of the flowers in the **Indonesia Permai Orchid Garden** (35,000 sq metres/8.6 acres). North of Ragunan Zoo, in the above-mentioned Taman Mini Indonesia Park there is another orchid garden.

The best chance of seeing the treasures of Indonesian birdlife close-to is on the **Pasar Burung,** the bird market. This is a nightmare for animal lovers. Large numbers of sometimes rare birds are kept cooped up in small cages. Other animals are sold here, too – sometimes even protected species. The place is teeming with mites and the number of sick animals is evidence enough that disease is rife here. Anyone who does want to visit the market on the Jl. Pramuka should try to go along with someone who can speak Indonesian.

The many **monuments** to be found in Jakarta reveal the recent history of the Indonesian Republic. The monument to the **Sukarno-Hatta proclamation** reminds people of the declaration of independence on 17th August, 1945. The monument was unveiled by President Suharto on 16th August 1980.

Many relics of Indonesia's struggle for liberation can be seen in the **Satria Mandala-Army Museum** in South Jakarta. Among other things there are antiquated examples of arms supplied by both the East and the West. A special place in the exhibition is given to the period of the struggle lasting from 1945 to 1949.

You can reach the museum on the bus from Stand M heading for Mangarai via the bus and bemo station Cililitan. If you ask the driver or a fellow-passenger, there's no danger of missing the museum.

For anyone with more time in Jakarta, a list of addresses worth knowing:

Tourist Information Offices in Jakarta

Directorate General of Tourism,
Jl. Kramat Raya 81.
Jakarta Regional Tourist Office,
Jl. Gatot Subroto (simpang
Jl. KH. Abd. Rochim).
Jakarta Metroplitan City Tourism Development Board,
Jl. Medan Merdeka Selatan 9, 19th.
Jakarta Visitor's Information Centre,
Jakarta Theatre Building
Jl. Thamrin 9.
Jakarta Visitor's Information Services,
International Airport Halim Perdana Kusuma 16.
Hotel Information & Reservation Centre,
Jakarta International Airport Halim Perdana Kusuma 16.

Taxi Companies

Blue Bird, Jl. Garuda 88.
Gamya, Jl. Tiang Bendera 62A.
Morante, Jl. Alaydrus 15.
President Taxi, Jl. D/7 Pekan Raya Jakarta.
Royal City, Jl. Mayjen Panjaitan.
Ratax, Jl. Kramat Raya 21.
Srimedali, Jl. Mayjen Sutoyo 15.
Steady Safe, Jl. Gondangdia Lama 22.

Car Hire Firms

Avis Rental & Reservation System,
Jl. Diponegoro 25.
Eustis Rental Car,
Phone: 352782.
Imperial Rental Car,
Jl. Raden Saleh I/12.
Inter City Taxi to Bandung "4848",
Jl. Prapatan 34,
Jl. Kebon Sirih 32.
Parahyangan,
Jl. Wahid Hasyim 13.
Metro, Jl. Kopi 2C.
Perkasa,
Jl. Merdeka Barat 18.

Bus Stations

Intercity Bus:
Pulogadung (For Eastern Areas),
Cililitan (For Southern Areas),
Grogol (For Western Areas),

Rawa Mangun (For Southern Areas).
City Bus:
Pulogadung,
Cililitan,
Grogol,
Blok M.,
Kampung Melavu,
Pasar Minggu, Manggarai,
Hawamangun, Tanah Abang,
Kota, Senen,
Tanjung Priok.

Train Stations
Jakarta Kota,
Jl. Stasiun Kota 1.
Gambir,
Jl. Merdeka Timur.
Pasar Senen,
Jl. Medan Senen.

Important Telephone Numbers

Information:	
Local	108
Trunkcall	106
Inter-island	105
Time	103
International	102
Telegram hint	109
Connection Requests:	
Trunkcall	100
International	101
Singapore/Jepang	104
Assistance Requests:	
Police	110
Fire	113
Ambulance	118
City Health Service	119

Post Offices
Central Post Office,
Jl. Pos Utara (Pasar Baru).
Gajah Mada Post Office,
Jl. Gajah Mada.
Jakarta Kota Post Office,
Jl. Fatahillah 3.
Menteng Post Office,
Jl. Serang 25.
Kebayoran Post Office,
Jl. Wolter Monginsidi 85.
Cikini Post Office,
Jl. Cikini Raya.

International Airlines
British Airways,
c/o Mandarin Hotel, 1st floor,
Jl. M.H. Thamrin Jakarta,
Phone: 33 32 07.
Cathay Pacific,
BDN Building, Jl. M.H. Thamrin no. 5 Jakarta,
Phone: 32 63 07, 32 78 07.
Borobudur Hotel: 37 01 08.
China Airlines,
Sancta Maria House,
Jl. Ir. H. Juanda no. 15, Jakarta,
Phone: 37 07 08, 35 44 48, 36 13 68, 35 15 64.
Garuda Indonesia Airways,
Jl. Ir. H. Juanda no. 15, Jakarta.
Phone: 37 07 09.
Borobudur Inter-Continental Hotel,
Phone: 37 01 08 ext. 22 41–22 42.
Japan Airlines, (J. A. L.),
Wisma Nusantara Building,
Jl. M.H. Thamrin, Jakarta,
Phone: 32 22 07 (5 lines), 33 39 09.
K. L. M. Royal Dutch Airlines,
Hotel Indonesia,
Jl. M.H. Thamrin, Jakarta,
Phone: 32 07 08 (5 lines), 32 00 34.
Lufthansa,
Asoka Hotel, Jl. M.H. Thamrin, Jakarta,
Phone: 32 06 32, 32 11 04, 32 34 00, 32 12 39.
Malaysian Airlines System,
BDN Building, Jl. M.H. Thamrin, Jakarta,
Phone: 32 09 09 (4 lines).

Philippine Airlines,
Borobudur Inter-Continental Hotel,
3rd floor,
Jalan Lapangan Banteng Selatan,
Jakarta,
Phone: 37 01 08 ext. 23 10–23 14–23 36.
Qantas Airways,
BDN Building, Jl. M.H. Thamrin no. 5, Jakarta,
Phone: 32 77 07 – 32 67 07 – 32 75 38.
Singapore Airlines,
Sahid Jaya Hotel,
Jl. Jend. Sudirman no. 86, Jakarta,
Phone: 58 40 21, 58 40 41.
Swiss Airlines,
Borobudur Inter-Continental Hotel,
Jl. Lapangan Banteng Selatan,
Jakarta,
Phone: 37 80 06, 37 01 08.
Thai International Airlines,
BDN Building, Jl. M.H. Thamrin no. 5, Jakarta, Phone: 32 06 07.
U. T. A. (Union de Transport Aeriens),
Gedung Jaya, Jl. M.H. Thamrin no. 12, Phone: 32 35 07 (3 lines).

Domestic Airlines
Garuda Indonesia Airways (GIA),
Jl. Ir. H. Juanda 15.
Mandala Airlines,
Jl. Veteran I/34.
Merpati Nusantara Airlines (MNA),
Jl. Patrice Lumumba 1.
Bouraq Indonesia Airlines,
Jl. Patrice Lumumba 18.
Pelita Air Service,
Jl. Abdul Muis 52.

Hospitals/Medical Care
Metropolitan Medical Centre,
Hotel Wisata, behind Hotel Indonesia Sheraton,
Tel.: 32 04 08–1 46/1 53.
Rumah Sakit Pertamina,
Jl. Kyai Maja, Kebayoran baru,
Tel. 70 72 11.
Rumah Sakit Carolus,
Jl. Salemba Raya 41,
Tel. 88 30 91.
Rumah sakit Cikini,
Jl. Raden Salen 40,
Tel. 34 00 90, 34 92 11.
Damajanti & Associates,
Jl. Diponegoro 14, Tel. 34 15 02.

Night Clubs
Apollo Night Club,
Jl. H. Agus Salim 31.
Blue Moon Night Club,
Jl. Gajah Mada (Hotel Gajah Mada).
Copakobana Night Club,
Jl. Pantai Indah Ancol.
L. L. C. Night Club,
Jl. Silang Monas (Jakarta Fair).
Marcopolo Night Club,
Jl. Teuku Cikditiro (Marcopolo Hotel).
New Flamingo Night Club,
Jl. Hai Lai Building Ancol.
Blue Ocean Night Club,
Jl. Hayam Wuruk 5.
Sea Side Night Club,
Ancol Dreamland.
Tropikana Night Club,
Jl. Manila Senayan Complex.
Concorde Night Club,
Jl. Thamrin (Kartika Plaza Hotel).
Sky Room Permai Night Club,
Jl. Gajah Mada (Duta Merlin).

Discotheques
The Pistop,
Jl. Thamrin (Sari Pacific Hotel).
Tanamur Disco,
Jl. Tanah Abang Timur 14.
Oriental Club,
Jl. Jend. Sudirman (H. Hilton).

Variety Shows
Hayam Wuruk Theatre,
Jl. Hayam Wuruk (Pasar Lindeteves).

Cinemas
Kuningan Theatre,
Jl. Rangkayo Rasuna Said.
New Garden Hall Theatre,
Jl. Bulungan 76.
Kebayoran Theatre,
Jl. Melawai V/36.
Kartika Chandra Theatre,
Jl. Gatot Subroto (Kartika Chandra Hotel).
Prince Theatre,
Jl. Jend. Sudirman.
New International Theatre,
Jl. Silang Monas.
President Theatre,
Jl. Merdeka Selatan.
New City Theatre,
Jl. Gedung Kesenian I.
Djakarta Theatre,
Jl. Thamrin 9.
Megaria Theatre,
Jl. Proklamasi 21.
Menteng Theatre,
Jl. HOS Cokroaminoto 79.
New Krekot Theatre,
Jl. H. Samanhudi 11A.
Ramayana Theatre,
Jl. Gunung Sahari 27.
Tim Theatre,
Jl. Cikini Raya 73.
Glodok Sky Theatre,
Jl. Glodok.
Jayakarta Theatre,
Jl. Hayam Wuruk (Jayakarta Tower Hotel).
Mandala Theatre,
Jl. Hayam Wuruk Plaza 108.
New Orient Theatre,
Jl. Mangga Besar 73–75.
Duta Theatre,
Senen Shopping Centre.

Shopping Centres
Pasar Baru Shopping,
Jl. Pasar Baru.
Glodok Shopping, Jl. Pancoran.
Sarinah Department Store,
Jl. Thamrin.
Jalan Sabang, Jl. Sabang.
Senen Shopping Complex,
Jl. Senen Raya.
Jalan Haji Juanda & Jalan Majapahit,
Jl. H. Juanda & Jl. Majapahit.
Pecenongang, Jl. Pecenongang.
Jalan Surabaya, Jl. Surabaya.
Blok M,
Jl. Melawai Kebayoran (Blok M).
Ratu Plaza, Jl. Jen. Sudirman.
Gajah Mada Plaza, Jl. Gajah Mada.
Duta Merlin, Jl. Gajah Mada.
Hayam Wuruk Plaza,
Jl. Hayam Wuruk.

Indonesian Food
Ayam Bulungan Restaurant,
Jl. Bulungan I/64. Keb. Baru.
Ayam Goreng Mbok Berek Restaurant (Ny. UMI),
Jl. Prof. Dr. Soepomo,
Jl. Panglima Polim Raya no. 93.
Ayam Goreng Ratu Restaurang,
Jl. Hayam Wuruk no. 81.
Gudeg Buk Tjitro (Yogya Food),
Jl. Cikajang 80, Blok 02. Keb. Baru.
Jakarta Coffee Shop Restaurant (Indonesian Food)
Jl. Thamrin (BDN. Building).
Griya Utarie Restaurant (Indonesian & European Food)
Jl. Melawai Raya 14 Blok M.
Koca/LCC Restaurant, Jl. Silang Monas (Jakarta Fair).
Marundu Restaurant (Indonesia Food),
Jl. Thamrin (Hotel Wisata International).

Roda Restaurant (Padang Food),
Jl. Matraman Raya 65.
The Propper Pot (Padang Food),
Jl. Sudirman (Wisma Metropolitan).
Sari Bundo Restaurant (Padang Food),
Jl. Ir. H. Juanda.
Natrabu Restaurant,
Jl. H. Agus Salim no. 29A.
Putri Duyung Restaurant,
Jl. Taman Impian Jaya Ancol.
Oriza Restaurant,
Jl. Gondangdia Lama 40.
Ratu Sari Restaurant (Bandung Food),
Jl. Pinangsia Raya (Glodok Plaza).
Tamalatea Restaurant (Makasar Food),
Jl. Krekot I/40G (Pasar Baru).
Angin Namiri Restaurant (Makasar Food),
Jl. K.H. Wahid Hasyim Ashari no. 49.
Happy Restaurant (Makasar Food),
Jl. Mangga Besar Raya no. 4.
Tan Goei Restaurant,
Jl. Besuki 1A (Menteng).
Senayan Satay House (Indonesian Barbequed meat on skewer's),
Jl. Pakubowono VI/6 Keb. Baru,
Jl. Kebon Sirih 31A,
Jl. Tanah Abang II/76.
Satay House Gajah Mada Restaurant,
Jl. Pecenongang No. 3,
Jl. Gajah Mada 71.
Sate Blora Cirebon Restaurant,
Jl. Pemuda 47 (Rawamangun),
Jl. Jend. A. Yani 11 (samping Bea Cukai).
Pepes Ikan Mas Majalaya Restaurant,
Jl. Senopati 19 Keb. Baru.
Sari Kuring Restaurant, Jl. Batu Cepter 55A.
Warung Selera Nusantara (Open 19.00–06.30),
Jl. Thamrin (Sarinah Building).
Tinoor Asli (Menadonese Food),
Jl. Gondangdia Lama no. 33A.
Jawa Tengah, Jl. Pramuka.
Ayam Pemudi, Jl. Melawai Raya.
Sari Kuring, Jl. Batu Ceper 55A.
Sate Pancoran, Jl. Pasar Minggu.
Pondok Surya, Jl. Cikini Raya.

European Food
Art and Curio Restaurant,
Jl. Kebon Binatang III/8A (Cikini).
Brasserie Le Parisien Restaurant,
Jl. Prapatan (Hyatt Aryaduta Hotel).
Cafe Expresso (American/European Fastfood).
Club Noorwijk Restaurant (Rijstafel and European),
Jl. Kemang Raya 3A Keb. Baru 12,
Jl. Ir. H. Juanda 5A.
Candy Steak House Restaurant,
Jl. Gajah Mada 32A,
Jl. Melawai VIII/2 Keb. Baru.
"George & Dragon" Pub & Restaurant, Jl. Teluk Betung 32.
Grunewald Restaurant,
Jl. Sidoarjo 1 (Menteng).
Haighland Grill Restaurant,
Jl. Thamrin (Asoka Hotel).
Jaya Pub Restaurant,
Jl. Thamrin (Jaya Buildung).
Le Bistro Restaurant,
Jl. KH. Wahid Hasyim 75.

Supper Clubs
Nusah Indah Supper Club,
Jl. Gatot Subroto (Kartika Chandra Hotel).
Nirwana Supper Club,
Jl. Thamrin (Indonesia Hotel).
The Oriental Club,
Jl. Gatot Subroto (Jakarta Hilton Hotel).

Tiara Supper Club,
Jl. Thamrin (Kartika Plaza Hotel).
Oasis Restaurant, Jl. Raden Saleh 47.
The Raffles Tavern Restaurant,
Jl. Sudirman (Ratu Plaza).
Pizza Ria Restaurant,
Jl. Gatot Subroto (Hilton Hotel).
Ramayana Restaurant,
Jl. Gatot Subroto (Hilton Hotel).
Rugantino Ristorante Italianno Restaurant,
Jl. Melaway Raya 28.
Jayakarta Grill Restaurant,
Jl. Thamrin (Sari Pacific Hotel).
Bistro Pondok Surya,
Jl. Cikini Raya.
Sahid Grill Restaurant,
Jl. Jend. Sudirman (Asoka Hotel).
Swiss Inn Restaurant,
Jl. Jend. Sudirman (Artaloka Building).
Sky Garden Restaurant,
Jl. Thamrin (Nusantara Building).
Taman Sari Grill Restaurant,
Jl. Gatot Subroto (Hilton Hotel).
Tankard Restaurant,
Jl. Melawai V/36 (Kebayoran Theatre).
Toba Rotisserie Restaurant,
Jl. Lap. Banteng Selatan (Borobudur Hotel).
The Ankerage Restaurant,
Jl. Merdeka Selatan (President Theatre).
The Club Room Restaurant,
Jl. Thamrin (Mandarin Hotel).
The Royal Orchid Restaurant,
Jl. Thamrin (Mandarin Hotel).
The Shakespeare Pub & Sandwich Restaurant,
Jl. M.H. Thamrin (Wisma Kosgoro).
The Stable Restaurant,
Jl. Jayam Wuruk 8 (Wiskma Hayam Wuruk).
Kem Chicks Restaurant,
Jl. Kemang Raya 3 Keb. Raru 12.
La Bodega Grill Bar,
Jl. Charingin (Charingin Shopping).
Green Pub (Mexican Restaurant-bar),
Jl. Thamrin (Jakarta Theatre).
New Zealand Steak House and Ice Cream, Jl. Gajah Mda No. 18A,
Tel. 62 60 06.
Balkan Grill House,
Jl. Raden Saleh 28.
Rice Bowl,
Jl. M.H. Thamrin (Nusantara Bld).
Aline Ropal, Jl. Cikini Raya 46.

Chinese Food

Brilliant Palace Restaurant,
Jl. Ir. H. Juanda 17.
Cahaya Kota Restaurant,
Jl. KH. Wahid Hasyim 9.
Dragon Garden Restaurant,
Jl. Godok Plaza.
Eka Ria (Yik Lok Yun) Restaurant,
Jl. Hayam Wuruk (Pasar Lindeteves).
Golden Pavilion Restaurant,
Jl. Thamrin 59 (President Hotel).
Hayam Wuruk Restaurant,
Jl. Hayam Wuruk 5.
Happy Garden Restaurant,
Jl. Glodok Plaza.
Hongkong Restaurant, Jl. Blora 27.
Istana Negara Restaurant,
Jl. Gatot Subroto Kav. 12 (Case Building).
King's Palace Restaurant,
Jl. Gajah Mada (Hotel Gajah Mada).
King's Coffee Restaurant,
Jl. Hayam Wuruk 114.
Moon Palace Restaurant,
Jl. Melawai VI/15A, Keb. Baru.
Phoenix Restaurant,
Jl. Hayam Wuruk (Wisma Hayam Wuruk).
Ruby Restaurant,
Jl. Ir. H. Juanda 4A.

Sim Yan Restaurant,
Jl. Hayam Wuruk 37.
Jade Garden, Jl. Blora 56.
Chez Rose
Jl. M.H. Thamrin (Nusantara Bld).

Seafood Restaurants
Atithya Loka Restaurant,
Jl. Gatot Subroto (Satria Mandala Museum).
Coca Restaurant,
Jl. Melawai VIII/2-A.
Dragon Gate Restaurant,
Jl. Ir. H. Juanda 19.
Ever Green Restaurant,
Jl. Batu Cepter 20.
Furama Restaurant,
Jl. Hayam Wuruk 72.
Gloria Restaurant,
Jl. Manggabesar Raya 67.
Jade Garden Restaurant,
Jl. Blora 5–6.
King's Restaurant,
Jl. Cikini Rava 10 B.
Mina Restaurant,
Jl. Jend. Sudirman (Sahid Jaya Hotel).
Perahu Bugis Restaurant,
Jl. Lodan Timur (Horizon Hotel).
Price Restaurant, Jl. Blora 69.
Ratu Bahari Restaurant,
Jl. Melawai VIII/4.
Yun Nyan Restaurant,
Jl. Batu Cepter 69.
Hotel Asoka,
Jl. M.H. Thamrin, Tel. 32 29 08.
Hotel Asri,
Jl. Pintu I Senayan, Tel. 58 40 71.
Hotel Airport International,
Jl. Kran V/20, Tel. 34 26 71.
Hotel Febiola,
Jl. Gajah Mada, Tel. 63 40 08.
Hotel Hasta,
Jl. Pintu IX Senayan, Tel. 58 18 34.
Hotel Interhouse,
Jl. Melawai Raya, Tel. 71 64 08.
Hotel Jakarta,
Jl. Hayam Wuruk 35, Tel. 37 77 09.
Hotel Metropole,
Jl. Pintu Besar Selatan 38,
Tel. 37 69 21.
Hotel Marcopolo,
Jl. Teuku Cikditiro 19, Tel. 37 54 09.
Hotel Menteng I,
Jl. Gondangdia Lama 28,
Tel. 35 76 35.
Kebayoran Inn,
Jl. Senayan 87 Blok S, Tel. 71 62 08.
Hotel New Golf Court,
Jl. Patal Senayan, Tel. 54 21 08.
Hotel Monas,
Jl. Merdeka Barat 21, Tel. 37 52 08.
Hotel Surya Baru,
Jl. Batu Ceper 44, Tel. 37 81 08.
Hotel Surya,
Jl. Batu Ceper 44, Tel. 37 81 08.
Hotel Sabang Palace,
Jl. Setiabudi Raya 24, Tel. 58 63 81.
Hotel Wisata International,
Jl. M.H. Thamrin, Tel. 32 03 08.
Hotel Dirgantara,
Jl. Iskandarsyah Raya 1,
Tel. 71 21 09.
Hotel GrandParipurna,
Jl. Hayam Wuruk 26, Tel. 35 09 12.
Hotel Gama Gundaling,
Jl. Pal Putih 197A, Tel. 35 42 51.
Hotel Melati,
Jl. Hayam Wuruk 1, Tel. 37 72 08.
Hotel Pardede,
Jl. Raden Saleh I/9–11,
Tel. 34 63 76.
Hotel Royal,
Jl. Ir. H. Juanda 14, Tel. 41 28 26.
Hotel Wisata Jaya,
Jl. Hayam Wuruk 123, Tel. 63 22 08.
Hotel Wisma Indra, Jl. KH. Wahid Hasyim 26, tel. 34 75 36.
Hotel Menteng II,
Jl. Cikini Raya 105, Tel. 32 55 93.

Japanese Restaurants
Kikugawa Restaurant,
Jl. Kebon Binatang III/3 (Cikini).
Yoshiko Restaurant,
Jl. Museum 1.
Kobe Barbeque Restaurant,
Jl. Blora 27.
Shin Yukari Restaurant,
Jl. Thamrin (Sarinah Building).
Yamazato Restaurant,
Jl. Thamrin (Hotel Indonesia).
Shima Restaurant,
Jl. Prapatan (Hyatt Aryaduta Hotel).
Keio Restaurant,
Jl. Lap. Banteng Selatan (Hotel Borobudur).
Jakarta Okoh Restaurant,
Jl. Lodan Timur (Hotel Horizon).
Jakarta Nippon Kan,
Jl. Gatot Subroto (Hotel Hilton).
Jakarta New Hama,
Jl. Jend. Sudirman (Ratu Plaza).
Furosato Restaurant,
Jl. Thamrin (Sari Pacific Hotel).
Ginza Benkay Restaurant,
Jl. Thamrin (President Hotel).
Hana Restaurant,
Jl. Hayam Wuruk 126.
Hanako Japanese Restaurant & Bar,
Jl. Melawai Raya 28.
Hay Thien,
Jl. Hayam Wuruk 80, Tel. 27 88 63.

Thai Food
Ayothaya Thai Restaurant,
Jl. Ir. H. Juanda 35A.

Indian Food
Omar Khayyam Restaurant,
Jl. Antara 5–7.

Korean Food
New Korean House Restaurant,
Jl. M.H. Thamrin 28–39.
Korean International Restaurant,
Jl. Melawai VI/3 Blok M.
Korean House Atache,
Jl. Ir. H. Juanda 31.

Buffet Restaurants
Torsina Restaurant,
Shangrila Indah Unit II,
Jl. Cileduk Raya, Keb. Baru.
Vic's Viking Restaurant,
Jl. M.H. Thamrin 31.
Golden Cross Bar & Restaurant,
Jl. Silang Monas (Gerbang Utara Jakarta Fair).

Noodleparior
Raja Mie,
Jl. Hayam Wuruk 106A.
Bakmi Gajah Mada,
Jl. Gajah Mada 92,
Jl. Melawai IV/25 Blok M. Keb. Baru.

Bakeries
Hongkong Bakery,
Jl. Hayam Wuruk 13A.
Holand Bakery,
Jl. Hayam Wuruk 95A,
Jl. Melawai VI/7 Blok M. Keb. Baru.
Krekot Baru Bakery,
Jl. S. Hasanudin 18M III, Keb. Baru.
Pan Merlino Cake Bakery,
Jl. Gajah Mada 156C.

Souvenir & Artshops
Arjuna Crafts & Shop,
Jl. Majapahit 16A.
Bali International,
Jl. KH. Wahid Hasyim 115.
Bali Kerti Souvenir Shop,
Jl. Gajah Mada (Duta Merlin).
Banuwati Artshop Java Boutique,
Jl. Semarang 14.
Djelita Batik Arts & Shop,
Jl. Palatehan I/37 Blok KV.
Djodi Art & Curios,

Jl. Kebon Sirih Timur Dalam 22.
Fine Art,
Jl. H. Agus Salim 57C.
Garuda Art & Curios,
Jl. Majapahit 12.
Handicraft Production Centre,
Jl. Rawaterate 2 Pulogadung.
Harris Art Gallery,
Jl. Puri Mutiara 41C
Home Art,
Jl. H. Agus Salim 41 B.
Indonesia Art & Curios,
Jl. Cikini Raya 63A.
Indonesia Bazar,
Jl. Gatot Subroto (Hotel Jakarta Hilton).
Jayakarta Centre of Crafts,
Jl. Wahid Hasyim 168.
Johan's Art & Curio,
Jl. H. Agus Salim 59A.
Kota Gendang Art & Crafts,
Jl. Ir. H. Juanda 8.
Lee Cheong NV,
Jl. Majapahit 32.
Majapahit Art & Curio,
Jl. Melawai III/4.
Oriental Art,
Jl. H. Agus Salim 57B.
Modern Jewels & Art Shop,
Jl. Ir. J. Juanda 14.
Pigura Art Shop, Jl. Palatehan I/41.
Prambanan Antique & Curio,
Jl. H. Agus Salim 35.
Pura Art Shop, Hl. Palatehan I/43.
Rattan Handicraft Centre,
Jl. Bangka Raya 11 Kemang.
Rieka's Atelier,
Jl. Buntu Gambir 10.
Sarinah Jaya Sarinah Department Store, Jl. Thamrin 11.
Shinta Art & Gift Shop,
Jl. Melawai VI/17.
The Banka Tin Art Shop,
Jl. KH. Wahid Hasyim 178.
Tony's Gallery, Jl. Palatehan I/31.
Urip Store Art Gallery, Percelain Antiques, Jl. Palatehan I/40.

Batik

Batik Keris,
Jl. M.H. Thamrin (Sarinah Department Store).
Batik Hajadi,
Jl. Palmerah Utara 46.
Batik Semar,
Jl. Tomang Raya 54.
Batik Semar,
Jl. Gajah Mada 67868.
Batik Berdikari,
Jl. Mesjid Pal VII Pal Merah Barat.
Batik Seni Indonesia B.I. Pekalongan,
Jl. Panglima Polim IX/17 Keb. Baru.
Batik Sidomukti, Wisma Indonesia Batik, Jl. Prof. Dr. Sahardjo 311.
Batik Danarhadi, Jl. Raden Saleh 1A.
Gabungan Koperasi Batik Indonesia (GKBI), Jl. Senopati 5,
Jl. Jend. Sudirman 28,
Jl. H. Agus Salim 39.
Nusa Batik Iwan Tirta,
Jl. Panarukan 25.
Batik Wijaya,
Jl. Panglima Polim Raya 65 I1.
Batik Pandu, Jl. A.M. Sangaji 17.
Sunjoyo Batik Indonesia,
Jl. Salemba Tengah I/3H.
Srikandi Batik Shop,
Jl. Cikini 90 (Hias Rias Shopping Centre),
Jl. Melawai VI/6 Keb. Baru.
Batik Aria,
Jl. K.H. Wahid Hasyim 129.
Batik Damaswijaya,
Jl. Kramat Raya 71.
Batik Ratna Dewi,
Jl. Melawai V/8.
Batik Toraja, Jl. Melawai IX/40.
Hariom's Batik Corner,
Jl. Pasar Baru No. 5.

How far is it to . . . ?

From	To	km
Jakarta	Bandung	187
	Banjar	350
	Bogar	58
	Ciemis	320
	Cilegon	111
	Cikampak	95
	Cirebon	260
	Garut	246
	Klaten	632
	Krawang	71
	Kudus	562
	Kuningan	295
	Labuan	160
	Majalengka	321
	Merak	125
	Pekalongan	390
	Purwakarta	113
	Purwokerto	433
	Sarang	95
	Semarang	500
	Solo (via Semarang)	605
	Subang	177
	Sukabumi	119
	Sumedang	226
	Surabaja	815
	Tasikmalaya	307
	Tegal	335
	Wonogiri	635
	Wonosobo	525
	Yogyakarta (via Purwokerto)	587
Bandung	Banjar	148
	Bogor	129
	Ciamis	126
	Cianjur	65
	Garut	62
	Kadipaten	80
	Krawang	111
	Merak	310
	Purwokarta	70
	Purwokerto	260
	Semarang	368
	Solo	470
	Subang	32
	Sukabumi	96
	Sumedang	45
	Tasikmalaya	122
	Tegal	205
	Yogyakarta	488
Yogyakarta	Banyuwangi	631
	Gombang	130
	Kebumen	109
	Kroya	165
	Magelang	45
	Purwokerto	185
	Purworejo	65
	Semarang	118
	Solo	66
	Sragen	96
Surabaja	Bandung	746
	Banyuwangi	290
	Blitar	170
	Cirebon	616
	Denpasar	411
	Jember	202
	Kudus	264
	Lumajang	140
	Madiun	161
	Magelang	384
	Padangbai	475
	Ponorogo	191
	Purwokerto	525
	Rembang	200
	Semarang	315
	Singaraja	383
	Solo	275
	Trengalek	193
	Yogyakarta	341
Denpasar	Banyuwangi	130
	Malang	417

Pulau Seribu – Thousand Islands

Anyone wishing to escape the hectic pace of the capital, Jakarta, will find a calm oasis on Thousand Islands (in fact there are only 112, 8 of which are inhabited). The centre of the archipelago is about 65 nautical miles off the coast.

Pulau Putri is the best known isle of the archipelago and can lay claim

to air-conditioned bungalows, a restaurant and a diving centre. Not far from Pulau Petri lies the **Pulau Mata Hari,** the sun island. Here there's less comfort but the atmosphere is more tranquil and romantic. Electricity and radio are frowned upon. Small, clean bamboo bungalows are dotted around this paradise island with its white, sandy beaches.

From the restaurant, which is built on stilts on the reef there's a wonderful view of the surrounding atoll. Because of the **coral reef,** the island is a popular holiday destination for divers. The hotel manager can supply oxygen tanks on request. The climate on the island doesn't vary much in the course of the year – average temperature: 28 °C/82 °F.

You need to book early to be sure of getting accommodation on the two islands.

Pulau Putri Booking Office:
Jakarta Theatre Building,
Jl. Thamrin 9, Tel. 35 93 33-4
Pulau Mata Hari Island Resort,
Jl. Prapanca Raya 24, Kebayoran Baru, Jakarta, Tel. 71 78 47.

You can get to the Thousand Islands by boat or plane. Flights can be booked at both of the above offices. Departure is from **Kemayoran Airport** at either 9 am or 3 pm and it takes 20 minutes to fly to **Panjang Island.** There you have to change for Putri or Mata Hari. Single air fare costs US$ 80 – if this is a little too expensive, the islands can also be reached from the marina in Ancol. The Agaphos Marine Department (Agaphos Office, Jl. Gajah Mada, Tel. 35 13 32) has weekend trips to Pulau Mata Hari for diving.

Lesser Sunda Islands – Nusa Tenggara

Bali is the best known of the islands of the Nusa Tenggara (Lesser Sunda Islands). For administrative purposes, the archipelago is divided into two provinces. The **Nusa Tenggara Timur** comprises **Sumba, Komodo, Flores, Timor** (as well as innumerable islets) and has a population of three million. The islands of **Bali, Lombok** and **Sumbawa** make up the **Nusa Tenggara Timur** and are home to 2.9 million people.

Apart from Sumba and Timor, the lesser Sunda Islands are all **volcanic. Rainforests** (which contain many types of Eucalyptus trees), **savannah** and **open grassland** dominate a landscape which loses much of its green during the very marked dry season. The influence of the **Australian climate** is unmistakable on the islands. The rainy season lasts from November until the end of May and during this time sea travel is hazardous due to the rough conditions similar to those around the South Moluccas. Because of pronounced low pressure, Timor is subject to whirlwinds, the so-called cyclones.

While the population of the western islands is mainly **Malayan,** there are **Melanesian** and **Papuan** groups in the central areas of Flores and Timor. Scientists can clearly make out australoid, veddoid and negroid features in the people of East Nusa Tenggara.

Belief in spirits and magic and the worship of ancestors still prevails in the villages. Although much of the population has been converted to Christianity in recent times, the people still remain faithful to traditions which have been handed down from generation to generation. The main centres of the **Islamic** faith are in Central and East Lombok and on Sumbawo. The very orthodox population here has strict rules with regard to clothing and these have not been relaxed for tourists. Those travelling on here after having spent some time on Bali (people there are generally more tolerant) should be aware of the important differences that an Islamic area will mean.

There are two main attractions for the tourist within the Nusa Tenggara (not including Bali, that is). The first of these is **Lombok** island. The West of the island is populated by **Hindus** and is said to have that "originality" which Bali has now somehow lost. The other attraction is the "Dragon Island", **Komodo,** home of the Komodo dragon (monitor lizard). Since access is both difficult and expensive, tourists usually visit in groups.

All the other islands represent new ground for the tourist and the arrival of strangers is always met with a great deal of curiosity – the children are especially interested. In this part of the Republic tourism does not as yet play a major role in the economy. The latter is still based very much upon **cattle** breeding and on crude **petroleum** (found in East Timor). There are also some **sulphur** deposits but the working of these is of little economic importance. Every type of industry found on the islands is, in fact, outdated and the social and economic framework of the country can only really be called moderate to good.

A regular **ferry and boat service** operates between Bali, Lombok and Sumbawa. On the other islands, however, things are more or less left to chance. (This is somehow the appeal of the Nusa Tenggara).

On Lombok, Sumbawa and Flores the **roads** (more or less surfaced) cross the islands from East to West. Sumba and the other islands can only really claim the beginnings of a road system. **Aeroplanes** do a lot but in the rainy season are often unable to land on some of the unsurfaced runways. The waiting list for destinations which are inaccessible by road is usually so long that prospective passengers run out of patience.

Komodo is one of the islands where the only way of getting about is on foot.

Bali

Area: 5,600 sq. km/2,162 sq. miles – 145 km/90 miles long and 80 km/50 miles at its widest point. Population: 2.8 million. Much celebrated in verse and prose, Bali is the best-known island of the Indonesian archipelago and, as a result, also the most endangered.

Although frequently described as the "Island of Gods and Demons", Bali is experienced by most visitors as an island of celebrations and joie de vivre. Those who knew the island before, however, will today notice a change for the worse in all sectors. The commercialization of temple rites and dances has taken on dubious forms, and the daily life of the Balinese, which is characterized by colourful ceremonies, may appear to some as a staged tourist attraction. As many holidaymakers consider a well-chilled beer to be a sign of civilization, it is not surprising that only a few of them give a thought to Bali's historical background and its impact on the lives of its people today. The culture of Bali has survived Islamization, colonialization and many natural disasters – the future will show if it can also withstand mass tourism. Those who would like to gain some insight into what makes the Balinese so unique and what makes them able to largely evade Western influence must forget everything they already know and open their minds to the mysterious. Those who succeed will be enriched by an experience they will never forget. The traveller who is alert and observant will discover remnants of the original Bali even in the areas given over to tourism. Off the much beaten tourist tracks, and certainly not only at the seaside, Bali has remained what Ghandi once called it: "The dawn of the world".

Bali is, at the same time, a densely populated and heavily agricultural island. Its decomposed volcanic soil is fertile enough for two to three rice crops yearly. A Balinese village resembles a cooperative society whose members can trace their ancestry back to a common forebear. The villagers are organized in a banjar, which regulates work and social life. Each married man has a voice in decision-making over such issues as the distribution of duties and the planning of celebrations. A village organization called subak is responsible for regulating the water supply and the irrigation system. One of the volcanoes that fertilizes Bali's soil is the active Gunung Agung, 3,142-metre/10,308 ft. high, which, like the ancient Greek's Mt. Olympus, is the home of the Balinese gods.

When Islam penetrated Java's Hindu-Buddhist culture in the 15th century, the Balinese princes remained true to the Hindu faith, which they had acquired four centuries earlier. The East Javanese rulers who withdrew to Bali to escape the extensive Islamization that was under way, enriched Bali's culture through the introduction of their own customs and institutions. Today, more than 90 per cent of Bali's 2.8 million inhabitants profess to Hinduism, or Dharma-Hindu Bali, as it is called here because of its Buddhist elements.

The Balinese are famous for their artistic talents. At an early age, children begin learning dance, sculpture, painting and woodcarving, and some even acquire a command of these art forms before reaching school age.

Bali's capital, **Denpasar,** a city of almost 200,000 people, offers many opportunities for shopping and sightseeing. Among its attractions are an interesting evening market, the Bali Museum and an academy where one can get an idea of the arduous training the Balinese dancers go through. The museum contains exhibits of Balinese art, crafts and architecture dating from prehistoric to modern times. Bali's international airport, Ngurah Rai, located approx. 5 km/3 miles south of Kuta, offers connections to Australia and Tokyo, as well as to Jakarta and the neighbouring islands.

Sanur, bathers' paradise and home to international hotels, lies a few miles south-east of Denpasar on a fantastically beautiful bay. A coral reef protects the coast, making the sea shallow, calm and ideal for non-swimmers. Everything imaginable is offered the holidaymaker who would rather not do without the comforts of home, but despite all the night spots, arts and crafts shops and souvenir stands, Sanur still gives the impression of being a quiet and restful resort. After the completion of an eight-storey hotel, the elders of the village set down a decree banning the further construction of buildings of this size, it being a sacrilege to construct anything exceeding the height of a palm tree. Thanks to the wisdom of the Banjar elders, Sanur has remained a holiday paradise rather than becoming a hotelier's dream come true.

The home of the Belgian painter, Bonnet, who worked here in the 1930's, is located in Sanur. It is administered by his widow, a celebrated dancer, and offers an in-depth look at the painter's life and works. By sailing-boat, pleasant trips can be made to the islands off the Balinese coast. Nusa Penida, for example, is a very dry island covered with karst formations, but it offers interesting sights, such as the Goa Karangsari, a cave and subterranean lake, and a number of temples.

Those who seek the surf and rolling waves are better catered for at **Kuta Beach,** whose long, virtually endless coastline and optimal surfing conditions have made it famous throughout the world. Kuta is frequented by predominantly young people whose presence is strongly felt in this former fishing village – the sound of their motorcycles in the early morning and late at night is especially unpleasant. In July and August, as well as in December, the resort is hopelessly overcrowded. Restaurants, bars and discos stay open until the small hours, and what is left of typical village life has long been relegated to the sidelines. Despite the continuous flow of tourists, the prices of food and lodging have remained surprisingly low. The tourist industry has also attracted the lower elements from Surabaya and Ujung Pandang, who have introduced theft and robbery to Bali. There also seem to be a number of globetrotters who try to enrich their travel purses by laying hands on other people's property. It is therefore best to be on one's guard.

Legian is a quieter resort located 2 km/1¼ miles north of Kuta. Those who really want to experience Bali, however, should head straight for the island's interior. West of **Singaraja** on the northern coast are several relatively new resorts which have yet to be developed for tourism. Here, accommodation is in the form of losmens (guest houses) and so-called homestays. **Lovina Beach** is the centre of tourism on this coast where the sand is somewhat darker than at Sanur or Kuta. Excellent diving areas can be found among the reefs off Lovina's coast. The temples in the area are all representative of the North Balinese style and have interesting reliefs. Here, food and lodging is especially good value. The port of Singaraja, which lies close by, is North Bali's most important.

Among Bali's many attractions, its sea temples are probably the most spectacular. The national sanctuary of **Tanah Lot** is one of the most beautiful. Situated on a black, volcanic rock offshore, it can be reached from Kuta and Legian on foot in three hours, or from Denpasar and Kediri by bemo. In their sea temples, the Balinese pray for protection from the evil spirits of the sea, and the ill-health and misfortune that they bring. The best time to see Tanah Lot is in the late afternoon when the bizarre silhouette formed by the temple and its odd-shaped rock, is especially conspicuous. The sea temple of **Ulu Watu,** situated on a precipitous cliff on the peninsula of Nusa Dua, is mostly frequented by surfers who take advantage of the extremely high waves in the area. The **Goa Gajah** (Elephant Cave) near Bedulu is one of the island's most ancient sights of interest. Carved out of a huge block of stone, the cave served as a Hindu monastery in the 11th century. A huge demon's head chiseled out of the rock guards the entrance, while outstanding carvings of plants, animals and people line the outside wall. The bathing pools opposite the cave were only discovered in 1954, when excavation work was carried out. From just below the cave, there is a beautiful panorama of the surrounding terraced rice fields.

The sacred spring of **Tirta Empul** near **Tampak Siring** is believed to have curative powers. From all over Bali, people journey here to seek protection and deliverance from illness. In commemoration of the spring's creation in the year 962 A. D. and the purification ritual that was prescribed at the time, a sacred stone is carried to the spring in an annual procession which takes place during the full moon in the fourth month of the Balinese year. On a hill in the immediate vicinity, stands the summer residence Sukarno had built in 1954.

The Holy Monkey Forest of **Sangeh,** a nature reserve 20 km/ 12½ miles north of Denpasar, is always full of activity. The friendly monkeys here soon learnt to connect the tourist with peanuts. Some of them, however, are more interested in sunglasses, cameras

Sri Dewi is honoured on Java and Bali as the godess of rice.

and hats than in nuts and bananas. Visitors especially captivated by this tropical island have been known to enter this forest deliberately displaying their passport and plane ticket.

Another of Bali's national sanctuaries, the Pura Taman Agun, which dates from the 17th century, is located in **Mengwi,** 11 km/7 miles away. This immense temple complex situated on high ground is one of Bali's most beautiful; however, since 1977, it has been closed to tourists. The wall surrounding the temple is sacred and may not be touched. The Puch Panataran Agung on the slopes of Gunung Agung near **Besakih** is the largest and most hallowed temple on Bali. The sight of the black merus against the huge backdrop formed by the volcano is especially breathtaking in the early-morning hours. The temple is maintained by the Balinese nobility, who make a yearly pilgrimage to this symbol of religious unity, turning it into the venue of an opulent celebration in honour of their ancestors. Once every hundred years, a religious celebration is held here, which is by far the island's biggest.

The immense caldera of **Mount Batur,** from which another, smaller volcano rises up, can be reached by way of Kedisan. The magnificent, unobstructed view from the village of Penelokan more than compensates for the arduous journey. This is certainly one of Bali's most fascinating regions, offering spectacular scenery as well as many interesting sights. The Bati Aga, considered to be the aboriginal inhabitants of the island, live in the vicinity of the volcano. Those who reach the crater's edge by early morning can then go on foot or on horseback to the lake and paddle to **Trunyan** in a dugout canoe. Here, the Bali Aga do not cremate their dead in the Hindu manner, but instead, they leave them out in the open to rot. Those who may have visited these aboriginals many years ago probably left with many pleasant memories. Today, however, as opposed to other Balinese who are distinguishable through patience, an even temperament and tolerance, these people are frequently cold, aloof and money-grabbing. Can tourism once again take the blame? Considering the development in other regions of Bali, this question cannot be ignored

Those intent on climbing the small, hissing Batur volcano should hire a guide at **Kintamani.** Six to eight hours should be calculated for the ascent and return journey. Then, to get to **Goa Lawah,** you have to leave the mountain area. In Klungkung, a visit can be made to the **Gerta Gosa,** or Royal Court of Justice, where the high court convened during the Gelgel Dynasty. The entire ceiling is covered with frescos painted in wayang-style and depicting the various forms of punishment allotted to lawbreakers.

Goa Lawah, the famous Bat Cave, is located not far from Kusambe. Its caverns, which are closed to the public, are said to extend all the way to the temple at Besakih. The cave itself is teeming with bats. They line the ceiling, and a thick layer of their excrement covers the floor of the cave as well as the roofs of the small shrines in the adjacent temple. In 1904, the princes of Bali held a conference here to plan action against the Dutch colonial forces. The measures taken were virtually ineffectual, however, and eventually caused the fall of several royal houses.

The beach at **Kusambe** is covered with black, volcanic sand. Travelling eastward, one is confronted increasingly with the effects of the 1963 eruption. The village of **Amalpura,** which used to be called Karangasem, has yet to recover fully from that eruption. Even today, the walls of many buildings are cracked and split. Because the name "Karangasem" was seen by the villagers as the bringer of misfortune, they renamed their village to prevent other disasters. Today, very little evidence remains of the volcanic origins of **Lake Braton** near Bedugul in Central Bali. The slopes surrounding the lake are heavily forested, providing protection and a home to many animals. The Bali tiger once lived here and in the western part of the island before it became extinct in the early 1970's.

Bali's Centres of Arts and Crafts

Those who pass through **Mas** on their way to Ubud will certainly notice many shops selling objects carved of wood. Here, high-quality work is still turned out by hand, but the growing demand for Barong, Vishnu and Garuda carvings for exportation as key-rings, chess figures and statuettes has given rise to a certain degree of mass production. The creative and artistically inclined Balinese have been forced to submit to customer pressure. For many tourists, quality is less important than a plastic tote-bag in which to carry home their souvenirs – and it did not take long for the Balinese to adapt themselves to this market. The beautiful masks and statues that take weeks to carve and paint were originally not intended for commercial or decorative use, but were created in honour of the gods. Today, however, art in the service of the gods has been mostly replaced by art in the service of the tourist's purse.

In the language of the Balinese, there is no word for "art" although it has been an intrinsic part of their daily lives for centuries. The people of the countryside have always maintained strong links with their traditional art forms, fully comprehending their symbolically veiled messages.

In **Celuk,** Bali's silver centre, there are large numbers of shops. The silversmiths who work in the village proper are always glad to carry out special orders.

Ubud is the island's cultural centre. In the 1930's, this village was the home of an artists' colony to which European artists such as Walter Spies and Rudolph Bonnet belonged. Today mostly local artists live and work here. The Balinese charm of this small village, as well as its beautiful surroundings, also attracts many tourists, who then spend time in Ubud's numerous art galleries. Quality and prices should be compared before a purchase is made, however. Those especially interested in the development of Balinese painting should visit Puri Lukisan, Ubud's art museum, which contains a valuable collection of paintings. Two kilometres west of Ubud lies a small forest inhabited by monkeys which are probably the fiercest and most savage on Bali. A small fairy-tale temple can also be found here, well off the beaten track.

Lombok

The Indonesian name for fiery red and green chilli peppers is "Lombok". The island's name can perhaps be traced back to the temperaments of its **Islamic** inhabitants, the Sassacks. In **Peresehan**-competitions in which the two opponents are armed with bamboo clubs and shields and attack each other viciously, something of this temperament comes to light. At one time the Peresehan was seen as a way of toughening up young warriors for battle. Today it is a sporting event which takes place all over Lombok on Independence Day.

15% of the island's population is of **Hindu Balinese** origin but tension between the Islamic and Hindu groups has less to do with religious differences than with the **bloody history** which they share. In return for support in their struggle against the Raja of Sumbawa in the early 18th century, the Lombok people allowed the Balinese to settle in the West of the island. Soon, however, the Sassacks found themselves oppressed and forced into slavery by the Balinese – and that on their own island.

The colonialists used this conflict between the two groups to their own advantage and in 1894 Lombok became part of the **Dutch colony.** The Balinese Raja of Mataram was exiled and the Crown Prince murdered.

Balinese cultural influences are still apparent in West Lombok. This, together with Lombok's geographical position (away from the main stream of tourists) has won the island the reputation of possessing Bali's former "originality". If tourist numbers continue to increase at the same rate as they have up to now, however, there soon won't be a great deal of this originality left on Lombok either.

The island, which covers an area of some 4,595 sq. km/1,774 sq. miles, is dominated by the 3,726 m/ 12,224 ft high volcano, **Rinjani.** A smaller volcano, Baru ("new one") stands in Rinjani's large crater but is not visible from the plains. West of the Baru lies the Segara Anak lake – the waters of which fill most of Rinjani's crater. On the northern shore of the lake there are hot springs. The people of Lombok have great faith in the healing powers of the springs, especially at full-moon. Once a year, at the **Pekelan ceremony,** not only Sassaks but also Balinese People make pilgrimages to the crater lake to pay homage to the gods. The Rinjani has the same religious significance to Balinese descendants on Lombok as does the Gunung Agung to people living on Bali itself.

Anyone wishing to **climb the Rinjani** should use the Bayan-Senaro route. In the Losmen Horas (losmen = guesthouse) in Ampenan hopeful climbers will be given help in both word and deed. The owner of the losmen, Mr. Batubara, knows the Rinjani massif better than any man.

The ascent begins with a 4–5 hour journey to **Desa Anyar** via Permenang and Tanjung. From Desa Anyar the road leads via **Bayan** to **Senaro.** Senaro's resident teacher will not only arrange for a guide but will also help with accommodation arrangements. The actual climb to the edge of the outer crater lasts about 8–10 hours. The path into the caldera (cavity at summit of volcano) is treacherous and to attempt to follow it at dusk, or once night has fallen, would be reckless – no experienced guide would do so. Groups usually spend one night at the edge of the crater and then begin the 3-hour descent the next morning. Since temperatures on the mountain can drop well below 10 °C/50 °F at night, it's advisable to take along a good sleeping bag and warm clothing. Anyone without these essentials will perhaps be able to hire them from the Losmen Horas in Ampenan. Climbing parties with sufficient equipment and food could spend a few days on the crater of the Rinjani.

People with no climbing experience should not try to ascend the Rinjani at the eastern edge of its crater. The ascent of the smaller volcano, Baru, is made more difficult by gases which are given off. This is most dangerous when clouds gather in the crater towards midday. (There is a danger of suffocation!)
Another route to the summit begins in the east and leads through Sapit.

The sides of the Rinjani massif, which are wooded up to 2,000 m/6,560 ft, stretch as far as the sea in the north. Between **Desa Anyar** in the north-west and **Labuhan Lombok** in the north-east, **difficult terrain** has meant there are few settlements and hardly any roads. The woods in the area do, however, contain teak which is felled. The **valley to the south** of the Rinjani has, on the other hand, been settled and the land cultivated. A modest road system links the towns and villages here.

Mataram, the administrative centre of West Nusa Tenggara, has now spread out into the towns of Cakranegara and Ampenan. The question of visas etc. can usually be sorted out in Mataram or in Denpasar (Bali) or Kupang (Timor). The "Kantor Imigrasi" (Immigration Office) in Mataram is on the Jl. Udayana, about 10 minutes from the airport.

Lombok offers both cultural interest and a wealth of scenic beauty. The island's colourful beaches are a great attraction. Near **Ampenan,** for instance, 10 km/6.2 miles of

beach stretch as far as the fishing village of Senggigi – more than enough to cope with even today's growing number of visitors. Another beach, **Pamenang,** lies 35 km/21.7 miles north of Ampenan. Many examples of Balinese culture are to be found along the coast near Ampenan. There are, for example, the temples of the **Pura Segara** and also the temple **Batu Bolang** which stands on a cliff overlooking the sea 20 km/12.4 miles from Ampenan.

From the **Gunung Pengsang** (8 km/4.5 miles south of Mataram) there is a wonderful view of the cultivated land and villages. Not far from the mountain top is an important (though not very impressive) Hindu temple in which a bull is sacrificed once a year at the harvest celebrations. The **Summer Palace of Narmada** (10 km/6.2 miles from Cakranegara), built in 1805 by the King of Karangasem (East Bali), is also worth visiting. The palace grounds contain terraced gardens, bathing places and a lake. In the mountains near Narmada (only 7 km/4.3 miles away) lies the town of **Saranadi.** Apart from a hotel with swimming-pool and sporting facilities, and an excellent view of the surrounding countryside (weather permitting) there is a **Balinese temple** about 3 km/1.8 miles from Saranadi which is especially interesting since it is a synthesis of **Hindu and Islamic motifs.** The temple of the Holy Eels isn't far from Saranadi either.

Cakranegara is known for its traditional woven fabrics, for which "ikar" dyeing is used. The weaving

mills are situated in the outlying districts of Cakranegara. Visits can be arranged. **Kota Raja** and **Loyok** are places which are famous for their fine **wickerwork.**

The **Taman Mayura,** a Balinese water palace is also situated near Cakranegara. The palace once served as a court of justice. The largest Balinese temple on Lombok is the **Meru temple.** Constructed in three sections, the temple was built by Prince Made Karang in 1720. As with all Balinese temples, the number of roofs shows to whom the Meru was dedicated.

With its sailing-boat harbour, **Ampenan** in West Lombok is a pleasant town and visitors often spend some time here. Because of this, there is a relatively wide choice of hotels and "losmens". Coaches and minibuses will collect guests on arrival, providing sufficient notice is given.

Travel to and from Lombok takes place as a rule by **ferry** from Lembar and Labuhan Lombok. **Lembar** (West Lombok) offers one ferry daily to and from Padang Bai (Bali). Bemos cover the 35 km/21.7 miles between Ampenan and Lembar in about an hour. **Labuhan Lombok** (East Lombok) has a ferry service to Alas (Sumbawa). Here again there is one ferry per day in each direction and the crossing takes about 3 hours. The distance between the two harbours can be covered in 2½– 4 hours, depending on traffic conditions. There aren't many hotels or "losmens" in Labuhan Lombok so it's a good idea to stay in Cakranegara. The "Stasiun Sweta", the central bus and bemo station, is in Cakranegara and links it with all the larger towns on the island.

Selaparang Airport is 2 km/ 1.24 miles outside Ampenan and offers flights to Bali and the islands east of Lombok.

Addresses of the Airlines:
Garuda, Jl. Langko 80, Ampenan, Tel. 2 37 62,
Merpati, Jl. Langsat 1 (GSA).

Sumbawa

Even today the eruption of the Krakatoa in 1883 (see "The Volcanoes") is considered to be the worst ever catastrophe of its kind – the effects of the eruption did, indeed, cause the deaths of 36,000 people. In comparison with Krakatoa, relatively little attention has been given to the **Tambora** which erupted on Sumbawa in 1815. Yet here 85,000 people lost their lives in tidal waves and famine and a cloud of pumice ash almost 9 times greater than at the eruption of Krakatoa was thrown up into the atmosphere. At that time no-one thought to connect the arctic Summer of 1816 with the eruption of Tambora the year before – we now understand the possible effects of such a mass of dust particles in the atmosphere. The 4,200 m/13,776 ft high fiery mountain was reduced to a jagged crater of 2,820 m/9,249 ft. Today this is the highest elevation on the otherwise dry and barren island.

Even 300 years ago Sumbawa was quite well-known for its extensive stocks of **sandalwood.** More recently the island has made a name for itself in the field of **horse-breeding** – the same is true of Sumba. Animals bred on these two islands are used all over Indonesia and the horse-drawn taxis (known as "andongs" in Central Java, "dokars" in West Sumatra and Lombok, and "benhurs" in the horses' homelands) depend upon them. They're also often to be seen taking a tourist to the foot of the Bromo (East Java). Breeding of Sumba horses does now take place in other areas but there's really no replacement for a Sumba horse bred on Sumba or Sumbawa.

Sumbawa's history tells of two linguistic groups which established **two separate states** on the island. "Sumbawa" was spoken by the population of the West and "Bima" by people in the East. Indonesia's national language (bahasa indonesia) has now resolved the former linguistic conflicts, but the original centres of the two states still exist. The people of Sumbawa are strict followers of the teaching of **Islam.**

After having been spoilt by the calm polite natures of the Balinese and Javanese people, the tourist is confronted with unrest and **aggression** on Sumbawa and Sumba. It is, for example, not unusual for traffic police to be kicked and punched while they go about their work distributing parking tickets. The fiery temperaments of the Sumbawa people come to light in the **Berempah.** This is sport similar to boxing but in which the wrists are bound with rice straw. The sharp edges of the stalks can wound badly.

It could well be that the temperament of the people also affects the way they drive...

Sumbawa's only **road** crosses the island from **Jareweh** in the West to **Sape** in the East. Places which are off the beaten track (and therefore interesting) can only be discovered and enjoyed on foot.

Sumbawa Besar, one of the main towns on the western peninsula, offers the best accommodation (neat and clean but not luxurious). While in Sumbawa Besar, try to visit the **sultan's palace** which is dilapidated although it was only built in the 20th century.

The **ferry** from Sumbawa's western harbour takes about 3 hours to reach Sumbawa Besar. The journey from here to Bima, the island's main port, takes more than 10 hours. Two **bus** companies run services to Bima but each company only operates on two days of the week – and these days change regularly. Up to date information about the bus services is only really available on the spot.

There are, of course, **flights** to Bima. Zamrud Airlines used to specialize in such inter-island air traffic within the lesser Sundas with two veteran aircraft, a DC 3 and a C 47. At the end of 1980, however, the company was forced to discontinue operations because of financial difficulties. A resumption of services at a later date was not altogether ruled out. At the moment, then only Merpati Airlines cater for short-haul flights within the Nusa Tenggara. There are flights from Sumbawa Besar to Bima and from Bima there is a connection to Ujung Padang on Sulawesi. De Havilland Twin Otter aircraft (which can accommodate 12–16 passengers) also fly to Ende and Ruteng on Flores. **Bima's airport** is 40 km/25 miles from the town.

To get to **Komodo,** island home of the Komodo dragon, you have to go by boat. The best place to find a boat heading to Komodo is **Sape,** the harbour on Sumbawa's east coast. The crossing is not cheap and with the arrival of more and more tourists in this part of Indonesia, chartering boats has also become more expensive. Overnight **accommodation in Sape** is only really possible courtesy of the police, or on one of the boats lying at anchor. Anyone arriving after nightfall will find Sape deserted – the local people go to bed early! The crossing to Komodo is only really possible between April and September. High waves and variations in the tides between the Sea of Flores and the Indian Ocean make sea travel in the rainy season a risky business. At this time of year there's hardly a captain who would make his boat available for the crossing.

Boats from **Bima,** Sumbawa's main harbour, rarely cross to Komodo. Mostly, shipping heads straight to Labuhanbajo or Reo on Flores. From Bima boats do head for Kupan on Timor. You'll need to arrange for a "surat jalan" (letter of permission to visit outer islands, available from the police) before buying your passage, however.

Sumba

Until recently the island of Sumba was almost completely cut-off from the outside world. This changed to some extent when the **Mahau Airport** was opened at Waingapu (the island's main town). Merpati Airlines now has flights to and from Denpasar (Bali), Ende (Flores) and Kupang (Timor) – that's to say flights are officially scheduled but really depend upon sufficient demand. So it's a good idea to check up on the date of your return flight as soon as you arrive on Sumba – otherwise, you might end up staying longer than originally planned. As far as access by **boat** is concerned, services between Waingapu and the outside world are infrequent.

Sumba, with its **dry, flat landscape** and lack of distinctive features, doesn't really fit into the usual picture of tropical Indonesia. This in no way means that it is not worth a visit, however. The **cultural traditions** of the island are still very much alive and the reputation enjoyed by the unique cloth woven by the islanders has spread far beyond the Indonesian archipelago.

Although similar versions of **Ikat dyeing** are found on Sumbawa, Kalimantan, Bali, Sumatra, Flores, Roti and other Indonesian islands, highly advanced weaving techniques on Sumba have made its cloth very popular.

Ikat cloth produced in **East Sumba** is mainly rust-coloured (kombu), this shade being combined with blue tones (wora) to produce very colourful motifs. The incredible range of effects achieved is possible because a different number of dye baths is used for each piece of work. The **motifs** themselves also vary a great deal. Mostly the Ikats feature the figures of men (on foot or on horseback), birds, snakes and octopus.

In **West Sumba** motifs are more **abstract** and the dominant colour is blue. The only designs which are immediately recognisable as coming from this region are those on scarf-like garments.

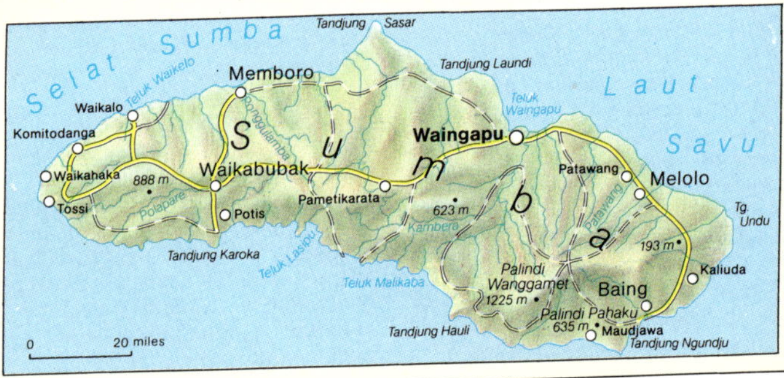

It's interesting to note that the articles of clothing woven on Sumba are **only ever worn by the men.** Both rectangular in shape, the "hinggi" is wrapped around the hips while the "kambu" is draped over the shoulders.

Transport can be a problem on Sumba, which is mostly made up of savannah and has a very small road network. The large number of small but powerful **horses** to be found on the island will make the choice of transport easier for anyone with riding experience. There is a limit to the endurance of the temperamental animals and any tourist who hasn't had much experience with horses should hire himself an islander who has. To have seen some part of Sumba's 11,000 sq. km/4,247 sq. miles on horseback is an achievement few can claim.

The **traditionally – built houses** in the **Mani village** on the north coast of Sumba are well known for their high, sloping roofs. In Mani and other villages in the area **harvest time** means **fascinating festivals** (these do include rather bloody sacrificial rites). Traditions live on the island. In West Sumba too, ceremonies take place in fairly quick succession. A central feature of them is the sea worm. If the worm is not included, or if it rots soon after being caught, the people believe there will be floods and a bad harvest.

It isn't only on Lombok and Sumbawa that traditional versions of what we know as boxing are found. High-spirited and really quite dangerous **fighting matches** also seem to be typical of Sumba.

The fists of the contenders are bound with straw and when the sharp edges of the straw come into contact with an opponent's body there is almost always bloodshed.

The "Pasola", **horse-back fights** which take place at the end of February or beginning of March, are not without bloodshed either. From galloping horses the contenders hurl blunt lances at each other – people

have been known to lose eyes, some even their lives. Venues for the "pasola": Wanokaka, Lamboya and Kodi.

A visit to Sumba should include:
Traditional Villages:
Tarung and Anakalang (both are near Waikabubak);
Rende and Wunumuku (near Waingapu).
Weaving Centres:
Prailin, Mangili and Melolo (Waingapu area).

Sumba – Distances in Kilometres.

WAIKELO										
11	WAITABULA									
47	36	WAIKABUBAK								
65	54	18	WANOKAKA							
12	37	1	19	TARUNG						
68	57	22	39	21	ANAKALANG					
184	173	137	155	136	116	WAINGAPU				
246	235	199	217	198	178	62	MELOLO			
253	242	206	224	205	185	69	7	RENDE		
284	273	237	255	236	216	100	38	31	MANGILI	
424	413	262	395	261	240	124	62	55	24	BAING

Komodo

Komodo, the "Dragon Island", lies between Sumbawa and Flores. The unusual formation of Komodo's mountain crests gives the impression that not only the monitor lizard but also the island itself is a survivor of primeval times.

With its thick leathery skin, red forked tongue and huge claws, the **Komodo dragon** (as the creature is still popularly known) does indeed look like the incarnation of the mythical beast. The awesome length of its body – up to 4 m/13 ft – astonished P. A. Ouwens when he first chanced upon the lizard in 1912.

The lizards are found on Komodo as well as on its neighbouring islands. They vary in colour from a greenish-yellow (the young lizards) through light brown and rust to black. Female lizards, which are on the whole smaller than the males, can lay up to 30 eggs. As protection against the voracious adults, the young monitor lizards have developed impressive climbing skills. No bird's nest is safe from them. Komodo lizards are deaf but have a highly developed sense of smell. They are also aware of the slightest movements around them, even at a fair distance – their vision is, however, not particularly keen.

Eels form the main diet of the lizards but if the opportunity arises, they will also hunt for roe-deer and small game. When temperatures become too hot the lizards retreat to caves or lie under overhanging rocks. It is not unknown for them to cool off in the sea. It is thought that around **2,000 lizards** live on the 300 sq. km/116 sq. miles island.

The island was originally **volcanic** and probably first emerged out of the sea at the start of the Pleistocene era. In 1980 Komodo was declared a **national park** – as were also the neighbouring islands, Padar and Rinca, where monitor lizards are also found. Komodo mainly consists of **rocky highlands,** the highest elevation being the 735 m/2,411 ft high Gunung Arab. In the rainy season (November to March) the coarse grass which covers the island is green, but in the dry season (July to October) it turns a yellowish-brown colour. Only lontar palms and zizyphus trees (typical vegetation of the lesser Sundas) can survive on Komodo's barren land during the dry spell.

The monitor lizards are most often seen in the **Poreng Valley.** This valley forms part of the hinterland of the semi-circular Loh Liang bay where water is found throughout the year – most other fresh-water sources dry up in the dry season. The best time for a visit to Komodo is May, when there's also enough drinking water about.

Just **500 people** live on Komodo – in a single settlement on the east coast, Kampong Komodo. The population of the island is strictly controlled by the government and is never more than 500. Should numbers exceed this figure, special moves are made to re-settle people elsewhere.

The "Wisata" and the "Floating Cottage" are to be found north of Kampong Komodo. Tourists can stay overnight here (40 beds are available).

People who visit secluded areas and remote villages in Indonesia should, in accordance with local custom, call upon the village leader (Kepala Kampong) first of all.

The **fishermen of Komodo** are descendants of people who were banished to the island from Flores. Fishing provides them with a living, but only just, and so they try to make something out of tourism, too. Besides providing **food and accommodation,** they will act as **well-informed guides.** Nowadays about 400–500 people visit Komodo every year. Most tourists stay no longer than 3 days – a **maximum stay of 5 days** has been laid down by the **Direktorat Perlindungan dan Pengawatan**

Alam (P. P. A. for short), the Indonesian Directorate of Nature Conservation and Wildlife Management, in Labuhanbajo. Anyone wishing to stay longer should ask at the P. P. A.'s main office in Bogor (Java). To avoid any delay, apply for your permit to visit Komodo in good time. You could even try applying before leaving home – enquire at the Indonesian Embassy or Tourist Board.

If you only decide upon a visit to Komodo once you're in Bali, the P. P. A. office in Denpasar will be able to issue the necessary permit (the office is open 7.30 am–11 am). You'll have to call at the police station as well (with 2 or 3 passport photos) and they'll provide you with your **surat jalan** (letter authorizing travel in the outer islands).

The last opportunity to get a visiting permit is the P. P. A. office in Labuhanbajo in West Flores. The permit will normally take 2–3 days coming through but, as the **area surrounding Labuhanbajo is beautiful,** this shouldn't be a problem. The Bupati (district officer appointed by the Minister of Internal Affairs) in Ruteng has quite a future planned for this pleasant coastal town. There are plans for an air-strip as well as a large hotel which could receive guests on their way to Komodo. There is a **fairly regular boat service** from Labuhanbajo to Komodo – provisions are taken to the island in this way. Prices are quite reasonable. **Provisions** for the trip to Komodo should be bought in Labuhanbajo at the latest (or even better in Bima).

Goats, which are used to lure the lizards out into the open, are very expensive on Komodo, although wild goats are in fact a real pest there. Anyone who buys his "scapegoat" on Flores and travels with it to Komodo (the crossing takes 4 hours) must reckon with growing fond of the animal. (Could this be where Komodo's wild goats come from?)

People who don't like sensations and don't want to spill "innocent blood" can avoid both and still catch sight of the Komodo dragons if they use some initiative. There are always enough tourists who visit the island with meat to bait the lizards between May and September anyway, and since the insatiable monitor lizards never move far from the traditional feeding grounds, you're almost sure to find them there even without bait.

Anyone who wants to see how the lizards devour the goats must be quick, however. The "feast" is over in no time, so have your cameras loaded and at the ready!

Komodo is also well-known for its unspoilt **coral gardens.** The most beautiful examples are to be found off the north coast. Swimmers have to be careful, however, as **currents** around the island can reach speeds of 4–5 knots. These currents are caused by the tidal differences between the Indian Ocean and the Flores sea. At low and high tides masses of water flow through the straights between the lesser Sunda islands. Engine trouble can turn into a serious situation in such conditions.

Flores

Flores was first sighted by a Portuguese sailor – he saw the thin strip of land which forms the eastern part of the island, and named it **Cabo de Flores** (The Cape of Flowers). This is the origin of the island's name.

It was this part of the island which was occupied by the **Portuguese.** Today people in the East of Flores have names and, indeed, facial features which are reminiscent of the Portuguese. These phenomena are even more evident on Timor, the island in the South East, which was a Portuguese possession right up to 1975, and where the influence exerted by this one time naval and trading power still lingers.

The island measures 400 km/248 miles by 80 km/50 miles. Of the **million people** living on Flores today, over 50% are **Roman Catholics.** The **Moslems** tend to live in the coastal area in the west of the island. **Animism** has not died out completely either. Here, as elsewhere in Indonesia, the religions of Islam and Christianity still show traits of older traditions. There is a concentration of **Melanesian** and **Papuan** peoples in the east, as a result of the many waves of immigrants. Looking at the island as a whole, though **Malayans** are in the majority.

In the towns on the coast, the people adopt a friendly, outgoing attitude towards strangers. This is not true in the island's interior, however. There, magic and ancestor worship still persist, and **the natives tend to fear the approach of white people.** If a white man is seen, then people simply stop whatever they're doing and take to their heels.

The greatest fear is shown by the people living in the **area around Maumere.** Their fear is based on a rumour which still circulates today. In order to build the islands road network, the Dutch had recruited large numbers of local people. Many of them died – some under the strain of the hard physical labour, some as the result of accidents. As it was a former custom amongst the local people to bury an enemy under the foundation of a new house, the islanders assumed that the Dutch were doing this too. Today many people still think that the heads of native workers lie buried beneath the old bridges.

Bearing in mind, that for the islanders, all white people are automatically Dutch, – (at whose hands they suffered), you would be well advised to be on your guard.

Children who attend a missionary school are usually much more trusting, however, due to their contact with European missionaries, and often laugh at their parents' behaviour. In the east of the island, though, the fear of white people has become so extreme, that the **visitor should leave a village** at the first signs of non-acceptance and hatred. In some villages east of Boganator, the inhabitants throw stones to keep white visitors at bay.

This may all sound very daunting, but it would be wrong to cancel your visit because of this – or for

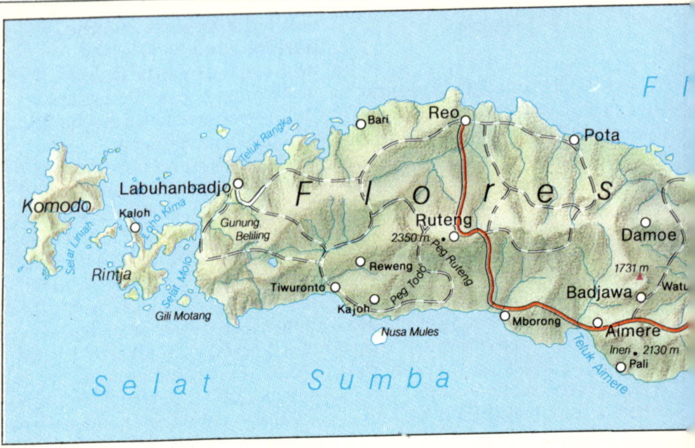

any other reason. Flores, with ist **marvellous scenery,** is often considered to be Indonesia's most attractive island. And apart from this, Flores has many interesting **traditions** to offer. Traditional music and dances aside, there are also the **Caci fighting tournaments.** Although there are similarities to the "Pereshan" performed on Lombok, the Caci competitors use whips with the shields instead of bamboo clubs. These tournaments only take place on special occasions in the Mangarai region.

Ikat weaving is very highly developed on Flores, and many visitors to the island buy cloth as a souvenir to take home. If you can't resist the temptation to haggle over the price, at least take into account that weaving is a difficult, demanding skill, and agree on a reasonable amount.

Tourism hasn't really got off the ground on Flores yet. As far as **accommodation** is concerned, the area around **Labuhanbajo** has made the greatest effort to meet the tourist's needs. Labuhanbajo itself is the place many people stop off at, on their way to Komodo. It lies on a road (some 705 km/438 miles long) which extends from the West of Flores to Waiklibang, in the extreme north-east of the island, with the worst section of road between Ruteng and Labuhanbajo. There are also **hotels and losmens** in the larger places along this road – e. g. in Ruteng, Ende, Maumere and Laruntuka. The area around Ende also attracts visitors who come to see the volcano **Kelimutu.**

If you're travelling from Ende to see the volcano, your best bet is to make for Moné and take the south

fork. It may be possible to rent a small overland vehicle in Moné.

Kelimutu has three lakes – one time craters – each of them a different colour due to the mineral composition of the water. One is deep red, one black and the other a greyish green. Don't risk bathing in them. The water in the green lake is said to have a high alkali content, and is particularly dangerous.

The early morning mist and the unspoilt landscape with its enormous ferns combine to lend the area an air of mystery. Local people firmly rooted in their old traditions would never enter this area. They believe Kelimutu to be the home of the deceased. The spirits of both young and old are said to inhabit the green and black lakes, and the sinners are thought to live in the red lake – they come out at dusk or at night time in search of suitable victims.

Today, **ten active volcanoes** dominate the mountaineous central area of Flores. Over thousands of years these volcanoes have shaped the island's romantic and wild-looking landscape. A further volcano worthy of mention, though it is no longer active, is located where Ipo Airport, Ende, now stands. This volcano has a rather startling appearance. It looks something like an elaborate sand-castle, with a regular pattern of grooves (the marks left by erosion).

During the **rainy season,** many areas are cut off, when streets and bridges are quite literally swept away. High seas along the south coast, also make it very difficult for ships carrying provisions to land. This can lead to a fuel shortage, which brings traffic to a standstill in some areas. Travel overland is virtually impossible in some months and people then turn to the more than adequate **air-service.** As a result, flights are often fully booked weeks in advance.

There are good connections by **boat** between the various coastal towns. People planning to travel to Labuhanbaja – a place barely accessible by land – often opt for a boat connection from the port of **Reo** (North-West of Flores). Reo, or the mountain resort of **Ruteng** are chosen by some people as starting points for the journey eastwards to the archipelago of **Solar** and **Alor.** From Ruteng it's possible to fly to Birma, Ende, Bajawa and Maumere.

In **Ruteng** which lies 1,200 m above sea level (3,937'), there is a technical school financed by Mission Airlines. The health problems that have to be dealt with in this part of the island are very much in evidence in Ruteng's small **hospital.** In spite of the difficulties they must contend with, the hospital is run with great enthusiasm.

Moné – is probably the best starting point for a visit to Kelimutu. It lies 52 km/32 miles to the east of Ende on a surfaced section of road leading to Maumere. From Moné, Kelimutu is a mere 12 km/7.5 miles away.

Wolowaru – can be reached by travelling south from Moné. Should you wish to spend several days touring this interesting area, Wolowaru's losmen offers suitable and pleasant accommodation.

Topu – and the other coastal villages of Nggela and Nduria are known for their unusual Ikat motifs. All three villages are surrounded by magnificent volcanic scenery.

Maumere – though it's a small, quiet port, there is a fairly good air-service from here. Merpati Airlines have 5 flights a week to Ujung Pandang from Waitopi Airport, using F 27's. Flights between Kupang on Timor and Maumere (3 per week) are often fully booked.
Some places near Maumere worth visiting:

Pantai Koka – an attractive beach close to the town.

Wuring – a fishing village built on stilts, which extends out into the sea and attracts many visitors. On the beach at Waiara, there are 11 bungalows, making a longer stay here feasible. If you are a good diver, you may feel like hiring diving equipment, to take a look at the marine life.

Lela, Sikka, Nita and Kotung – are all villages where the one-time presence of the Portuguese is still evident today. Another somewhat older remnant of the past is a 2 m/78' long tusk, said to be from some kind of mammoth, that might once have lived on Flores.

Ledalero – an anthropological museum where you can find out more about the culture of Flores.

Compang – a village located 7 km/ about 4¼ miles from Ruteng, and typical for the area, with regard to its layout. The straw-covered roofs which used to reach the ground, are constructed today to finish above the entrance.

Wang Bua – is located 13 km/ – 8 miles away. There is an old cave here, which was once used as a dwelling-place.

The Tanaka Peak – a mountain which is 2,500 m/8,202′ high. There is a fantastic view from here in the early morning.

If you plan to drive **across land** from **Ruteng** to **Ende,** then be prepared for a long journey, or having to turn back because of heavy rain. Should you reach **Bajawa,** which lies halfway between Ruteng and Ende, you can always make for **Padhamateda airstrip** and complete your journey by plane. Despite money being short, every effort is made to keep the road to the airstrip in good repair. The speed-limit for vehicles is between 30 and 50 km/h or 19–31 mph. Some places to visit around Bajawa – not forgetting the old part of Bajawa itself: **Wairana** – a mountain village, in a marvellous location, 25 km/15.2 miles from Bajawa. There are many traditional villages nearby, which are worth a visit.

Bena – is one such typical village. Some of the traditional ceremonies that are performed here go back to megalithic times.

Ende – is the most important town on Flores. There are **2 flights** per day to Kupang from Ida Airport, and there is also a restricted **boat-service** to Waingapu (on Sumba).

Wolotopo – weaving is carried out here and in the surrounding settlements. It was first introduced to Flores by pirates, who came to Flores from New Guinea on their raids. Later weaving also spread to the coast of Irian.

Ikat weaving in Irian still forms part of the bride's dowry today as is also the case in the islands east of Flores. The fabrics are usually over 150 years old, and the traditional patterns are still to be seen today in Wolotopo.

Larantuka – is a beautiful old **port,** located in the far east of the island, 140 km/87 miles east of Maumere. Here, too, the **Portuguese** have left their mark. Their influence can not only be seen in the large number of houses decorated with stucco work, but also in the religious practices that are upheld, such as the processions on Good Friday, and other Catholic religious festivals.

Ships sail from here to the **Solar** and **Alor Archipelago.** The **flights** that use Gewajangtanah airstrip, provide links with towns on **Flores** and **Timor.** Places you should visit in the surrounding area:

Kawalibu, Lewokluok and Lewoloba – villages where traditional ceremonies are still performed, and

Flores – Distances in kilometres.

	LABUAN BAJO	PANTAI PEDE	PUNCAK RANAKA	RUTENG	DANAU RANAMESE	AIMERE	BAJAWA	BENA	BOAWAE	ENDE	DETUSOKO	KELIMUTU	MONI	WOLOWARU	SIKKA	NITA	LEDALERO	MAUMERE	WAIARA	HOKENG	KONGA	LEWOKLUOK	LEWOLOBA	LARANTUKA	WATOWITI
PANTAI PEDE	3																								
PUNCAK RANAKA	120	117																							
RUTENG	137	121	28																						
DANAU RANAMESE	142	139	46	18																					
AIMERE	218	215	122	94	76																				
BAJAWA	257	254	161	138	115	39																			
BENA	282	275	182	154	136	60	21																		
BOAWAE	298	295	202	174	156	80	41	62																	
ENDE	382	379	286	258	240	164	125	146	84																
DETUSOKO	415	412	319	291	273	197	158	179	117	33															
KELIMUTU	448	445	352	324	306	230	191	212	150	66	33														
MONI	434	431	338	310	292	216	177	198	136	52	19	12													
WOLOWARU	447	444	351	323	305	229	190	211	149	65	32	25	13												
SIKKA	531	528	435	407	389	313	274	295	233	149	116	109	97	84											
NITA	519	516	423	395	377	301	262	283	221	137	104	97	85	72	14										
LEDALERO	521	518	425	397	379	303	264	285	223	139	106	99	87	74	16	2									
MAUMERE	530	527	434	498	388	312	222	294	232	148	115	108	96	83	27	11	9								
WAIARA	553	550	457	429	401	325	286	307	245	161	128	121	109	96	38	24	22	13							
HOKENG	562	559	466	438	420	344	315	377	315	231	198	191	179	166	108	94	92	83	70						
KONGA	629	626	533	505	487	411	372	393	331	247	214	207	195	182	122	108	106	97	84	14					
LEWOKLUOK	642	639	546	518	500	424	385	406	344	260	227	220	208	195	137	123	121	109	99	29	15				
LEWOLOBA	660	657	564	536	518	442	403	424	362	278	245	238	226	213	155	141	139	130	117	47	33	18			
LARANTUKA	667	664	571	547	525	449	490	431	369	338	252	245	233	220	162	148	146	127	124	54	40	25	7		
WATOWITI	677	674	581	553	535	459	420	441	379	295	262	255	243	230	172	158	156	147	134	64	50	35	17	10	
WAIKLIBANG	705	702	609	581	563	487	448	469	407	323	290	283	271	258	200	186	184	175	162	92	78	63	45	28	18

where ancestor-worship is practised. **Weaving** is also widespread.

Podor – has a small shell museum, with some very rare exhibits.

Lamalera – is a **whale-hunting** community. Though it is situated on Lembata, it can be reached easily from Larantuka.

Unfortunately, though some might find the traditional methods used very fascinating, these people are killing a marvellous species of animal, which international whale-hunters have already decimated and made an **endangered species.**

Timor

In 1975, the eastern section of the island was granted **independence** by Lisbon, after having been a **Portuguese colony** for centuries. The events that ensued made an island which might otherwise have been described as being "at the back of beyond", into the focus of attention in the field of international politics. Indonesia followed the forming of a new government with interest, but was afraid that the strategic position of the island could be misused and Timor was therefore incorporated into the **State of Indonesia** as the **27th province.** The **conflicts** that erupted between government troops and the supporters of independence (Fretilin) resulted in the death of countless people on both sides.

Today, despite giving the impression of being a peaceful island, the province is still regarded as something of a **powder-keg.** Tourists must have **special permission** to visit the area and permits are not always granted.

The **scenery** and **vegetation** bears little resemblance to that found in the remainder of Indonesia. Though at one time, sandalwood was a major export commodity, the wood can only be exported in small quantities today, due to indiscriminate felling, which has left behind large areas of savannah grassland. This is now used for **cattle-breeding,** which the Dutch first introduced in 1930.

The **western region** is very **mountainous,** and in the extremely dry period from May to September, it turns into a desert-like area, dusty and scorched. Evergreen **rain-forests** are found mainly in the higher areas in the **East.** Visitors would be well advised to come to the island towards the end of the rainy season **(February/March is ideal).** During the rainy season, from November to March, there can be so much rain that it becomes virtually impossible to travel on the island. February/March is, by the way, also the time that the fermented syrup from the Lontar Palm (Borassus flabellifer) is drunk in particularly large quantities.

Most of the **Timorese people** live in the **coastal areas** and work as **fishers** and subsistence **farmers** – i.e. producing only enough for themselves. The island's original inhabitants – the Antonis – are of austronesian-melanesian descent. They are of small build with

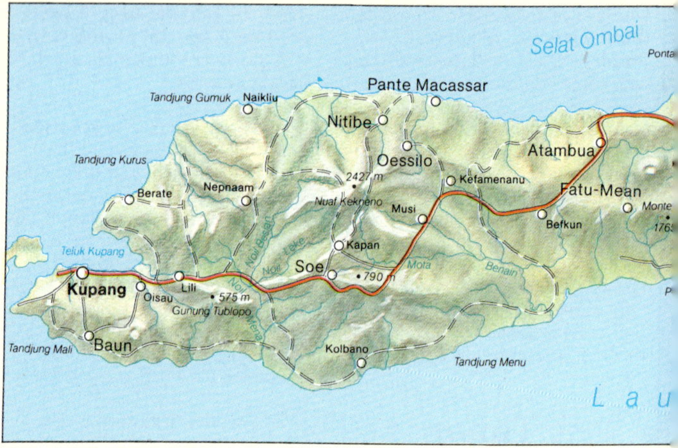

curly hair. The men not only still hunt with bows and arrows, but also use the blow-pipe. And in the South-East of Timor, wooden missiles are used like those employed by the aborigines in Australia.

The island's **roads** are generally in bad condition, and many areas can only be visited on foot. However, where driving is possible, bus services do exist.

Kupang is the largest city in the Nusa Tenggara with a population of about 100,000. It has the virtue of being a **commercial and administrative centre,** with important institutions such as schools and hospitals – features which have proved a great attraction. This accounts for the city's **multi-racial population.** Chinese, Sabunese, Rotinese, Kisarese, Sobrese, Alorese, Adonese, Javanese, Arabs, Eurasians and of course Atari, all live here.

Kupang has a long **history.** In 1791, **William Blight,** the captain of the Bounty landed in Kupang after a journey of 3,500 nautical miles in a small sloop. The mutineers, who had put him out to sea near Tofua, probably never dreamt that he and his followers would reach Kupang (which was even then a **Dutch trading post**). On his return to England, he supervised work on the "Pandora", and once it was seaworthy, put to sea to track down the mutineers. In fact only a few of them were actually captured, and later court-martialled in England.

The sleepy town did not emerge from its century old history until the

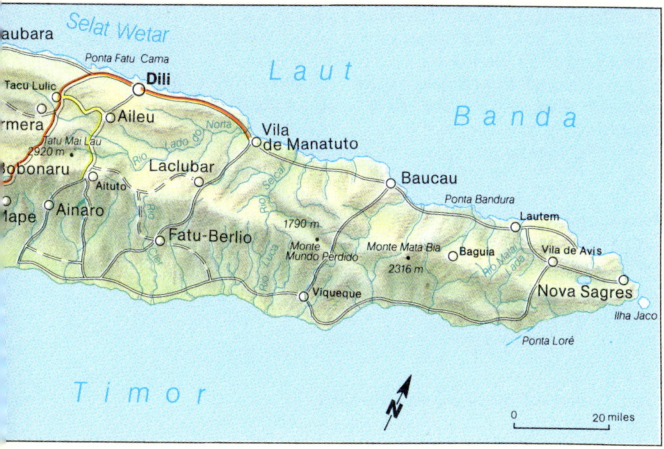

early 70's, when electric street-lighting was installed. Sights you should visit in Kupang include:

The Pantai Laisiana – lies near to Kupang. Ideal for a dip in the sea.

Kelapa Lima – lies on the road to El Tari Airport. Remains of the last war with Japan are to be found here, including a shore-battery.

Mantasi – an old village, where the family grave of the Taebenu, an old Raja-family, is found.

Camplong – is a popular bathing resort, and also an important market town. Australia has given financial backing and sent experts for an agricultural project, designed to improve irrigation, increase crop-yields and stocks of trees, and ensure better water supplies.

Atapupa – lies close to the former border with East Timor. From this large specialized port, shipments of cattle are sent direct to Singapore and Hong Kong. There are also regular connections with Sumbawa, Flores and Bali.

Other places on Timor:

Soe – capital of Central Southern Timor, known for its pleasant climate and high quality fruit.

Niki-Niki – is located nearby, with its old royal graves.

The Isana region – a name which has spread for beyond the shores of Timor, due to the intricate and finely woven cloth produced here.

Atambua – the capital of the Belu region in W. Timor, was once the crossing point on the border with E. Timor. **(Tourists are not, at the moment allowed to travel to Atambua).** In the vicinity of this small, quiet town there are hot mud pools.

Since **Kupang** is the largest port in Nusa Tenggara, there are good connections by **boat** to Surabaja and Jakarta, as well as to Ujung Pandang, Ambon and Sorong.

Flights to Kupang are provided by **Garuda Airlines.** They also have a flight to Denpasar on Bali.
Merpati Airlines provides several services from Kupang – e. g. flights via Maumere to Ujung Pandang, or via Maumere and Waingapu to Denpasar, and the other airports in Nusa Tenggara.

West Timor – Distances in Kilometres.

KUPANG									
10	LASIANA								
54	44	CAMPLONG							
110	100	56	SOE						
139	130	85	29	NIKI-NIKI					
197	189	145	89	60	KEFAMENANU				
217	208	163	107	78	18	OELOLOK			
287	278	233	177	148	88	70	ATAMBUA		
312	303	258	202	173	113	95	25	ATAPUPU	
319	310	265	209	180	120	102	32	7	TELUK GURITA

The Island of Sawu and Roti

Sawu (or Sabu) is a beautiful island. It is not, however, easy to reach, and is probably out of the question for the average holidaymaker, with six weeks to spare. What's more, a fair amount of know how and stamina are needed if you are to avoid making any social blunders in your dealings with a people who have a great respect for tradition. People here are never in much of a hurry. They take their time and they expect visitors to do the same. Popping into a village to take some photos and then leaving again, is therefore looked on as strange.

Sawu has strong ties with Java, going back to the time when Hinduism was the prevalent religion there. Indeed they view themselves as the **children of Java and Hinduism.**

The **Lontar palm** plays an important role in the day to day life of these people. At some times of year, the palm's syrup (thickened by boiling) constitutes their main source of food.

The **clothes** worn by the people of Sawu are made from cloth they have woven themselves, and are not just reserved for special occasions. Charcoal, and plant-sap are used to achieve the traditional colours of dark-blue, beige and rust. Most of the colours are fast, but in the case of Sumba cloth (Ikats) you should always ask.

Seba is the main town on Sawu. There are **boat connections** between Seba and the ports of Waingapu (Sumba) and Kupang (Timor). Only **private accommodation** is available on Sawu.

The island of **Roti** is located near the southern tip of Timor, 100 km/ 62 miles east of Sawu. The **boat** journey from Kupang to Roti takes 3 hours. **Merpati Airlines** also has a regular air service to Roti, using twin otter planes. Today, many Rotinese people live in Kupang.

For those who remain on Roti, however, the **Lontar Palm** is an important feature of their day to day life – just as it is on Sawu. The possibilities of making food and drink from the tree have really been exhausted to the full, and the fermented juice of the palm – (tuak) – flows like wine on Roti.

The Solor and Alor Archipelago

Solor – situated between Flores (to the west), Adonara (to the north) and Lembata (to the east).

The **whale-hunting** community of Lamakera lies on Solor's east coast. During the hunting-season, which runs from May to September, the men only put out to sea in their small open boats when a whale is sighted. After the whale has been slaughtered, it is brought on to land

and processed by the entire village. The catch is then divided up, according to a system of rules laid down by the older members of the community. Whale-meat and blubber are then exchanged for rice and vegetables in towns in the island's interior.

On the north coast of Solar stand the remains of a fortified **Dominican monastery,** Benteng Henrique, built in the mid 16th century. Today, only 35% of the entire monastery still exists.

Adonara – today a centre for pearl fishing, but the island was once known for the constant **feuds** that took place between its various tribes. For years the Dutch tried in vain to resolve the conflict. However, the people responsible for death and actual murder were usually given protection by the other inhabitants and thus evaded capture. Tension still exists today between the mountain dwellers and the tribes that inhabit the coastal regions.

Alor – an island north of Timor, whose main town is **Kalabahi.** Mission Airlines has flights from Kupang (Timor) to Alor, but they are not intended for tourists. There is, however, a **regular boat service** between Kupang and Alor. Alternatively, you can travel from Larantuka (E. Flores) via Balauring (Lembata).

The island has caused linguistic experts many a headache. There are **60 languages** on Alor, many of them Papuan, and some are only spoken by 2 or 3 people. In some areas the economy is still based on barter, for example using Ikat cloth.

An air of mystery still surrounds the large number of bronze kettledrums found on Alor. They originate from North Vietnam's Dongson culture and were once used for ceremonial purposes. Decorated with Hindu motives, these attractive drums are an essential part of the brides dowry, without which the marriage could not take place. Another point – the people very rarely part with these Moko drums no matter how persuasive you are.

Lembata – the second largest island (after Alor) of this small archipelago, east of Flores. The population is mainly made up of **Melanesian** and **Papuan** people, and the landscape is characterized by extensive grassy areas, interrupted by numerous volcano cones. The scenery in the eastern part of the island is particularly beautiful. To visit Lembata you must have **written permission** from the police authorities in Larantuka (E. Flores). Some of the missionaries are willing to offer private **accommodation.**

Sumatra

The name of this island is a modified form of the former Latin designation, suma terra (black earth), which can still be found on old navigational maps. This name referred to the dark, fertile soil whose high crop yield astonished the first Europeans who came here. Later, it was discovered that this earth contained valuable natural resources such as petroleum and lignite, as well as bauxite, tin and other ores. The second-largest Sunda Island measures 470,000 sq. km/181,467 sq. miles – it is 1,770 km/1,100 miles long and 400 km/248 miles at its widest point – and has a population of about 23 million. Travelling to Sumatra from overpopulated Java or Bali, one is struck by the expansive, deserted stretches of land. The island is divided into nine provinces. The largest concentration of population is in North Sumatra, which has 115 people per square kilometre/298 per sq. mile; the lowest is in Riau with 23 people per square kilometre/59 per sq. mile. In spite of the fact that settlers from overpopulated Java are being relocated here within the framework of transmigration programmes, one can travel distances of 50 or 60 kilometres/31–37 miles on this island without seeing a single village.

Along the west coast lies the Bukit Barisan, a mountain range including 50 volcanoes, 20 of which are active. The highest, the Kerinci, has an elevation of 3,805 metres/12,483′. Many rivers spring up from its slopes and flow through the broad plains of eastern Sumatra before reaching the marshy coast where they empty into the sea. Between the mangrove swamps of the east coast and the mountains of the west coast stretch vast rainforests, where there are leopards, tigers, tapirs, rhinoceroses, elephants and orang-utans. In the rivers, an occasional crocodile can still be found. Despite the existence of crocodile farms, the animals are still hunted for their skins, which are made into shoes and handbags in Singapore.

Nice beaches are hard to find on the east coast because of the alluvial rivers that empty into the sea here. The islands that dot the coastline, however, offer lovely beaches covered with fine, white sand of the sort that is otherwise only found on the west coast, where the fury of the sea is checked by coral reefs and island groups.

Because clouds coming in from the ocean are halted by the over 3,000-metre-high/9,842′ peaks of Bukit Barisan, the climate to the west of this range is mostly very rainy and hot. Less than 10 per cent of the entire area of the island has been developed for agricultural use.

Tobacco, tea, coffee, sisal, oil palms and rubber trees are grown here in addition to rice. Cigar smokers will be familiar with Sumatran tobacco, which has always stood for high quality and a "good smoke".

A planned trans-Sumatran highway from Banda Aceh in the north to Teluk Betung in the south is still at the drawing-board stage. Owing to the difficult terrain, only a small portion could be completed so far. During the rainy season, many rivers flood their banks, washing away bridges and road-surfaces. Another problem in mountainous areas are landslides that block the already weakened roads. In the summer, however, you can travel by bus from one end of the island to the other. Allow 12–18 hours for the section of road between Sibolga and Padang, depending on the type of bus. (Roads going straight from A–B are few). For those in a hurry, Sumatra also has a dense network of air traffic routes.

Although its population is composed primarily of Malayans, the island is nevertheless interesting from an ethnological point of view. North Sumatra is the home of the Gayo, the largely Christian Batak, and the Acehnese, who have often struggled for political independence. Near Bukittinggi in West Sumatra live the matriarchal Minangkabau. The southern and eastern parts of the islands are largely inhabited by Malayans, from whose vernacular, Melayu, the Indonesian language is derived. Everywhere on this island, there are groups of people living in seclusion known as the "orang asli". Kubu, Sakai, Bonai, Baruk and Mantang are the names of just a few of these tribes – each has only between 500 and 2,000 members.

The many Sumatran cultures with their mysterious origins and colourful present-day interpretations of traditions make this island of proverbial scenic beauty a travellers' destination of a special kind.

Sumatra – a lot more than "black earth"!

Aceh Province

This is Sumatra's (and Indonesia's) north-westernmost province. Marco Polo landed here on his return voyage from China in 1292, and later brought news back to Europe of this distant land which even then was ruled by a Moslem prince. Aceh has always been a fiercely independent province that has not shied away from warfare to protect its interests. As early as in the 16th century, Aceh was making life difficult for the Portuguese in Malacca and had involved Holland in a colonial war which was to last over 200 years and cost countless lives. In July of 1904, Colonel van Daalen, who was known for his relentlessness, succeeded in pacifying the province – but only superficially. Even after Indonesia had gained independence, Aceh's goal of an autonomous Moslem state remained alive. The separatist spirit which flared up after the Republic's formation had to be quelled by military means. Today, Aceh enjoys special political status, as is shown by the fact that, among other things, **Islamic Law** applies here.

The laws set down in the Koran have fundamental significance for the rigidly Moslem Acehnese: Ramadan, the month of fasting, is strictly observed here and at this time, restaurants remain closed during the day. Despite the fanaticism of the Acehnese, women here enjoy more rights than women in other Islamic countries. As her dowry, a girl receives a house from her parents which then remains in her exclusive possession. If the parents cannot afford it, the young couple takes up temporary residence in the home of the bride's parents until the new house can be built. As a guest in his parents-in-law's house, the young bridegroom usually has very little to say.

As the province of Aceh was for centuries the gateway to the Malay Archipelago for Arab, Persian, Turkish and Indian traders, the influence of these peoples on the commerce and culture of the province and its capital, **Bandah Aceh,** has been quite significant. This city, whose markets were at one time filled with wares from all over the world, also attracted philosophers and scholars, in particular Arabs, some of whom gained a considerable degree of authority and influence. One of them was Habib Abdoerrachman, who was in the service of the sultan of Johore. After arriving in Aceh, he quickly became the teacher and counsellor of the local sultan, and up to the end of 1878, successfully led many battles against the encroaching Dutch. Aceh experienced its political and cultural golden age, though in the 17th century under Sultan Iskander Muda.

Today, Banda Aceh is a neat and peaceful city which rarely sees tourists. It does nevertheless have a number of attractions. At the stadium, there are football and wrestling matches to see. Information about these and other **sporting events**

From left to right: a "parang" – an all-purpose knife; a dagger; three swords. The hilts are made of stag-horn and ivory.

can be obtained at the hotel reception desk or the Governor's Office. The **Aceh Museum** displays everyday articles of the past and present. The **Baturrachman mosque** and the well-kept Dutch cemetary nearby are also worth seeing; as a rule, however, non-believers are barred from entering mosques which are used for worship. Another point of interest is **Gunongan** – this palace with pleasure gardens situated on the banks of a river was built by an Acehnese sultan for his princesses. There are many beautiful beaches in the vicinity of the city whose white sand and clear water quickly help one to forget the hectic life back home.

Lampuk, located only a little over 10 km/6.2 miles from the city, is one of these. In the hinterland, the mountains rise up to elevations of over 3,000 m/9,850 ft. These are the Gayo Highlands, the home of the **Gayo people,** an ehtnic group related to the Batak. Although they were converted to Islam in the 17th century, these people never completely gave up their animist beliefs; instead, they blended Islam with their ancient tribal rituals and formed a syncretic religion. Near Bireuen, the Gayos cultivate tobacco. **Lake Tawar** is located in the midst of the Gayo Highlands. Those who plan to spend some time here will have no trouble finding accommodations as there are three hotels in the lakeside village of Takengon.

A visit to the **Gunung Leuser Nature Reserve** is a definite must for all nature lovers. Although the major part of this reserve lies in Aceh Province, it is best reached from Medan in the province of North Sumatra. From Medan, the road leads past Brastagi to Kotacane in the Alas Valley. The PPA office responsible for park administration is located near Tanah Merah, 2 km/1.24 miles north of Kotacane. In order to visit this and all of Indonesia's nature reserves, one must obtain written permission from the PPA head office in Bogor, West Java (the address is Jl. Juanda 9). The Gunung Leuser Reserve contains 176 species of mammals, 520 species of birds, 194 species of reptiles and 62 species of amphibians. Indigenous animals such as the elephant, the rhinoceros, the tiger, the leopard, the tapir, the gibbon and the orang-utan make this area a treasure trove of Sumatran wildlife. The plant life in this reserve has hardly been studied. As is the case with many of Indonesia's wildlife parks, Gunung Leuser is threatened by road construction, illegal settlements and slashing and burning. Due to the lack of surveillance personnel, the felling of trees on the outskirts of the parks can barely be kept under control.

A minimum of ten days ought to be set aside for a visit to this park; those who do not have this much time should at least visit the **Bohorok Orang-utan Rehabilitation Centre** on the eastern edge of the reserve. It takes about 2½–3 hours to get to the centre from Medan. Orang-utans, recaptured from smugglers or confiscated from "private zoos", are prepared here for a life in the wild. Bohorok is not a tourist attraction, but rather a place where painstaking efforts are being made to assure the survival of these magnificent apes. Often, the valuable work is hindered by masses of tourists. The responsible nature lover should act in a way that will not disturb the animals and should stay no longer than one hour (there are many other more suitable places for picnicking). Although this project is supported by the World Wildlife Fund and the Frankfurt Zoological Society, the centre barely has enough money to cover its costs. A contribution as your "souvenir" of the place would be a good idea!

Banda Aceh's **Blan Bintang Airport,** located 15 km/9.3 miles from the ctiy, offers connections to Jakarta, Medan and the island of Sabang; the latter can also be reached by **ship** from Banda Aceh. Sometimes there are ship connections to Pulau Simeulus off Sumatra's western coast as well; from there, boats sail every now and then for Nias and Sibolga.

North Sumatra – Sumatra utara

North Sumatra is home to high mountains and volcanoes, to a spectacular crater lake, an abundance of waterfalls, vast palm oil, rubber, coffee and tobacco plantations and the many fascinating tribes of **Batak** people. The territory of the Batak people extends around Lake Toba – covering 1,700 sq. km/656 sq. miles, the largest lake in South-East Asia. The area has been extensively developed for tourism – and because of its many facilities for sport and relaxation, it has already become a popular destination for weekend excursionists from Malaysia and Singapore.

Another of the many reasons for the lake's great popularity is, however, that it is the home of the spirited and lively Batak people. Their villages are hidden away among the alpine vegetation that surrounds this lake, whose beautiful location makes it one of Indonesia's most magnificent attractions. Two thirds of the approximately 1.5 million Batak are Christians and have their own church. Despite the influence of Christianity, however, they have still kept alive many elements of their animist past, evident e.g. in their funeral rites and other solemn observances. The Moslem Bataks, who belong to the Mandailing group, are concentrated around Tapanuli. The Batak are divided into further groups, all living isolated from one another in terms of dialect, customs and architecture. The traditional houses of the Karo and the Toba Batak are especially interesting. They are built without nails and provide a pleasant indoor climate even during the hot midday hours. Karo dwellings have square foundations and can house up to 100 people. Besides the Karo, who live around Brastagi, and the Toba, who live in the vicinity of the lake and on the island of Samosir, other well-known Batak tribes include the Simalungun of Pamatang Siantar and

the Pak Pak of Sidikalang. Their villages are inhabited by numerous extended families which together form a so-called huta. Several hutas unite to form a marga, whose members can trace their lineages back to a common ancestor. Earlier, Batak society was split into three classes: nobility, peasants and slaves. Their ancient faith taught them that harmony was the highest goal. It was for this reason that thieves, murderers, adulterers and other lawbreakers who attempted to upset this harmony were condemned to the worst fate imaginable. To be eaten by one's fellow villagers was considered the ultimate form of degradation and a just punishment for the perpetrators of such calamitous offences.

In order to guard their society from outside interference, the Bataks closed themselves off from the world around them and managed to maintain their isolation until the beginning of this century. Today, they form the largest Christian community in Indonesia.

According to government statistics, almost one third of Indonesia's total revenue comes from North Sumatra. **Plantations,** most of which are government-owned, account for the bulk of the province's income. Multinational concerns such as Uniroyal and Goodyear own rubber plantations here as well. As a result of the drop in rubber prices on the world market (a trend which continued until a few years ago), many rubber tree forests were cleared and oil palms planted in their place.

Tobacco was first planted here in the middle of the last century, at which time it quickly won worldwide fame under the name "Deli Tobacco". With the introduction of this cash crop, the local people's rights to the land, which they worked by a system of crop rotation, were lost along the wayside. The **colonial government** summarily confiscated all unused land – this included all fallow land too. In this way, the colonialists, who were smart enough to include the Sultan of Deli in their underhand dealings, took possession of arable land which was already cleared and ready to be leased to private businessmen and plantation companies. The local population, which lived only by subsistence farming, found itself in great difficulties. As the labour force soon proved to be too small for the high-profit plantations, Chinese labourers were brought into North Sumatra to work in atrocious conditions. As most of these plantation coolies were kept like slaves, large-scale escape attempts often occurred. In order to put a halt to this, the government in Batavia allowed the plantation owners to take drastic measures – these ranged from imprisonment and floggings to the execution of fugitive coolies. Because social tensions on the plantation often had a negative effect on profits, fundamental improvements were finally initiated at the beginning of the 20th century. At the close of the year 1918, plantation workers were each contributing an average of 11.64 Dutch guilders annually toward their medical care. The money was used to cover the cost of maintaining and running the infirmaries, to pay the salaries of the doctors and nurses and to cover administrative expenses.

The capital of the province of North Sumatra is the cosmopolitan city of **Medan,** the population of which includes Arabs, Indians, Malayans and Chinese who have come to seek their fortune in this prosperous region which is, among other things, the world's second-largest producer of natural **rubber.** From the port of Belawan, located 26 km/ 16 miles from the city, plantation products are exported to every corner of the globe. In the near future, Medan's **Polonia Airport,** located close to the city's centre, is to be expanded to handle long-distance flights from Europe. As well as con-

nections to Gunung Sitoli (Nias), Banda Aceh, Pakanbaru, Padang, Palembang and Jakarta, the airport already offers international flights to Singapore, Penang and Kuala Lumpur. The addresses of the airline offices in Medan are:
Garuda, Jl. Jend. Suprarto 2
Merpati, Jl. Katamsu 37
MAS, Jl. Imam Bonjol 17
SIA, Jl. Imam Bonjol 16
For information on boat connections apply to the Pelni office on Jl. Palang merah in Belawan.

Although Medan hardly makes a good impression on most tourists, it does eventually reveal its positive sides to those who stay here long enough. It is good to know that the city houses 15 **foreign consulates.** Among others:
Great Britain, Jl. Imam Bonjol 18, Tel. 32 29 45,
United States, Jl. Imam Bonjol 13, Tel. 32 22 00.
Tourist information can be obtained at the tourist office on Jl. Palang merah 66. For questions concerning **visas** apply to the Kantor Imigrasi on Jl. Jend. A. Yani 74.

But Medan offers a great deal more than just administrative offices. For those who enjoy good food, for example, there are Indian, Indonesian, Chinese and Padang **restaurants.** Local delicacies can also be savoured at one of the many food stands which open up along Jl. Selat Panjang and the Taman Ria Park after 6 pm. Those who like to dine in the atmosphere of the "good old days" should go to the Tip Top Restaurant on Jl. Jend. A. Yani 92. In addition to delicious meals, tasty baked goods are also available here. Although the air-conditioning in the Hoover Mandarin Restaurant on Jl. Mangkubumi 18 is so effective that a sweater must be worn, the quality of the food will more than make up for the chill. The Micado on Jl. Prof. Yamin 236H also offers excellent Chinese-Indonesian food.

Colonial architecture still defines the character of many parts of Medan today. One of the city's most imposing structures is the **palace of the Sultan of Deli**, also known as Maimoon Palace, built in 1888. The sultan, who, as we know, was on good terms with the Dutch colonial government, built this stately residence with their financial support. In a small building set apart from the palace, a holy canon can be seen, a model of which is on exhibit in Jakarta's National Museum. This canon (called Si Jagur) is said to bestow fertility upon any woman who touches it.

The great **Mesjid Raya Mosque** lies within sight of the Deli Palace. Medan's oldest mosque, the **Gang Bengkok,** was partly built with stones taken from old Hindu and Buddhist temples. Medan's oldest **Chinese shrine** (built in 1870) can be found on Jl. Pandu. There are also **Hindu and Sikh temples** in Medan. The Medan **Garnizoen** dates from 1873. A former Dutch fort, it is now occupied by a military garrison. This unimposing building which is terribly in need of repair is located on Jl. Kapt. Maulana Lubis. Near Deli Tua on the outskirts of town, there are remains of a **16th century fort** which was once destroyed by the Acehnese.

Many striking buildings dating from colonial times are located on **Lapangan Merdeka** (Freedom Square) which was at one time the place to see and be seen. Today, it appears a bit untidy. In 1874, the **Witte Societeit** (White Society Club) opened its doors here. As its name suggests, its main purpose was to uphold the principles of segregation. Now a bank occupies the building which once housed this club. The **Grand Hotel Medan,** formerly called the Hotel Granada Medan, was once the best address on the square. The first building constructed by the Europeans was completed in 1869 for the **Dutch** tobacco magnate, Nienhuys. This building now houses the P. N. P. Tobacco Co. A fountain now stands in Nienhuys's honour in front of the post office. The **British** also contributed to Medan's architectural profile: the Harrison & Crossfield Building, the seat of the British rubber company, was, up until a few years ago, the tallest building in Medan.

Medan's environs offer a number of interesting sights as well. At **Kota Cina,** 7 km/4.3 miles outside the city on the road to Belawan, there are ruins from **Hindu-Buddhist** days. The foundations of an ancient temple as well as 9th-century stonemasonry were discovered here in 1971. Those who enjoy visiting zoos will find one 4 km/2.5 miles from the centre of the city. Animals from many parts of the Republic can be viewed in the rather antiquated enclosures of the Mangasatwa Zoo. Information about the **crocodile farm** located 6 km/3.7 miles from the city can be obtained at Jl. Palang Merah 112 in Medan. Those who consider, though, that these reptiles (which are all too frequently kept in cramped enclosures) are the victims of a (dated) fashion trend, will find little pleasure in such a visit. More worthwhile, on the other hand, is a visit to the **botanical gardens** in Sibolangit, 43 km/27 miles south of Medan on the road to Brastagi.

Hornbill – mainly found on Sumatra.

On the way, you'll pass the village of **Binjei** (22 km/13.6 miles from Medan), known for its aromatic rambutans which are sold from countless fruit stands set up along the road in the months of July and August.

From Medan, there are two ways of reaching **Lake Toba:** either by the road to Brastagi which passes through beautiful countryside, or by the road that leads to Pematang Siantar and continues on to Prapat – here you'll see endless rows of rubber trees and palms.

Going from Medan to Lake Toba by way of **Brastagi** (or Berastagi) – takes us through the territory of the **Karo Batak.** The Karos differ from the other Batak tribes in a number of ways: they speak a different dialect, they build their houses in a different way – even the people's natures are different – but they are friendly in any case. Brastagi is a good starting-point for excursions in this region: it has a more scenic location and offers a better choice of accommodation than the district's administrative centre, Kabanjahe. Owing to its elevation (1,300 m/ 4,268 ft), Brastagi can get quite cold at night. **Mt. Sibayak,** a volcano which is cracked open on one side, can be climbed in about four hours from the nearby village of **Semangat Gunung.** Sturdy footwear and an early start are very important. One of the typical Karo Batak villages is **Lingga,** which can be reached by "oplet" from Kabanjahe. Earlier, up to 100 people lived in the square-shaped Karo dwellings, now, the search for employment has separated many families. A beautiful road leads from Kabanjahe to the Karo village of **Barusjahe,** 15 km/ 9.3 miles away. Not a single nail was used in the construction of this over 250-year-old village. In the shelter of the steep, protruding roofs of the adat houses, women still crush rice as they did in the olden days.

A number of interesting excursions can be made into the countryside surrounding Brastagi. **Lake Kawar,** situated at the foot of Mt. Sinabung, can be reached by bus; arrangements for overnight stays can be made with the people who live there.

The other route to Lake Toba from Medan is on the road to Prapat via Pematang Siantar. A visit to **Pematang Siantar,** approximately 130 km/80 miles south-east of Medan, is to be recommended since the largest community of the **Simalungun Batak** is found here. Though the town's museum concentrates on Simalungun culture, the collections on display give the visitor a good, general impression of other Batak cultures as well. It is open daily except Sunday from 8 am–12 noon and from 2 pm–5 pm. And in order to see examples of Simalungun culture, a visit to the **palace of the Rajah of Simalungun** in Pematang Purba is, in fact, more rewarding. Of all the Batak tribes, the Simalungun have distanced themselves the most from their original way of life – it is hard to imagine that, only 35 years ago, this palace was a centre of courtly life. Thirteen pairs of buffalo horns remain here in memory of the thirteen generations of Simalungun kings, the last of whom died in 1945. Each of the thirteen kings resided here with twelve wives, who all had their own cooking area. The palace complex consists of a guesthouse, a throne room, a courtroom (with an ancient Batak calendar) and the living quarters. These buildings, which were restored in 1945 and are still guarded by their original stone house gods, convey a rather sterile image of this once-flourishing proto-Malayan culture.

In the vicinity of Siantar, there are a number of **transmigrasi** villages which date from the earliest days of this national resettlement project. People from rural Java have been living for many years now in villages with names like Kampung Java.

Prapat is the centre of tourism on **Lake Toba** (which lies at 800 m/ 2,625 ft above sea level). This clean little town on an inlet on the lake's east bank offers a wide selection of accommodation – but those looking for a place to stay should also consider the hotels in **Tuk Tuk** and the losmens in **Ambarita** and **Tomok** – all on Samosir Island in the middle of the lake. Each of these villages is linked with Prapat by ferry, but services are not regular. On market days (usually Saturdays), half-fare is charged.

Lake Toba owes its appeal not only to its beautiful surroundings and the Batak culture present there, but also to the 400 sq. km/154 sq. mile island of **Samosir** in its centre. It is here, where the magnificent landscape and the fascinating local culture blend perfectly, that the heart of Toba-Batak country is to be found. Sadly, most package tourists spend only a few hours here because of busy schedules. The crystal-clear water of the lake reflecting the green of the pine trees along its deserted shores makes a stay here a pleasant and relaxing experience. However, since it is really worth the effort of getting to know the culture and way of life of the Batak tribes, a visit to Lake Toba purely for the purpose of recreation would be a pity. It goes without saying, however, that the island will not reveal all its secrets to the visitor in the space of a three or four-week holiday.

European explorers first set foot on Samosir Island towards the end of the 19th century. Travel reports of the time do not leave any doubt in the reader's mind that the Batak were determined to ward off all influence from outside. Even colonial police forces had trouble establishing themselves in the district around Lake Toba. Samosir Island remained the last bastion of the Toba Batak, but this too was eventually taken. (Missionaries were influential in this.)

Today, there are no traces of xenophobia left among these people, who once were forced into the island's interior by peoples who migrated after them. (That the tourist industry has re-animated much of the traditional ill-will towards foreigners in South-East Asia is a fact that cannot be denied, however.) Today, the traveller here is still often met with a friendly "Horas!" which is Batak for "Welcome!" or "How are you?". Only in places like Tomok, Tuk Tuk and Ambarita, where tourists usually arrive in droves, is this greeting dying out – a greeting, by the way, which should not only be answered, but may even be called out first.

The following villages on Samosir deserve special mention:

Tomok is one of the two most frequented villages on the island. The stone **sarcophagus of King Sidabutar,** the last pre-Christian Batak ruler, can be reached by following the road which leads from the lake and runs past the souvenir stands. The stone coffins of a son and a grandson of this legendary king also lie here under the hanging branches of a majestic hariara tree. The few animistic Batak remaining, believe that the king is still among them, ready to help whenever needed. Obviously, however, he has not been able to protect their culture from decline. Corrugated sheet metal now in use and marring the beauty of their traditional dwellings testifies to this decline. But then, what is the use of a beautiful (if dilapidated) house built of natural materials if it cannot keep out the rain? The horrors of modern civilization have already made themselves quite apparent in many a Batak village: the heads of the "ulus" which once decorated the gable of every house and protected it from theft, fire and other calamities are often sold to tourists as souvenirs nowadays, and the black, red and white ornamentation on the façades of the houses are now seldom renewed.

There is a "pasangrahan" or government lodge and meeting hall 16 km/10 miles from Tomok which, when not in use, will put up tourists; otherwise, there are "losmens" in Tomok.

Those who cannot or will not do without motorized transport can rent a motorcycle – the odds on the completion of a circuit around the island are unfavourable, however, due to poor road conditions, particularly in the southern part of the island. Some have supposedly made it, but certainly at the expense of peace and tranquility. From Tomok, it takes 1–2 days to walk to Pangururan on the western side of the island.

Tuk Tuk, the other popular tourist resort here, owes much of its attraction to the Tuk Tuk Hotel. For the traveller on a lower budget, there are many "losmens" here as well. Small, low-priced restaurants and "warungs" continually take pains to satisfy their mostly western clientele by offering everything from spaghetti bolognese to smörgasbords! Tuk Tuk's position on a peninsula makes it an excellent vantage point from which to enjoy a fantastic view over large areas of Lake Toba.

Ambarita is less touristy and it is thus more peaceful than the other two villages. Just next to the landing pier, there are two Batak houses which can be leased by tourists.

The walled-in courtyard of the local **royal residence** also served as a court of justice until the beginning of this century: the judges who pronounced sentence from the moss-covered stone table here were not afraid of meting out the death penalty in certain cases. (The people of Ambarita have an amazingly candid attitude toward their village's past.)

A beautiful waterfall can be reached in a 1½-hour-walk from Ambarita. To the left of the falls, a steep trail leads up to the top and continues into the island's interior. Monday is market-day in the north-shore village of Haranggaol, and the village is accessible by ferry from Ambarita on that day only.

Simanindo possesses one of the most beautiful king's houses in the entire Batak region. Cultural events such as performances of the **tor-tor dance** often take place here. The entire village, including the adat house which contains a small museum, has been carefully restored. Another specialty of Batak culture, the **sigalegale dance,** can sometimes be seen here. A life-sized wooden puppet attached to a box is brought to life using the strings attached to it. Normally, this puppet is only made to dance in the event of the death of a sole male heir (i. e. the mediator between the living and the dead members of the family).

Tao, the island of flowers, lies not far from Simanindo off the northern coast of the over 50 km/31 mile-long island of Samosir. The clean inn here makes for a pleasant stay.

Pangururan, on the island's western coast and connected to the mainland by a bridge, can be reached from Simanindo by bus – as the road is very poor, however, it is better to take the boat. On the mainland, 5 km/3 miles from here, there are hot springs.

One of North Sumatra's greatest scenic splendours can be found near **Tongging** on the northern end of Lake Toba: the **Sipiso-Piso Waterfall** cascades down a precipice behind the village. From a look-out point which can be reached on foot from Tongging in one hour, there's an unforgettable view of the falls and the lake. Tongging should be approached by way of Kabanjahe and Seribudolok.

Along the road from Prapat to Balige and on to Sibolga, the observant traveller will be rewarded with many interesting sights. The road to Balige is flanked on both sides by traditional Batak villages nestling in the shelter of dense bamboo groves. **Lumban Garaga,** idyllically situated amidst ricefields just over a mile from the road to the right, is sometimes visited by tour groups; **Lumban Binaga,** further up the road to Balige and to the left, is, on the other hand, known to only a few. Traditional woven fabrics are still produced by the old women of this village.

Those who wish to visit the 200 m/656 ft **Sigura Gura Waterfalls,** the largest in South-East Asia, will need a special permit: there are plans to use the falls as part of a hydro-electric plant which is to provide power for a bauxite foundry.

Sibolga, on Sumatra's western coast, is the port of embarkation for **boats to Nias,** but apart from an old mosque and spectacular sunsets, the town has nothing of special interest to the tourist. An **airline service** to Nias was initiated in 1977, but because Nias's airport (near Gunungsitoli) is quite far from the touristically interesting southern part of the island (which can only be reached by boat from Gunungsitoli anyway) many people still prefer to take the boat direct to Teluk Dalam in South Nias. As the boats used for this 18–22 hour long crossing are not always suitable for ocean travel, tourists must obtain a **permit** from the harbourmaster (syahbandar) before embarking – his office is in the "pelabuhan besar" (the big port) from where ships leave for Gunungsitoli. Up until 1976, this formality was not necessary, but accidents involving smaller vessels without a radio on board led to the introduction of this regulation. The decision of the harbourmaster depends on the capacity of the boat in question as well as the amount of technical equipment it has on board. The small vessels which sail from Padang to the Mentawai Islands generally will not carry tourists.

Nias

The island is located south-west of Central Sumatra and measures 130 km/81 miles by 50 km/31 miles. Though the megalithic structures found on Sumba, Flores and Sulawesi are still an important feature of people's lives there, Nias is regarded as the most significant **megalithic culture** of them all. In South Nias, the people go about their daily lives, surrounded by these imposing stones from an ancient culture.

Today, experts are able to say with certainty that the Nias's culture originally developed thousands of miles away in the **Assam region of North East India.** Even today, the inhabitants of this area, the **Naga,** have stronger cultural links with the Niah than any other people do. The Naga, a race of small people, migrated to the above areas from South China in about 2000 B.C. This accounts for the language on Nias differing so much from that spoken on Sumatra.

On Nias itself the customs vary greatly from village to village. This is not so much due to the geography of the island, as to its early history. In the **North of Nias,** which is thinly populated, and has large areas of flat **swampland,** you will only find **single round houses** on stilts. In the **South,** however, the **villages** are spread out, and have wide roads, with a surface covering of large stones. Most of the villages are located on mountain tops and can only be reached via huge flights of stone steps. To reach **Bawamataluo** for example, which is one of the largest and best known villages, you have to climb more than 700 steps.

At the centre of each village square, a haphazard arrangement of **obelisks, stone seats** (some of which are decorated) and **dolmen** (megalithic graves) dominate the scene. It must be said, however, that less reverence is shown towards these stone monuments today. Indeed most of the villages are now **Christian.** At one time, however, the stones were the means of increasing a **person's rank.** It was customary for the man having a stone erected to bring several pigs to be sacrified. In earlier times the sacrifice was human. The stone graves, built in phallus form, were supposed to ensure lasting fertility. For others, though, they were the permanent reminders of powerful former ancestors, or could provide physical and mental strength for battle.

The Niah men, who are **polygamous,** had a stone grave erected for each new wife. (These graves were decorated with symbols of female sexuality.)

To attain the highest rank of all, it was necessary to have a great deal of power and many possessions. Large numbers of pigs were required for slaughter, and there was the additional expense of the obligatory celebrations.

The villages in Southern Nias were based on a **hierarchical system.** The head of this hierarchy could only be someone whose mother also came from a family of chieftans. It was also possible for the **chieftan** to hand this position on to his children. This also applies, by the way, in the case of **priests.** Both chieftan and priest belonged to the highest group of society – known as **si ulu. Si ila** was the name given to the normal citizens. The third group, referred to as **sato,** were treated as slaves and led fairly restricted lives. A member of "si ila" unfortunate enough to owe money to someone from the "si ulu" often slipped down to the "sato" class. The "sato" were also the people who might be sacrificed, when a house was being built, though this fate was generally reserved for enemies taken prisoner during a military expedition.

Statues of ancestors

The Niah, known for their **courage** in battle, hit upon the idea of building columns (over 2 metres (6½ ft high) to "simulate" the walls and palisades which generally surrounded enemy villages – and practised jumping over them! Some of the men may be willing to demonstrate this athletic feat, for those who are interested, providing it's not raining and the stones aren't wet.

The first attempt of the **Dutch** to subjugate the Niah ended in them being driven from the island, and it took a great deal of effort on their part to break the resistance of this diminutive race of warriors.

War dances, which are still performed in some villages on special occasions, and in full battle dress, clearly show that the Niah have retained their warrior temperaments. Two items of battle-dress worn are the "Kalabubu" – a neck ring, which is the sign of a successful hunter – and a metal or leather "armour" jacket.

The adornments worn in battle, which used to be made of brass and small pieces of coconut shell (burnt to harden them), have sadly lost their original significance. Now, once treasured family heirlooms are sold to tourists. Ornaments made of gold are seen rarely, nowadays. Tin painted yellow, has taken its place.

The **women** on Nias are highly-respected. However, strict regulations are in force with regard to relations between men and women before marriage. These are designed to prevent immoral sexual behaviour. At one time, girls had to sleep under the watchful eyes of older women.

Today, many outside influences have found their way to the island, which covers 4,800 sq. km/1,853 sq. miles. Many old traditions have had to give way to jeans, portable radios and James Bond films.

In South Nias, people were only allowed to walk parallel or at right angles to the fronts of the houses. Running was not allowed, even if it rained, though exceptions were made in the case of war or fire. People who failed to comply with this were beaten. Today, people are (fortunately) never in such a hurry that they have to run.

The rites and ceremonies surrounding births and deaths conform to the **Christian** norm, yet in 1935 the Niah were reported as still practising head-hunting.

When, in **April 1973,** Nias was officially opened to the **tourist trade,** the people had great expectations of the development that was planned. So far, their expectations have not been fulfilled. Since the luxury liner, MS Prinsendam went up in flames off the West Coast of America, tourist trade has quietened very much. (The Prinsendam had been making regular runs since 1974). The majority of people who now come here, travel alone and are not deterred by the rather complicated journey. Nias's **poor communications network** is often (rightly) given the blame for the drop in tourist figures. On the other hand, this lack of development has meant that large areas of the island remain **unspoilt by tourism.**

The extensive **road network** which had been built in colonial times was swallowed up by forests in the years following independence. A section in the south, which was cleared and repaired in 1976, had, by 1979 become a mass of pot-holes due to heavy tropical downpours. A further problem, which is the result of poor supervision, is that tar destined for the road-building scheme tends to become side-tracked for other projects. The poor stretch of road in the South merges with primeval forest close to Hilisimaetano.

There is a further **system of roads** in the area around **Gunungsitoli,** and, though it is not yet completed either, it is in better condition. Gunungsitoli's nearest airport is 30 km/19 miles away. **Binaka Airport** is small, however, and at present only Islanders (seating 7 passengers) fly there – from Medan and Siboliga (North and West Sumatra). As there is no through road from here to the south of the island, journeys southwards must be made by **boat.** However, the attractive and varied coastline does in part compensate for the length of the journey (8 hours).

Once you arrive in Teluk Dalam, you are faced with the problem of finding **accommodation.** If you are lucky enough to acquire one of the few losmen beds, don't expect anything too comfortable. Accommodation is easier to find in Gunungsitoli. There, hotels and losmens come closer to the standard of hygiene we expect.

Whilst you are waiting for a boat connection to the South, why not take advantage of this opportunity and look at houses in the area, which are typical of the **oval shaped adat houses** found in North Nias.

Little now remains of this culture, but several of these amazing constructions are still to be seen on a hill near Hilibawedesolo – 13 km/ 8 mi. away from Gunungsitoli. German Missionaries who first came here, over 80 years ago, dismantled many of the houses, and took their "souvenirs" home when they left.

The most important and interesting places on Nias are:

Teluk Dalam – is located in the far south of the island. Ships wishing to drop anchor here can experience great difficulties at certain times of day due to large waves – shipping is, without exaggeration, at the mercy of the Indian Ocean.

The small port of Teluk Dalam, which extends back to the surrounding hills, is dominated by the church (a red building). There is nothing here to remind one of the megalithic culture.

If the boat you're travelling on is full, then it is advisable to hurry along to the "Cusit" at the east end of the main street. This **losmen** may be simple and not particularly clean, but it does have the greatest number of tourist beds. If they had more money at their disposal, the inhabitants of Teluk Dalam would be more than willing to have further hotels and restaurants built. The **roads** around the town, which are in a very bad condition are used by lorries and bemos.

Hilismaetano – lies some 16 km/ 10 miles inland and can be reached along a fairly well surfaced road. In the daytime, the village with its 140 "Adat" houses is like a ghost-town. The chair at the southern end of the village, which is made of stone, was once used to carry the chieftan. The last chieftan of the ruling tribe was somewhat of a revolutionary, who introduced many new ideas and also refused to build his house in the accepted style.

Bawamatalua – translated into English, this means something like "hill of sunshine", and it is one of the **largest and most important villages.** Bawamatalua, which is laid out in the form of a "t", can be reached by **bus from Orahili,** and then on foot – there are **480 steps** to climb before you reach the village entrance.

The **chieftan's home** "Omo Namada Laowa" is the largest of its kind on Nias. You must, of course, ask for permission if you want to visit it. Inside the house there is a series of **platforms** of different heights for the chieftan's people. Each person is designated a platform in accordance with his rank. The top platform is reserved for the chieftan and his wife.

This house with its 16 m/52 ft high walls, which is built on wooden pillars 1 metre in diameter has a roof made of sheet metal. If the government provided the necessary cash, the village chief would immediately replace this with the traditional one of palm-fibre. Money is also badly needed to restore the **unique carvings** inside the houses. It is to be hoped that the government will not neglect these marvellous examples of **Niah culture** for much longer. Otherwise it might be too late. Bawamatalua is also known for its **folklore** eg. the Faluaya and Tulo Tulo dances.

Hilisitare – can be reached on foot in 4–6 hours. The village is steeped in **folklore,** and dances etc. are usually performed on request, with great care being taken to keep to the original costumes. For this reason, the dancers don't wear garments of man-made fabrics. The people are very lively and remain true to the old spirit of Nias.

Gomo – is regarded as the place where the "orang niah" originated. According to the legend of their ancestors, they are said to have come down from heaven.

Gomo lies approximately halfway between Gunungsitoli and Teluk Dalam. It can only be reached on foot across **difficult terrain,** and you must be prepared for a journey of 2 days at least. The outstanding feature of this village is the artistic and very impressive masonry which has since become very rare.

Lagundri – is located in the far South-West of Nias, and has often been called a **surfer's paradise.** It was first "discovered" by Australians and Americans, who described it as having perfect conditions for surfing. Now the former fishing village has grown into a small tourist resort with several losmens and snack-bars. The **traditional villages** of Botahili and Milimaeta lie close to Lagundri's sandy, palm-lined beaches. Lagundri could only ever be reached on foot, but now the government has made **plans for a street and hotels** to be built.

Sadly, people are likely to recognize too late that the growth of a tourist culture will inevitably mean that the culture of the ancestors is forgotten.

West Sumatra – Sumatra barat

Padang is the capital and major port of the western province of Sumatra and in bygone days was the main town in the land occupied by the **Minangkabau** – a tribe noted for its matriarchial society. Even today, although the region is for the most part Moslem, the role of the male is not, as is usual for this faith, predominant. In contrast to the usual position of the mother in Indonesian homes, in Minangkabau households, she is the controlling and guiding force. The most important male figure for the children is not the father, but rather the mother's oldest brother. Decisions concerning marriage and inheritance are also made by the women, and when a man marries, he becomes part of his wife's household. While not feeling oppressed in this matriarchal society, many Minangkabau men try to marry women from other ethnic groups. The determining factor here is probably the lack of power in making decisions and the lack of material possessions.

The richly-decorated Minangkabau family houses are characterized by curved roofs thatched with palm. These roofs resemble the horns of a water-buffalo. The symbol, and the name, Minangkabau, which means "victorious bull", is commemorative of a legendary siege by alien troops in which a fight between two buffaloes eventually brought victory to the Minangkabau people. Their homeland lies in one of the most beautiful and fascinating regions of the country, which is, as a result, one of the most visited areas of Sumatra. Here, there is an ever-changing panorama of virgin rainforests, fertile valleys, immense volcanoes, deep gorges, blue lakes and sandy beaches: a haven for nature lovers who do not mind travelling long distances on foot and can do without first-class hotels.

Major exports from West Sumatra are timber, rotan and damar resins and, in contrast to other Sumatran provinces, it is completely independent of rice imports; quite the opposite, in fact – West Sumatra exports excess produce to other parts of the land. In spite of the fact that agriculture here has been self-supporting for years, enormous sums have been granted in development aid to support a project that introduced not only potatoes but also insecticides and artificial fertilizers.

Padang can be reached by land, sea or air, and from **Tabing Airport,** 10 km/6.2 miles away, there are direct flights to Medan (N. Sumatra), Pekanbaru (E. Sumatra), Palembang (S. Sumatra) and Jakarta; there are also Garuda flights to Singapore and Kuala Lumpur on a weekly basis. Ships of the Pelni and Arafat Lines maintain more or less regular services to Jakarta from **Teluk Bayur port** in the south of Padang, and the same trip can be done by bus, although then it takes three days and three nights. Other **overland connections** serve Bengkulu, Pekanbaru, Tanjungkarang, Palembang, Sungaipenuh, Padangpanjang, Prapat and Medan. Instead of taking the bus to **Bukittinggi,** only 80 km/50 miles away, why not go by train? Pulled by an old steam engine, it's a journey that proves to be an experience in every sense of the word: in something like 5 hours you'll travel past gulches and through tropical rain forests and finally reach the town that lies some 900 m/2,953 ft above sea level, heart of Minangkabau country. There is only one big but: the train doesn't always take the same route, and occasionally Kayutaman is the end of the line!

Still, before taking off to explore the back contry you really should take some time to discover the delights of Padang's surroundings.

The fabulous palm fringed coastline south of Padang has names like **Air Manis** (3 km/1.86 miles away), **Pantai Nirvana** (8 km/5 miles) and **Pasir Putih** on Bungus Bay (24 km/15 miles from the city). The only accommodation available is private. Anyone looking for that Robinson Crusoe feeling just once, or once more, should avoid **Pulau Pisang** (Banana Island) on Sundays, when it seems as if all Padang is taking part in some kind of mass picnic! The small islands south of Padang, reached by hired boat from Muara, offer a better chance of solitude.

Another worthwhile visit is to the ancient port of **Pariaman** where the Tabut Festival takes place once a year in memory of Mohammed's grandsons.

To enjoy the rich scenic beauty of West Sumatra you simply have to include a trip to the highlands in your itinerary. The pearls of the high country are **Danau Singarak** and **Danau Maninjau,** lakes where losmens and hotels tempt you to linger for a few restful days and offer many and varied opportunities for aquatic sports as well. South of Solok, near Alahan Panjang, there are two other lakes **Danau Diates** (upper lake) and **Danau Dinawah** (lower lake). They are a bit off the beaten track, but this is something of an advantage since it means that they have remained unspoiled.

Most of us are familiar with those concrete paths of the western world which are supposed to make things easier. But maybe we will still be able to adjust to pure unspoiled nature in this part of the world, instead of expecting change in "our" direction.

The drive from Padang to **Solok** is along one of the most picturesque roads in West Sumatra, likely to lead to fits of frustrated fury on the part of the hobby photographers sitting in the fast-moving tourist buses.

Trains go to Solok as well, along a route that is just as lovely and this is a good way of getting your first impressions of Singarak Lake as the train puffs along its whole length. **Padangpanjang** one of the stops along the way, is the highest railway station (1,400/4,593 ft) in Indonesia. This is another place, like **Batusangkar** that has less tourist traffic than Bukittinggi (present-day centre of the Minangkabau culture). At one time, however, Batusangkar was the seat of the tribal rulers of this people, and in nearby **Limakaum** and **Pariangan** there are still old communal houses, with the loveliest of them all, at **Sulitair** east of Singarak Lake, still inhabited today. Much of the artistry of the traditional houses has been robbed of its fascination by the glare of corrugated tin roofs.

In spite of the bustle, you'll probably find it hard to tear yourself away from **Bukittinggi,** for the atmosphere of the town more than proves that the heart of the Minangkabau country beats here. It is – and anyone who's been here will more than agree – one of the nicest, most appealing and hospitable towns in Indonesia.

The Dutch gave the town the name **Fort de Kock,** after the fortifications built here in 1825 during the Padri war by a general of that name. From the ruins of the former fort on the hill above the town there is a fantastic view of the countryside surrounding the volcanic peak of the 2,891 m/9,485 ft high Gunung Merapi – which, by the way, has namesakes in both Central and East Java.

The old **zoo,** specializing in Sumatran fauna, lies at the highest point in town, and here too, in an Adat house, is the **Bundo-Kandung Museum,** with a valuable collection of ancient national dress, splendid jewellery and interesting items of everyday life. Going in the opposite direction you come to **Panorama Park** where you can get wonderful views of Sianok Canyon (Ngarai Sianok) and, some distance away, Gunung Singgalang. During the Japanese occupation, tunnels were burrowed under the park and there are guided tours through these.

A special landmark in Bukittinggi is a clock tower in the main market place known as "jam gandang". The town itself is the second biggest in West Sumatra and even boasts a university. Horse drawn carriages as taxis are typical for the streets, and there are plenty of opportunities for interesting excursions to the surrounding countryside.

One of the most dramatic sights in West Sumatra is **Sianci Canyon.** A river flows between the 100 m/328 ft high, steep sides, snaking down to the rice fields that cover the valley. The canyon is at its most impressive in the early hours of the morning, just after the first cock crows, when the light of dawn throws the immense shadow of the distant **Singgalang Volcano,** onto the mist-filled valley. In the heat of the midday sun the peak of this volcano is wrapped in cloud. You can reach **Kota Gadang** on the other side of the canyon in just an hour on foot. This town is not only famous for its artistic silver work, but also as the birthplace of many Indonesian government ministers, diplomats and intellectuals.

Another canyon with breathtaking views is **Anai Valley** – the valley is a national park and is covered with rain forests. There's an observation platform on a viaduct and you can look down to the Anai river flowing far below and also see part of the railway lines that disappear into a tunnel here.

From **Puncal Lewang,** 30 km/18.6 miles west of Padang, there is a wonderful view of **Maninjau Lake.** There are 44 hairpin bends in the road from the peak down to the lake that was formed in a crater caused by volcanic eruption. The small town **Manijau** on the shore of the lake has losmens and boats for hire. Anyone with enough time can wander round the whole lake in 3 days along well trodden paths.

At **Harau Valley,** 15 km/9.3 mi. away from Pavakumbah, north-east of Bukittinggi, there's any number of waterfalls, especially during the rainy season, rushing and tumbling in an area which the government was far-sighted enough to declare a nature reserve. The valley is the habitat of tigers, leopards, tapirs, kancils and other animals. Another interesting reserve, **Rimba Panti,** 100 km/62 miles from Bukittinggi on the road to Medan, has rare lowland and alpine flora and large numbers of animals including some tigers. Before the road turns off into the park you travel through Bonjol, that lies right on the **equator.**

Near **Ngalau Kamang,** 15 km/9.3 miles from Bukittinggi in majestic countryside, there are caves that once served as hideouts for the Tunaka Nan Renceh during their battles with the Dutch.

The colourful **markets** in West Sumatra take place on different days of the week, with one of the biggest at **Payakumbuh,** which is famous for its woven baskets and rotan wares. At the markets the women from the surrounding villages meet for "business and gossip". Another small town renowned for its skilled **handicrafts** is **Panadai Sikat,** near Padangpanjang, where the silk and gold woven brocades really do catch the eye. The men of the idyllic village don't lag far behind their womenfolk in skill, excelling in wood carvings.

Another worthwhile place to visit in West Sumatra is the site of the 11th century ruins at **Muara Takus,** about halfway between Bukittinggi and Pekanbaru. These are the most significant pre-Islamic remains in Sumatra. Although the style in general reveals strong Buddhist influence, there is a strange lack of depictions and effigies of Buddha. The temples were once part of a city which spread over more than 10 sq. km/3.8 sq. miles and which is still today surrounded by the remains of earth walls. Maligai Stupa dominates the site where the biggest structure measuring 20x30 m/66'x98' is the poorly preserved Candi Tua.

It would be a mistake to think that only Muara Takus has uncovered secrets. Small towns and sites throughout West Sumatra have their secrets, too, and these are still awaiting discovery.

Minang Festivals

The Tabut Festival

The Minangkabau who are, with few exceptions, **Moslems,** celebrate a festival unique in the Moslem world at Pariaman, 36 km/22.4 miles north of Padang. The Tabut Festival takes place here once a year in the first month of the Islamic moon calendar, Muharram. It is held to honour the memory of Hassan and Hussein, two of the prophet Mohammed's grandsons, who fell in battle on the Kerbala Plains.

Legend has it that a Bouraqu, an Islamic version of the winged horse of Greek mythology, Pegasus, was sent to earth to rescue their souls. In memory of this heavenly intervention each district makes its own Bouraqu which is carried in triumphant musical procession to the sea. Having reached the shore, the Bouraqu's end is less heroic, for the spectators jump into the sea in a mad scramble to grab as many parts of the cardboard horse as possible – the imitation gold jewellry festooned round Bouraqu's neck is the most coveted prize of all. If the cardboard effigies of two districts should meet on the way to the shore, there's a violent battle with "horsepower" supplied by human hands. Often, all that remains to be borne to the sea afterwards are bits and pieces. The festival is also famous at places far from West Sumatra. A Bouraqu is not only carried in the Tabut Festival today but also in other processions as well, for instance at independence celebrations.

Bull Races and Bull Fights

Just before the ploughing season starts some Minangkabau villages stage bull races, using a normal field as a track. As a bonus, the surface soil is turned over at the same time. The "jockey" perched on a ploughshare steers the bull by pulling its tail and, during risky attempts at overtaking, the temperamental Zebu bulls often try to get rid of their tormentors by rubbing them off against an opponent. More often than not the races end in a rich harvest of bruises instead of the hoped-for rich harvest of rice… and competitors often end up spending a few days at the nearest PusKesMas (Pusat Kesehatan Masyarkat = health centre)!

Bull fights take place once a week after the harvest and have a long tradition in West Sumatra. These are not only seen as trials of strength between the bulls but also a major means of promoting communication among the villages.

Before the fights start – which, by the way, don't as a rule end in bloodshed – the elders discuss particular farming and communal problems. When the battle finally does get underway, emotions run high among the spectators. The oxen on the other hand often fail to see any reason for all the excitement and – in spite of all their owner's efforts – simply go on placidly chewing the cud. If they do finally let themselves be spurred into action, the public goes wild. The beaten bull, when it manages to break away, often takes the shortest route to safety right through the mass of people, and what were originally cries of excitement often turn into cries for help.

Duck Racing

The duck races at Limbuku are, as far as the emotions of the spectators are concerned, hardly any less spectacular. They only take place at this village close to Payakumbuh and are a sort of marriage market as well since they draw all the eligible young girls of the neighbourhood. The specially bred ducks, which are unable to fly, cover the stretch in a kind of half-flying, half waddling gait that leads to fits of helpless laughter on all sides. Many a duck that can't be stopped at the finishing line not only wins the race but makes its escape from the cooking-pot too.

Kite-Flying Competitions

Making huge paper kites is not just something for children in West Sumatra. Competitions are arranged from time to time in which the highest flyer, much to the dismay of many an airline pilot, is the winner.

The Mentawai Islands

The peaks of a ridge of mountains emerge from the Indian Ocean west of Sumatra and form the Mentawai Islands. This group of islands includes North and South Pagai, Sipora and Siberut, which, with a surface area of 4,500 sq. km/1,737 sq. miles, is the largest island.

When approaching **Siberut** by ship from Sumatra there's nothing to see at first except a flat, dark strip in the blue shimmering distance. Slowly, as the ship gets closer and closer, the island seems to stretch across the whole horizon. Gradually the rain forests which rise from the mangrove swamps and a few grey sandy beaches along the island's hilly coast take shape. The confusion of wide spreading jungle giants is shrouded in mist especially in the early morning, and all you hear, apart from the surf, are the plaintive cries of hornbills gliding over the tree tops, or the call of a cicada, which penetrates the otherwise complete and utter silence.

And perhaps this is why the stranger's first impression of Siberut is more off-putting than inviting. Although the island only lies around 150 km/93 miles from the provincial capital Padang it escaped 20th century influence until the beginning of the sixties; **neolithic cultures** were able to survive until recently in its **primeval forests** which still cover 65% of the land today. What is strange is that the other islands north-west and south-east of Siberut, including Engano, have widely differing cultures although they lie in the same geographical position. Whilst parts of the Mentawai group show indications of stone-age cultures with a democratic structure, on Nias there are polymorphic bronze age societies with hierarchial structures. The other islands also have specific cultural features. On **Simalur,** for instance, one can find **Malayan-Islamic** communities.

Present-day tourists are witnesses to **changes** on the islands west of

Sumatra, changes which are not only driving a wedge between the generations but also between man and nature. For sometime now **timber companies** have been active on the Mentawai Islands and their operations threaten not only the flora and fauna but also the living conditions of the natives as well.

Encounters with real aborigines are rare on arrival at one of the two main towns on Siberut (which can be reached only by ship). **Sikabaluan** in the north, and **Muara Siberut** at the southern tip of the east coast, are chiefly inhabited by members of the Minangkabau tribe of West Sumatra famous for their matriarchial social structure. These people monopolize trade with the mainland, primarily in rotan and other products of the rain forests. The visitor will only rarely have the opportunity of making contact with the shy natives. The latter still show their own ethnic characteristics: their blue-black hair is twisted into a knot; their thinned eyebrows – not only as a sign of beauty – lend their normally open and friendly glance a somewhat piercing aspect: their bodies, generally tattooed with traditional designs are hidden under tattered western clothing – gifts from administration and missions, as a "symbol of progress".

Compared with the "civilized" people who live in Muara Siberut and show unmistakable signs of suffering because of the unhealthy climate and diet of the area, the Mentawaians (the product of generations) give the impression of being light-footed and agile. Their fairly good health and slim, almost always athletic physiques are evidence of an active life dictated by the natural hardships of the jungle. Only the feverish glitter of many an eye betrays the curse of the islands – malaria, which claims many lives every year.

Fortunately clothes are only the rule in the coastal regions since otherwise the number of skin diseases would soar in the excessively humid climate. In those places, though where the Mentawaians live under the eye of the law, the usual leaf-skirts and bark loincloths have been ousted by the poor, uniform trappings of civilization – more of a bane than a blessing compared with the rough natural fibres of their traditional dress. These can be renewed at regular intervals and there are none of the problems involved in western clothing. The people cannot produce the clothes themselves (this means dependence upon manufacturing countries) and cannot keep them clean if soap is not supplied at the same time.

It is clear then that a visit to bigger towns means overcoming obstacles for these people who still live in the traditional way. When they do go, although they are naturally lively and uninhibited, the general impression is that they are under restraint in the Sikabluan and Muara Siberut of today; they are indeed outsiders. The greater the influence exerted by the west (tourism) in Mantawai becomes, the greater the gulf between the two worlds will be.

In recent years officials have been more and more unwilling to allow

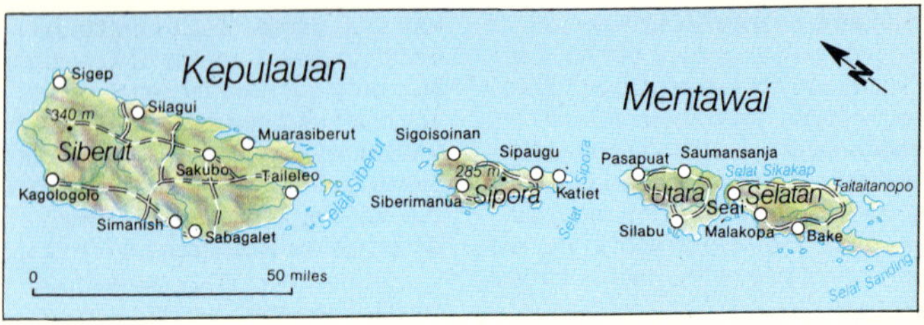

strangers to visit Mantawai, the prevailing opinion being that the impression given by the natives is at odds with the image of a striving, developing Indonesia.

It is strange that opinions in the last century were entirely different – perhaps because life close to nature held more fascination then. **Sir Stamford Raffles,** who led **British** intervention in Dutch East India during the Napoleonic wars, showed special interest and affection for the Mantawaians and their culture. In a report he wrote: "Formerly I intended to write a book to prove that the Niassans were the most contented people on earth. Now I have to acknowledge the fact that the people of the Mantawai Islands are even more admirable and probably much less spoiled than we". In the same way, the hobby ethnologist **Maass** of Berlin gave his book on the Mentawai, published in 1902, the title "Among the Gentle Savages". What is remarkable is that the word "savage" only appears in the title. The work – written with a great deal of feeling – reflects the author's empathy with, and respect for, the culture of these people. When it is borne in mind that many travel books of the time were marked by a lack of insight and chauvinism, Maass's book becomes even more of a small miracle.

At present, feelings of cultural superiority determine outside opinions of the Mentawaians. To get your own impressions of the patriarchal society, you really have to follow the rivers that snake through the island to the remote interior.

People who once lived in variations of the long house, the so-called "uma", have been resettled – on government orders – in single houses in the coastal regions. But even in the new villages, **communal life** based on the group (which is now itself called "uma") and within the original principles of equality still prevails. Inherited titles and positions which mean privilege or subordination are unknown on Siberut. Decisions are only reached after general discussion and in major matters the community of the "uma", comprising several families, stands as an entity, excluding no-one.

Major matters would include the choice of a **rimata** (someone who leads religious affairs and conveys the community's decisions to the outside world), building an "uma", clearing forests, or the problem of a tree that falls by chance in the village area. When any of these take place a period of rest – **punen** – is ordered, during which all kinds of everyday jobs and activities become taboo. The village is cut-off from the outside world, its isolation marked by a cordon of palm leaves and woven garlands, and outsiders (including tourists) are not allowed to enter.

When less solemn but none the less important events take place involving only one family (illness, marriage, birth, adoption or even making a new canoe), a family punen (known as **lia**) is called. Numerous taboos imposed at times like these, make it hard for anyone involved to cope with everyday life. The men play a major role, and this is one of the reasons why the young men tend to put off marrying for as long as possible. Instead, they enter into a sort of open marriage – **rusuks** – with the partner of their choice. There are no religious rites, but even so, the couple still have to follow certain set rules. Men living in "rusuks" with a woman are not permitted to set up the sacrificial baskets usual in family homes (lalep). But an advantage at this stage is that the couple are not tied to each other in any way. Only when marriage finally does take place is there complete monogamy – at this point the new family father has to meet all his duties in connection with the "lia".

These "rusuk relationships" are common throughout Siberut and some of the neighbouring islands and are fully accepted socially. Meals may only be taken together when the marriage has been formally solemnized, however. Mantawaian culture is in some ways less well developed than that of the Dayak of Kalimantan or the Toraja of Sulawesi, although they all number among the ethnic group of ancient Malayans. Developments have taken place in different spheres and at different rates. The inhabitants of Mentawai are, for example, famous for their splendid, well-proportioned canoes (up to 12 m/39½′ long) whereas pottery and weaving are unknown. Agriculture, which doesn't include rice, is very basic and is carried out for the most part along the frequently flooded banks of the rivers. **Cultivated plants** include **sago** – a staple food of man as well as pigs and chickens – **root vegetables, bananas** and **coconut palms,** plus plants that provide the poisons for arrows. Pigs and chickens are kept as domestic animals although slaughtering only takes place on special occasions and eggs are hardly eaten at all since they eventually become valuable livestock. Hunting and fishing more than ensure supplies of valuable protein, however. Bows and arrows, nets and spears, and dogs (always present in large numbers in the "uma") are all used in hunting.

Proof that the people on the Mentawai Islands try to live in complete harmony within the community and with nature around them, is demonstrated by their custom of begging forgiveness for their action before they slaughter a domestic animal or kill their hunted prey. This is something which stems from their religious concept of the world and its taboos, which also play a part in the belief of being one with nature. They believe that everything in their environment possesses a **soul** and it is in keeping with this belief when they seek reconciliation with the river after fishing with poisoned roots to paralyze the fish. And even inanimate objects: stones, houses and rainbows have souls, and are respected because of this.

They believe too that when a soul leaves the human body, the person dies. Thus when any one seems to be threatened with death the **medicine-man** (sikerei) is called to try, with the relatives aid, to hold the soul fast and drive out evil, outside influences. His powers lie in going into a trance – a state believed to enable him to contact supernatural forces. This not only brings him great personal respect but material benefits as well: women by the way can also become sikerei.

At one time, the Indonesian authorities displayed very little understanding for Mentawaian customs, and regarded them as heathen practices. For this reason both the training and practice of the sikereis were banned. Bead decorations, the traditional long hair, tattooing and other outward expressions of their culture were regarded as primitive and forbidden under threat of punishment. Even the "uma" with their strong social roots were no longer permitted. What was aimed at, was **resettlement** of the people in the **coastal regions,** where they would be within reach and more accessible for civilization. Many groups migrated to isolated jungle regions to escape the influences of administration and missionaries. These were missionaries who, at the beginning of the century, had made enormous efforts to eradicate the work of the medicine men, and whose records with completely biased information were responsible for the distorted picture presented to the outside world. The inhabitants of Siberut held fast to their traditions however, and by the

Tatooed medicine man on Siberut, hunting monkeys.

start of World War II the missionaries had only been able to baptize around 10% of the islanders.

In the meantime, the Biblical command to go out and tame the earth, applies here too.

In spite of the fact that intellectual circles in Indonesia are slowly acknowledging the fact that the unconditional adoption of western thought and ways of life will be at the cost of the cultural variety and thus the identity of the republic in the long run, indiscriminate felling and **development programmes** are continuing their destructive course on the Mentawai Island. On the other hand sentimentality and romanticism won't pave the way to a bright future for the islands west of Sumatra, but a great deal of understanding for their cultural heritage will need to be shown. Projects launched with great enthusiasm by the **World Wildlife Fund** and **Survival International** aimed at giving nature and man on the Mentawai Islands a chance of survival have met with little understanding. A nature reserve originally planned to cover 100,000 hectares to protect the cultural integrity of the Mentawais, has shrunk more and more with time. Wide tracks of mud, churned up by the bulldozers felling timber, run through large sections of the, at one time officially approved, reserve. The first uprooted people, torn out of their traditional way of life have already migrated to the coast, and it perhaps won't be long before they are seen, begging or unemployed, on the streets of Padang, searching for a future that was once assured by tradition.

Only when the word "culture" assumes more importance than development, which is sometimes for development's sake, will Mentawai, a group of islands from the past, have something of a future.

Shipping services from Padang to Siberut and the Pagai Islands are very irregular. Boats from Pelubuhan Muara are too small and haven't been permitted to carry tourists since 1977. There are bigger boats from Teluk Bayur, a few miles south of Padang, but the same thing applies, they are irregular; and a round trip can be a time consuming undertaking. The wait for a ship can be as long as two weeks, there are no hotels, and only a slim chance of accommodation at a house owned by the wild life authorities at Muara Siberut.

Another obstacle to be overcome is the amount of red tape involved in getting **permits** to visit the Mentawais. Although the governor's office in Padang insists that none are necessary, if you arrive on the islands without one, you won't be allowed to travel into the interior. When you do finally succeed in getting a permit, and actually reach the islands, then you have to entrust the island authorities (for a fat fee) with the organization of canoes and guides. Lone tourists are unwanted. Any gifts for visits to the village should be bought in Padang, and it is advisable that arrangements for supplies are made here as well.

Bengkulu

This is the most isolated of Indonesia's provinces and during the rainy season overland travel connections often break down completely. The city of the same name was occupied by the British for more than 150 years. In 1685 they founded a factory here which they soon had to defend by building a fort, which was then named York. Around the middle of the 18th century a French fleet succeeded in destroying many of the British possessions, and it was only in 1818 when the English governor, Sir Stamford Raffles, revived the pepper trade, that the town gained some of its former significance. Sir Stamford was also responsible for having Marlborough Fort built, known today as Benteng Malioboro. This fort is now used by the army, in the same way as many other old forts in Indonesia, but can still be visited. Inside the compound stand the gravestones of former British commanders. There is a fine view of the city and harbour from the walls of the fortress. In 1824 the British exchanged Bengkulu for Malacca a Dutch possession.

Most Indonesians still remember Bengkulu today as the place where former president Sukarno was interned for nine years by the Dutch in 1933, for his activities as a freedom flighter.

Other sights worth seeing in the city and its surroundings are the lovely beaches and botanical gardens, Dendam Taksuda, where with any luck you can see the huge raffelsia in full bloom between September and November.

And if you're interested in fish markets there's another one to see in Bengkulu.

The province has at present some one million inhabitants, including large numbers of Javanese migrants who have settled here in recent years. And there's quite a number of things to interest the tourist.

In the Pasemah Highlands, the individualists may like to look at huge Bronze Age monuments, which have an added touch of mystery since the full significance of this one time cult-site has never been completely unraveled.

A large national park, Kerinci, in the north-west of Bengkulu will certainly appeal to nature-lovers with the 3,000 metre/9,842′ Kerinci Volcano that gave the park its name. The protected area covers some 1,484,600 hectares with differences in height ranging from 50 to 3,500 metres/164′–11,483′ above sea level. Sumatra shows itself at its wildest here with regard to both wild animals and landscapes. It is indeed tragic that the existence of this park, to be reached from Padang, Jambi and Bengkulu, is threatened by illegal land seizure. Four-wheel drive vehicles are needed on the park's roads. Sungau Penuk, reached from Jambi via Bangko, in around 22 hours, is probably the best starting point for a visit.

Bengkulu can be reached by air from Jakarta via Palembang and there is a night-train every evening from Lubuk Linggau 120 km/74 miles away. There are also bus services to and from Padang, Bukittinggi and Palembang.

Jambi

Jambi province, with a population of 1.3 million lies on the east coast of Sumatra, facing the Straits of Malacca, a fact that no doubt contributed to people of other nationalities settling in the area. The resulting racial tension is however barely noticeable to outsiders. The city of the same name, Jambi, with a population around 155,000, is on the Batanghari, Sumatra's longest river. Apart from possibilities for extending visas, a few shipping connections and dense rain forests in the vicinity, the town hasn't much to offer the tourist, and most of them only travel through to make boat connections to Singapore or Jakarta. Should you wish to do this, it's particularly interesting to travel to the capital by Bugis sailing ship. The ship takes about 2–3 weeks and more often than not has a cargo of timber.

A boat trip along the Batanghari offers a further bonus of penetrating Kubu territory and that of other nomadic tribes. Not much official toleration is shown in Sumatra for the way of life followed by these primitive peoples and resettlement programmes were carried out that gave rise to immense health problems. Unaccustomed to civilized peoples and with no immunity towards the diseases, they were decimated by childhood illnesses (measles, etc.) and tuberculosis. Of the people still alive today, 85% of what were once widespread tribes are now settled in one place.

Only a very small number were able to find sanctuary in the dense rain forests and understandably they shy away from any contact with civilization.

Some decades ago a professor set out on an expedition to find those Kubu people still living in the wild. Finally he had to abandon his search and be content with tribe members living in settlements. It does indeed seem at times that the last Sumatran forest nomads, living in complete isolation, really have vanished from the face of the earth. Hardly any wonder, for apart from their abandoned huts, they leave no traces in the forests. The use of iron or pottery utensils is unknown to them, and their practical, sparse, clothing is still made from tree bark – although one or two items of "civilized" wear have found their way to them too. If a member of the tribe dies, be it of illness or even old age, they break camp immediately and move on, and in doing so, avoid any risk of infection, more or less by chance.

Kubus regard plants and animals of their forest home, both as friends and gods. And the people of Jambi believe they can really understand the language of the forest and its life. One thing is sure, it's something we have long forgotten, if we ever knew it at all!

There are flights from Jakarta, Pelembang and Medan to Jambi. Addresses to contact:
Garuda Airlines, Jl. Dr. Wahidin, Jambi,
Telephone: OT 2 20/2 20 41
Merpati Airlines, Jl. Damar 55, Jambi.
And there are bus services to Palembang, Padang and Bukittinggi.

Riau

With a population of 2 million certainly not the most densely populated province of Indonesia, but rich, because of its vast oilfields. The main fields, connected by pipeline to the refineries at Dumai, are close to the provincial capital Pekanbaru. Singapore, that centre of finance and commerce, has always exerted great influence on this province and its 1,000 offshore islands, although these are mostly uninhabited, or only used for short periods by fishermen.

Rain forests and mangrove swamps cover the greatest part of the land and there are only a few roads leading to Pekanbaru, Dumai, Jambi, Bukittinggi and Padang. Otherwise, transportation is only possible on the great navigable rivers of East Sumatra.

Air-transport, still in its infancy, is concentrated at Simpang Tiga Airport, 10 km/6 miles from Pekanbaru, with airstrips at Dumai, Batam and Tanjung Pinang. Although there is a direct flight to Singapore from the capital, most tourists prefer to travel by Merpati Airlines to Tanjung Pinang and take a ferry from there to the island state.
Airport offices:
Garuda Airlines, Jl. Jend. Suirman 207, Pekanbaru,
Telephone: 2 10 26,
Merpati Airlines, Jl. Hos. Cokroaminoto 18, Pekanbaru,
Telephone: 55 85.

Pekanbaru, 160 km/99 miles up the Siak River, cannot be said to conceal its wealth. Dollars from oil have ensured that public buildings are more impressive than in other places, but on the whole the town doesn't have much to offer apart from fairly pleasant surroundings, shopping and the chance to take care of official business, visas, etc.

Rain forests in the vicinity of the oil boom town are interspersed with pipelines and wells, but for all that have remained the home of rhinos and tigers and sometimes traces are even found of bears, tapirs and elephant: these are often seen in the early hours of the morning crossing the country roads. The forests of Riau are still home to several animistic tribes with numbers estimated between 10,000 to 15,000 in all. The Sakai, a nomadic tribe like the Kubu, and Jambisals are concentrated around the neighbourhood of Dumai. Oil companies with drilling-rights here, attempted to settle the Sakai near the oilfields to ensure a steady supply of labour, and there's no doubt they would have made ideal workers for the swampy oil-fields, accustomed as they are to the extremely humid climate of the rain forests. However, the blood of the nomad runs through their veins and only very few took the jobs offered.

Tanjung Pinang is a small but important trading centre on Pulau Bintan and you can reach Singapore from here in just four hours by ship. Its closeness to the free-port, plus the almost impenetrable confusion of small islands, have made the area a haven for smugglers: and not only smuggled goods are well received – TV programmes from the City of the Lion are too. There is a fine panoramic view of the town, built in some places on piles, and of the surrounding islands, from Gunung Bintan. Bintan hasn't much to offer apart from its nice beaches. On the other hand, the seemingly modest neighbouring island of Penyenget was once capital of the Johore-Riau sultanate whose powers extended over the Riau and Lingga archipelago, the Malaysian states of Johore and Pahang, and great parts of Sumatra.

There's very little evidence now of the power that was once Penyenget's, apart from the graves of a few sultans and their ruined palaces. The island is completely inhabited by Malayans and has no social and economic structure whatsoever.

Other islands too show the remains of ancient palaces and graves of former inhabitants. On Pulau Birma Dewa, around 20 km/12 miles from Tanjung Pinang, there are the remains of a palace whose walls are decorated with ceramic work, known locally as "Istana Piring" or "Kota Piring".

If you want to become acquainted with the outer islands of the Riau archipelago, some with wonderful beaches, pay a visit to the Pelni Line in Tanjung Pinang at Jl. Temiang. You can get all the information you need on boat connections, but without at least 4 weeks at your disposal it's something not really worth thinking about.

Buses in Sumatra

Anyone who has ever travelled the whole length of Sumatra by bus has a tale to tell, no doubt full of exaggerations and hair-raising details, of an unforgettable experience and all that went with it.

But even without the exaggeration the tale will still be one of trips lasting hours and long waits, heat, dust, cold, wet, pot-holes, sick-bags, narrow seats, spicy, burning food, hunger, thirst, chickens, goats. dour and friendly passengers, and the wildly, romantic, splendid scenery of Sumatra.

During the rainy season the tale will have to be supplemented with talk of mud, cloudbursts of almost biblical dimensions, landslides and washed out bridges to contend with, and so on. There's hardly a listener who will be able to picture just what such a "bus marathon" through Sumatra means. The 2 main reasons tourists – usually those travelling alone – embark on these trips at all are time and money.

For they have nothing in common whatsoever with holiday or study tours. Buses on long distance routes are privately owned with the best operated by A. N. S. or A. L. S. with relatively comfortable Mercedes Benz vehicles (assembled in Indonesia) and air conditioning (when it works) which is a blessing during the day and a curse at night in the cool higher regions! These buses are only rarely booked out, but reservations in advance are advisable. Towards the end of Ramadan, shortly before the Lebar festivals, all seats are booked well in advance; all Sumatra (and Indonesia) is on the move. Since seats in buses, trains and planes are at a premium then, the best idea is to find some nice restful place far, far, away from all means of transport and to stay there! If a tourist should by chance get a bus ticket shortly before these celebrations, then more often than not it's only as a reserve for any passenger who just might not turn up. And even when a booking has been confirmed there is still a danger of someone else taking the seat if you don't get there hours in advance. This applies especially to those places away from the main bus station; and if you insist on your rights (a seat) this more often than not brings the cup (read bus) to overflowing.

If you want to be sure of a certain degree of safety and comfort, avoid the old, low Chevrolet buses like the plague (standing upright is an impossibility) and in the dry season they fill with dust that creeps in through the rust holes in the floor. Then there is the matter of doors and seats, the former, 2 or 3, are all on the left hand side, the seats however are all of the long bench type, and that means anyone sitting on the outside right has to go through antics that would be the envy of a contortionist to get out.

The space between the seats is calculated on the amount of legroom that Indonesians need. Since luggage is also crammed behind the seats, anyone with long legs will have great difficulties clambering in at all.

Although the seats at the front next to the driver do mean more room taking a seat somewhat further back might be preferable, even if you do have long legs, unless of course you have nerves of steel and can remain impervious to close-ups of risky overtaking and numerous "near-misses". The fiery temperamental style of the drivers is hardly a surprise if you take into account the amounts of hot, spicy food they consume during their 4 or 5 meal breaks at the Padang restaurants along the route. And another thing, since your baggage probably means as much to you as your neck, you should keep your eye on it. Pickpockets love nylon rucksacks, with their masses of side pockets, so easy to slit open. So if you can't keep your baggage within sight inside the bus, it's better to have it up on the roof under a tarpaulin, and then you have to keep your eyes open when people are getting out, or if the bus stops for some length of time. All this doesn't, however, mean that you have to mistrust everyone in sight.

What influences bus travel most of all in this part of the world is the weather. It's better to give the south of Sumatra a miss during the rainy season.

Sumatra's Climate in Brief:
North of the Equator:
Dry season: May to December
Rainy season: October to March (very heavy downpours)
South of the Equator:
Dry season: April to October
Rainy season: November to February (very heavy downpours)

South Sumatra and Lampung

Although 75% of Indonesia's oil is found on Sumatra, the oilfields here only constitute a very small percentage of national production. The reason for this apparently distorted picture is the giant Minas oilfield at Riau which has to date supplied 300 million tons and according to the latest studies will supply another 700 million tons.

Only one of the more than 10 oilfields owned by the state run oil company, Pertamina, in South Sumatra yields more than 10,000 tons a day. Other sources, for instance Jatibarang in North-West Java, yield more than 45,000 tons daily. But there are hopes of further finds at the east coast of South Sumatra. The provinces of South Sumatra and Lampung were already in colonial times a transmigration region for people from overpopulated Java and today the rain forests still have to make way for housing projects. Forestry with commercial felling is also stripping the land bare in other places. An almost unavoidable result of these developments are unpleasant encounters between animals and settlers, and for this reason between 15th November and 31st December 1982 a giant drive took place in an attempt to resettle more than 200 elephants in a special reserve set aside for them with more than 75,000 hectares. With the help of police and army the animals were driven to the safer region 50 km/31 miles from Palembang between the rivers Air Sugihan and Air Padang. A water-filled ditch was made 20 metres/66′ wide and 23 km/14 miles long to prevent the herds pushing their way back into settled areas and it can only be hoped that this was not an isolated attempt to save Sumatra's some 1,700 elephants.

The best place to see the elephants is at Way Kambas Reserve near Sukadenas on the east coast and they can be spotted from quite some way off. The swampy marshlands, inaccessible during the dry season, can be reached by canoe in the rainy season. Way Kamba Reserve is best explored by boat via the many rivers, from the coastal town of Labuhan Meringgi. The PPA headoffice in Tanjung Karang is answerable for this area and are willing to help tourists in any way possible.

Tanjung Karang is also the starting point for tourists from Java who are journeying down the whole length of Sumatra, it's also where the Trans Sumatra Highway starts, planned to cover 2,700 km/ 1,678 miles, although to date only a few stretches have been finished.

Twice daily there are ferries from and to Panjang, the port near Telukbetung. The trip from Merak in West Java via the Sunda Straits to here takes 5 to 6 hours. If you arrive in Panjang by ferry a little late in the day then the best bet is to spend the night in Telukbetung or Tanjung Karang as there's a better choice of accommodation more in keeping with western standards.

Sumatra's roads are notorious among tourists and many of them prefer to take the train from Tanjung Karang. These have 2nd or 3rd class carriages and go to Palembang, the provincial capital of South Sumatra, twice daily. The better of the two trains is the Sivijaya Express, but it costs over twice as much as the Rajabasa. Another train connection, 3rd class only, with Sindang Marga, goes from Palembang via Perabumulih to Lubuk Linggau. The train journey to Palembang takes a little over 10 hours.

This town, with 650,000 inhabitants, was originally intended as capital of the Srivijaya realm. The one time metropole, frequented by merchants from East Asia and the Mediterranean, flourished culturally and financially at the beginning of the 11th century until it was conquered in 1028 by a south Indian potentate. The once flourishing city lost its fame. Then the kingdom of Srivijaya was divided into eight princedomes in the 14th century and its powers were seized by Malacca. In the meantime, the town, whose libraries and seats of learning were the intellectual heart of South-East Asia from the 7th to 11th centuries, has regained some kind of economic significance with pepper, timber, handicrafts, tin and oil.

Cultural remains of the Srivijaya kingdom are found in the museums, of which Rumah Bari is the best, and are evident in the customs of Palembang's people.

The colourful, frenetic, activities at the wide Musi river, spanned by a huge steel bridge, makes it one of the most interesting places in town. Another place where there's plenty to see is the Pasar Ilir (pasar=market)

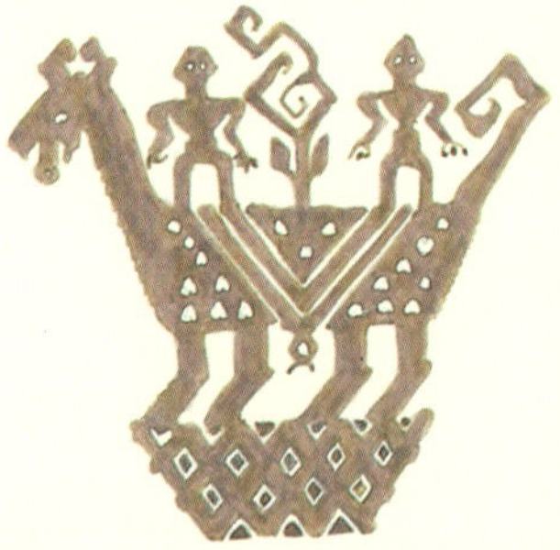

Figurative decoration on a ship's sail.

2 km/1.2 miles downstream: a market where a lot is sold that many a person didn't want to be rid of!

An old Dutch fort built towards the end of the 18th century is used by the army today, but it can be viewed with the commander's permission. Since Palembang has become a major junction for traffic by land, sea and air, several industries, mainly chemical, rubber, shipbuilding and machine making, have sprung up alongside the oil refineries. Not something that is likely to tempt tourists to linger.

There are flights from Talangbetuhu Airport, 17 km/10½ miles north of the town, to and from Jakarta, Singapore, Telubetung, Tanjung Pinang, Pekanbaru, Padang, Medan, Bengkulu Jambi and other places.

Airline addresses:
Garuda Airlines, Jl. Kapten Rivai 20, Tel.: 2 29 33, 2 20 29
Merpati Airlines, Jl. A. Rivai, Tel.: 2 16 04, 2 60 51

If you are looking for good boat connections then travel to Muntok on the west coast of the tin island Bangka. A Pelni ship, Tampomas I, that runs between Jakarta and Medan, docks here too.

Hotels

Of all the Indonesian islands, Java and Bali offer the widest selection of accommodation. Jakarta has several "5-star hotels" and other towns on the two islands also offer many establishments which would come under the remaining categories. The majority of hotels are air-conditioned and in the big hotels travellers will find all the comfort, luxury and peace they could wish for.

Many tourists, however, prefer **small hotels, cottages** or **losmens,** since the atmosphere in them is on the whole informal and makes contact with the local people easier. On the smaller outer islands, however, accommodation can be a problem. Often it's the local teacher, priest, policeman or missionary who is prepared to take in strangers – at a cost, of course. Anyone who wants to travel around independently or who plants to visit sparsely populated areas should take a light-weight tent with them.

Details of hotels given in this travel guide are based on information from the Indonesian Ministry of Communication and Tourism.

N. B. * = Hotel with star rating.

Price Group
1 = 2,000– 5,000 Rp
2 = 5,000–10,000 Rp
3 = 10,000–20,000 Rp
4 = over 20,000 Rp
(per night/single)

For further details contact an Indonesian Tourist Office (Addresses, see Useful Information) or the Information Office of an Indonesian Embassy.

Hotels in Sumatra

Name/ Address	Price Group	No. of Rooms	With WC/Bath	Km to Airport	Km to Bus	Km to Train
North Sumatra						
Brastagi						
Rudang** Jl. Sempurna Brastagi Tel. 43	2	40	40	–	–	–
Bukit Kubu* Jl. Sempurna 2 Brastagi Tel. 2	2	21	21	65	2	66
Medan						
Danau Toba International**** Jl. Imam Bonjal 7 Medan Tel. 32 70 00	4	280	280	1	1	1
Garuda Plaza Hotel*** Jl. Sisinga-mangaraja 18 Medan Tel. 32 62 55	4	170	170	3.5	26	2
Pardede International** Jl. H. Juanda 14 Medan Tel. 32 38 66	4	46	46	2	3	4
Angkasa* Jl. Sutomo 1 Medan Tel. 32 12 44	3	19	19	1.5	0.5	0.2
Sumatra Jl. Sisinga-mangaraja Medan Tel. 2 49 73	2	36	36	1	1	1

Name/ Address	Price Group	No. of Rooms	With WC/Bath	Km to Airport	Km to Bus	Km to Train
Parapat						
Natour Hotel*** Jl. Marihat 1 Parapat Tel. 41012/ 41018	3	75	75	176	0.2	48
Atsari Hotel** Jl. P. Samosir Parapat Tel. 41219/ 41275	4	55	55	176	0.2	48
Budi Mulya* Jl. P. Samosir Parapat Tel. 41216/ 41485	2	28	28	174	–	48
Karona Jl. Gereja Parapat Tel. 46	2	14	14	176	–	46
Pematang Siantar						
Siantar*** Jl. W.R. Supratman Tel. 21091/ 21667/ 21736 Pematang Siantar	3	85	85	130	1	1
Sinar Baru Jl. Bukit Barisan Pematang Siantar Tel. 79	1	13	13	134	2	1
Pulau Samosir						
Toba Beach* Tomok/Samosir Tel. 24850 (Medan) Tel. 41802 (Parapat)	4	40	40	176	–	–

Pulo Tao Cottage Pulo Tao/ Samosir Representative: Jl. Ampera 9, Medan/ Glugur darat Tel. 2 08 60	4	10	10	184	–	–
Tuk Tuk Hotel Tuk Tuk/ Samosir Representative: Jl. Samosir Parapat Tel. 2 39 81	3	28	–	–	–	–

South Sumatra

Lubuk Linggau Lintas Sumatra* Jl. Yos Sudarso 21 Lubuk Linggau	2	24	24	–	0.5	1
Palembang Swarna Dwipa*** Jl. Tasik 2 Palembang Tel. 2 23 22, 2 13 55, 2 28 11	4	82	82	12	4	5
Puri Indah* Jl. Merdeka 38 Palembang Tel. 2 06 85, 2 69 12	3	37	37	12	3	5
Rivano Jl. Kol. H. Barlian Palembang Tel. 2 33 25	3	20	–	6	6	10
Sintera Jl. Jend. Sudirman 8 Palembang Tel. 2 06 14/ 2 16 18	2	75	66	12	1	5
Sri Wijaya Jl. Jend. Sudirman 48 Palembang Tel. 2 61 93	2	14	–	12	2	5
Tanjung Pandan Martani* Jl. Pantai Tanjung Pandan	1	30	–	–	–	–
Pangkal Pinang Geulis Jaya Baru Jl. Deputi Amir 12 Pangkal Pinang Tel. 755	3	14	–	–	–	–
Ranggi Jl. Jend. Sudirman Lembawai III/ 1–38 Pangkal Pinang Tel. 429	2	14	14	6	2	–
Karya Bhakti Jl. Jend. Sudirman Pangkal Pinang	1	16	16	7	–	–

West Sumatra

Bukit Tinggi Dymens International*** Jl. Nawawi 1–5 Bukit Tinggi Tel. 2 37 81/ 2 27 02/2 10 15	3	54	54	85	1.5	0.5
Benteng* Jl. Benteng 1 Bukit Tinggi Tel. 2 25 96/ 2 11 15	2	18	18	85	0.8	–
Denai Jl. Rivai 26 Bukit Tinggi Tel. 2 14 60	1	15	15	83	1.5	2
Limas Jl. Kesehatan 34 Bukit Tinggi Tel. 2 26 41	1	22	22	83	2	–
Yani Jl. Jend. A. Yani 101 Bukit Tinggi Tel. 2 27 40	1	14	14	82	0.5	1

Padang Mariani International** Jl. Bundo Kandung 35 Padang Tel. 2 20 20/ 2 26 34	3	33	29	10	1	3.2
Aldilla* Jl. Damar No. 2 Padang Tel. 2 39 62	2	15	15	7	1	5
Wisma Bougainville Jl. Bgd. Azis Chan 2 Padang Tel. 2 21 49	2	15	15	7	1	1.5
Wisma Femina Jl. Bgd. Azis Chan 15 Padang Tel. 2 19 50	1	12	12	10	1	1.3
Minang International Jl. Diponegoro 17 Padang Tel. 2 17 19	1	30	30	10	0.5	–
Maninjau Parawisata Maninjau Indah Maninjau Tel. 16	2	18	18	113	–	–
Singkarak Jayakarta Singkarak	1	16	16	100	–	–
Riau						
Pekanbaru Sri Indrayani** Jl. Bangka 2 Pekanbaru Tel. 2 18 70/ 2 34 61/2 37 10	3	53	53	12	1	–
Anom* Jl. Gatut Subroto 3 Pekanbaru Tel. 2 26 36	2	14	14	–	–	–
Kelabang sakti Jl. Diponegoro 53 Pekanbaru	2	11	11	–	–	–
Bintom Jl. Tangkuban Prahu Riau	1	14	14	–	–	–
Dharma Utama Jl. Sisingamangaraja 2 Riau	1	52	18	–	–	–
Rengat Bintang Tujuh Jl. Terminal Bus Rengat Tel. 93	1	32	18	25	–	–
Lampung						
Lampung Marco Polo* Jl. Dr. Susilo 5 Lampung Tel. 4 15 11	3	81	81	26	1.5	2.5
Kota Bumi Lampung Jl. Cokro Aminoto	2	25	–	78	0.8	0.1
Tanjung Karang Ria Hotel Jl. Dewi Warna 7 Tanjung Karang Tel. 5 39 74	2	24	24	25	3	0.2
Kurnia Dua Jl. Raden Intan 75 Tanjung Karang Tel. 5 29 05	1	30	30	26	1	2
Wijaya Kesuma Jl. Dr. Susilo Tanjung Karang Tel. 5 21 63	2	12	12	2	2	3
Teluk Betung New Jakarta Hotel Teluk Betung Jl. Belanak 28	2	50	50	28	1	2
Shintana Jl. Selat Berhala 95 Teluk Betung Tel. 4 29 41	1	12	12	28	–	–

Kalimantan (Borneo)

With an area of approximately 740,000 square kilometres/285,700 sq. miles, Borneo is the world's third-largest island. The North of the island is made up of the Malaysian states of Sarawak and Sabah, as well as the tiny sultanate of Brunei. Kalimantan, the Indonesian portion of the island, covers an area of 539,460 square kilometres/208,285 sq. miles. This island, which is divided up among three sovereign nations, appears on maps under the name of "Borneo", which is thought to be a corruption of Brunei.

At present, approximately 6.5 million people live in the southern part of the island, which is divided into the provinces of Central, East, South, and West Kalimantan with their capital cities of Palangka Raya, Samarinda, Banjarmasin and Pontianek.

The great rivers of this island – which is very mountainous in parts – are its only communication routes. With the exception of a few roads in the vicinity of the provincial capitals, the area has no road network to speak of and relies heavily on river and air transport. However, as flying is too expensive for the majority of the population, the bulk of Kalimantan's passenger and cargo traffic depends on inland navigation. The over 700-kilometre/434 mile-long Mahakam which empties into the sea near Samarinda, as well as the southward-flowing Barito and the westward-flowing Kapuas, are the largest river systems on the island. Their navigability is, however, limited by rapids and, in the dry season, by low water levels, The tides make quite a difference in the coastal regions, but do not pose a problem for river navigation on the whole.

Plans for a "Trans-Kalimantan Highway" are in the making, but those who know the island well are aware of the great difficulties that would have to be overcome.

Borneo's vast swamplands and its mountainous interior have always made life difficult for explorers, the first of whom arrived at the beginning of this century. The once so impenetrable rainforests, however, have thinned out considerably over the years. In 1983, a fire destroyed 3,75 million hectares (9.3 million acres) of rainforest in what is considered to be the greatest environmental disaster of the century. In this enormous area, as well as in regions which have been totally cleared of vegetation by the logging companies, an intensive reafforestation programme will have to take up the battle against soil erosion. So far, efforts made in this direction have been unsatisfactory. Diluvial rainfall has already washed away the soil's thin layer of humus, thus rendering large tracts of land unsuitable for cultivation. Such areas become overrun by elephant grass ("alang alang"), the lushness of which fools only the uninformed into thinking that the land is once again fertile. In reality, "alang alang" must first be cleared away - an almost impossible task due to its heavily tangled mass of roots. In most cases, this precludes any further use of the soil.

As Kalimantan does not exhibit any volcanism, its soil is not as fertile as that of Java or Bali. In many areas, though, a lush paradise with a rich assortment of plants and animals presents itself to the beholder. The variety of trees, flowers (including dozens of different varieties of orchids), lianas and other plants is nothing short of spectacular. With the help of the ten nature reserves here, one can see for oneself that the word "forest" can have many different meanings. In addition to the sparse mountain forests, the mangrove belts along the coast and the "kerangas" or heath forests, there are also vast peat forests whose rivers and streams are the colour of very strong tea because of the peaty soil. Many rainforests grow on top of a saturated layer of silica sand, much like plants grown using the hydroponic method. Supported by an army of saprophytic fungi, bacteria and insects, the plant kingdom here has found its own answers to the poor soil. Vegetables would have a hard time thriving here: only those plants which can adapt to their surroundings are able to exist on a permanent basis. This applies to all forms of life – including those of the animal kingdom, represented here by mousedeer, orang-utans and other apes, deer, bears, leopards, argus pheasants, hornbills, crocodiles, as well as elephants and rhinoceroses. In the rainforests of Borneo there is little or no place for those forms of life which seek to adapt their surroundings to their own needs. Only the tribes of hunters and gatherers who roam through the bush as nomads know how to live in harmony with their surroundings – all others end up destroying the delicate balance of Nature. The Dyak people, for instance, often clear land for farming by burning the existing vegetation, cultivate the land and then move on when the soil cannot support further growth. If this practice could at least be limited, the rainforest would be able to recover from these violations and take possession of the land again. It takes a long time, however, before the original concentration or variety of life forms is again reached. More especially in the coastal regions, but in the interior as well, the use of machinery has completely destroyed any chance of a regeneration of the rainforest. Plans to use these areas for transmigration projects are not likely to be put into effect owing to the especially poor soil there.

At present, the majority of Kalimantan's population lives in the municipal centres along the coast where the Chinese and the Malays wield considerable influence. The indigenous Dayaks, who make up 42 per cent of the entire population of Borneo, still live along the rivers of the island's interior. The Indonesian government is trying to abolish their traditional "longhouses" (which are sometimes occupied by more than 150 families) and replace them with single-family houses, which indeed are becoming more and more common. In a number of "scientific" studies, the Dayaks' form of social organization was referred to as a type of primitive communism – this understandably led to allergic reactions on the part of the government following the attempted coup of September 1965. According to the government at the time, a show of power was absolutely necessary.

Today, Dayak youths hire themselves out to timber companies or go to the cities in search of fortune. Most of them do not make it beyond menial jobs, however. The children of wealthy Dayaks, who are not so much a rarity as one might think, can be found at Indonesia's universities or even in far-off Europe where they study medicine, engineering, forestry and many other subjects. Even though, in their cases, progress has only just supplanted the past, each one of these students hopes for a white-collar position after completion of his studies.

The timber and petroleum industries, which presently dominate the region's economy, have already handed out most of their management posts to Japanese, Americans and Europeans with the necessary know-how; the government, however, is seeing to it that local specialists are afforded a chance as well. (From an economic point of view,

A Dayak tribesman with blow-pipe and "mandau", the traditional sword of the Dayaks.

Kalimantan, which is very rich in natural resources, still receives too little attention.) Coal, petroleum and, to a lesser degree, natural gas reserves are being exploited along the eastern coast. For quite a time now, a refinery in Balikpapan has been handling the processing of the crude oil, and while gold and iron ore are being mined in the western part of the region, new oil deposits and even diamonds are being discovered in the south.

In contrast to the Malaysian states of Sarawak and Sabah and the freshly independent sultanate of Brunei, there is very little tourist activity in the Indonesian portion of the island. Those who wish to travel across Kalimantan by way of the rivers, need, above all, time – endless amounts of it!

The tropical **climate** of the island is characterized by a rainy and a dry season. The sun predominates from April to September, but does not preclude the possibility of heavy tropical showers during these months. In the period from October to March, diluvial rainfall occurs at regular intervals. This is, however, the best travel time for butterfly and orchid lovers. It is somehow hardly surprising that the blossoming of the orchid coincides with the appearance of countless butterflies of magnificent beauty and variety.

Note: Those who wish to explore the entire island of Borneo and plan a **border crossing** into the Malaysian states of Sarawak and Sabah should bear in mind that the border between Kalimantan and Sarawak is officially closed to foreigners. The only legal way in is on the twice-weekly Merpati flight from **Pontianak** to **Kuching.** Those who wish to enter Sabah, may do so at the border, however. There is also a flight from **Tarakan** to **Tawau** in Sabah. Boat connections between the Indonesian and Malaysian portions of the island also exist. There is even a ferry between **Nunukan** and Tawau – the crossing takes one night.

The Dayaks

The approximately 300 different tribes who live in Borneo's vast interior are grouped together under the blanket term, "Dayak". With 390,000 people, the **Iban** are most strongly represented in Sarawak, but groups belonging to this tribe can also be found in the northern parts of West and Central Kalimantan. A characteristic feature of Dayak culture is their architecture: they build so-called "longhouses" which can be 15 metres/49'3" wide and up to 150 metres/492'5" long. Earlier, when the younger generation did not go to the cities in search of work, the total number of people resident in one longhouse often exceeded one thousand. The Indonesian government regards this form of cohabitation as being behind the times and has long been advocating the construction of single-family houses. Even though communal life is greatly prized among the Dayaks, individual families do have their own rooms in the longhouses, where they sleep or prepare meals. There is usually an open platform extending the entire length of the back of the house where laundry is hung out to dry or other household tasks are carried out, but the covered veranda on the side of the house facing the river is the heart of the community. Here, people stroll back and forth, relax, work on handicrafts and enjoy themselves. During the evening hours, things can get quite lively on the veranda or "ruai", as the Dayaks can always find something to celebrate. The chief or "tuai rumah", who is chosen by the elders of the community, lives in the centre of the longhouse. His is not a hereditary position: if the "tuai rumah" makes a wrong step, he quickly loses his authority. While he is responsible for the internal and external affairs of the village, the "shaman", or medicine man, is responsible for the mental, physical and spiritual welfare of the people. The Dayaks who live in the vicinity of the great rivers are Christians (on the surface, at least) but those living in the mountainous regions near Sarawak and Sabah are still animists. In other areas, there are longhouses which are occupied by both animist and Christian or Moslem families.

A Dayak girl in traditional dress.

Most longhouse communities live from the cultivation of pepper and rubber. Hunting and fishing also contribute to their livelihood. Along the Skrang River in Sarawak and the Mahakam in East Kalimantan, tourism provides an additional source of income. In some circles in our society it is considered chic to visit former headhunters; for other people, it satisfies a need to show courageousness. Our own standards and values have undergone such changes over the years that when we use them on primitive peoples, we end up making false judgements. While napalm bombings are advocated by many as an expedient way of exerting power, head-hunting, which had its roots in the religious and spiritual life of those who practised it, is considered primitive and inhuman. It has already been proven, however, that "civilized peoples" do not always decry such "base practices": after having initially banned head-hunting in Borneo, the British encouraged the native people to hunt "Japanese heads" during the Second World War.

The Dayaks, who stopped collecting human trophies long ago, are not at all bloodthirsty at heart – this is exhibited by the fact that before slaughtering a domestic animal, a Dayak will talk to it, explain his intentions and beg forgiveness.

The social organization of the many Dayak tribes can vary considerably: while the cheerful and light-hearted Iban have a liberal, democratic and highly cooperative social system, the **Kayan** and **Kenyah** tribes, who practised slavery well into this century, are ruled by powerful aristocrats. These tribes are also known for their artistic wood carvings and metalwork which are marketed throughout the island.

The tatooing of the skin, a widespread practice among the Dayaks, has been banned by the authorities as an antiquated custom. In the cities, however, no one pays attention to this law, and it is not enforced anyway. The wearing of long hair (popular in the cities but forbidden among the Dayaks) as well as the sporting of anchors and nude women on the arms and torso is seen as a sign of modernity and progress.

Those who want to experience Dayak life close-to should spend some time with them, but always bear in mind that, although their hospitality is proverbial, it should not be taken advantage of. A useful gift (see the chapter on the Asmat region) is not a tourist's ploy, but rather a traditional gesture.

Things to Keep in Mind When Visiting a Longhouse:

1. A longhouse is not a museum. Do not enter without having asked permission first. The stairs leading up to the veranda should be regarded as part of the house as well.
2. Shoes should be removed before entering a longhouse. Those who

Dayak shield.

would like to show their good will and be on the safe side should also remove their socks.

3. Never refuse the welcoming drink. Take a small sip of the "tuak" (palm or rice wine) and decline with thanks when you have had enough.

4. The above applies to food as well.

5. The food and drink offered should always be accepted with two hands at the same time. A single outstretched hand is regarded as a challenge.

6. Never tease or torment the animals! According to Dayak belief, this could bring on floods, bad harvests and other disasters.

7. A white flag flying over a longhouse signifies a period of taboo. During this time, strangers are not welcome.

8. Gifts should be reciprocated immediately in kind. Do not worry! You will not be put in an embarrassing position.

East Kalimantan – Kalimantan Timur

The boomtown city and port of **Balikpapan** is the most important oil centre on the island's east coast. Since the majority of the oil-drilling licences have been given to American companies, it is not surprising that the U.S. dollar sets the tone here – nor is it idle rumour that skilled foreign workers can earn a great deal of money. This is borne out by the extortionate prices demanded of these non-Indonesians for luxurious necessities, prices way out of reach of the ordinary people. The traveller who is looking for the unique in Balikpapan will have to be satisfied with the glaring contrasts between the life of the Indonesians there and the unreal environment within which foreigners exist. Balikpapan has nothing to offer the tourist, however.

From **Sepinggan Airport,** 8 km/ 5 miles outside Balikpapan, there are **connections** to Jakarta, Surabaya, the island of Sulawesi and into Kalimantan's interior. Samarinda, which lies 120 kilometres/74 miles away, can also be reached from here – trips on the Mahakam River start there. Those who want to save money can take the **bus** from Balikpapan, (it also stops at the road leading to the airport) or travel by taxi. Those who are curious as to what a secondary forest looks like, or what erosion is, will find vivid examples of both of these along the way. After a journey of 1½ to 2 hours, which also takes one past small settlements and pepper gardens, the road ends in **Loa Janan** on the **Mahakam. Samarinda,** which lies on the other side of the river, can then be reached by ferry. This provincial capital lies in the delta of the Mahakam, which has a width of up to 4 kilometres/2½ miles and is navigable by sea-going vessels. The fact that Samarinda is a timber centre becomes clear when one notices that the river is full of meranti and kerung logs tied together to form rafts. They are processed in

the sawmills located on both sides of the river in the vicinity of the city. For **tourist information** in Samarinda, apply to: Kantor Parawisata, Jl. Batur 1.

Those who are not particularly interested in visiting Samarinda but would rather embark immediately on the **boat trip up the Mahakam** should take a car from Loa Janan to **Tenggarong,** 30 km/19 miles upriver. The **sultan's palace** that once stood here was then the oldest in existence. In 1936, the Dutch replaced it with the "substitute palace", but as the prince had twenty wives, his new abode soon became too small. Today, it is a **museum** (open Mon–Thurs 9:00 am–5:00 pm, Fri-Sun afternoons only). Tenggarong lies on the edge of the Kutai Basin, where the Mahakam forms a wide delta. In order to keep dry despite frequent flooding, the people here build their houses on stilts.

Many boats set sail from Tenggarong on the journey upriver. The cost of the trip is based on the speed of the boat. With a speed of up to 60 km/h (37 mph) and a fare of more than Rp 100,000 per day, the speed boats are not recommended for anyone travelling alone.

Ordinary boats need 18–20 hours for the trip to Muara Muntai; the speed boats do it in one-third of the time. **Muara Kaman,** on the right bank of the river, is presumed to be the site of the former centre of a kingdom established by the Hindu king, Mulawarman, in the 4th century A.D. The kingdom, which is thought to have had commercial ties with China and Arabia, probably survived into the 17th century. In Sebulu, a short distance beyond, there is a **rehabilitation centre** where **orang-utans** are prepared for their return to the wild.

The region surrounding the **Jempang Lake** is both fascinating and diverse. If one ends up with the slowest type of boat, the trip there could take more than two days; however, at leisurely speeds, one has a chance of seeing the freshwater dolphin, or ikan pesut, which can be found in the Mahakan as well as in the Jempang and **Semayang Lakes.** The lake region lies in the land of the **Benuak Dayaks.** The boat makes a stop in **Tanjung Isuy,** and then from **Melak,** a short distance further upriver, it is easy to reach the **Padang Luwai Nature Reserve,** which is 16 kilometres/ 10 miles away. Melak also has a small airstrip that is served by mission and charter airlines only. Most tourists come here hoping to meet a Dayak tribe and get an invitation to spend a night in a longhouse. Very few come for the **orchids** for which this reserve is famous. Those who are interested in the more than 70 species of orchids that grow here, however, should make the journey toward the end of the rainy season. The permit to visit Padang Luwai is obtainable at the PPA office in Bogor (West Java).

Many scenically rewarding outings can be made from Melak as well as from Tanjung Isuy. A recommended hike leads south-west from Melak to the picturesque village of **Barong Tongkok** which can be reached in a matter of four hours. After a night spent in one of the losmens there, the hike continues past Dayak villages and on to **Tering,** which lies on the river. This leg of the hike takes seven hours, excluding stops. **Longiram** lies an hour away from Tering, but can also be reached by boat from Tenggarong in two days. Those who imagined the Mahakam to be a great, untouched jungle river may be a little disappointed with what they will have seen, for up until now, the river will have been flanked by secondary forests and busy little Moslem communities – the logging companies and Malayan settlers staked their claim on this region decades ago. Those who want to advance on into Borneo's primordial heart will have to continue upriver to **Longbagun** – this is where the real adventure begins.

Between Longbagun and **Longpahangai,** comes the next important stop. There are three dangerous rapids which must be negotiated. The boats, which are necessarily smaller than those used on the lower course of the river, will have to be carried.

Dayak tribes living here include the **Bahau,** the **Modang** and the **Kenyah Dayaks;** missionaries have

The Chinese: A Powerful Minority

The Chinese presence in Indonesia goes back to colonial times when they were first brought in by the Dutch as plantation labourers. Their passion for gambling often cost them their wages, which were, by the way, intentionally paid out in advance. Hopelessly in debt, the "coolies", as they were called, were frequently reduced to serfdom. Later, thanks to their business know-how, they were recruited in large numbers to handle the retailing of colonial and European goods. From the onset, the Indonesians were at a disadvantage due to their general unfamiliarity with modern means of payment. Conditioned by Buddhism, Hinduism and Islam to see the calculation of interest as something evil and forbidden, they were not able to compete with the Chinese in the mercantile world. This socio-economic imbalance was further aggravated by the fact that the Chinese enjoyed many privileges in the class society of the Dutch East Indies. Before long, they were seen as an extension of the colonial apparatus. The privation endured by Indonesians in many areas of the land was often worsened by the merciless practices of many Chinese money-lenders, which, in most cases, met with the approval of the colonial administration. Sceptical of the Indonesian nationalist movement, the largely loyalist Chinese rejected and even opposed Indonesian independence. The former nationalist leaders, who today hold high posts in business, politics and the bureaucracy, have still not completely forgiven the Chinese for their former attitude.

Chinese entrepreneur, around 1890

Although about 60 per cent of the country's economy is controlled by the Chinese, this minority (3 per cent of the total population) still does not enjoy equal rights in Indonesia. They may not publish their own newspapers, run their own schools or form their own political parties. In addition, the "tiong hoa" residing in Indonesia must give up their Chinese citizenship as well as their Chinese names.

The government, however, is aware of the fact that the Chinese, who distinguish themselves as traders, shopkeepers, bankers, engineers, plantation owners and artisans, are indispensable to the Indonesian economy. What is usually ignored, however, is that they have also enriched this nation of many peoples with their own fascinating culture.

The Chinese in Indonesia, representing many different regions of their homeland, have concentrated themselves in certain provinces according to their ethnic origin. The Teochu, originally from the Chinese province of Swatow, live in East Sumatra and Riau where they specialize in market gardening and retailing. The Hakka people from the mountainous province of Kwangtung were originally employed in Dutch mines; now they live on the islands of Bangka and Biliton as well as in West Java and Kalimantan, where they are known as skilful tradespeople. The Hokkien Chinese, who are concentrated in West Sumatra and on the eastern islands of the republic, have distinguished themselves as merchants and traders. Many Chinese have become well integrated into Indonesian society through marriage or their work. These so-called peranakan Chinese have developed their own customs, their own cuisine and they even speak their own unique dialect.

The fact that differences still exist between the Indonesians and the Chinese became frightfully apparent after the attempted coup d'état on September 30th, 1965. In its violent aftermath, between 200,000 and 400,000 Chinese lost their lives. They were ostensibly accused of being communist agitators and instigators, but it was obvious that prejudice and envy played an important role. It is the hope of many today that the rising standard of living will succeed in starving out these negative human emotions.

been active among them for almost thirty years. Longpahangai is difficult to reach and the traveller cannot count on regular connections, but it is a very scenic area that lends itself to extensive hikes. Besides, from this point on, the river places no more obstacles in the way of the traveller – at least as far as rapids are concerned. During the dry season, the river can become so shallow that all traffic is forced to come to a halt, and when it rains, the water level in the upper reaches of the Mahakam can rise by several metres in a matter of a few minutes (non-swimmers beware!).

Having come this far, one should pause to reflect on the fact that Longpahangai lies a good 500 km/ 310 miles away from Tenggarong, the point of departure. Very few people are willing to take the hardships of such a journey upon themselves – a journey which, if the worst comes to the worst, can take more than a month. The scenery around the upper reaches of the river and the many opportunities for observing animals, however, are generous rewards for the effort spent. Those who are especially daring, however, can attempt to cross the entire island, but an undertaking of this nature should never be ventured on alone. A command of Bahasa Indonesia is also necessary for communicating with local guides. Those who reach the upper course of the Kapuas after having crossed the **Müller Range** can look back on a journey which lasted two months.

To get to know the real Borneo, one must journey to the upper-course of one of its major rivers: this doesn't only apply to the Mahakam. For instance, travelling up one of the rivers which flow together near Muara Kaman, a lot of territory has to be crossed before Dayak villages are sighted. It will be necessary to travel on the Sungai Telen via Muara Ancalong to Muara Wahau and to search the tributaries there as well. **Muara Wahau,** for example, is a village which can already boast more single family houses than long-houses. By the way, those who remembered to bring along a pan can try their luck sifting for gold in the **Sunga Telen.** In and around Muara Ancalong, **Punan** tribes-people can sometimes be spotted. These nomadic hunters and gatherers are shy and prefer to live in the darkness of the jungle. Attempts on the part of the government to get them to settle down have mostly failed – and when they did succeed, disease came along and undermined their efforts. The Punan are the true rulers of the island, for they are truly at home in the jungle. They can also be found along the rivers which flow into the sea near the island of Tarakan.

This oil island is connected to Samarinda and Balikpapan by air and to Pare Pare and Ujung Pandang by sea. From **Tarakan,** there are also boats going south to **Tanjung Selor,** which lies at the mouth of the **Sungei Kayan.** Boat trips on the Kayan as well as on the **Berau** take one into the territory of the Kenyah and Kayan tribes, whose societies are organized in classes. These tribes also still practise teeth-filing.

South Kalimantan – Kalimantan Selatan

The provincial capital of South Kalimantan, **Banjarmasin,** lies at the mouth of the **Barito River.** This city, which is criss-crossed by canals, is often called the Venice of Kalimantan. Here, an early-morning visit to the floating **Kuin Market** is especially worthwhile. Not far from here lies the **Pulau Kembang** in the Barito River. This island is inhabited by half-tame monkeys. Wild members of their species, on the other hand, can be found on the **Pulau Kaget,** five kilometres/3 miles away. The proboscis monkey – unique to Borneo – lives here on a 270-hectare/667 acre reserve. Not only Banjarmasin but virtually all of South Kalimantan lies in a swamp. This was once the domain of the **orang banjar** whose piracy made the mangrove-covered coasts unsafe until the mid–1950's. Today, the Banjar are ardent Moslems who go on pilgrimages to Mecca each year in droves.

It has already been mentioned that diamonds have been found in Southern Kalimantan; however, it is a little known fact that there is a small diamond market in the town of **Martapura** not far from Banjarmasin. Diamonds are found near the village of **Cempaka,** among other places, but most of them are sent abroad to be cut and processed as the necessary experience is lacking here. The diamond industry employs over 30,000 people. There are many shops in Banjarmasin offering precious and semi-precious stones at reasonable prices; those who plan to spend larger sums of money, however, ought to bring along some knowledge of gems.

Banjarmasin's airport (20 km or about 12½ miles from the city) can be reached from Jakarta, Semarang and Surabaya; Tarakan and Balikpapan are included in its air service time-table as well. Balikpapan can also be reached **overland** from Banjarmasin via **Rantau, Barabai** and **Tanjung.** If money is not an issue, it is best to take a jeep-taxi as they are designed to handle the rough terrain. The fare is twice the amount charged for other vehicles, but, especially in the rainy season, it is money well spent. Fascinating boat trips can be made on the **Barito** and **Kahayan** rivers which,

The **monsoons** determine the climate of the whole of South and South-East Asia. The word monsoon comes from the Arabic "mausim", meaning season.
On the left: South-East Monsoon – dry, prevails May to October.
On the right: West Monsoon – wet, prevails November to April.

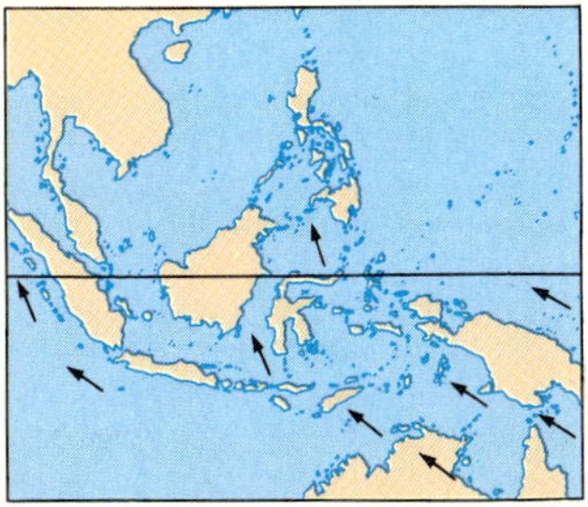

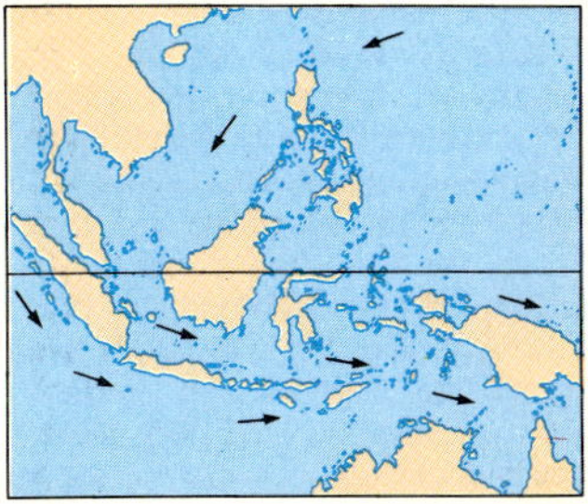

with their tributaries, form a dense river network that leads deep into the island's interior. Maps of the area are unreliable; only experienced boatmen make reliable navigators.

Central Kalimantan – Kalimantan Tengah

Central Kalimantan covers an area of 156,610 square kilometres/ 60,467 sq. miles and has a population of 850,000. The cultural diversity of its people and the natural splendour make this area a popular tourist region. Under Sukarno, the provincial capital of **Palangkaraya** was to have become the capital of the entire island. However, this project, which was designed to win prestige, was never completed. Palangkaraya has a surprisingly well-laid system of roads; only the Soviet-built, 35-kilometre-long highway ending in the jungle seems unnaturally long. The best route of access to Central Kalimantan is the **Barito River,** which is navigable for almost 750 kilometres/466 miles. The boat trip from Banjarmasin to Palangkaraya takes twenty hours; with the more expensive speed boats, however, the trip can be made in six to seven hours. Although the river route is far more interesting, there are also flights from Banjarmasin and Balikpapan to Palangkaraya.

West Kalimantan – Kalimantan Barat

Founded in 1771 by an Arab named Syarif Abdur and lying directly on the Equator, West Kalimantan's provincial capital, **Pontianak,** is the largest city on Borneo. A large portion of the province's almost 2.5 million people are descendents of Chinese people brought in at the beginning of the 18th century to work in the mines. Today, the province is the second-largest rubber producer after North Sumatra. Rubber plantations dot the banks of the 1,150 km/ 715 mile long Kapuas, the island's longest river. **Putussibau,** which lies 820 kilometres/509 miles inland, can be reached by boat in about one week to ten days (small aircraft also fly there).

There are **groups of Iban** living in West Kalimantan (mostly north of the Kapuas), but these people, who were at one time known as Sea Dayaks because of their coastal piracy, are primarily at home in **Sarawak.**

For foreigners, the only way into this Malaysian state is by plane – there are two flights weekly from Pontianak to **Kuching.** If you plan on spending a few days in Pontianak, you should pay a visit to imigrasi (immigration office) and the police; otherwise, they will pay a visit to you, in which case difficulties will have to be reckoned with.

Hotels in Kalimantan

Name/ Address	Price Group	No. of Rooms	With WC/Bath	Km to Airport	Km to Bus
East Kalimantan					
Balikpapan					
Balikpapan Hotel* Jl. Garuda 2 Balikpapan	4	33	33	–	–
Grand Park Hotel* Jl. Pangeran Antasari Balikpapan Tel. 2 29 41/2 29 42	3	37	37	15	10
Hotel Benakutai**** Jl. Pangeran Antasari Balikpapan Tel. 2 18 13/2 18 04	4	220	220	6	6
Tirta Plaza Jl. D. I. Panjaitan XX/5152 Balikpapan Tel. 2 23 24/2 23 64	3	29	29	–	–
Bahtera Jl. Gajah Mada SK 1347 Balikpapan	2	32	32	–	–
Kaltim Jl. Kampung Baru Tengah Balikpapan	1	18	–	–	–
Samarinda					
Mesra** Jl. Pahlawan 1 Samarinda Tel. 210 11/2 10 13/ 2 10 14	4	53	53	2	2
Lamin Indah* Jl. Bhayangkara Samarinda	3	18	18	–	–
Jakarta II Jl. Dewi Sartika 2 Samarinda Tel. 2 38 95	3	32	32	–	–
Sewarga Indah Jl. Jend. Sudirman 42 Samarinda Tel. 22 06/2 20 67	4	69	69	3	0.5
Tarakan					
Tarakan Plaza Jl. Yos Sudarso Tarakan Tel. 501/502/503	4	44	44	4	–
Wisata Jl. Jend. Sudirman 46 Tarakan Tel. 221	2	22	22	–	–
South Kalimantan					
Banjar Baru					
Loktabat* Jl. Ahmad Yani (km 33.5) Banjar Baru Tel. 28 03 84	2	30	30	7	7
Anggrek Jl. Ahmad Yani Banjar Baru Tel. 64	2	19	19	7	7
Hotel Banjarbaru Jl. Ahmad Yani Banjar Baru	1	25	25	7	7
Banjarmasin					
New River City* Jl. Martadinata 3 Banjarmasin Tel. 29 83	3	48	48	25	1
Sempaga* Jl. Mayjen. Sutoyo S-292 Banjarmasin Tel. 24 30/27 53	2	25	25	25	5

Anda Jl. Letjen. Suprapto Banjarmasin Tel. 20 06	2	11	11	25	1
Rahmat Jl. A. Yani 9 Banjarmasin Tel. 43 22/44 29	2	41	41	25	–
Sewarga Jl. Cempaka 1/No. 2 Banjarmasin	3	17	17	25	6
Central Kalimantan					
Palangkaraya Salendra Jl. Halmahera 42 Palangkaraya Tel. 213 92	2	13	–	1	3
Virgo Jl. A. Yani 78 Palangkaraya Tel. 212 65	3	21	–	2	2
Muara Teweh Barito Muara Teweh	3	12	–	–	1
Gunung Sintuk Muara Teweh	2	–	–	–	–
Sampit Beringin Sampit	2	–	–	–	–
Faisal Sampit	2	–	–	–	–
Mutiara Sampit	2	12	–	7	–
West Kalimantan					
Pontianak Dharma* Jl. Imam Bonjol Pontianak Tel. 47 59	4	56	56	17	2
Orient Jl. Tanjungpura Pontianak Tel. 26 50	3	67	67	17	1
Pontianak City Hotel Jl. Pak Kasih Pontianak Tel. 24 96	3	16	16	18	0.7
Ketapang Pasifik Jl. Merdeka selatan Ketapang Tel. 66	3	11	–	5	–
Singkarang Kalbar Komplek Pasar	2	33	33	145	0.5
Palapa Jl. Ismail Tahir Singkarang Tel. 234	2	37	37	145	2

Sulawesi

Owing not only to its unique scenic beauty, but also to the fascinating culture of its people, as shown by the ornate design of their dwellings and their colourful ceremonies and celebrations, Sulawesi has quickly become a popular destination for travellers to Indonesia. The fourth-largest of the Indonesian islands measures 227,654 sq. km/87,897 sq. miles and has roughly 11 million inhabitants. Sulawesi still frequently appears in atlases under the name "Celebes", which comes from Ponto dos Celebes (Place of the Infamous), the name the Portuguese sea-farers gave the island because of the many pirates they encountered here. The bizarre shape of this island, which is often compared to an orchid because of the arrangement of its peninsulas, endows it with an extremely long coastline, which provided shelter to countless pirates up until the close of the 19th century. The island is divided into the provinces – North, Central, South and East Sulawesi with the capital cities of Manado, Palu, Ujung Pandang and Kendari.

Presently under construction, Sulawesi's network of roads does not yet offer any through overland routes. Those who wish to travel from Ujung Pandang in the south to Manado in the north will find it necessary to go part of the way by plane or boat. Some of the roads shown on the maps actually exist only on the drawing board. Only in the areas that have been developed for tourism, namely, the south with Toraja Land and the north with its diving centers, are there adequate traffic routes. For a visit to the less-frequented central and eastern provinces, time and a working knowledge of Indonesian is necessary. Accommodation there is only suitable for lovers of the outdoors, for whom the land and the people are more important than comfort. While the southern and eastern provinces are marked by dry climate and covered with savannahs, there are vast rainforests in the central and northern parts of the island, where the vegetation shows a clear resemblance to that of the eastern Indonesian islands. Sulawesi's fauna includes a number of species which can be found nowhere else in the world, for example, the babirusa (a small wild boar), the anoa (dwarf buffalo) and the makaken (small but gorilla-like). The coral reefs which lie off the island's spectacular sandy coasts provide shelter to a dense and diverse marine population; those in North Sulawesi, in particular, attract many divers. The interior is predominantly mountainous (the 3,450-metre/11,318′ high **Rantekombola** is the island's highest elevation). While only the craters of long-dead volcanoes remain in the south, active volcanism affects the north, where geysers, solfataras and stratum volcanoes dominate the scenery.

The island is inhabited by a host of indigenous tribes such as the Bugis, the Makassans, the Torajas, and the Seku, Loinang, Rongkang, Balantak, Minahasa, Mori, Muna, Wana and Toala tribes. At the time of their discovery toward the end of the last century, the Toalas were still living a Stone-Age existence. Now, most of the tribes, the most well-known being the Bugis and the proto-Malayan Toraja, live somewhere between the Neolithic and the Bronze Ages, although signs of the "plastic age" are also evident.

South Sulawesi

Ujung Pandang, the capital of the province of South Sulawesi, can be reached direct from Jakarta and Denpasar on one of the many flights daily to Hassanudin Airport, 20 km/12 miles outside the city. As the island's largest and most important port and centre of trade, the city also offers good boat connections to Kalimantan, the Moluccan Islands and Irian. The many fortress ruins of Ujung Pandang, which is known in the history books as Makassar, stand as reminders of the city's once heavily contended position. The city, which was once a stronghold of the kings of Gowa, was conquered by the Dutch admiral, Cornelius Speermann, in 1667. Its fortifications (renamed **Fort Rotterdam** by the Dutch) can still be visited today. Prince Diponegoro, who led the people's uprising in Java from 1825 to 1830, died here in exile. His tomb is located on the street named after him. The museum that has been established inside the fort, features outstanding Chinese porcelain and unique musical instruments. At the beginning of this century, a further fortification, **Fort Ujung Pandang,** was built by Sultan Aladdin.

This city, which presently has 750,000 inhabitants, has been growing by leaps and bounds in the past few years. New districts with wide avenues, hotels and administration buildings have sprung up in the vicinity of the pier, just outside the old town centre, whose colonial-style buildings date from the 17th and 18th centuries. Although people of many different ethnic groups are to be found in this city, the Bugis and Makassans predominate. Characteristic of the Bugis are their schooners, which can be seen in the hundreds lying in anchor in **Paotere Harbour.** These vessels, which measure up to 30 metres/98′ in length and 12 metres/39′ in breadth, are still used for the bulk of the cargo traffic between the islands. One of the city's landmarks is the **lighthouse** near the harbour which is over one hundred years old. The combined **orchid garden/seashell museum** on Jl. Mochta Lufti 15A is also worth visiting. Several other tourist attractions lie in the environs of the city. In the museum at **Sungguminasa,** 8 km/5 miles from Ujung Pandang, the crown of the Gowa kings is displayed. The remains of the former **Sultan's Palace,** as well as a number of interesting tombs dating from this period, are, to some extent, well preserved.

For those drawn to the water, there are several islands lying off the western coast of South Sulawesi that can be easily reached from Ujung Pandang. Island-bound vessels, which usually have to be chartered, depart from a quay near **Wisma Ria.** Worth visiting are **Lia Lia** and **Boletambu** and **Samalona. Kayangan** is not as interesting but can be seen on a stop-over to Boletambu. For a visit to these islands, an early start is necessary. Boletambu, whose inhabitants are fishermen by trade, is excellent for snorkling and swimming. On this small, circular island, the arrival of a stranger is treated as a major event. Tourists will find themselves constantly pursued by the curious and friendly eyes of the islanders, for whom they are a rare sight. Even the collecting of shells can quickly turn into a general celebration. The shells found may not all be perfect specimens, but they will certainly be difficult to carry home! Live specimens should be avoided, though. As a result of the lively trade in seashells, which have become a popular souvenir, many species are in danger of becoming extinct.

For those who would rather not take a boat trip, there is a lovely beach near **Barombong,** 20 km/12 miles south of Ujung Pandang, which, however, is quite crowded at the weekends. Bantimurang, a nature reserve located 40 km/25 miles from Ujung Pandang, can be reached by way of Maros. During the rainy season, a visit here is especially recommended because of the butterflies, present in large numbers at this time. Other interesting sights include a waterfall and stalactite caverns. For those who choose to stay awhile, accommodation is simple but good.

The village of **Cikorok,** situated 800 metres/2,625′ above sea level, enjoys a pleasant, high-altitude climate. The small, clean guest houses here encourage an extended stay. Market-day is twice a week in nearby **Malina.** Scattered tribes of hunters and gatherers, which show evidence of the culture of the ancient Veddoid people, still live in the south-eastern portion of the peninsula. The government is making an effort to settle these semi-nomadic Toala people. The port of **Pare Pare,** near which lies the shipbuilding town of **Pallingo,** is on the road that leads to Toraja Land. This is where the Buginese schooners are built. From Pare Pare, ships sail almost daily to eastern Kalimantan.

Toraja Land (Tana Toraja)

At present, the Toraja highlands, 340 kilometres/211 miles north of Ujung Pandang, can only be reached after a seven to ten hour bus ride; in future, however, a small airport near Makale should eliminate the hardships of this journey. Because of the truly spectacular scenery along the way, one should travel there (or back) during the day. Deep gorges, mountain slopes covered with sparse vegetation, rice fields, rainforests, coastal swamps overgrown with nipa palms and cockpit karst are just a few examples of what the ever-changing landscape has to offer along the way. **Makale** and **Rantepao** are the two main centres here. The latter is especially well-situated: from here, many tourist sites can be reached on foot. A wide range of accommodation – from losmens to simple tourist hotels – is available here, but during the months of June, July and August, and later, in December and January, beds can become scarce.

Of the 700,000 Torajas, approximately 50 per cent are Christian, while only 5 per cent are Moslem. The remainder are followers of **Aluk Todolo,** a cult based on ancestor worship. Remarkable-looking buildings with curved roofs covered with bamboo shingles characterize Toraja villages, where dwellings and granaries stand side by side. Perfectly symmetrical patterns are carved on the building-fronts and painted black, red, yellow and white.

The cult of ancestor worship forms the centre of the spiritual and cultural life of the Torajas, for whom only the hereafter has significance. Their strong sense of identity has led them to consolidate Buddhist, Hindu, Islamic and Christian influences into one syncretic religion in which the creator-god Puang Matua plays the central role. Birth, death and burial are the most important events in the rather unreal lives of the Torajas. Funeral rites are precisely defined. After being embalmed and wrapped, and bound into a bundle, the body of the deceased is laid out in his home. The soul of the deceased is believed to remain alive until all religious rites – including the slaughtering of buffalos and pigs – have been carried out. Depending on one's status in the multi-level Torajan caste system, the number of animals sacrificed could range from one or two, to several hundred. The meat of these offerings is later distributed according to traditional custom. The deceased, accompanied by the spirits of the sacrificial animals, arrives in **puya,** the hereafter, where he is elevated to the status of half-god. At the end of the festive funeral celebration, characterized by dancing, bull fights and communal feasting, the body is buried in a grave hewn out of a cliff. If the deceased was a member of the nobility, a life-sized wooden image is carved to house his soul and to protect the living from evil spirits. These statues (tau tau) are placed in niches below the burial ground, from where their rigid, often expressionless faces gaze out over the vast countryside. The graves at **Lemo, Londa** and **Kete Kusu** are considered the most outstanding, and are therefore the most frequented. After burial, the actual mourning period begins. Close family members are forbidden to eat rice for ten days. Strangers are welcome guests at Torajan celebrations, which always include an abundance of food and drink. The most popular alcoholic beverage in Toraja Land is a wine made from the fermented juice of the **enau** palm. Here on Sulawesi, it is called **balok;** in other parts of the country, **tuak.**

Those who get the opportunity to attend a Torajan funeral should bring along a little something for the host (tobacco, cigarettes, a pound of rice). In this case, the giving of gifts is not an objectionable tourist vice, but rather, it is customary practice. One should also avoid making derogatory comments when witnessing the slaughter of a buffalo. The death of these animals (usually brought about by the thrust of a sword or a lance) marks the end of a normal and active life spent in the company of caring human beings. The death of an animal in one of our slaughterhouses, on the other hand, is nothing more than the technologically programmed termination of a purely utilitarian existence spent vegetating in the undignified imprisonment of a stockade.

The extraordinary physical splendour of the Toraja highland alone makes the long journey there worthwhile. For those not interested in paying only a cursory visit to the Tana Toraja and its people, a longer stay than the customary three to four days will be necessary. Currently, most tourists just "drop by" for a short visit from Bali, in which case it is no wonder that many of its cultural and physical highpoints are overlooked. The rarely-visited mountain village of Batutumonga, for instance, should definitely be included in one's itinerary. This village, which lies 20 km/74 miles away from Rantepao, and can be reached on foot in four to five hours, or by jeep over a rocky road in two, offers a fantastic view of the surrounding mountains and valleys which is particularly

Torajan houses decorated with buffalo horns; the horns which come from sacrificed bulls indicate the wealth of the owner.

breathtaking at dawn. The house of the village teacher functions as a sort of tourists' inn with the kindly manner of its host more than making up for its lack of comfort. Apart from its magnificent surroundings, however, the village itself is uninteresting, but if one rises before sun-rise and heads west toward Lokomata, one can witness a spectacle of colours so lavish that it can by all means compete with the sunrise over Mt. Bromo. Those who have carried along a tripod up until now will be glad they did! The road to Lokomata (3 kilometres/1¾ miles away) leads past a valley whose slopes are covered with rice terraces and dotted with gigantic monoliths, one of which houses the cliffside graves of Lokomata. A sacrificial clearing surrounded by menhirs can be found in a small bamboo grove not far from this huge block of stone. On the slopes of Gunung Sesean, which appears on the right-hand side of the road as one continues on to Pangala, lie many traditional Toraja settlements which are accessible only on foot. Surrounded by bamboo thickets, they can hardly be spotted from a distance, but the dull rumble of the rice crushers heard mornings and evenings allows them to be pinpointed.

In the vicinity of Pangala, which is already quite off the beaten track, there are a number of interesting Toraja villages whose inhabitants have re-embraced their ancient religion (aluk todolo). From here, you can hike to Mamasa by way of Awan, Bolokan and Bittung (which can also be reached from Makale), or you can return in one day's time to Rantepao by way of Lolai. A travel permit (surat jalan) is required for excursions around Mamasa, and it is advisable to take along a guide: unlike Rantepao and Makale, hardly any English is spoken here, and there are neither hotels nor losmens. As the local people always bring along a gift for the chief or elder of a village in which they spend a night away from home (usually as the guests of the chief), the foreign traveller who plans a similar venture should stock up well on tobacco, cigarettes, rice, sweets (still the opiate of young and old), batteries or other suitable items. In order not to be mistaken for Santa Claus, one should avoid presenting the gifts personally; instead, one should place them conspicuously out of sight, and then change the subject. It is better not to wait for a word of thanks – your host has already been embarrassed enough.

Those who are not very good walkers and prefer to take the jeep to Batutumonga, Lokomata and Pangala should stop in the village of Palawa along the way. It is located just beyond the turn-off to Pangala and is one of the loveliest village complexes in Torajaland. For a small fee, you can spend the night in the chief's house, which is located in the older, elevated part of the town. Those interested in Torajan weaving should visit the village of Sadan, 4 kilometres/2½ miles north of Palawa. The prices charged for woven fabrics here are far below those charged in the souvenir shops of Rantepao.

Torajaland's most celebrated tourist attractions can be found south of Rantepao: the cliffside graves of Londa, for instance, which are guarded by wooden images called tau tau, are located 6 kilometres/3¾ miles away. Before proceeding to Londa, however, one can stop at Keté Kesu, which is on the road to Sullukang. Directly behind this village, which is known for its woodcarvings, there is a gravesite under an overhanging cliff whose tau tau figures (among the most magnificent in all Torajaland) can be viewed from as close as one metre away. The remains of decoratively carved wooden coffins said to be 400 years old lie scattered about as well. Those tourists who once thought they had found a goldmine of souvenirs here (including life-size tau tau figures from Londa) ended up having to appease the spirits of the desecrated site by sacrificing a buffalo and a pig – the financial means to this end had to be cabled from home.

As the gravesites of the Torajas are also sites of ancestor worship, one should behave there as one would in any cemetery: with reverence and consideration. This applies to the gravesite at Londa as well, which is located at the foot of a steep limestone wall. Here, there is a beautiful group of tau tau figures lined up on a wooden balcony. Little children earn pocket money by providing tourists with torches or petroleum lamps for their visit to the neighbouring catacombs. In one of the smaller ones, a pair of lovers lie buried – lovers who committed suicide in answer to the irrefragable adat rules prohibiting marriages between aristrocrats and commoners. Old, beautifully-worked wooden coffins lie in the shadow of an overhanging rock. (The afternoon is the best time for taking pictures of Londa). Lemo, 5 kilometres/3 miles further down the road to Makale, is probably the most famous and most photographed burial site in Tana Toraja. Life-size statues of the dead stand in galleries hewn out of a 60–70 metre/37–43′ high face of rock. Although in a motionless pose, some of them appear very lifelike. This and the other burial sites mentioned are still in use today, as can be seen by the caves now being painstakingly hewn out of the rock. Those with more time at their disposal should explore the area around Lemo's burial sites: enormous expanses of karst, beautifully patterned rice fields, bizarre rock formations and picturesque villages all add to the fancifulness of this landscape. Amateur photographers are not the only ones who will have a field day here.

Those who feel the desire to take a cool dip in a pool should repair to Tilanga, 10 kilometres/6 miles southeast of Rantepao, where there is a natural swimming-hole fed by a clear mountain stream. On the way to Tilanga, you pass the village of Sullukang, which despite its many objects of interest (menhirs, ancestor images, and burial caves) is seldom visited by tourists. The large festival grounds or rante which are used for princely funerals are also little known. Those who leave Rantepao in the direction of Makale will notice the many make–shift but richly decorated Toraja houses just outside the city limits. They are used to accommodate the thousands of funeral guests. Special notice should be paid to the giant menhirs in the centre of the festival grounds – how old they actually are has never been exactly determined. Those who leave Rantepao and head east to Palopo will pass through expansive bamboo and evergreen forests. Torajan culture is prevalent in this region as well.

Larger and busier than Rantepao, Makale is another good base for excursions in Tana Toraja – large tour operators, in particular, prefer this village because of its wider choice of accommodation. Both villages have interesting markets which take place once every six days – Rantepao's pasar is, however, more traditional.

Bantukalando, located between Makale and Sangalla, boasts of a king's palace and a rante. Some of its residents are well-versed in the traditional art of weaving and are happy to demonstrate their abilities. More palaces can be found near Kandora (5 kilometres/3 miles from Makale). The ruins of Puan Marinding, located 8 kilometres/5 miles south of Mengendek, as well as many other tangible reminders of former times, are shunned by the local people during the twilight hours. Tourists, on the other hand, usually stay away because of their remoteness. The hot springs at Makula (near Buntukalando) will be a welcome sight to those who are exploring Torajaland on foot!

South-East Sulawesi

The south-eastern province would hardly be known were it not for the Kendari gold and silver jewellry produced there: experts agree that the skill and dexterity of the silversmiths here far surpasses that of the craftsmen in Yogyakarta. Filigree work spun from silver threads whose delicacy comes close to that of cobwebs never ceases to amaze local and foreign visitors alike. One of the economic cornerstones of this province, whose capital carries the name of the craft which made it famous, is agriculture, which is highly productive thanks to the fertility of the soil. Rainfall, however, is not always abundant because this part of Sulawesi is affected by the dry climate of Australia. The economic impact of South-East Sulawesi's nickel deposits, which are presently being exploited under the supervision of the Americans and the Japanese, has been felt far beyond its provincial borders.

Tourism is only just being developed in South-East Sulawesi, but the region's vast cultural diversity is instrumental in spurring on its growth. In addition to the various ethnic groups living in the peninsula's interior, there is a coastal people who deserve special attention. The Bajau, or "sea gypsies", live from, with, and on the sea and have very little to do with the land; they differ from the region's other ethnic groups in language (they speak Samal dialects) and way of life. The estimated 35,000–40,000 Bajau live in villages scattered throughout the southern Philippines, in north-eastern Borneo, in northern and eastern Sulawesi as well as in many parts of eastern Indonesia. Their settlements in South-East Sulawesi can usually be found either on remote coasts or near Bugis' settlements along the Gulf of Bone, the Straits of Tioro and Butung, on the island of Wowoni and along the Kendari Bay and northward to the Salabangka Islands. Whether a settlement consists of a collection of boats or a group of thatch-roofed stilt dwellings, the lives of its inhabitants remain closely linked to the sea. Because they consider the meat of land-dwelling animals to be unclean, the Bajau eat only fish and vegetables; not being farmers themselves, they barter a portion of their catch for agricultural products. Trade relations between the people living inland and the Bajau have not always been as free from difficulties as they are now: although the Bajau are nominal Moslems, their neighbours consider them to be heathens.

Nowadays, the government is trying to encourage them to give up their nomadic way of life. Their day-to-day life, however, does not follow the calendar, but rather, the phases of the moon. Many Bajau do not even know what year it is, or how old they are. They live according to the demands of the sea: if a swarm of fish is sighted or only just presumed to be in the vicinity, the villages come alive, regardless of the time of day.

Kendari, the capital of the south-eastern province, can be reached by Merpati Airlines or Garuda Airways from Jakarta and Surabaya via Ujung Pandang. An alternative way to get there is to take a ferry from Bone or Palopo (both in South Sulawesi) to Kaloko, from where there are buses to the capital.

Central Sulawesi

Palu, the capital of Central Sulawesi, can be reached from Ujung Pandang by Merpati Airlines. Tourists are still a rarity in this town of 43,000 inhabitants, and the ones who do show up are usually on their way to Manado or Poso by plane, or are waiting for a boat to Kalimantan.

Most visitors who come to Central Sulawesi do so on account of Lake Poso. Coming from Torajaland by way of Palopo and Wotu, one can reach Pendolo on the southern tip of the lake by means of a brand-new road which has only recently been completed. The 1,400 metre/4,593'-deep lake surrounded by rainforest, lies in the heart of a region which is also inhabited by Torajas, whose culture, however, differs from that of the Torajas of South Sulawesi. Interesting hikes can be made in the vicinity of the lake: one may catch a glimpse of a babirusa, or, with a little luck, even encounter an anoa, a rare dwarf buffalo. Boats ply regularly between Pendolo and Tentena on the northern tip of the lake; from there, the 60 kilometres/37 miles to

Poso take three hours by bus. Three additional lakes in the south-eastern part of Central Sulawesi are also worth visiting; these three, Lakes Matana, Towuti and Mahalona, can be reached from Malili on Bone Bay. The best way to get to Malili is by boat from Palopo or Wotu, as the overland connections are rather poor. The boat from Palopo takes about eight hours. Malili is the headquarters of a mining company which works a nickel mine in Soroaka on Lake Matana. Soroako now has its own airstrip, but it is served mostly by Merpati charters. Most vehicles which run between Lakes Matana and Towati belong to the mining company, so that those who prefer not to walk, will have to hitch a ride. The sight of the many foreigners here (employees of the mining company) can give the newcomer the impression that this is a booming tourist zone. In reality, however, this lake district is very remote: isolated groups of proto-Malayan peoples live here, of whom very little is known. What is known, however, is that their number is steadily decreasing as a result of outside influences. The way of life of the Tobela, for instance, – a tribe indigenous to the districts north-east of Malili and around Lake Matana – has lost much of its original character. This region is nevertheless worth visiting. The following excerpt from the travel diary of a German explorer who travelled through Central Sulawesi in September of 1911 may serve as encouragement: "At last, the road began to descend. Imagining the lake behind every bend in the road, I crossed a ridge with hurried steps. Suddenly, Lake Matana lay before me, sparkling in the most splendid shade of azure blue. This singularly beautiful landscape of a lake with many inlets, framed by a magnificent range of mountains, elicited from me a cry of joy: the sight of the lake beckoning from out of the depths of the valley – a sight beheld by not quite a half a dozen Europeans before me – signified the fulfilment of a long-cherished, unavowed hope and desire and, at the same time, sealed the success of my travels in Celebes." – Prof. A. Grubauer.

As far as the lack of accommodation in this area is concerned, not much has changed since those days. For many Americans employed by the mining company, however, a visitor from the civilised world is a welcome change of pace.

North Sulawesi

The smallest of Sulawesi's four provinces covers some 25,786 sq. km or an area of 9,956 sq. miles and is divided into the districts of Minahasa, Bolaang Mongondow, Gorontalo and the Sangir-Talaud Islands, whose culture differs very much from that of the three mainland districts. The province extends over a portion of the northern peninsula that is mostly no more than 50 kilometres/31 miles across, but is more than 500 kilometres/310 miles long.

Beautiful and diversified, North Sulawesi has something for everyone. Hissing volcanoes, hot springs, white, sandy beaches that seem to go on for ever, green and blue lakes, virgin rainforests sheltering a unique animal kingdom, friendly, open people with a love of colourful celebrations. And there are the world-renowned sea gardens of Bunaken, Manado Tua, Mantehage and Siladen. These are just a few of the many attractions this region has to offer. Sulawesi Utara is not completely unknown in international diving circles – the Nusantara Diving Club as well as other newly-established diving centres report interest from all over the world. Therefore, it goes without saying, that stringent regulations are necessary for the protection of the marine world here. Divers, for instance, must obtain a diving permit before going off on their own. In addition to diving enthusiasts from France, many Japanese and even Australians (who have the matchless Barrier Reef just outside their door) come to Manado, the provincial and commercial capital of North Sulawesi, to pursue their hobby. The city has a clean and neat appearance. Poverty and class distinctions seem to be non-existent here, which cannot be said for other parts of the republic. As Indonesia's top producer of copra (17,000–19,000 tons a month) and an important supplier of cloves, North Sulawesi has been able to provide the financial basis for its own industrial development. Most of its people are Christians and very open to Western ways. Western attire, which has largely replaced traditional dress, reflects an aspect of the Manadoan character which has made the local women famous throughout Indonesia. The women from Manado are ranked no. 2 in the "Top Ten" ratings of suitable brides. Their rivals, the women of Solo occupy first place. Here as everywhere else, on the other hand, the qualities of the husbands seem to be beyond discussion.

Europeans first came to North Sulawesi in the 16th century. The Portuguese and, later, the Spanish, operating from the Philippines, brought Catholicism to the Minahasa people of the region. At the end of the 18th century, however, not long after the Dutch had established themselves here, Protestantism began to spread and the majority of the people converted to the new religion. The cooperation between the Minahasa and their colonial masters was so successful that after Indonesia became independent, it took a while for the Minahasans to accustom themselves to the new political reality. At the end of the 1950's, when a rebellion against the central government broke out in North Sumatra, Sulawesi's northern province followed suit. Bombs over the capital city of Manado were Jakarta's way of warning the renegades.

Today, approximately 200,000 people live in the city. While life in Sulawesi's other towns and villages comes to a standstill at sundown, Manado by night is a place of lively social activity. Excellent Chinese and seafood restaurants, offer many opportunities to eat well at low prices. Aside from its cheerful and pleasant atmosphere, however, Manado has nothing of special interest to offer.

The city can be reached from many different directions: part of Indonesia's domestic air-network, it can be reached by plane from Jakarta or Surabaya via Ujung Pandang, as well as from Bakikpapan and Banjarmasin. Although Manado is officially a gateway to and from the Philippines, regular flights are still rare. Bouraq and Merpati fly to Davao on south-eastern Mindanao only when the need arises. As the government of the predominantly Catholic Philippines has been waging a war against separatist Moslem rebels on this large island to the south for many years now, they regard any traffic between Mindanao and the Islamic neighbouring states of Indonesia and Malaysia with some suspicion. Moslem groups in these two countries do provide their rebellious fellow-believers with weapons; as a rule, however, they are smuggled in on copra and fishing boats from Borneo and Sulawesi. Ships in the territorial waters of the southern Philippine Islands are subjected to strict controls at the hands of the local authorities. This is why adventure trips which take the form of inofficial border crossings on smuggling vessels, can all too easily end with a spell spent in a Philippine jail. Mention should be made of the plane connections from Manado to Gorontalo on the southern coast of the northern peninsula, to the Sangir Talaud Islands, and the twice weekly connection to Ternate in the North Moluccas. The port of Bitung, east of Manado, offers boat connections to Java, Kalimantan, the North Moluccas and Irian. Information on prices and time-tables can be obtained in Bitung from:
Pelni Lines, Jl. Suprapto, Tel. 23 71;
Sriwijaya Lines, Jl. Kol. Soegijono, Tel. 29 41;
Gesuri Lloyd, Jl. Tikala 1, Tel. 26 67.
Buses running between Manado and the port take about one hour; bemos take a little longer. Both buses and bemos leave from the bus terminal at Jenkie Market in Manado.

Many interesting excursions can be made in the immediate and not-so-immediate vicinity of the provincial capital. The mountain village of Tomohon has a pleasant, windy, climate and many low-priced losmens which might encourage you to extend your stay. Mt. Lokon, an active volcano which forms the backdrop to this village, can be climbed from here without any problem, but it is advisable to take along a local guide. And do remember that volcanoes emit poisonous gases. Volcanism is also the reason for all the hot springs in this region: the best known thermal waters can be found at Kinilow and Lahendong, a few kilometres from Tomohon. An attempt is being made in North Sulawesi to harness the heat of the earth's interior – heat which often reaches the earth's surface here – for energy production. In the case of these geothermal projects, water is piped into the glowing-hot lower stratum, thus producing steam, which is then used to power turbines.

In Tara Tara, 30 kilometres/ 18½ miles south of Manado, Minahasan dancing is fostered and cultivated. Every Sunday afternoon at 3 o'clock, performances are held in which sometimes more than 200 dancers and musicians participate. In addition to the Maenqket, the Cakalele, a war dance also common to the Moluccas, is performed, while the kolintang, a Minahasan orchestra composed of bamboo instruments, provides the accompaniment. The 400 years of Minahasan culture shine through every dance step and every resonant tone produced by this orchestra. For a fee, the chief of Tara Tara can also arrange smaller performances during the week.

Those who are interested in Minahasan culture will find that, besides dance performances and century old stone sarcophagi, there is not much else to discover. These oddly-formed stone coffins, in which the dead were once buried in a seated position along with weapons, jewellery and Chinese porcelain, have a square base and a lid shaped like a Chinese temple. The most beautiful warugas, as they are called, can be found at Airmadidi; some can be found at Kema and Sawangan as well, but these are not quite as well-preserved. Although the Minahasans saw the warugas as the dwelling-place of their ancestors, some could not resist the temptation to plunder them. Today, these tombs, which for the most part contain the remains of former leaders, are held in veneration by the people. The provincial museum, located on Jl. Ki Hajar Dewantara in Manado, has interesting exhibits of Minahasan artifacts as well as rare objects from the Portuguese, Spanish and Dutch colonial periods.

The village of Pinabetengan, 50 km/31 miles from Manado in the district of Tompaso, holds great significance for the Minahasa people. A few kilometres outside the village, there is a stone block covered with mysterious characters and script which have never been deciphered. According to Minahasan lore, the batu (stone) of Pinabetengan marks the spot where the forefathers divided their territory between their descendants in order to secure peace for northern Sulawesi. The Minahasa people were thus divided into the following eight tribes: Tombulu, Tounsawang, Tonsea, Ponosaken, Toulour, Bantik, Pasan Ratahan and Tountaboan.

Despite the fact that the Minahasans were not opposed to Dutch colonial rule (as has already been mentioned), two of the most celebrated Indonesian freedom fighters lie buried in Sulawesi Utara – both of them, however, died here in exile. One of them was Imam Bonjol, who led the resistance in West Sumatra. After an almost 30-year struggle, he died in exile in Pineleng, 8 km/5 miles from Manado, in 1837. His sarcophagus is shaped like the Minangkabau dwellings of West Sumatra. The Javanese national hero, Kiay Mojo, whose supporters followed him into exile, lies buried in Kampung Jawa. This village, which is located near Tondano, is said to be inhabited by the descendants of these resistance fighters. The anniversary of his death is observed every year in festive fashion. One of the most famous celebrations – and one which attracts viewers from all over Indonesia and abroad – is the Toa Peh Kong, which dates from the 14th century and is celebrated by the Chinese of North Sulawesi. This spectacle, which takes place every year in the middle of February, two weeks after Chinese New Year, includes parades, dance and theatre performances and demonstrations of traditional forms of self-defence. Hotel reservations are recommended. The Confucian temple of Klenteng Ban Hian Kiong is located on Jl. Panjaitan in Manado's Chinatown. This building, which was originally constructed in the earlier part of the last century, was rebuilt by the Chinese residents of the quarter, in 1974. Many Chinese temples were destroyed during the political disturbances of 1965, but only a few have since been reconstructed. In many cases, the rubble was used for the construction of housing.

For the most part, rubble is all that remains of the period of colonial conquests as well. While the ruins of a 16th-century Portuguese fort can be found in Kema, there are traces of the Dutch in Kawarukan. During the last war, even the Japanese had entrenched themselves here. Many of these places are steeped in legend. The village of Airmadidi (air mendidi = boiling water), for instance, is supposed to have been frequented by nine angels who came here to bathe on nights with a full-moon. As so often happens, a demon stole the clothes of one of the angels, who was then forced to spend the rest of his life as a mortal on earth; thus, the inhabitants of this village see themselves as the descendants of a celestial being. The people who live around Lake Tondano (600 metres/1,968′ above sea level) have similar stories to tell. This lake, which is located 30 kilometres/19 miles south of Manado, can be reached by bus via Tomohon. Accommodation in the form of losmens are available in several of the villages scattered about the lakeside. Eris and Tandengan are both tourist resorts which are frequented by local people at the weekend. The coast is a better bet for those who want to do some swimming, though. Near Tanawangko and Tombariri, 18 kilometres/11 miles from Manado, lies the "white, sandy beach" of Tasik Ria. This well-known weekend resort offers boats for hire, as well as the opportunity to go waterskiing.

Near the port of Bitung lies the Tangkoko Batuangus Nature Reserve – a must for all nature lovers. A visitors permit can be obtained without any problem from the PPA (Perlindungan dan Pengawetan Alam – office of conservation) in Manado. As wild animals are to be found here in large numbers the patient observer is sure to make some interesting encounters. Anoas, hornbills, black makakens, maleos, deer, wild boar and marsupials are only a few of the unique species that can be found in this park. Unfortunately, however, the practice of illegal expropriation of parklands has placed their survival in jeopardy. The measures taken to protect the marine-gardens are, in many areas, inadequate as well, but in view of the fact that divers have distin-

Brief description of North Sulawesi's best-known diving centres:

Location	Diving Conditions	Marine Fauna	Current/Temp.	Comments
Bunaken (island)	Reef extends down 90 m/295′ visibility up to 50 m/164	Varied coral growth; countless species of coaral; hawksbill turtles; ocean fishes.	Weak to moderately strong; ± 24° C/75° F	Inhabited island; ideal for swimming; western part covered with mangroves; approx. 30 min. from Malalayang/ Manado.
Manado tua (island)	Some gaps in the coral growth; reef extends down 60 m/197′; visibility 40–50 m/ 131–164′	Diversity of fishes not as great as off the coast of Bunaken.	Weak to slight; ± 25° C/77° F	Inhabited; inactive volcano; from a hill there is a fantastic view of the islands and the mainland. Near the beach the sea is too shallow for swimming; danger of injury due to sharp corals; approx. 35 min. from Manado.
Mantehage (island)	Formation of reefs less pronounced; visibility 35–40 m. (115–131′)	Sharks, barracudas and other large fishes; dolphins.	Slight; ± 24° C/75° F	Coast covered with mangroves; Bajau village; approx. 75 min. from Manado.
Bitung	Open water; max. visibility 12 m.	Tunas, sharks, dolphins.	Moderately strong; 18°–23° C (64°–73° F)	Japanese hulk 35 m/115′ under; only for divers with open-water experience.
Pantai selantan	Slightly sloping sea floor; visibility 25–30 m. (82–98′)	Tunas, sharks, dolphins, some corals.	Moderately strong; 20°–23° C (68–73° F)	Suitable for novice divers; good opportunities for fishing.

For further information contact: Nusantara Diving Club, Malalayang, I.P.O.Box 15, Manado/Sulawesi utara.

guished themselves world-wide as nature conservationists, they should not hesitate here to report any incidences of destruction to marine life to the PPA in Manado or to the head office in Bogor – or even better, to both. PPA (Directorate of Nature Conservation and Wildlife Management)
Jl. Juanda 9, Bogor, West Java.
Visitors' permits for Indonesia's nature reserves are obtainable at the PPA's main office, which is located to the left of the main entrance to the botanical gardens in Bogor.

Since there are no roads leading from North Sulawesi into the central part of the island, only a few travellers come to Gorontalo in order to catch a boat or a plane to Poso on the opposite bank of the Teluk Tomini. Gorontalo can be reached from Manado by bus along a Korean-built road which passes through Inobonto, Maelang and Kwandang, all on the northern coast. Those who are not in a hurry should turn off the road at the sleepy, coastal village of Inobonto (this Tagalog name reveals the nearness to the Philippines) and head toward the district capital of Kotamobagu. A serpentine road follows the Mongondow River (which lends its name to the district of Bolaang Mongondow) through woodlands and into the mountains. Because of its elevation, Kotamobagu enjoys a pleasant climate.

Excursions can be made to the village of Bilalang, 5 kilometres/3 miles away, and to Lake Moat and the sulphurous volcanic crater nearby. Accommodation in the form of losmens are available. The many mosques in this district show that the majority of its people are Moslems; even the fishing villages near Inobonto are rigidly Islamic. This does not mean that visitors of other faiths are not welcome here, though. Travellers who may have discovered an interest in old forts while on the Moluccas should not miss the ruins of the old Portuguese fortification in Bintuna near Inobonto.

During the rainy season, Gorontalo is often difficult to reach overland; in particular, the 70 kilometre/43 miles-long stretch from Kwandang to Gorontalo which leads past lake Limboto can be very difficult to negotiate during this time. Due to the small number of foreign visitors, the police at Gorontalo do appreciate people coming and introducing themselves. Those who plan to stay for a while will have to use their initiative.

Those waiting here for plane or boat connections should take up lodgings on Lake Limboto: the best view of this large expanse of water can be enjoyed from Dahawalolo, 11 kilometres/7 miles away. Here, as well as in Utapato and Batudia, there are hot springs, and daytime temperatures are likely to make most people search for ways of cooling down. Other villages in the vicinity of Gorontalo which are worth mentioning are Tapa and Kota utara, where handwoven kerawang clothing is produced, and Kota barat, where Fort Otanaha is located.

The kings of Gorontalo, who had more problems with their colonial masters than did their neighbours to the north, the Minahasa, once entrenched themselves here against the Dutch.

By the way: No one should leave the province of North Sulawesi without having tried one of its three culinary specialties. These delicacies, which are not exactly inexpensive, may not be enjoyed by Moslems, however. They are:
tikus utan goreng – fried wood rat
lawa pangang – stewed bat
gulei anjing – spicy hot dogmeat.
Those who feel overwhelmed by the choice are best off trying a little of everything.

Sangir-Talaud Islands

The Sangir (also spelled "Sangihe") and Talaud island groups, extend into the extreme northern reaches of the Indonesian archipelago and up to the Philippine territorial waters. The district includes 77 islands, 56 of which are inhabited, and has a land area of 2,273 sq. kilometres/878 sq. miles and 32,000 square kilometres/12,355 sq. miles of territorial waters. The population of 250,000, 90 per cent of which are Christians, exhibits a fascinating variety of customs and practices.

The main islands of the Sangihe group are Sangir Besar, Siau, Biaro and Tagulandang. The Talaud group includes the main islands of Karakelang, Salibabu, Nanusa, Kabaruan and Miangas as well as many smaller islands. The capital of the Sangir-Talaud Islands is Tahuna, located on the island, Sangir Besar. The northernmost island lies only 150 kilometres/93 miles from the island of Mindanao, but there are no official connections between this small archipelago and the large Philippine island. Tahuna offers accommodation in the form of losmens. Manado can be reached from Naha Airport, 21 kilometres/13 miles outside the town. There are also boat connections between Tahuna and the mainland port of Bitung.

For information about ships from Gorontolo contact:
Surya Shipping Co.,
Jl. Hati Mulia 3/34
Sriwijaya Lines, Jl. Hati Mulia 3/34
Gapsu Lines, Jl. Pertiwi 5

Airline offices:
Bouraq Airlines, Jl. Jend. A. Yani
Merpati Airlines, Jl. Jend. A. Yani

For information about the provinces of North Sulawesi contact:
North Sulawesi Regional Tourist Office,
Jl. Martadinata 11, Manado.

It is a good idea to inquire about the exact dates of the clove harvest, for during this time, the tourist could experience a number of inconveniences. Not only are hotels, shops and offices closed, but schools close for the "harvest holiday" as well.

Hotels in Sulawesi

Name/ Address	Price Group	No. of Rooms	With WC/Bath	Km to Airport	Km to Bus
South Sulawesi					
Bantaeng Wisma Ahriani Jl. Raya Lanto Bantaeng Tel. 36	1	28	8	–	–
Bone Pasanggrahan Jl. Taman Bunga Bone	1	11	4	0.7	–
Bulukumba Sinar Fajar Jl. H. A. Sultan 27/29 Bulukumba Tel. 68	1	12	–	–	–
Gowa Malino Jl. Endang 10 Gowa Tel. 15	2	15	15	–	–
Pare Pare Gandaria Hotel Jl. Bau Massepe 171 Pare Pare Tel. 210 93	1	13	13	–	–
Kartika Jl. Lompobattang 110 Pare Pare	3	12	12	–	1
Pare Indah Jl. Lompobattang 116 Pare Pare Tel. 218 88	2	12	10	–	1
Yusida Jl. Pinggir Laut Pare Pare Tel. 218 13	2	14	14	–	2
Palopo Adipati Jl. Pattimura 2 Palopo Tel. 129	1	21	19	60	1
Rio Rita Jl. Jemma 18 Palopo Tel. 130	1	12	12	59	1.5
Ujung Pandang Raodah*** Jl. Khairil Anwar 20 Ujung Pandang Tel. 70 55, 70 75	4	96	96	21	6
Grand Hotel** Jl. Jend A, Yani 5 Ujung Pandang Tel. 58 81, 58 82	3	65	65	21	5
Alaska Hotel* Jl. S. Saddang 52 Ujung Pandang Tel. 71 38	1	40	18	25	5
Benteng* Jl. Ujung Pandang 9 Ujung Pandang Tel. 2 21 72	2	30	30	26	6
Kenari Pantai Jl. Semba Opu 283 Ujung Pandang Tel. 8 21 83	2	15	15	22	5
Purnama Jl. Pattimura Ujung Pandang Tel. 2 29 90 - 38 33	2	28	21	22	7
Tiatira House Jl. Dr. Sutomo 25 Ujung Pandang Tel. 2 89 48	3	10	10	21	5
Wajo Ayuni Jl. Puang Rimagalatung 18 Wajo Tel. 9 Senkang	1	12	8	–	0.2

South-East Sulawesi

Kendari Kendari Beach Hotel** Jl. Sultan Hasanuddin 44 Kendari Tel. 219 88	4	26	26	20	–
Arnin's Hotel Jl. Jand A. Yani 55 Kendari Tel. 216 15	3	15	15	30	1
Kolake Wonua Beringin Hotel Kolake	2	–	–	–	3
Pinrang Buana Jl. Hasanuddin 89 Pinrang Tel. 82	3	15	12	–	2
Purnama Jl. Hasanuddin 76 Pinrang Tel. 76	1	10	10	–	2
Polmas/Mamasa Wisma Anda Jl. A. Yani Polewali	1	12	12	–	1
Soreang Jl. K. H. A. Saleh Polewali	1	12	–	–	0.3
Selayar Harmita Jl. Haijam 17 Selayar	1	11	–	–	–
Sinjai Linggarjati Jl. Pramuka 1 Sinjai	1	18	4	–	15
Nusantara Jl. Kesatuan Raya 73 Sinjai	1	12	2	–	1
Sanrego Jl. Hasanuddin 27 Sinjai	1	15	4	–	0,5
Soppeng Aman Jl. Merdeka 48 Watansoppeng	1	11	8	–	2
Makmur Jl. Kemakmuran 66 Wetansoppeng Tel. 36	1	10	10	–	1
Tana Toraja Indra Jl. Pasar 63 Rantepao	2	14	14	24	1
Victoria Rantepao	2	12	12	24	1

Central Sulawesi

Luwuk Kawanua Jl. Niaga II Luwuk Phone 77	1	12	–	–	–
Ramayana Beach Jl. Dr. Sudary No. 7 Luwuk Phone 338, 502	3	15	15	12	1
Palu Bumi Nyiur City H.* Jl. Letjen S. Parman 24 Palu Tel. 210 75, 210 76	2	15	15	5	4
Wisata* Jl. S. Parman 39 Palu Tel. 379	2	15	15	15	4
Angkasa Raya Jl. Danau Poso Palu	1	27	–	7	0.5
Buana Jl. R. A. Kartini 6 Palu Tel. 214 76	1	12	10	4	1.5
Fahmil Jl. Jend. A. Yani I Palu	2	11	11	6	1
Garuda Jl. Hasanudin 33 Palu Tel. 48	1	14	11	4	1

Latimojong II Jl. Gaja Mada Palu	1	10	10	7	1
Palu Beach Grand Park Hotel** Raden Saleh 22 Palu Tel. 217 67, 211 26	4	55	55	7	5
Pattimura Jl. Pattimura 18 Palu Tel. 217 75	1	16	10	4	1
Taurus Jl. Hasanudin Palu	1	14	7	5	1
Viscana Jl. Pattimura 57 Palu Tel. 213 75	2	10	10	4	2
Poso					
H. G. H. Jl. Hasanudin Poso Tel. 436	1	19	19	5	3
Hok Jl. Wolter Monginsidi Poso	1	12	–	15	3
Nels Jl. Yos Sudarso 9 Poso Tel. 12-386	1	12	6	15	2
Samangat Jl. Wolter Monginsidi Poso Tel. 69	1	12	–	13	2
North Sulawesi					
Manado					
Kawanua City Hotel*** Jl. Sam Ratulangi 1 Manado Tel. 5 22 22	4	100	100	13	14
Angkasa Raya* Jl. Kol. Soegijono 12 Manado Tel. 20 30	3	20	20	14	1
Manado Inn* Jl. 14 February Manado	3	10	10	14	1
Tentram Jl. Serapung Manado Tel. 31 27	2	12	–	13	3
Yepindra Jl. Sam Ratulangi 37 Manado Tel. 40 49	3	16	16	12	1
Tomohon					
Indraloka Jl. Raya Tomohon	–	–	–	–	–
Wisma Merdeka Jl. Raya Tomohon Tomohon	–	–	–	–	–
Tondano					
Wisma Nusantara Jl. Toar Kampung Tounkuramber	–	–	–	–	–
Tamaska Jl. Tataaran Tondano	–	–	–	–	–
Kotamobagu					
Kabela Jl. Mayien Sutoyo Kotamobagu	1	14	–	195	1
New Plaza Hotel Jl. Mayien Sutojo Kotamobagu	2	10	–	195	–
Ramayana Jl. Adampo Dolot Kotamobagu	1	10	–	195	–
Gorontalo					
Asparaga Centrum H. Jl. Kartini Gorontalo Tel. 122	3	18	18	25	0,5
City Hotel Jl. Jend. A. Yani Gorontalo	2	10	10	25	25
Irene Jl. Medan Gorontalo	2	10	10	25	1

The Moluccas

Land area: 87,100 sq. km/33,629 sq. miles. Territorial waters: 763,911 sq. km/294,946 sq. miles.

Composed of 999 large and small inhabited and uninhabited islands, the Moluccas make up only about 4 per cent of the total area of Indonesia. Together with Sulawesi, they form an area of transition between the Eurasian and Australasian plant and animal kingdoms. To the north, these islands are bordered by the Philippines; to the west, by the almost 5,000-metre/16,404′ deep Moluccan Sea and by Sulawesi; to the south, by the Lesser Sunda Islands and by Australia; and to the east, by New Guinea. The province of the Moluccas (capital: Ambon) is divided into three administrative zones. The North Moluccas include the islands of Halmahera, Morotai, Tidore, Ternate, Bacan, Sula and Obi. The Central Moluccas are made up of the islands of Ceram, Banda, Ambon and Buru, and the South-East Moluccas consist of the islands of Wetar, Babar, Tanim bar, Kai and Aru. Many of the islands (particularly those of the North Moluccas) are of volcanic origin, and most of them are mountainous (on Ceram and Halmahera, the mountains reach heights of up to 3,000 metres/9,842 feet). Many areas of the Moluccas enjoy a pleasant maritime climate with temperatures varying between 24 °C/75 °F and 29 °C/84 °F during the dry season – (September to March), and between 19 °C/66 °F and 22 °C/72 °F during the rainy season (April to August). As the sea is very rough at this time, and traffic between the islands comes to a halt as a result, it is better to visit the Moluccas in the period from September through March.

As a link between the Malayan and Melanesian cultures, the Moluccan archipelago is of great ethnological and anthropological interest. These islands are peopled by dark-skinned proto-Malayan Alfuros, the original inhabitants of the Moluccas, and by lighter-skinned Malayans – descendents of deutero-Malayan immigrants. The Spanish, Portuguese and Dutch colonists also left behind more than just their names. Approximately 1,250,000 people live in the Moluccas, which has an average population density of 13 inhabitants per square kilometre/34 per sq. mi. While much of the population in the North Moluccas and in the coastal regions of the Central Moluccas is Moslem, the South-East Moluccans are, for the most part, Christians. On the island of Ambon, the two religions are more or less equally represented, but most aspects of life are governed by a adat system known as pela. More often than not, Christians and Moslems will assist each other in the construction and repair of their churches and mosques.

The inaccessibility of many of the Moluccan islands has allowed them to retain their special brand of exotic beauty up to the present day. Even though the number of foreign visitors is increasing steadily each year, it is still too early to speak of Moluccan tourism. People in the tourist industry, however, see a promising future in the area of marine tourism (many of the volcanic and coral islands are sourrounded by lovely untouched submersed gardens), provided that roads etc. and facilities for tourists can be built. However, as long as three to seven days of one's valuable holiday time must be sacrificed in order to obtain the special travel permit (surat jalan) needed for the Moluccas, and then additional days possibly be lost waiting for plane or boat connections – these islands will continue to attract only the tireless individualists. Although they are among the twelve touristic destinations in Indonesia that are being promoted by the government, public officials here have little experience in dealing with tourists. Indeed many tourists, faced with suspicion, or even disapproval beat a hasty retreat back to Java or Bali. Those who remain unmoved by the lesser problems of daily life, however, will discover a truly fascinating island realm that is little-known and, for the most part, undeveloped.

Owing to the spice trade, the Moluccas were, at one time, the focus of European colonial interest. By the 19th century, however, clove, nutmeg, pepper and cinnamon exports had declined considerably. Now, the economy of the former "Spice Islands" is based on cattle breeding, fishing and the growing of copra, cocoa and sago. Today, the ruins of numerous forts or bendengs bear witness to the bitter power struggle that went on between the Spanish, the Portuguese, the British and the Dutch East India Company over the monopoly of the spice trade. Many of these forts still bear the marks of their former occupants. Travellers with an interest in history come here to view these vestiges of a not particularly pleasant past, the most interesting of which can be found on Ambon, Saparua, Bandaneira, Ternate and Tidore.

In the 1970's, Moluccan colonial history acquired an unexpected sequel: After their attempt at establishing an independent South Moluccan republic had failed in 1950, the Moluccan rebels, most of whom had been members of the colonial army and police force, were evacuated to Holland, where they were relegated to civilian status. After it became clear that the Dutch would not support them in their struggle for autonomy, as had initially been promised, the Moluccans, who were not prepared to live in permanent exile, took to violence as a means of protest. In the final act of this colonial tragedy, trains were hijacked and hostages taken. The exiled Moluccans are now split up into numerous groups each pursuing its own aims, but despite this, and despite increased efforts on the part of the Dutch government to integrate them, their dream of an independent Moluccan state has not yet died.

The Central Moluccas (Maluku Tengah)

Land area: 37,701 sq. km/14,556 sq. miles.
Territorial waters: 265,316 sq. km/102,438 sq. miles.

The major part of the century-long battle for control over the spice trade was fought out on the Central Moluccan islands, where this power struggle between European nations claimed many lives – especially among civilians. The native population of a number of islands – the Bandas, for example – was virtually wiped out. On Ambon alone, the ruins of more than forty fortresses testify to this relentless struggle for power. The money that – according to a colonial adage – literally grew here on trees, soon brought discord and corruptness to the new rulers, who found it increasingly difficult to counter the resistance that was flaring up on Ternate and the islands around Ambon. By the close of the 18th century, however, coffee, tea and cocoa had succeeded in outranking spices in importance in world trade. The interest in the Spice Islands more or less died out, and the Moluccas went into a kind of economic hibernation that lasted until the second world war.

There are approximately 500,000 people in the Central Moluccas, headed by a bupati or regent, who administers this district from the capital of Masohi on the island of Ceram.

Ambon – City and Island

Those who begin a Moluccan tour on the much-celebrated island of Ambon will encounter many of the region's scenic and historic attractions right from the start. The name of the island is believed to come from the word apon, meaning "plantation". Indeed, Ambon was one of the first Moluccan islands to be occupied by the Portuguese and used as a plantation. The beginnings of the city of Ambon can also be traced back to the Portuguese, who established the fort of Kota Laka on this spot in 1577. The Dutch, who eventually supplanted the Portuguese as a mercantile power, renamed it Fort Victoria. Dominating the waterfront, the large, forbidding walls of this fort, clearly show to what ends the Europeans went to defend this island in the 16th century.

As this benteng now houses a military barracks, a ban on picture-taking is in effect and tourists with cameras are closely monitored. It has not yet occured to the military authorities, however, that when a panorama shot is taken from the hill where the Tiahahu Monument is located, there is no preventing either the walls or the interior of the barracks, also appearing on the picture. Those who would rather not risk their films being confiscated, however, are better off adhering to the rules, which here, are more rigorously enforced than in other parts of Indonesia. With a little luck, one can obtain a permit from the military authorities to visit Fort Victoria and a permit to take pictures as well. To save time, these should be requested along with visitor's permits for the other Moluccan islands.

Ambon City, with approximately 85,000 inhabitants, enjoys the status of an autonomous provincial capital. The appeal of this city lies principally in its lovely setting. From the hill in the suburb of Karang Panjang where the memorial to **Martha Christina Tiahahu** stands, one has a spectacular panoramic view of Ambon Bay and the illuminated city, which is especially striking at dusk. Martha Christina was a freedom fighter who fought alongside her father against the Dutch colonial regime and died while being transported to Java with a shipload of prisoners. Near her monument stands the House of Assembly where the elected representatives meet in session. Another monument commemorated to the Moluccan people's struggle for freedom is that of Thomas Matulessy, also known as Captain Pattimura. On March 5, 1817, he and his followers took Fort Duurstede on the little island of Saparua, east of Ambon. Betrayed by one of the local rajahs, he was later caught in an ambush and taken prisoner. Before he died, he said to his Dutch executioners, "I wish you all a pleasant stay". Those who wish to learn more about the history of the Moluccan islands can visit the Siwa Lima Museum, located on Taman Makmur Hill, which contains objects of historic and ethnographic interest from all over the Moluccan archipelago. Another of the city's attractions is the tourist village in Karang Panjang where demonstrations of folk dances and traditional

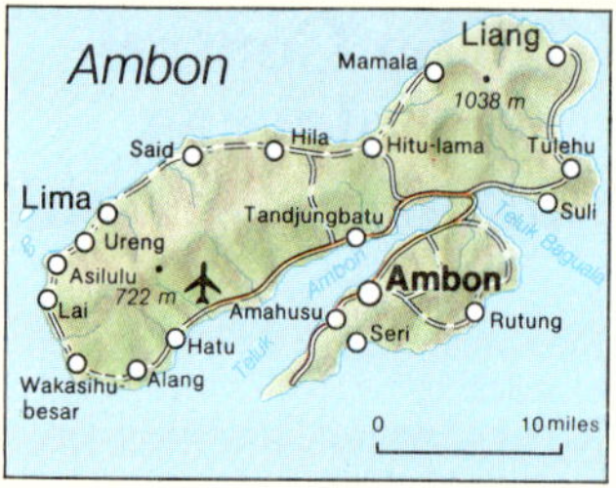

crafts can be viewed at the weekends or by arrangement. Moreover, the village is complemented by a lavish garden where Indonesian and, in particular, Moluccan flora grows in abundance. Orchid lovers will be glad to know that several endemic species of their favourite flower can be admired here. Laka Airport, 50 kilometres/31 miles from the city, is the centre of island to island air traffic here. From Jakarta, Ambon, which lies on one of Indonesia's main domestic airroutes, is served by the following: Garuda Indonesian Airlines (twice a day), Merpati Nusantara Airlines (twice a week), Mandala Airlines (twice a week) and Pelita Air Service (once a week). From Ambon, Merpati flies to the following Moluccan destinations: Taliabu (Sula Islands), Tual (Kai Islands), Saum Laki (Tanimbar Islands), Amahai and Bula (Ceram), as well as to Jailolo and Galela (Halmahera) via Ternate. Bandaneira and Dobo (Aru Islands) are further destinations planned. During the rainy season (April to August), not only is shipping badly affected, but the unsurfaced landing strips of many small airfields take such abuse

Pela or "United We Stand"

Pela, which actually means "brother", is a form of adat or common law which dates back to the 15th century. It is still very much alive on the Moluccas today and has even been kept up by the Moluccans living in Dutch exile. **Pela** signifies a form of alliance between two or more villages. In the 15th and 16th centuries, as a result of the infiltration of Christianity and Islam into Moluccan society, a great deal of mistrust and emnity arose between individual villages. In order to bring peaceful co-existence back to the adherents of the two religions, the pela confederations were formed. Genuine pelas follow a strict code of laws and principles which endows them with the necessary strength to win the daily battle for survival. One law, for example, bans marriages between members of the same confederation – such a union is looked upon as incestuous. The rights and responsibilities of pela members are precisely laid down: the pela oath covers wartime support as well as mutual assistance in house-building, planting and harvesting. Earlier, the village chiefs often sealed the vow by entering into a form of blood brotherhood with one another.

The many forms of pela, regardless of how strict they are, place no obstacles in the way of religious affiliation. Alliances exist between Christian and Moslem villages whose inhabitants even assist each other in the building of their churches and mosques. In the last three decades, however, the pela movement has lost some of its vitality. The cult of the individual, which is embraced by many young Moluccans today, and the search for employment, which sends many young people to other part of the republic, are the causes of a drastic change in attitudes. The Moluccan exiles in the Netherlands, however, are as loyal as ever to their pela system, which provides them with the warmth and support of a close-knit community. The financial burden of weddings and funerals as well as the economic obligations of the community are all borne by the pela. It remains to be seen, however, whether the pela can solve the many problems which arise from the Moluccans' desire to return to their homeland.

from the weather that they become unfit for use over long periods of time. The larger seagoing vessels are not however affected by the inclement weather. For information on inter-island connections, it is best to apply to the harbourmaster, who keeps up to date with the ever-changing time-tables. The tourist office, located in the Governor's Office on Jl. Pattimura, only offers general information.

Sightseeing Trips on Ambon
The island of Ambon, whose two peninsulas, Hitu and Letima, were at one time separate islands, offers its visitors an array of sightseeing opportunities. Owing to the poor network of roads, however, it is not possible to plan all sightseeing trips as one-day excursions.

In the village of Hila on the northern coast, one can view an old Portuguese church which bears an inscription in Dutch, and the block-house, "Amsterdam", whose walls are threatening to collapse under the grip of a banyan tree. From here, the immense island of Ceram can be recognized in the hazy distance. Those who take an early boat to Letima can visit Fort Rotterdam which is in better repair than Hila's fort. The fact that this is an important clove-growing region is especially obvious during harvest-time when each breath of air is filled with the lovely, aromatic fragrance coming from the endless rows of cloves left out in the streets to dry.

In the days before the arrival of the Europeans, Soya, which lies within two hour's walking distance of Ambon, extended over the area that now includes that city. The attractions of this historically important village include a Portuguese church dating from 1817 and a holy water jug which is said to replenish itself. The villagers regularly fetch water here because it allegedly has the power to protect them. On the road from Soy to Erma over Mt. Serimau, one has a fabulous view of Ambon's southern coast. Once in Erma, one can continue on to Naku and Hatalia, which are both inhabited by descendents of the Portuguese – the local dances strongly resemble those common in Portugal in the 16th and 17th centuries. Between **Naku** and **Batu Itam** lies a fantastic waterfall which should not be missed. Ambon also has many beautiful beaches for those who prefer to swim in the sea. The problem lies in choosing one of the many possibilities. The following is just a selection of the island's many beach resorts:

Natsepa, 14 km/9 miles from Ambon, accessible by taxi or bus. White, sandy beach that is especially wide at low tide; crystal-clear water; popular at weekends.

Toisapu, 18 km/11 miles from Ambon, opposite Natsepa. Quieter, more isolated beach; accessible by boat from Passo.

Latuhalat, located on the southern coast of Letima. Particularly suited to snorkling; because of sharp corals, shoes should be worn.

Amahusu, located on the southwestern coast of Ambon. Offers a lovely view of the peninsula Hitu; beautiful coral formations close to the beach; outriggers can be hired.

Namalatu, 16 km/10 miles south of Ambon City. Clear, calm water, white sand; coconut palms and a motel run by the provincial administration are condusive to an extended stay.

Waime, located near the bay opposite Ambon City. Not always clean; offers a lovely view of the city, especially at dusk; private accommodation available.

Marthafons Cape, located opposite the naval port of Halang, therefore often oil-infested. Pertamina cottages and other accommodation available.

Pulau Pombo, an uninhabited island east of Ambon accessible by boat from Waai or Tulehu. Beautiful beaches and underwater gardens. Many species of birds have found nesting-places in this as yet unprotected nature reserve. In the middle of the island lies a pool whose water level rises and falls with the tides. Whether or not it remains a refuge for animals depends on each individual visitor. By the way, it should be obvious that disposing of used plastic and tin, is of no benefit to the environment.

Ceram

Called "Nusa Ina" (Mother Island) by its inhabitants, Ceram (Seram) is the largest of the central islands. The peaks of its mountainous interior reach heights of up to 3,000 m/ 9,842′. But unlike the southern coast which is rocky and precipitous, Ceram's northern coast is covered by vast swamplands. Roads are limited to the area around Amahai and Maohi. In Ceram's primeval forests, some of which are impenetrable. Alfuro tribes have been able to keep their traditional way of life up to the present day. A lack of the patriotic spirit so common on the Moluccas, however, is demonstrated by the fact that the island administration regards these people as "backward". When asked about the future of Alfuro culture, an administrative officer on Ambon once replied, "We have built a lovely museum for them". While Malayan groups live mainly in the west and on the densely-populated southern coast, the Alfuros, whose name stems from the Portuguese word, fora, or "outsider", live in the almost accessible eastern interior. The members of the Nalulu or Borera tribes are, to some extent, still hunters and gatherers. Boys are taught how to handle a bow and arrow at an early age. The generous and friendly attitude that these people have toward strangers contrasts strongly with the reserved manner of the coastal inhabitants. Those who wish to venture into the eastern part of the island will have to use coastal shipping. The trip from Amahai to the outer reaches of the island takes two to three days by

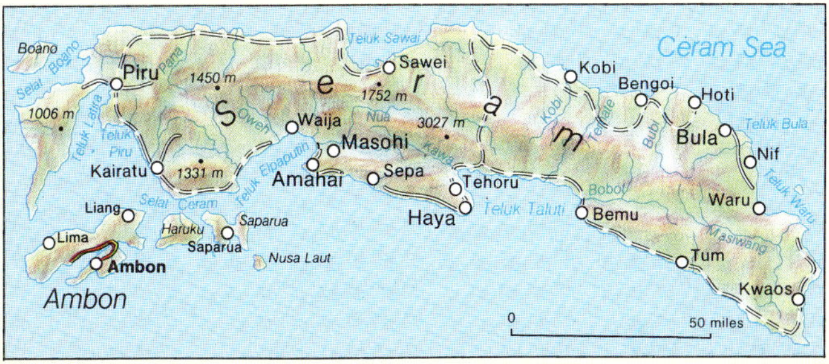

small craft. A hike of several day's duration must also be reckoned with. As one to two months are needed for serious travel on this island, most undertakings of this nature run aground for lack of time.

Ceram's main sources of income stem from tourism and petroleum, and it is hoped that further oil deposits in the eastern coastal shelf will bring even more capital to the island. The entire import-export trade is currently based in the district capital of Masohi, which can be reached from Ambon by plane or boat.

Travel on Ceram is often made difficult by a lack of normal accommodation, but the missions, as well as the police, are usually happy to assist in an emergency. What generally holds true for the large Moluccan islands also applies to Ceram: many of the attractions have yet to be documented. This means that the discovery of historic and topographic points of interest is left to the exploratory spirit of the visitor. Ceram is internationally famous for its varied and colourful birdlife, but even the remaining signs of the colonial period make a visit worthwhile. Indeed, many are still languishing under thick layers of vegetation, waiting to be discovered. **Fort Campelo,** built by the Dutch on the western tip of the island in 1616, is only one of many fortress ruins here.

It is not possible to mention here the many beautiful beaches on Ceram's almost 1,000 kilometre long/621 mile coast – discover them for yourself! The following are a few suggestions for the immediate vicinity of **Amahai:** Ruta Beach, Piru Beach, Uneputtih Beach, Elpaputih Beach, Soleman Beach and Koako Cape. All can be reached by car from Masohi or Amahai. Another point of interest near Amahai is the **Kawa Pool** which is connected to the sea by a stream and is believed to contain sacred fish. Often it is the local people who draw the visitor's attention to attractions of this nature which are rarely mentioned in the travel guides. In cases like these, knowledge of the Indonesian language is useful.

The Banda Islands

The nine small, volcanic (some active) islands that lie 160 kilometres/99 miles south-east of Ambon are known as the Banda Archipelago. Their past is a dark page in Dutch colonial history. In 1609, an admiral by the name of Pieter Verhoeffe was sent to the Banda Islands, whose abundance of nutmeg made them a desirable object, on behalf of the Dutch East India Co. He was to take the entire archipelago and secure it by means of a fortification, but the islanders succeeded in luring him into an ambush and murdering him. The Dutch continued their colonization efforts in spite of this setback. **Fort Nassau** in Bandaneira was their first stronghold on the islands, but the local population very quickly deserted the area around Nassau, leaving no-one behind to harvest the nutmeg. For this and other reasons, Governor-General Jan Pieterszoon Coen entered the scene in 1619. This man, who had been a member of Verhoeffe's crew and had witnessed his murder, proceeded to take ruthless measures. Through the use of muskets and cannons, more than two thirds of the population of the Bandas was wiped out. Those who survived but could not escape, were shipped to Java as slaves. The shortage of workers that resulted from this loss of lives was gradually remedied through the use of Timorese slaves, Papuans, contract workers from Java, Chinese and Macassans. Nutmeg, which originally grew only on the Bandas, was soon transplanted to other areas of the Moluccas, thus causing the colonial interest in these islands to dwindle.

Today, the Banda Islands have the air of a world where time has stood still. **Bandaneira,** the islands' main port, is a quiet, idyllic little town with old churches and houses built by the Portuguese. Opposite the harbour stands the 670-metre-high/2,198′ volcano, **Gunung Api,** which still shows signs of activity. It is not necessary, however, to climb to the rim of the crater to enjoy the splendid view of the city that this mountain offers. Another panoramic view can be enjoyed from the walls of **Fort Belgica,** located not far from the pier. In contrast to this benteng, 80 per cent of which is intact, the afore-mentioned **Fort Nassau** is in very bad repair. The old **Dutch Protestant church,** on the other hand, is well cared for and still in use today. The former **residence of Jan Peterszoon Coen** can also be visited. Those interested in other historical buildings can see **Fort Hollandia** on the neighbouring island of **Lantor** and an old blockhouse on Ay Island. The volcanic island of **Manuk,** 80 km/50 miles south of Banda, serves as a nesting-ground for many marine birds. Here, one findes an untouched undersea world that has not yet been harmed by dynamite fishing, as is the case in other parts of Indonesia.

Since the Banda islanders are a very hospitable people, the lack of regular accommodation here should pose no real difficulties. It should be understood, however, that payment is expected. With the steadily increasing number of visitors, where would this otherwise lead to? Although boats operate between Ambon and the Banda Islands on a fairly regular basis, the number of visitors here each year is not yet excessive.

Buru

This island with an area of some 2,000 sq. km/772 square miles can be reached from Ambon by plane in just under 45 minutes. Being a penal colony, it has long been inaccessible to tourists, but today, the special permit needed is usually granted. The island is covered mainly with dense eucalyptus forests and savannahs overgrown with alang alang grass. Crocodiles can still be found in the **Wai Apu** and other rivers, and during the rainy season, Buru is visited by a veritable plague of mosquitos – to the great discomfort of its inhabitants. Chinese, Javanese and Arab immigrants live along the coasts, while Alfuro tribespeople live in the mountainous interior. The Waeloa, Rama and Waejapo people, who were once feared as headhunters, live mainly around **Lake Wakolo,** which lies 670 metres/ 2,224′ above sea level. Very little is known about these dying tribes; owing to the island's special status, researchers are usually not granted permission to enter.

The island's economy is based mainly on timber and the production of minyak kayuputih, an essential oil obtained from a certain species of eucalyptus. Besides finding world-wide use in pharmaceutics, this oil is the main ingredient of the well-known ointment, Tiger Balm.

Those who enjoy hiking, studying plants and animals, and do not fear the encounter with primitive cultures will discover many gems in this otherwise rough and uninviting countryside. Because of the irregularity of plane and boat connections between Ambon and the Burunese town of **Namlea,** however, those planning a visit should have ample time at their disposal.

Saparua

Saparua is a small island with a varied history, west of Ambon, which owes its special significance to Pattimura's conquest of **Fort Duurstede.** This relatively well-preserved fortification is still mounted with cannons. A 17th century church, as well as a number of other ruins, can also be visited. **Waisisil Beach,** now a resort, was the site of Pattimura's first victory against the Dutch. Saparua can be reached by boat from Tulehu or Waai, both on the eastern coast of Ambon in three hours.

Haruku

Haruku, located between Sapurua and Ambon, was once an important spice-growing island. Its tourist potential lies in a Portuguese fort, lovely beaches and a hot sulphur spring that provides a natural cure for skin ailments. The island can be reached from Ambon and Saparua.

Nusa Laut

Lovely beaches and hot sulphur springs can also be found on this island, whose inhabitants regard the curative powers of the sulphurous water with high esteem. Nusa Laut can be reached by boat from Saparua.

The North Moluccas (Maluku Utara)

Land area: 32,000 sq. km/12,355 sq. miles.
Territorial waters: 207,381 sq. km/ 80,069 sq. miles.

The North Moluccas, with its 353 islands is divided into 20 subdistricts. This region has an average population density of 17 inhabitants per square kilometre/44 per sq. mile. Volcanism characterizes the topography of many of the islands. Vast areas of the larger islands – Halmahera, Obi and Taliabu, for example – are still covered with tropical rainforests, which are now being commercially exploited to some extent. Only in these remote areas, which at one time were beyond the reach of outside influences, was the local population spared any suffering during the chaotic days of the colonial power struggless.

In the 16th and 17th centuries, the North Moluccan islands were virtually the sole suppliers of cloves. The Dutch East India Co. looked for ways to break this monopoly, but owing to the combined efforts of the sultanates of Tidore, Ternate, Bacan and Jailolo, it was only with great difficulty that they were able to establish themselves in this region. They never succeeded, though, in putting a complete stop to the smuggling trade that flourished between the North Moluccas and Macassar on Celebes. The Dutch East India Co. carried out predatory raids or so-called hongi tours into the North Moluccas, in an attempt to destroy the clove plantations. Central Moluccan village chiefs were obliged to aid these incursions by supplying ships and crews. Their unrelenting struggle for power against their Spanish and Portuguese rivals also brought the Dutch into North Moluccan waters. After countless battles in which the native population usually took the stronger side, the Dutch were eventually able to satisfy their lust for power. In 1663, the Spaniards abandoned Tidore, their last stronghold in the North Moluccas. Every ensuing incident of rebellion was quelled by the Dutch with unbelievable force. Arnold de Vlamingh, who led the "pacification" of the North Moluccas, was known and feared for his mercilessness. The fear of the people was so great that they were even prepared to kill their own leaders in order to escape the Dutchman's wrath. In 1655, for example, the people of Kelan offered de Vlamingh the head of the Prince of Ternate in order to save their city from destruction. The city was spared, but its people lost their freedom.

Today, Ternate is an important centre of administration. The economy of the North Moluccas is based on fishing, timber and spices. Owing to the popularity of kretek or clove cigarettes in Indonesia, the demand for cloves is on the increase. On Ternate, Tidore, Moti and Makian, there are almost 500,000 cengkeh (clove) trees spread out over an area that comprises 300,000 hectares. Ternate is the centre of sea and air traffic in the North Moluccas – Merpati Nusantara Airlines offers connections from Ambon and Manado (North Sulawesi). The following list can serve as a point of reference:
Ambon-Ternate, five times a week.
Ternate-Galela, twice a week.
Manado-Ternate, twice a week.
Shipping is relatively well-organized in the North Moluccas.

Ternate

Practically circular in shape, the island of Ternate has an area of approximately 40 square kilometres/ 15 sq. miles. Three volcanic peaks, the highest of which rises up 1,830 metres/6,003′, dominate its interior. The city of Ternate hugs the side of the 1,721-metre-high/5,646′ active volcano, **Gamalama,** whose cone contains three crater lakes. Although Ternate has great regional significance, it has a rather sleepy, and therefore relaxing, atmosphere.

Thanks to the trade contacts formed between Arab merchants and the North Moluccans long before the arrival of the Portuguese, the population today is 90 per cent Moslem. The sultanates of Ternate and Tidore, which ruled over vast areas of the eastern Indonesian islands, used their political influence to bring in the new religion. The **sultan's palace** on Ternate, which dates from 1234, serves today as a museum. From here, one has a lovely view of the harbour. The high concentration of forts and blockhouses bears witness to the strategic significance the island had during the 16th and 17th centuries. The following is a brief list of the most interesting fortifications:

Fort Oranje, Ternate City. Erected by Madeliede in 1607; 60% of the structure has been largely destroyed.

Fort Gamalama, 20 km/12 miles outside the city. Dates from the 14th century; only 20% of this fort is in good repair.

Fort Toleko, located in Dufa Dufa, 2 km/1¼ miles from Ternate. Erected by the Portuguese admiral Albuquerque in 1511; 30% of this structure is in fair condition.

Fort San Pedro, dates from 1522; 30% of this Spanish fort is well-preserved.

Fort Kaya Nerah, located in Kalumata. This British fort is basically in the same state of repair as Fort San Pedro.

Fort Kastella, located near the village of Kastela, is said to date from Magellan's days. Those who think they have now seen all of Ternate's forts are mistaken. The Portuguese fort of Sao Palobeo is only one of many fortifications erected to guard the spice plantations.

One is never far from the sea on Ternate and there are many opportunities for swimming, but deep water should be avoided by all but the best swimmers because of the strong currents at many beaches. Two of the most beautiful, **Ngade** and **Sulamendaha,** boast of crystal-clear water and a beautiful reef. In many places along the coast, the effects of a volcanic eruption that occured 250 years ago are still very evident. At **Batu Hangus** (Burnt Rock), for example, great rivers of lave flowed into the sea. Those interested in seeing more volcanic landscape can take a boat to **Mataira,** a volcanic island situated between Ternate and Tidore. Those who like to walk will discover even more of Ternate's natural beauty. For example there is **Lake Laguna,** lying a mere 7 km/4 miles from the city (of course, it can also be reached by car), and **Lake Tolire** lies some 24 km/15 miles away. Another attraction – and one that most tourists miss – is the **Afu clove tree,** 5 kilometres/3 miles from Ternate. Three hundred and fifty years old, this tree must have experienced the bulk of Ternate's colonial past.

Tidore, with an area of 50 square kilometres/19 sq. miles, is slightly larger than its sister island, Ternate. Large and small craft sail regularly and frequently from Ternate to Tidore's main port of **Rum.** Like Ternate, Tidore is dominated by a volcano – one which rises up 1,739 metres/5,676′ above sea level. There is

always something going on here – especially on market days, i.e. on Tuesdays and Saturdays. From Rum, the city of **Tidore** can be reached after a short drive. Besides the old city wall and other remnants of the past, this city can also boast of – what else – a number of forts. However, very little is left of the former glory of this sultanate, whose power once extended to New Guinea.

Halmahera

This is the largest and least-explored of the northern Moluccan islands. In shape, it resembles the larger island to the west, Sulawesi. Each of its four peninsulas has a mountainous interior that is still largely covered with tropical rainforests. Owing to the fact that most of the island was spared the visits of European merchant fleets, much of the people's traditional way of life has remained intact. Even the influence of the sultanates of Tidore, Ternate and Jailolo extended only as far as the coastal regions of the island – the nomadic tribes of the interior were hardly affected at all. While most native Moluccans speak languages belonging to the Malayo-Polynesian group, on Halmahera, some Papuan dialects are also spoken.

In **Jailolo,** which can be reached by plane from Ternate, one can see the ruins of a 13th century **sultan's palace,** as well as visit typical adat houses which can be found in the city's environs. Most of this island's historic remains date from the recent past, however. At **Kao Bay,** for example, which can be reached from **Tobelo** by motorboat, the remains of a Japanese military base can be seen. The bullet-ridden landing craft on the beach and the airplane wreckage scattered in the sea and in the jungle bear witness to the massive use of heavy combat material during World War II. On the island of Meti off the coast of Halmahera at Tobelo, traces of former combat can also be found. Of the island's many scenic attractions, the five lakes near **Galela** deserve special mention. **Lake Duma,** which is also located in the subdistrict of Galela, is worth visiting for its lovely surroundings.

Like Irian Jaya, Halmahera is a place to spend an active or an educational holiday. Those who come to the Moluccas for the first time, however, will find themselves confronted here with formalities that are otherwise only customary in Irian. It often happens that one must first register with the police before being sent to the Kantor Immigrasi. In most cases, one must then fill out forms stating the purpose of one's journey and the planned route. Depending on the town and the authority, one to two passport photographs are needed to complete the process. Answers to the renewed queries about one's age, occupation, marital status and children, as well as to the ubiquitous question, "How do you like it here in the Moluccas?", serve merely to satisfy the curiosity of the probing official.

Morotai

As an Allied defense base and, for a time, the headquarters of General McArthur, Morotai experienced much heavy combat during World War II. Even the Japanese had an air-base here. Today, the island is a producer of copra, damar resin and rattan.

Large coconut plantations dominate this heavily forested island, whose inhabitants' traditional way of life was largely destroyed by the war. Morotai can be reached by plane via Tobelo.

Bacan

This island is situated west of the southern tip of Halmahera. At one time a powerful sultanate, Bacan, together with the other surrounding principalities, once ruled over vast areas of the North Moluccas. The **sultan's palace,** one third of which is still intact, dates from the 13th century. **Fort Barneveld** is another of Bacan's historic sites. The islanders still fear the ghosts of the soldiers formerly stationed here. When there is a full-moon they allegedly hear soldiers marching, and commands being given. Today, Bacan is known for its high-quality cocoa. From the summit of the **Sibela volcano,** a beautiful view of the island can be enjoyed.

Sula Islands

Located in the south-western corner of the North Moluccas, the islands of Taliabu, Monggoli and Sanana may lie far off the beaten track, but not far enough to have deterred the Japanese logging companies, who have established themselves here. Taliabu islanders construct fascinating adat houses. Plane and boat connections are rather irregular.

The South-East Moluccas (Maluku Tenggara)

Land area: 27,451 sq. km/ 10,599 sq. miles.
Territorial waters: 320,470 sq. km/ 123,733 sq. miles.

The South-East Moluccas is made up of 287 islands and islets of which approximately 200 are inhabited. This region, which is divided into eight subdistricts, has a population of 23,000 and an average population density of 12 inhabitants per square kilometre/31 per sq. mile. The South-East Moluccas were little-affected by the colonial power struggles. It was not until the start of this century, when the missionaries began with their work here, that the people's strong cultural self-image became subject to outside influences. Today, the majority of Christians can be found among the coastal population, while animism still flourishes in remote areas. Up until a few decades ago, a class society made up of aristocrats, commoners and slaves still existed on a number of the islands west of the Kai group. Even as late as the early 20th century, raiding parties were still being sent out to the Aru Islands and New Guinea in search of slaves, and still today, the descendents of slaves are considered socially unacceptable. While the people of the southern islands grow sago as a staple food, on the islands between Alor and Tanimbar, rice is grown by the dry-rice method of cultivation. The island's economy is based on fishing, pearls and timber (ironwood and rattan). The flora and fauna here show a marked similarity to those of New Guinea and Australia: marsupials such as kangaroos and cuscus, birds of paradise and several species of cockatoo can be found here. Fortunately, many areas of this region have been declared nature reserves. These protected

Spices: The Stuff of which Dreams were once made

The Europeans searched many years in vain before finally finding the legendary Spice Islands in the late 15th century. Before that, their aromatic treasure, which was worth its weight in gold in 15th and 16th century Europe, was only obtainable through trade with Arab coasters. Many European rulers dreamed of possessing these islands and the power and wealth that would come with them.

The commotion that surrounded these once-coveted islands has long since died down. Today, however, the cengkeh (**clove**), which was originally endemic to the North Moluccas, has achieved new significance due to the popularity of kretek cigarettes, as well as to its use in pharmaceutics. Clove trees require very little care – keeping the area around the tree free of weeds promotes growth and simplifies the bi-annual process of gathering the harvest of fallen buds. Cloves, which are harvested late, are marketed as lower-quality, less-aromatic pulong. It takes eight to ten years before a clove sapling blossoms for the first time. A mature tree yields approximately five to six kilogrammes of buds/11–13 lbs, (the going price per kilo is about Rp 8,500). On Ambon and Ternate, model boats, houses and other constructions are built entirely out of cloves; this craft dates back to the last century. The tourist with a toothache will be glad to know that sucking on a few whole cloves brings relief. Dentists, too, are aware of the pain-killing properties of clove oil.

The **nutmeg** (pala) tree, originally native to the Banda islands, is also very easy to grow. Five years after being planted, the young tree bears fruit for the first time, but not until twenty years later does it reach its normal level of production. Then, it will continue bearing fruit for up to eighty years. The pala nuts, whose green peach-like shells are also used, can be harvested all year round. It is the pit of this fruit that is the actual nutmeg; its fibrous covering is mace. The white colour of whole nutmeg comes from a calcium solution that was first used during colonial times to render them unfit for use as seed. Only later was it discovered that this calcium layer did not impede germination, but rather, that it kept the nutmeg fresher longer. In the 17th and 18th centuries, the price of nutmeg was much higher in England than it was on the European continent. Ladies wore them as fragrance in gold or silver lockets around their necks; gentlemen spiced their grogs with nutmeg which they carried around with them in a small box complete with a grater.

areas are located on the following islands:

Tanimbar Islands:
Muswatar (7,500 ha)
Nustaran (3,200 ha)
Anguwarmasse (800 ha)

Aru Islands:
Baun (13,000 ha)
Enu (reservation planned)

Other Islands:
Gunung Api (80 ha)

It is usually necessary to charter a boat to get to these islands. A permit to enter the nature reserves can be obtained from the camat or district authority, or at a local office of the P. P. A. (Directorate of Nature Conservation). Guest-houses operated by the P. P. A. can be found in some reserves. Visitors to the southern Moluccan Islands should not be too demanding in their choice of accommodation. Proper lodgings can only be found in the administrative centres. In other locations, missions, schools and the police are often happy to be of assistance. Transport facilities are only available on Kai Kecil.

The Kai Islands

Not quite beyond the reach of civilization, **Dumaatuban Airstrip** near **Langgur** on Kai Kecil can be reached from Ambon, from Saumlaki (Tanimbar) and, possibly in the future, from Dobo (Aru Islands). **Tual** on Kai Kecil (Kai Ketji) is the administrative centre of the South-East Moluccas, and **Elat** on Kai Besar (Greater Kai) is the capital of

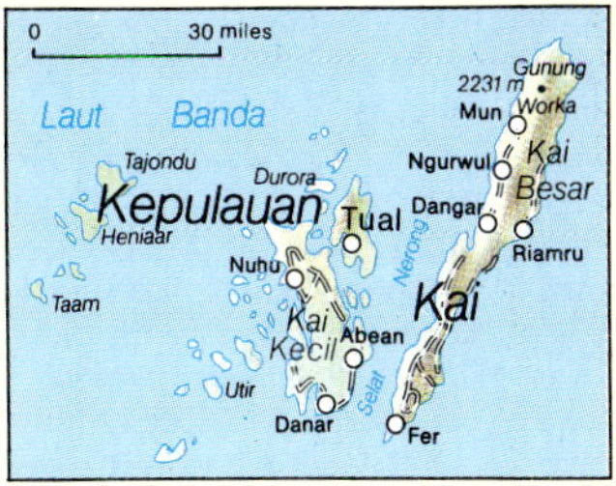

the Kai Islands. The normally heavy traffic in South-East Moluccan waters comes to a halt during the rainy season. From April to August only vessels with greater tonnage can ply the routes to and from Ambon all year round. During the dry season, there are also connexions to Kaimana (Irian). Only Kai Kecil can boast of an adequate network of roads – and a public transport system, however, rudimentary. With the exception of mountainous Kai Besar, the Kai Islands all evolved from coral growth. They have a total land area of 900 square kilometres and a population of 22,000. There are Kai people among the Moluccans living in Dutch exile as well, but in contrast to their compatriots, they have been able to adjust themselves relatively well to life in Holland.

Owing to their abundance of dazzling white beaches, the Kai Islands have great tourist potential. The scenic beauty of the mountainous island of **Kai Besar,** however, is considerably more varied. The eastern coast of the island (approachable only on foot over a mountain ridge) is especially interesting from an ethnological point of view: descendents of the survivors of the Bandanese massacre live here. For those without some knowledge of Indonesian, a visit to the Kai Islands will not be without its problems. Many older people still speak Dutch, however, it that is of any help. Two points of interest that deserve special mention are the pearl farms in **Difur** on the island of Dullah, and the **Luat Cave** on Kai Kecil. Inscriptions have been found on the walls of this cave, the nature and origin of which are still unknown.

The Tanimbar Islands

These 62 large and small islands – famous beyond their borders for the larat orchid – are often called the Lelemuhu Islands after the local word for "orchid". The population of this island group is made up of a mixture of Melanesians, Papuans and Negritos; its largest community is **Saumlaki** on Jamdena. Until only a few years ago, these people were still hunting with blow pipes. Hair design was once an important part of the traditional dress of many tribes. Their magnificent ceremonial and battle array, however, is now a thing of the past and can only be admired on the few old photographs that still exist. Today, Tanimbar islanders are famous for their high-quality weaving. In addition to teak and ironwood trees (which have attracted a few large timber companies), sago and coconut palms dominate the island landscape. From the ports of **Saumlaki** and **Larat** (on the island of the same name), goods "made in Tanimbar" are exported.

There are relatively good boat connections between the islands of this large group, but sightseeing here must be done on foot. On the island of Jamdera, pedestrians need not watch out for motorized vehicles, but rather for herds of buffalo – each year a good handful of people

are literally "taken by the horns". Those who do not let themselves be deterred will be rewarded with stalagmite caves. (**Bangruti, Weritibun** and **Bangdas caverns** are the best known), appealing scenery, lovely beaches and many interesting villages. The beaches on Tanimbar are really too numerous to mention, but it should not be difficult to find the one which suits one's wishes. It must be mentioned, however, that these waters are populated by sharks.

The Aru Islands

It was here in the 1850's that the naturalist Alfred Russel Wallace wrote down his observations on the distribution of flora and fauna in the Malay Archipelago. The fact that two areas of distribution overlap in this island group was certainly no coincidence. Cassowaries, birds of paradise, cuscus and kangaroos are found here alongside deer and small game. The presence of the latter two, however, is likely due to human hands. These islands, the majority of which are flat and swampy, are inhabited by another creature which is quite common to the tropics: the mosquito. It can turn a visit to the Aru Islands into an unforgettable experience!

Even today, the isolated position of these islands south-west of New Guinea still poses problems. **Dobo,** on the small island of **Wamar,** can be reached by boat from the Kai Islands only once or twice every two months. The culture of the coastal inhabitants strongly resembles that of the Kai people, but Negrito, Papuan and Aboriginal cultures prevail in the interior. Pearl oysters are found in the waters surrounding the islands and cultured pearls are produced on farms located along the coasts. Even the rare black pearl is cultivated here.

Babar

This island has large forests of spruce trees. Ten kilometres/6 miles from the village of **Tepar,** there is an eight-metre-high/26′ geyer whose activity is dependent on the tides. The mountain near the villages of **Yatoke** and **Wakpapapi** contains a holy cave – the skulls of ancestors as well as grave objects are kept in its guarded vaults. The cave located near **Potar Besar** once served the people as a place of refuge.

Hotels in the Moluccas

Name/ Address	Price Group	No. of Rooms	With WC/Bath	Km to Airport	Km to Bus
Ambon					
Abdulalie* Jl. Sultan Babullah Ambon Tel. 20 57, 20 58	2	39	39	36	1.5
Amboina* Jl. Kapten Ulu Paha Ambon Tel. 33 54	3	10	10	36	1
Cendrawasih* Jl. Tulukabesy Ambon Tel. 24 87	4	12	12	36	1
Eleonoor* Jl. Anthony Rhebok Ambon Tel. 28 34	3	10	10	37	1
Mutiara* Jl. Raya Pattimura Ambon Tel. 30 75, 30 76	3	12	12	36	0.5
Anggrek Jl. Jend. A. Yani Ambon Tel. 139	1	24	24	36	1.5
Irama Jl. Sultan Babullah Ambon	2	10	10	37	1
Ramayana Jl. Sirimau Ambon Tel. 33 69	2	10	10	36	0.5
Sylvana Jl. A. M. Sangaji Ambon Tel. 29 65	3	11	14	36	0.2
Halong Inn Cottages Halong Ambon Tel. 21 52	3	15	15	16	6

Name/ Address	Price Group	No. of Rooms	With WC/Bath	Km to Airport	Km to Bus
Monalisa Tantui/Ambon Tel. 26 67	3	75	75	32	5
Ternate					
Anda Baru Jl. Ketilang 49 Ternate	3	–	–	4	0.3
Chrysant Jl. Ahmad Yani Ternate Tel. 377, 210	3	10	10	5	1
Indah Jl. Busouri 3 Ternate Tel. 217	4	10	10	5	1
Sejahtera Jl. Lawa 21 Ternate	1	12	–	4	1
Banda					
Naira Jl. Pantai Banda	–	–	–	–	–
Ceram					
Mess „Ole-Sio" Jl. Salahutu Masohi	–	–	–	–	–
Losmen Mah rani Jl. Kasturi Masohi	–	–	–	–	–
Kai-Islands					
Rosemgen Jl. Karel Satsuitubun Tual Kai Kecil	–	–	–	–	–
Mirah Boarding House Tual Kai Kecil	–	–	–	–	–

West Irian / New Guinea

Total length: 2,350 km/1,460 miles.
Irian Jaya: 375,000 sq. km/144,787 sq. miles.
Papua New Guinea: 398,000 sq. km/153,668 sq. miles.
Between the Equator and Australia lies the immense island of New Guinea – the world's second largest after Greenland. Politically, the island is divided in two parts: to the east of the boundary formed by the 141st east meridian (with a slight deviation along the course of the Fall River) lies Papua New Guinea, a sovereign state since 1975; to the west lies Irian Jaya, a province of the Republic of Indonesia since 1969.

New Guinea, rugged and inaccessible, is still a mystery to many. Traversed by an over 5,000-metre-high/16,404′ windswept mountain range covered, in part, by perpetual snow, it is also one of the last great domains of the tropical rainforest. Oppressive, damp heat, high temperatures and floodlike rains predominate in the lowlands and deltas, fog and low-lying clouds alternate with intense sunshine in the central highlands. Here, too, low temperatures can play an unexpected role. In some mountain valleys, the climate can be anywhere between hot and humid, to icy cold.

Some call it the last frontier, others see it as a relic of the Stone Age since its inhabitants live self-sufficiently and close to nature and until a short time ago, were still using stone implements. In addition to the 800,000 native inhabitants of Irian Jaya, who call themselves Papuans, there are 400,000 migrants from Indonesia's western provinces. Despite its fantastic beauty, the island can be very inhospitable and driven by excessive ambition, many adventurers, explorers and missionaries met their deaths here, struck down by fever or exhaustion. Earlier, they were often sent out to punish natives held responsible for the disappearance of Europeans. These dark-skinned inhabitants adorned with feathers, bones, teeth and the like, fit only too well into the picture handed own to us of wicked, cannibalistic natives. Their alleged existence, however, can only be traced back to the character of their "discoverers" or to the shrewdness of the "gutter press" and the film industry. Even the 1961 disappearance of Michael Rockefeller after a raft accident on the south-western coast of New Guinea was attributed to cannibalism, by tabloids eager for a rise in circulation. Those with knowledge of the island often paint an albeit exotic, but less sensational picture of the land and its people. Only now are

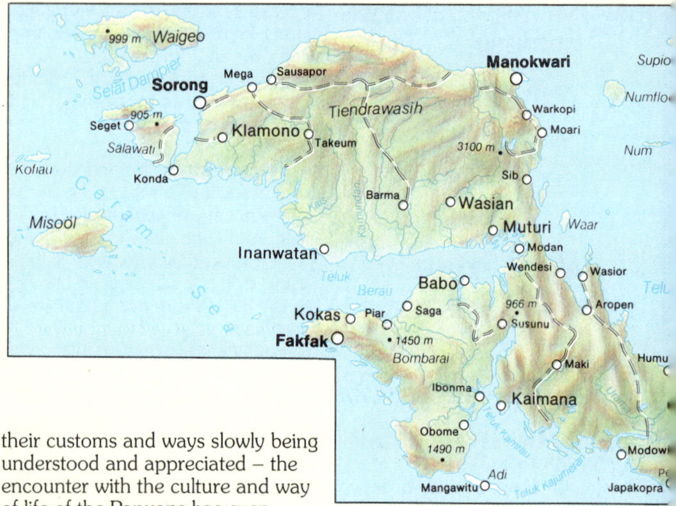

their customs and ways slowly being understood and appreciated – the encounter with the culture and way of life of the Papuans has even given some visitors to New Guinea a new perspective on their own lives. Until only a short time ago, one could encounter tribes living in isolation in hard-to-reach mountain valleys, subsisting as hunters, gatherers and tillers and using spades, hoes, picks and axes fashioned out of wood, stone or bones. New Guinea today, however, is an island of enormous contrasts. Western influence, which is gravely altering the make-up of the land and its people, is gaining more and more ground. Roads and tourist facilities originally found on the coastonly, are now advancing further and further inland. Ambitious building projects will provide a network of roads connecting Irian's northern and southern coasts. Along these roads, the government plans to resettle Indonesians from the overpopulated areas of the republic. The indigenous peoples have already made it clear, however, that they will not allow their land to be expropriated. Wherever it is still possible, several missions have therefore taken it upon themselves to secure for the natives the deeds to their land. As the infrastructure grows, so too does the number of tourists. While only a small amount of travellers have come to Irian in the last few years, in Papua New Guinea, the tourist industry already represents an important source of income. It has become obvious, however, that many tourists see the country as a prehistoric human zoo and that they come here "for the thrill of it" rather than out of any genuine interest. Owing to this,

Biak
Sorenarwa
Mamberamo
Apauwar
Sarmi
Randowaja
Betaf
Tarawesi
Demta
Jajapura
Barapsi
Wonti
Waren
1340 m
Pegunungan von Rees
Irian Jaya
Enarotoli
Pegunungan
4234 m
PK. Jaya
5030 m
Peg. Sudirman
4730 m
4595 m
Wamena
Maoke
Peg. Djajawidjaja
Uta
Mimika
Apimu
Kokonau
Timuka
Agats
Mindiptana
Tanamerah
Ostjanep
Birab
Masin
Pirimapuan
Kepi
Asike
Arafura
Sea
Mapi
Abemarre
Muting
Naroob
Jabowa
Kolepom
Okaba
Kumbe
Merauke
Komoran
10 miles

the government's initial interest in the lucrative tourist industry has since given way to a certain degree of reticence. In order to keep up appearances, the ambitious developing nation of Indonesia does not exactly try to promote contact between tourists and the so-called primitive peoples. Therefore, the interested traveller must display more than good intentions, understanding and tolerance, if he wants to achieve his objective and arrive at the destination of his dreams.

Cassowaries – large flightless birds related to the emu.

New Guinea's History

Scientific studies have shown that the first migrations to New Guinea occurred during the last ice age about 50,000 years ago, made possible by the then-existing land bridge between Asia and Australia. The Tasmanian and Australian peoples probably reached the Australian continent over this route as well. New Guinea's many ethnic groups, who had arrived at different times and lived isolated from one another because of mountains, swamps and forests, were able to retain their **cultural individuality.** To a certain degree, this explains the fact that over 1,000 languages are spoken on the island today. New Guinea ceased being a stepping-stone between Asia and Australia when, at the close of the Ice Age approximately 12,000 years ago, the sea level rose by 120 metres/394′. As a result, further cultural influences remained at a minimum. It was also unnecessary for the islanders to develop new forms of social organization. While domestic swine, still a status symbol for the highland people today, were evidently being bred as early as 6,000 years B. C., the cultivation of tropical tubers doesn't seem to have begun until 2,000 years later. Although the earliest stone implements found – albeit implements of rather indistinct form – date back to the year 10,000 B. C., lentil-shaped ax blades of the type that were still in use a few years ago, could not have been in use before the year 3500 B. C. The distribution of high-quality **pottery** (socalled Lapita ceramics) over Melanesia began 500 years later. At the time when the **Lapita civilization** reached its zenith (around the year 1500 B. C.), new methods of navigation and fishing were being developed by the peoples of the coastal regions.

It has been established that the Bronze Age first made its entry into northern New Guinea in the year 1000 B. C. The irrigation ditches still so typical of highland farming today were introduced in the first century A. D. and contacts with the islands to the east, were first seriously developed one thousand years later. Although the coastal areas of this huge island were known to Chinese and Malayan seafarers long before the arrival of the first European explorers, the western world did not even learn of the existence of this distant land until the beginning of the 16th century. The **Portuguese** seafarers d'Abreu and Serrano are thought to have sighted New Guinea in 1512. Their countryman, Jorge de Menezes, was definitely there in 1526, however – on a voyage from Malacca to Ternate, he drifted off course and spent five months near Warsai on Bird's Head Peninsula waiting for fair weather. He called the newly-discovered land Ilhas dos Papuas, or "**Island of the Curly-Haired**". A short while later, the **Spaniards** started arriving. During two attempts to reach Mexico by sailing eastward from the Moluccan island of Tidore, Alvaro de Savredo Ceron went ashore at several points along New Guinea's northern coast in the years 1528 and 1529. Proposals concerning the profitable exploitation of the newly-discovered territories were rejected by Charles V. of Spain.

1545 is probably the most significant date in the history of the island. In that year, the Spaniard **Ortiz de Retes** landed there by chance and gave it the name **Nueva Guinea** – its inhabitants reminded him of those of African Guinea, whom he had encountered on a previous voyage. In the ship's log he wrote: "I have discovered a new land of Negroes." One hundred years passed before the discovery was made that this "land" was an island. Up until then, it was assumed to be part of Australia. At the beginning of the 17th century, the Spaniard Luis Vaez de Torres discovered the passage between Australia and New Guinea that still bears his name: the Torres Strait. At the same time, Dutch vessels first appeared in New Guinean waters. The **Dutch East India Company** had entrusted Captains Schouten and Le Maire with the task of mapping new coastlines. Jan Carstensz, sent to New Guinea by the Dutch governor of Ambon, returned from this voyage in 1629 with a sensational report: from the coast, he had seen enormous mountains covered with ice and snow. At first, his tales of snow near the Equator were popularly attributed to rum, but soon they were confirmed by other seafarers as well. Mountains and glaciers did indeed exist only 600 kilometres/373 miles south of the Equator. It was not until 1962 that the highest peaks of this range, including the 5,030 m/16,502 ft. high Jayawijaya, formerly known as the Carstensz Pyramid, were finally scaled – by an expedition under the leadership of Heinrich Harrers.

The coming of the Europeans was of little significance to most coastal Papuans. Those suffering under the slave trade carried on by the neighbouring Moluccan sultanate of Batjan, saw the white visitors as a threat as well, and often treated them with reticence and even hostility. The fact that they offered resistance to these alien intruders (who were more often than not armed to the teeth) led to rather gory place-names on the first maps of New Guinea. Until the 20th century, maps were resplendent with names like Murderer's or Killer's River – names which paint a one-sided picture of the island and its inhabitants. The initial power that the Dutch wielded in New Guinea diminished temporarily in the 18th century. Spurred on by the lucrative spice trade as well as by strategic and scientific interests, many **European nations** sent expeditions into New Guinean waters; too. The use of French and English in the new maps added to the confusion already caused by new entries and new place-names. Philip Carteret, Louis Antoine de Bougainville, James Cook and John McCluer made large contributions to the knowledge of New Guinea. The captain of the Bounty, William Bligh, whose fate at the hands of the mutineers is well known, managed to reach the Dutch trading post of Kupang on Timor after a 3,500 mile sea-voyage which took him and the eighteen others, crowded in the longboat, through the Torres Straits. During this harsh journey, as well as on a subsequent one commissioned by the British Admiralty, he prepared exact sketches of New Guinea's southern coastline which proved useful to ships' captains in the decades to come. By engaging in intrigues with local princes, the **British** succeeded in winning sovereignty over the western part of the island in 1794. The Napoleonic Wars in Europe made it possible for them to maintain their authority there until 1828. In that year, the **Dutch,** after having claimed a large part of New Guinea as their territory, established their first stronghold on Triton Bay. In less than eight year's time, however, fifty per cent of the men stationed there had succumbed to fever, and the fort had to be abandoned.

August 24, 1828 saw the fixing of the Dutch colony's eastern boundary. In 1875, after a minor correction, it was officially set at 141° east longitude. Thus, in the interest of colonialism, New Guinea was split, and, in the interest of colonialism, it was to stay that way. Although the English had been farming in South-Eastern New Guinea for quite some time, it was not until 1883 that the Union Jack was hoisted there. In 1884, **Great Britain** and imperial **Germany** divided the eastern half of the island between themselves. On November 3 of that year, the previously established German New Guinea Company was entrusted with the administration of the north-eastern part of the island, as well as of the Bismarck Archipelago and parts of the Solomon Islands and Micronesia. The term "colony" was replaced by the term "protectorate" and the area was named Kaiser Wilhelm's Land. Its rich soil yielded coffee, cocoa, cotton and tobacco – products which were renowned in Europe for their high quality.

Missionary work began in New Guinea in the mid-19th century and was intensified in ensuing decades. Today, there are more than sixty different missionary groups at work on the island spreading the Christian faith. Some have become wiser over the years and, more tolerant of the traditional beliefs of the Papuans, place agricultural projects and medical care in the forefront of their activities. Unfortunately, they are still the exception.

It was not until the end of the 19th century that the **intensive exploration** of the island's interior began. German, British and Dutch expeditionary troops penetrated the unknown bush by way of the rivers Sepik, Hy and Mamberano. It was clear to the Papuans that these were not courtesy visits, but rather, shows of power on the part of the colonial forces. Although most of the encounters were peaceful, opposition to foreign rule did begin to mount. It was, however, more the severity of life in the tropics than the resistance of the inhabitants that brought colonial expansion to a halt in some areas. In 1895, the Imperial German Navy began mapping eastern New Guinea using modern cartographic methods. In 1906, the Dutch completed their mapping of the western area.

Immediately after the outbreak of World War I, Germany's colonial possessions on New Guinea were confiscated by **Australia,** which had already been granted the south-east portion of the island by Great Britain in 1906. On September 13, 1914, after a short skirmish with German colonial troops, the Australians raised the British flag over north-eastern New Guinea. A small German unit, however, with the support of the native population, waged a four-year guerilla war against the Australians in the central highlands. Today, very little remains of the former German presence in New Guinea. The word "raus", which is used by speakers of Pidgin English when showing someone the door, however, is a relict of the course manners which must have been prevalent in colonial days.

In 1927, Australia began exploiting the **gold deposits** discovered in the Bulolo Valley. Owing to the fact that the necessary machinery could only be transported into the jungle by aeroplane, New Guinea became one of **aviation's pioneer zones.** In those early days of development, the businessman Cecil Levine had an entire town flown into the jungle in four all-metal fuselage Junkers G 31. On 6,000 flights between Bulolo and the coast in less than three years, 5,000 tons of freight and 7,000 passengers were transported. New Guinea Airlines, which was founded then, was the first to introduce flight insurance for its white passengers. Papuans were carried uninsured for one shilling per pound of body weight. It was logical that the Papuans who lived in the seclusion of the highlands would mistake the first aircraft they saw for birds descending from the realm of spirits and ancestors. A reception party made up of the bravest men would present the spirit-bird with gifts and even venture to inquire about the creature's sex. Today, aviation is an important feature of the regional development of New Guinea. Obviously, these "big birds" quickly became a familiar sight.

The years of intensive exploration produced some sensational discoveries, notably the discovery in 1936 of the Wissel Seas (now the Paniai Lakes) by the Dutch pilot Wissel, and the discovery of the **Baliem Valley** in 1938. With the outbreak of **World War II,** however, this development came to an abrupt end. Following their attacks on Dutch East India and the Philippines, the Japanese attacked New Guinea in January 1942 to secure for themselves the island's vital raw materials. The Commander-in-Chief of the Allied forces in the South-West Pacific, General McArthur, decided to liberate New Guinea first, before going on to the Philippines. A bloody jungle war then broke out between the Australians and the Japanese. In the attempt to keep the Japanese units who were advancing over the Kokoda Trail, from reaching the southern coast, 15,000 Australian soldiers lost their lives.

During the war years, the Papuans, who rendered indispensable services as pathfinders and porters, were recognized for the first time, if only by force of circumstances, as fellow human beings and friends, and were treated as equals. Their personal needs, however, were incidental to the interests of the warring nations. The war years saw the burgeoning of a cult among the Papuans, which was given new stimulus by the air-dropping of supplies to the Allied troops: the **cargo cult.** The parcels which floated down to the earth on parachutes and landed in forest-clearings, contained wondrous items thought to be gifts from powerful ancestors. When these objects sent from the other world, did fall into the hands of the soldiers for whom they were meant, the Papuans attributed this to an error in delivery or even to theft. With the cargo cult, the seeds of selfesteem (and thus, of Papuan **nationalism**) began to grow. Its force was soon felt by the Japanese, whose cruelty made them especially unpopular. When they were denied food supplies by the Papuans, they retaliated by burning villages to the ground.

The eastern regions of New Guinea were the first to be liberated. When, in April 1944, the Japanese were defeated in the west as well, the island's customary stillness returned for a short time. On their return, the Dutch, eventually forced by world opinion to recognize the **sovereignty** of the Indonesian Republic, initially hung on to West New Guinea. Although the territorial demands of Hatta and Sukarno were originally restricted to the Moluccas, a conflict arose over the

Dutch part of New Guinea on the occasion of the transfer of sovereignty on December 27, 1949. By 1952, Sukarno was determined that West New Guinea should be included in the **Indonesian state.** The Netherlands felt, however, that the unique identity of the island, as manifested in its many languages and cultures, could only come into its own through self-rule. For this reason, they encouraged the application of Article 73 of the U.N. Charter which calls for the support of liberation movements in countries dominated by colonial powers.

Alarmed by growing Indonesian demands, the Dutch, despite the knowledge that the end of the colonial era was fast approaching, began stepping up social expansion in Dutch New Guinea. In the wake of the exploitation of the island's natural resources, new settlements emerged in the coastal regions. It became increasingly evident that the island was one of the richest sources of raw materials in the world. After the discovery of new oil deposits near Sorong, refineries were built.

It had long been known that the southern slopes of the Carstensz Mountains were rich in **copper.** More exact probings brought to light a 33-million-ton supply of copper ore. Owing to the volatile political situation, however, the Dutch decided, for the time being, not to invest money in the mining of these deposits. Sukarno's policy of confrontation became more rigorous from day to day. The deportation of Dutch citizens and the confiscation of Dutch industries brought no results, so military action was taken. The attempt on the part of Indonesian airborne troops to invade West New Guinea failed, however. While the Netherlands hastily dispatched troops to reinstate the status quo, New Guinea, with equal haste, was preparing itself for **independence** – Sukarno, however, demanded the immediate surrender of the territory. The **United States,** which under the Kennedy Administration was striving for better relations with Indonesia, withdrew all support for the Dutch in the New Guinea question. This dealt the deathblow to the **Luns Plan** which was submitted in 1961 and called for the placing of West Guinea under U.N. mandate and a subsequent plebiscite on the question of independence. The **Brazzaville Resolution,** which was adopted instead, called for bilateral negotiations which eventually did lead to a solution. On behalf of President Kennedy, the American diplomat Ellsworth Bunker, devised a new plan which ultimately helped avert an all-out war. The **Bunker Plan** called for a short period of interim rule under the United Nations, followed by the temporary transfer of authority over the region to the Indonesian government. After seven years, the people were then to determine their future by means of a plebiscite. The Papuans, who had already been anticipating independence, had to content themselves with this decision for the time being. On August 15, 1962, the Dutch Prime Minister, de Quai, took leave of his former dark-skinned countrymen with the following words: "Continue working for the welfare of your people. The thoughts and good wishes of the Dutch people will accompany you in this endeavour. May God protect you!"

After seven months of provisional rule under the United Nations, the Republic of Indonesia took control of West New Guinea on May 1, 1963 and changed its name to West Irian. The word "irian" comes from the Biak-Numfoor language and roughly means "hot land". Indonesia had been promulgating the use of this name for several years because its letters form the acronym of Ikut Republik Indonesia Anti Nederland – "**Follow the Republic of Indonesia against the Netherlands!**"

The city of Hollandia, founded in 1910 and subsequently the seat of the Dutch governor-general, was first renamed Kota Baru (New City) and then, Sukarnopura, and finally, Jayapura.

Meanwhile, in the **East,** development ran along a quieter course. The area had become a U.N. trust territory administered by Australia. At the instigation of a United Nations commission, parliamentary elections were held there in 1964. Of the 54 elected delegates, 38 were native New Guineans.

As a result of violations against the U.N. agreement which stipulated that Papuans were to be appointed to high government posts in Irian, disturbances broke out, followed by the formation of a resistance movement. In 1969, the referendum that was to decide the political future of West Irian took place as stipulated in the treaty between Indonesia and the Netherlands. The manner in which the referendum was carried out, however, became the object of much controversy. Out of the approximately 450,000 enfranchised Papuans, only 1,025 were selected to do the voting. After the news of their unanimous decision to remain a part of Indonesia was made public, unrest broke out which had to be quelled through the use of military force.

In 1972, after two years of intense work, the **Freeport Copper Mine** was inaugurated. From the mine, located on the southern face of the Carstensz Mountains, a 100-km/62 mile-long road leads to the mouth of the Tapoka River where a special port has been constructed. West Germany and Japan are the main customers for Indonesian copper ore. During the inauguration ceremony, West Irian was renamed Irian Jaya.

Papua New Guinea (or Papua Niugini) gained independence in 1975 following the ratification of its constitution. PNG is now a sovereign state within the British Commonwealth and a member of the United Nations.

From time to time, rebellions have flared up in Irian against the central government in Jakarta which have provoked the dispatch of military units to this outpost of Indonesian authority. In 1977, for instance, a revolt broke out among the Dani tribes of the Baliem Valley at the time of the Indonesian parliamentary elections. The resettlement programmes for migrants from Sulawesi, the Moluccas and Java have also lead to social tension in Irian, which is occasionally evident in outbreaks of violence. Most of the province's 800,000 native inhabitants live in the interior, while the 300,000 immigrants from other parts of the republic have settled mainly along the coast, thus determining the make-up of the villages there. While the gap between the native population and newcomers from the western provinces is in danger of widening in Irian Jaya, the 2.2 million citizens of Papua New Guinea are striving harder than ever to maintain national unity. The line of demarcation once set by the Dutch at longitude 141° East is, today, closely patrolled from both sides. Despite occasional flare-ups between PNG and its neighbour, Indonesia, the two countries maintain diplomatic relations which each other.

Tribal Life in New Guinea

Despite the fact that approximately 600 different languages are spoken on New Guinea, tribal life throughout the island is fairly uniform. For instance, the rank of tribal chief is not hereditary. A chief who is not up to the challenge of his post or who usurps privileges is usually forced to take his hat, or rather, his feather, and leave. The motto: "Equal rights for all" applies here as well. In the interior, the largest social unit is the village, or community, which is usually headed by more than one chief. As a group, women have a say in decision-making as well. Because their ability to bear children guarantees the continuance of the tribe, they enjoy social recognition as well as their husband's esteem.

Although a man must barter his most valuable pieces of property, i.e. his pigs, in order to get a bride, he does not view his wife as a possession, as popular belief would have it. Early in life, young girls are prepared by their mothers for the responsibilities of everyday life; their male contemporaries, however, are indulged a little longer.

Ancestor worship stands at the centre of Papuan belief, which is frequently based on the conception that all new life comes from death. This explains the Asmat people's cult of head-hunting, which was practised to ensure the continuance of the tribe. The concept of the balance of life and death is not only limited to human existence, but encompasses the whole of Nature as well. Although the Papuans have frequently been accused of being cannibals, this has never been definitively proven. As a rule, so-called eye-witness reports turn out to be pure sensation. The eating of the heart and liver of an enemy killed in battle, which has been documented by a number of missionaries, is, on the other hand, an ancient ritual which has many precedents in the history of civilization. It is thought to have been customarily practised in an ancient society which our western humanistic tradition holds in high esteem – that of ancient Greece. The eating of the ashes of a cremated body, as practised by several tribes, has likewise nothing to do with cannibalism or necrophilia. This act, which is bound up in the mythology of the people, is the expression of a close tribal bond which includes even the souls of the deceased. Such behaviour may seem extreme to us, but it is part of a complex view of the natural world that even anthropologists, after long and extensive studies, cannot entirely comprehend. To attempt to evaluate an ancient culture by using bits and pieces of scientific data is a risky undertaking which can easily lead to prejudiced assumptions. The visitor to New Guinea should therefore not try to evaluate, but instead, should merely try to understand.

Among the Papuan peoples, warfare and ancestor worship are closely intertwined. In spite of the fact that Papuans have an obligation to the spirits of the dead to wage war against enemy villages, the two sides still carry on trade with each other and celebrate weddings together. In the past, hostilities would sometimes escalate to such a degree that the only thing a tribe could do to avoid total destruction was to flee. When mutual warfare threatened the true essence of the tribes, however, recourse was often taken in the form of a peace treaty.

Not all tribes are warlike, however. Particularly among the tribes of hunters and gatherers found mainly in the dark of the forests, there are tribes who avoid encounters with other human beings, when at all possible. New Guinea is aptly called an **anthropological and ethnological treasure trove** because new, as yet unknown tribes, are continually being discovered. With the aid of research projects, these tribes are then catapulted into the 20th century – or into oblivion. This usually happens sooner than expected. For instance, there is not a single trace remaining of the Tapiro pygmies who once lived in the

Manioc – the Papuans produce flour from the tuberous roots of this tropical plant.

region around the Paniai Lakes. It is assumed that they were wiped out by a disease that was introduced from the outside.

In New Guinean villages, many tasks, such as house-building and the clearing of fields, are performed jointly – even old people are included in the work whenever possible. No-one takes charge, and no orders are given. No division-of-labour agreements are made – each participant simply knows what he has to do and does it. Steel blades are now widely used in addition to the traditional implements such as rodent teeth and chips of bone and rock. Bamboo splinters, an all-purpose tool, are also still in use. With them, hair is trimmed, pigs are cut up and umbilical cords are severed. Durable and costly timber must be brought in from the outside. While working, the highland people like to sing, but the only musical instrument they know is the Jew's harp, which they play with passion. Drums are common among some coastal tribes, but they are only played on special occasions. In Irian, celebrations are not only a part of worship, but serve to deepen neighbourly relations and the sense of community togetherness as well. Often trade is carried on at the same time.

The Papuan's traditional economic system is based on a special unit of currency, namely the **cowrie shell,** the value of which is estimated according to form, size, colour and age. Today, however, the shells are gradually being supplanted by paper money and coins. Now they play a minor role in the commercial transactions of the Papuan highlanders, but at one time, they were valued as much as gold. Their size, weight and hardness, plus the fact that they were difficult to come by, made them appear to be a suitable form of currency – and not only on New Guinea, but in many other parts of the globe as well. In Irian Jaya, four different shells are in use. While Cymbicum diadema and Nassa immersa are used only for decorative purposes, Cyprea moneta serves as legal tender. On the other hand, there are many colourful and beautifully patterned shells that have no value whatsoever in the eyes of the Papuans. Until just a few years ago, in remote areas, an entire pig could be had for a genuine cowrie. Its appearance, however, had to conform to the locally accepted conception of one. Because their value was determined in part by their shiny-white enamel surface, "counterfeiters" from the coastal areas would bleach the shells in acid to enhance their value. During the Japanese occupation, and later, in the wake of the many expeditions, this traditional money system was undermined by inflation. Great amounts of cowrie shells were brought into circulation, thus causing the prices of normal commercial commodities to increase drastically. In addition to its economic function, the cowrie also serves as an amulet against infertility and disease. Moreover, because of its resemblance to the vulva, it is believed to possess magic powers which have a positive effect on pregnancy and birth. The delicate relationship between man and his ancestors and man and his environment, as manifested in the use of such amulets, has already been essentially disturbed. The advocates of modern development see the cargo cult as proof that these people want more than anything else to follow the path of large-scale consumption and increasingly take on western ways. With this postulation, however, we are far from the truth. The industrialized world today, moreover, is no longer in a position to guarantee everyone the kind of life it presents, much less to guarantee that it will last.

Trips to Irian

The expression "mass tourism" is as yet unknown in Irian Jaya. The lack of comfortable hotels and the inevitable hardships of travel in this area do not exactly make it a popular travellers' destination; indeed, very few travellers, be they alone or in groups, venture out this far. Many people undertake a trip to Irian with an array of misconceptions, including the one that the Papuans will add a touch of adventure to their holiday. The experience of responsible tour operators shows that it is not genuine interest in the lives of the native peoples, but sensationalism that sends most tourists on their annual jungle adventure. Later, when the tales are told around the home fires, the storytellers often forget to mention that they could not have covered the distances that they did without the services the local people provided as porters, guides and hosts. It should be borne in mind that it is not easy for the Papuans to comprehend the modern world and the changes it brings; great mental flexibility is demanded of them in order that they may weigh its merits against those of their own traditions. In view of this fact, one should be sure about one's reasons for going, as well as about the consequences of such a visit. Those who decide to venture into such remote areas should know that sign language is not the appropriate basis for a carefully planned encounter with a strange and isolated culture. Particularly in New Guinea, unintentional violations of local taboos could cause offense and misunderstandings. A knowledge of basic Bahasa Indonesia, in which many Papuans are fluent, is therefore indispensable for the traveller to Irian. This effort will be rewarded by a more profound insight into the habits of the people and a better understanding of their customs and attitudes – as far as this is possible within the limits of one's own perception. Those who cannot find the time to acquire a working knowledge of the language should plan their trip with an experienced and responsible travel agent whose tour guides are capable of conveying the unadulterated facts. Unfortunately, however, the spontaneous and generous hospitality of the people, when experienced on an organized tour, often appears to be a service included in the price of the trip.

Getting to Irian

The cities of Jayapura, Timuka and Sorong, as well as the island of Biak, can all be reached from Jakarta by Merpati Airlines and from Surabaya,

The Cargo Cults

According to the beliefs of the Oceanic peoples (to which the Papuans belong), the goods that the white people possess are actually gifts sent down from the realm of their ancestors. Although these goods are meant for everyone's benefit, they are constantly being "embezzled" by white men. While waiting for justice to prevail, so-called cargo cults were formed – religious movements whose origins do not only go back to these people's first contacts with "cargo-rich" Europeans, but also to their own religious past. The prophets of these movements promise their followers happiness and prosperity – some elements of the Christian faith are also included. For the most part, these are sectarian groups who practise a type of ritual magic, in the hope that it will have a positive effect on their lives. In any event, the sheer amount of cults (approximately 300 and all basically alike) shows that their underlying message, which is generally an all-encompassing one, is of elementary significance to the people of New Guinea. Although the cargo cults usually offer no answers to vital questions of timely importance, they have served to strengthen the Papuans own sense of worth and helped them to develop a sound concept of self. As New Guinean art shows, this movement also brought about a release of creativity. It is easy to presume that the cargo cults are based purely on materialistic attitudes, but the matter is actually far more complex than that. The goods that the cult followers long to possess are of a more practical than frivolous nature, although a small status symbol or two does appear now and then on their lists. Imitating our way of life, however, lies far from their intentions.

Ujung Pandang and Ambon by Garuda. Those who wish to enter from Papua New Guinea are forced to take the once-a-week flight from Wewak to Jayapura because of a lack of roads connecting the countries. Travel by boat to and from Irian should only be considered by those who have enough time at their disposal. For the Surabaya-Jayapura route, served by the state-run Pelni Lines, one should calculate 10–14 days depending on the number of intermediary stops.

The fact that 80 per cent of Irian is covered by dense rainforests already suggests the difficulties with which the traveller has to contend. While the jungle in the lowlands and deltas, through which countless large and small waterways wind their way, is often swampy and malaria-infested, in the highlands, it covers steep and treacherous mountains. Owing to frequent earthquakes and heavy rainfall, landslides have often occured to which many a village has fallen victim.

Walking tours from the coast to the central highlands have the character of an expedition and must be cleared with the police and military authorities. As even short distances here require day-long marches that all too often take one through uninhabited areas, a tent and sufficient provisions are best taken along. Don't skimp on supplies. (Porters get hungry, too!) And after all – people are used to share and share alike. Since most travellers have about a four-week holiday at their disposal, only short trekking tours will be mentioned here. In order to undertake such a trek, one need not be a survival expert. Good physical condition, the ability to make do with little, and some experience in the tropics are, however, useful.

The destination of most trekking tours is the Baliem Valley in the heart of the highlands. The environs of the Paniai Lakes are being visited more and more frequently as well, but only as far as the authorities allow. The Casuarina Coast to the south is, on the other hand, only suitable for boat tours.

Official inner-Irian routes are served only by Merpati. From Biak, there are connections to Monokwari, Sorong, Fak Fak and Nabire. From Nabire, one can fly to Muanemani, Enaritali, Hometo and Ilaga. From Jayapura's Sentani Airport, there are one or two flights daily to Wamena. Other places served are Merauke, Bokondini and Ok Sibil. The smaller airstrips in Irian are served mainly by two mission-affiliated airlines which will occasionally carry tourists as well. Despite the fact that the Protestant MAF (Missionary Aviation Fellowship) has the larger fleet of aircraft and pilots at their disposal, they are only prepared to transport tourists under certain conditions. The Catholic AMA (Associated Mission Aviation) seems to be more accommodating, but does not always have seats available.

The number of flights that actually get off the ground each week depends on the weather. The early-morning hours are best suited for flying because of good visibility and low turbulence. At other times of the day, clouds can gather without warning, making flying in the mountainous interior of New Guinea more dangerous than in any other place in the world. The number of plane-crashes each year is proof of this. Many of the approximately 250 airstrips are not easy to land at; many are located on mountain slopes, in ravines or in the jungle, and are only grass- or gravel-covered. In addition to Cessnas, Islander and Twin Otter STOL (short take-off and landing) aircarft are used, to facilitate take-offs and landings where airstrips are short. These aircraft can carry between 5 and 16 passengers depending on size and cargo.

Travellers who wish to fly to their own time-table, or to land in almost inaccessible areas will have to charter an aircraft. For a twin-engine Islander, one must be prepared to pay about 400 US$ an hour. In addition passengers pay the cost of the plane's return flight (to its base). "Airfast", which specializes in charter flights, has offices at Jayapura's Sentani Airport.

A special permit is required for travel in the province of Irian Jaya. This surat jalan, as it is called, can be obtained from the police authorities in Jakarta or Jayapura. To avoid any unpleasant surprises in Jayapura, however, the application should be made in Jakarta. The following travel agencies can also furnish one with a permit in a matter of one to three days for a small fee: Agaphos, 16 Jl. Gajah Mada; and Natrabu, 29A Jl. Haji Agus Salim, both in Jakarta. People wishing to apply direct should write to: Dinas Intel Pol (Mabak), Jl. Sudirman Gedung Veteran, Jakarta pusat, or Polisi (MABD), Jl. Trunojojo 3 Jakarta.

Trekking and Equipment

There's no such thing as bad weather, just bad equipment – very true of Irian. Since the success of a wilderness trek depends to a great extent on the choice of equipment, this should be given careful attention during the planning of the trip. It should also be borne in mind that a trek should not be undertaken alone.

Since "sightseeing" in Irian takes place on foot, a good pair of comfortable, medium weight hiking or mountain boots with a heavy tread is the factor which determines the success or failure of the entire undertaking. When the trek begins, it will soon become apparent whether the right choice was made or not. Water-repellent spray, four pairs of comfortable ski socks and an extra pair of shoelaces should also be included. For crossing swamps and streams, waterproof overshoes can come in very handy. In addition, training shoes should be taken along to relieve the feet on easy stretches of roads and during rest breaks.

A good, weather-proof, lightweight tent equipped with a mosquito net eliminates the nightly search for quarters and allows one to be more roughly independent. Iglo tents weighing 2.5 to 3.5 kilogrammes, 5½–7½ lbs, offer more space and comfort than do pyramid tents. Regardless of whether you have a tent or not, you should not miss the unique experience of spending a night in one of the traditional dwellings of the highland people. When you emerge after the first night, much weakened by a slight case of smoke poisoning and attacks from various insects, it will not be long before you come to appreciate your tent!

Just as it takes practice to appreciate the experience of spending the night in a tribal hut, bivouacking in the rainforest also requires two to three days of acclimatization. Aside from mosquitos, there are usually no other nightly visitors that will rob one of one's sleep. Especially in the lowland jungles, all the fun of trekking can be lost, at least for a time, if leeches appear on the scene. They locate our position through the odour of lactic acid in our perspiration, as well as by the heat radiated from our bodies. The only means of protection from these pests lies in the camouflaging of the characteristic odours which we, as warmblooded creatures, have. Besides rubbing the skin with the

Le Roux and the Mountain People of Papua

The Dutchman Le Roux, came to know the interior of New Guinea through a series of expeditions he made between 1926 and 1939. Roux belonged to an age which believed that every culture and race discovered outside the "civilized" world, was made up of primitive, incapable beings in need of help and protection. It was an age that viewed colonialism as something acceptable, and indeed a matter of course.

Roux expressed very different sentiments in his significant work on the mountain people of Papua, as the following extract shows: "Though this "Stone-Age man" (people saw the Papuans as a very backward race) Ki gimujakigi, was thrust prematurely into 20th century Ambon, he did not for one moment behave like a helpless child in his new, modern world. No, rather he showed a great capacity for adapting himself to his new milieu. Would a European, transplanted from one of our large cities to a Papuan village, display a similar ability to survive?

And is the Ekari tribe really so unreliable, so underhand, and selfish as Post would have us believe in his book? Aren't we the selfish ones – selfish in our behaviour towards the Papuans? They certainly never asked us to come, and yet this did not deter us from coming. And now we expect them to be obedient servants, forever at our beck and call. We

liquid from boiled-down tobacco leaves, smearing the clothes with plain soap has also proven to be effective. It is also best to wear long-sleeved shirts and long trousers in such areas. If a leech does attach itself to the skin, it is best to loosen it with a burning cigarette or to wait about ten minutes after which time it drops off by itself. Tearing them off only leaves behind wounds which take a long time to heal and can easily become inflamed.

Those who plan to bivouac, but have no previous experience, should first consult a good handbook on survival in the tropics. Such a book can teach one about jungle orientation, safe fire-building and more. Alternatively, ask a Papuan to act as guide, and he will provide you with practical instruction in survival techniques. It is amazing what human hands are capable of doing without the aid of mechanical implements – with them, the Papuans can make ropes and nets, build bridges, huts and fires and much more. As far as protection against mosquitos is concerned, however, they have not devised anything better than the smoke from a fire. Nowadays, malaria- and filaria-carrying mosquitos are no longer found exclusively in the lowlands. In view of this fact, it is easy to see why it is imperative to bring along a mosquito net. This have them constantly running after building materials for biwaks, houses and churches, and, as if this weren't enough, they have to keep us supplied with provisions. Need we be surprised, if for example the Ekari, for a variety of reasons we cannot begin to comprehend, become tired of acting as servants and general "dogs-bodies"? Does it not speak in their favour that they have proved to be shrewd businessmen in their dealings with us, in striving to gain every advantage they possibly can of these strangers who have come to destroy their community?

Are we in future, going to accuse these people, who are as yet untainted by civilization, of failing to comprehend our western norms, morals and customs, or blame them for leading a quiet, carefree life? Don't we have to admit that many of us yearn to be released from the restrictions imposed upon us by state and church?

I have lost my heart to the simple mountain people of Papua, and I feel that it is my duty to defend them against claims made by people, incapable of fully appreciating their different manner of thinking, or of understanding their ideas on morals and propriety, and who attempt to judge their life-style using western norms."

Le Roux never lived to see his three-volume work published. He died on September 8th, 1947, whilst going over the manuscript for his book, "De Bergpapaos van Nieu Guinea en hun woongebied". Today his book remains of great significance to anthropologists.

does not, however, mean that you should abandon other preventive measures against malaria. (A suitable mosquito net is one that hangs on only two hooks and is designed for individual use – that way, you only have yourself to blame if you are bitten. The use of single nets also pays off when travelling partners become separated.) The use of insect sprays gives additional protection, but one should beware of introducing new consumer habits to the indigenous population. Empty or half empty aerosol containers carelessly discarded, or given away can be hazardous to the health of the local people – especially when they attempt to uncover the secret of the hissing sound produced by this object from another world by attacking it with sharp implements or submitting it to a sort of trial by fire. For the same reason, disposable lighters should be kept out of innocent hands. Those who have medicines left over at the end of their trip will find that the health centres (PusKesMas) and missions will be glad to have them. The leaflet with information on application and dosage should always be included. It should be kept in mind that medicines should only ever be placed in competent hands.

Irian's health centres being few and far between, one could do the people a great service by treating the injuries they acquire in rough terrain many of which are slow to heal. A first-aid kit should include a sufficient amount of dressings and disinfectants. Even though such assistance has a more symbolic than medicinal value, it leaves everyone involved feeling happier. Because the native people often take the white visitors for miracle healers, one's services are sometimes requested in more serious cases. Since most travellers are not professionals, adminster first aid as far as possible, but arrange for the transport of the patient to a mission post.

For many of us, snakes are the stuff of nightmares, but if one is not atually searching for reptiles in Irian, one is hardly likely to see them. Although only 20–30 per cent of all untreated bites are fatal, the trekker must be well prepared, as the lack of hospitals is a factor which must also be considered. Temperature-sensitive serums can do more harm than good when used improperly and are best left alone. A snake-bite kit, obtainable at sports shops or from camping outfitters, however, will furnish the necessary first aid – provided it is always at hand and one knows how to use it. In order to counteract the initial physical reactions to the snake venom, large doses of vitamin C can be administered (5,000–10,000 mg every two hours). Finally, drinking strong coffee will help to stimulate the circulation.

Drinking large amounts of fluids has a positive effect on the course of the illness. The patient should lie quietly, keeping the affected area in a position lower than the rest of the body. Important: In order to keep time on one's side, all snake bites should be regarded as poisonous and treated accordingly. Precious time is lost in the frantic search for and identification of the culprit.

The type and amount of provisions to be taken along depends on the character and duration of the tour planned. Besides instant soups and tinned meat and fish, high-fibre foods such as müsli should also be brought along. In view of the fact that the inland inhabitants often suffer from protein deficiency, one should think twice before buying up their last pieces of meat to satisfy one's own nutritional needs; instead, a supply of protein tablets (of the kind taken by high-performance athletes) should be to hand. Mineral drinks, which counteract mineral loss caused by heavy perspiration, are another type of special food which can prove very useful. For a balanced diet, sweet potatoes, sugar cane and perhaps fruits can be obtained on the spot – provided the harvest was plentiful. Since the lowlands offer poor growing conditions for vegetables, multi-vitamin tablets may be necessary in the event of an extended stay. For a tour of up to two weeks, such precautionary measures are superfluous.

A petroleum or kerosone stove is only necessary in the alpine regions which are rich in grass and moss but devoid of trees; on shorter tours, a stove only adds unnecessary weight. Besides, as a rule, liquid fuels may not be taken aboard commercial aircraft.

Obviously, a good pocket knife and compass as well as a powerful torch with a set of replacement bat-

Conch Shells or Paper Money?

The Papuan people are very familiar with the ins and outs of conch-shell money. Shells are hardly ever used today as a means of payment but in many areas they have retained their symbolic and religious significance. Dealing with modern money – for the most part, notes with a face value of Rp. 5,000 and Rp. 10,000 – is still a major problem for the Papuans. Depending on their method of counting (this may involve the use of fingers, toes, and other parts of the body, or stones and knotted string) certain tribes only count up to 5, 10, 13 or 20. At market, traders from other areas often make a profit at the expense of the mountain Papuans. It is common knowledge that they are unable to calculate the amount of change owing to them where large notes are concerned, and this fact is exploited again and again. Children who now attend school have a much better understanding of money than their parents.

Many Papuans make a point of not accepting 5,000 and 10,000 Rp. notes. They will usually accept 500 and 1,000 Rp. notes, but in many areas people prefer the red 100 Rp. notes above all. Coins are not very popular amongst these highland inhabitants, as they tend to lose them very quickly. (Is this because they have no trouser-pockets?).

Taking all this into consideration, it is important that the visitor take an adequate supply of small notes with him. Another point to bear in mind is that porters and guides prefer to be paid daily, when they have finished their work.

teries are musts on a trek. Even if mountain climbing is not on the agenda, a mountaineering rope of at least fifty metres in length can be very useful for crossing rivers and streams, descending into caves, hanging hammocks or laundry, and securing gear. For proper orientation in the bush, a detailed topographical map is indispensable. Unfortunately, they are hard to come by. The ONC map (Operational Navigation Chart), reference no. M-13, with a scale of 1:1,000,000 in the 1971 revised edition is an excellent orientation guide for the trekker, although it is meant for aviation purposes. The many white areas on the map designated "data incomplete" suggest that even the available information should not necessarily be taken at face value. This applies in particular to the rivers as their courses constantly change in the lowland areas. Another useful but hard-to-find map is: **Nederlands Nieuw-Guinea,** 1:1,750,000 published by Topografisk, Delft 1959. Strips of transparent tape placed over the folds of a map will keep it from tearing. Those who plan to tour only the Baliem Valley can get by with a sketch.

Another thing to remember is that the best advice ends where excess weight begins!

Arithmetic of the Highlands

Although mathematics might not mean much in New Guinea's interior, the people have long since solved their day-to-day calculation problems. The numbers which form the base of their mathematical system not only exist as written figures, but are also represented by parts of the body. An explanation of the system used by the Dem people from the Nogolo valley is given below:

1 =	ama	= thumb
2 =	dingi	= index finger
3 =	juda	= middle finger
4 =	amagime	= ring finger
5 =	emea	= little finger
6 =	jagakot	= ball of the tumb
7 =	jasige	= back of the hand
8 =	jagaja	= wrist
9 =	jagabua	= lower arm
10 =	jaga mungkut	= elbow
11 =	jaga bua moak	= upper arm
12 =	jengkegenggu	= shoulder
13 =	jemenuak	= chest

The left hand is used to indicate the appropriate number. Very often the other side of the body is used to count up to 25 (left thumb).

However in the Moni's system:

1 =	nana	= thumb
2 =	kindo	= index finger
3 =	dagupa	= middle finger
4 =	mugu	= ring finger
5 =	kiu	= little finger
10 =	anegi	= both hands (fists) together
20 =	ane baro	= hand and feet

When the fingers are used, each finger is bent into the palm after it's been named.

Some Moni and Ekari tribes count up to 100. This is no great surprise in the case of the Ekari, who are very adept in matters connected with trading. They often use conch shells or knotted string for counting.

The Baliem Valley

The date is June 23, 1938. The Guba, a CAC long-range seaplane, brings an expeditionary team headed by Richard Archbold into the virtually unexplored central highlands of New Guinea. The heavy rumble of the twin Pratt & Witney thousand horse-power engines, adds motion to the already-charged atmosphere in the cabin. The pilot, G. G. Rogers, stares fascinated at the scenery before his eyes. He sees the foliage drawing threateningly close: initially resembling a lush carpet blanketing the surface below, it soon rises up to touch the wings of the tiny aircraft in the form of rugged folded mountains. Following the course of the valleys, the small seaplane disappears in the immense cloudcovered mountain realm. Then the plane penetrates the last veils of haze, and a wide sundrenched valley stretches out before the astonished eyes of the Guba's passengers. (The valley is at 1,700 m/5,577′ above sea-level.) In its centre, a silver ribbon of a river winds its way toward the eastern horizon. From the air, the countryside below looks like a giant Garden of Eden – a patchwork of small fenced-in hamlets containing round and rectangular-shaped huts surrounded by neatly tended gardens and an extensive network of irrigation canals. While the seaplane prepares to land on a calm stretch of water, a storm of arrows rain down upon it… The pictorial documentation of this event can be viewed in New York's Museum of Natural History. Richard Archbold called it "Grand Valley", but now it is known as the Baliem Valley after the river that runs through it.

Since the mid-1970's, this area has been developing at a rapid pace. Wamena, a small police-base founded by the Dutch in the 1950's and supposedly named after a famous tribal chief, recently acquired a paved airstrip. In the last few years, more than fifty vehicles have been flown in by the airforce, although this settlement possesses less than ten kilometres/6 miles of roads. The indigenous Danis, considered by many to be a Stone Age people, fortunately have not allowed their encounters with the 20th Century to change them greatly. Dressed in grass skirts or kotekas, they seem to live on undeterred, in the tradition of their forebears. The increase in the volume of air traffic, as well as the use of even larger planes, however, provides for a constant influx of new developments. Cement-mixers, generators, refrigerators, television sets and motorcycles are only a few of the items that have found their way into the Baliem Valley. Our consumer-orientated society has also left its mark here: a discarded tin can which would have been fought over by the Danis a few years ago is now usually left lying on the ground unnoticed.

In addition to the many migrants from Sulawesi (mostly Makassans) who come for the pleasant climate and fertile soil, today more and more tourists are discovering the now easily-accessible Baliem Valley. Because the old Hotel Negara (now the Nayak), which housed Heinrich

Harrer during his 1962 expeditions, no longer met the needs of so-called adventure seekers, the state-run Pertamina Oil Company erected the Baliem Cottages (in the style of the local men's houses) ten years ago; since then, however, the ravages of time have spared very little of their original luxury.

Taking Wamena as the starting point, many day excursions can be made into the surrounding areas, although the radius of activity is rather limited. Equipped with a tent, however, one can move freely in the Baliem Valley (20 x 80 km/12 x 50 miles), as long as one has official permission. The only point of interest that Wamena itself has to offer is a daily market where the various Dani tribes sell their produce and handicrafts. Established by the Indo-

nesian government to familiarize the Danis with our economic system, this market has achieved a certain degree of fame due to its variety of wares and the different kinds of visitors it attracts. While the Danis offer their high-quality farm produce under the canopies in the centre of the market, the migrants from Sulawesi sell everything from plastic buckets to tinned vegetables in the surrounding shops. Those who plan to replenish their food supply at the market should compare prices well. The crops that the Danis grow also provide for the towns of Biak and Jayapura where the soil and climate are less suitable for farming. In fast-growing Wamena, the Papuans, who earn pocket-money doing odd jobs, frequently appear to be no more than onlookers. People not officially resident in the community must leave by sunset (tourists excluded).

The most celebrated tourist attraction in the Baliem Valley is the mummy located at Akima, a village west of Wamena which can be reached from there on foot in two to three hours. After a contribution has been given to the village elder (the amount of which keeps pace with inflation), the seated mummy can be viewed. In recognition of the Mummy of Akima's enormous contribution to the growth of Irian tourism, a stone pavillion was placed on the outskirts of the town by the Minister of Tourism to display this cultural relic. The village chief, however, whose mummified grandfather attracts hundreds of tourists each year, was ordered by the spirit of his deceased relative to move the mummy back to its original place, so the pavilion stands empty. Aside from bringing pecuniary blessings to the village, this powerful ancestor also ensures that the soil is fertile, the men are strong and the women are beautiful. Now, however, the mummy shows signs of being worm-eaten and the future no longer looks so bright to Hulolik, the Akima chief.

The road to Jiwika which passes Akima, is now negotiable by car, but the beauty of the countryside and the charm of its people can only be experienced by the hiker. The main road offers no difficulties and is easy to find. Jiwika is also the starting-point for a visit to the saltspring located at the threshold of the Pass Valley. Here, and in another spring near Hetigima, the Danis use an ancient method to obtain this mineral which is so valuable to them. Strips of the inner bark of trees, as well as banana stems which have been beaten to a pulp, are left in the well to soak up the brine, after which they are carried home to be dried and then burned. Then, the ashes are blown away carefully, and the salt remains. This home-made salt with a smokey flavour is frequently preferred by the Danis to the industrially-produced kind.

Travelling west from Jiwika, the bat-filled cave of Kontilola can be reached in about three hours. There are cave-drawings here, as well as a subterranean lake accessible by a path that leads straight down into the cave. To get to the cave located near the village of Minimo northeast of Wamena, one must cross a 60 m/197′ long wire-cable suspension bridge. Another bridge, the Pikke, has a modern reinforced-steel construction. The most impressive Dani suspension bridges are located in the eastern part of the valley where the Baliem River falls at great force into the gorge near Kurima. The trek along the Baliem and into the lowlands is one of a high degree of difficulty, as shown by Heinrich Harrer's account of his expedition along the right bank of the river. Those who decide to attempt it, however, should stay on the left bank, keeping in mind that wide detours will nevertheless have to be made around topographical obstacles.

The Danau Habbema, a lake on an uninhabited plateau overgrown with scrub, can be reached after a hike of one to two days. The debris of the camp-site left behind by the Archbold expedition in 1938 can still be found on the banks of the lake – an example not to be followed. Not far from the lake, the Trikora Peak rises up 15,518 feet. Once always covered by snow, it now has only a snow-cap as the result of sudden climatic changes. Only experienced mountaineers should attempt this climb: its smooth rock face has been the undoing of a number of mountaineers alread\

So far, many tourists have been delighted by the fascinating landscape of the Baliem Valley as well as by the sincerity and friendliness of its people. Unfortunately, however, rumours about a planned reservoir which would occupy the entire valley continue to circulate.

As a help with orientation, it's useful to know the following Dani terms:

pigu = easterly direction
uwabu = southerly direction
agindoga = westerly direction
koma = northerly direction

Pronunciation may vary a little.

The Danis

The tribes belonging to the Dani linguistic group inhabit the immense Baliem Valley as well as the many smaller valleys in the region. Their number is estimated to be between 80,000 and 100,000. Ethnologists believe that they left Asia before the Polynesians, but did not arrive on New Guinea until after the Australian peoples – but many other theories abound as to the origins of these dark brown, medium-built Melanesians with negroid features. The Danis' way of life is similar to with that of other highland peoples, but the structure of their society is unique; their families and communities are organized along different lines. As opposed to other peoples, they do not live in open-villages, but rather in fenced off hamlets with gardens. Within the enclosure, which is often disguised by bushes and shrubs, there are round family houses and houses for the men as well as rectangular kitchen buildings and barns. The men's houses, which can only be entered through a very low door, are usually situated in a commanding position on the village square. Their roofs consist of a 10–20-centimetre/4–8″ thick layer of thatching which privides excellent protection against heavy rainfall; their floors, which are raised 30–40 centimetres/12–16″ off the ground, are made of boards. In the middle of the round houses, a fire is kept burning day and night on a clay pit. As these constructions are not equipped with vents, the smoke escapes by seeping through the thatched roof. Owing to this smokey, stifling air, many Danis suffer from bronchial and eye disorders. Men and boys from the age of six sleep in the men's house – women are barred. Their domain is the family house, which is where marital life takes place. A man is obliged to erect a house for each of his wives as well as to provide each with her own cooking fire in the kitchen-building. He also has to ensure that each wife has a plot of land large enough to feed her and her children. In a society where the women greatly outnumber the men, polygamy offers many women a family life and support – something that would not be possible if monogamy were practised.

Men and women share the work in the fields; the men take on the more strenuous tasks of clearing, breaking up the soil and digging out irrigation canals, while the women do the tilling and harvesting. The Danis' diet consists mainly of sweet potatoes, bananas, yams, beans, sugar-cane and pandanus. As a source of protein, the pig plays a very insignificant role, as slaughterings take place only on rare and special occasions. Wam or pig is the most precious possession of the highland peoples and plays an important role in their rituals. The Danis even consider these four-legged, grunting creatures as members of the family, and go so far as to give them names. Dani tradition calls for a woman to amputate a finger up to the first joint as a sign of grief over the death of a favourite pig. The pig banquet (isatare to the Danis; pesta babi in Indonesian), which is the highpoint of the social and religious life of many highland tribes, takes place at intervals of three to ten years (sometimes only once in fifteen years), at which time up to 1,000 animals are killed. Given the Danis' relationship to the pig, however, these feasts cannot be compared to similar events in the West. Slaughterings also take place in the event of war and in celebration of births and deaths. The pig's flesh is cooked along with several types of vegetables, over hot stones in a pit, which is prepared by the women; the men are responsible for slaughtering (by arrows) and dressing the animals. Owing to the lack of proper meat-inspection facilities, the swine tapeworm (Cacing pita), which was introduced to West Irian a few years ago, has been able to spread like wildfire. In humans, which serve as intermediate host, the worm causes prolonged illness coupled by epileptic seizures ultimately resulting in death. Important: As the temperature in the pits is rarely high enough to kill all the parasites in the meat, one should only eat pork one has prepared oneself, or even forgo eating it altogether.

In conjunction with an isatare, weddings, initiation rites and celebrations in honour of the ancestors often take place. In Dani society, there are special rules governing matrimony: a distinction is made between two exogamous classes, namely, the waija and the wida; thus, bride and groom may not belong to the same group. Since the children are born into the same marriage class as the father, and maternal relatives are ineligible as marriage partners, the possibility of a marriage between blood relatives (endogamy) is ruled out from the start. Boys and girls are instructed in the facts of life at an early age and generally choose their marriage partners themselves. If a girl accepts a boy's offer of matrimony (which is usually conveyed through a female relative), her family is presented with a determined

Extract from the Dani ABC of Good Manners

The tribes of the highlands like to see friendly, laughing faces. Anyone with a friendly, open nature who has mastered a few words of the language will definitely be popular here.

In the Baliem valley the people greet each other with "Lauk". The only exception to this is the way in which men greet other men – here "nayak" is used. The pronunciation of "nayak" varies according to area. Variations include "narrak" and "nalak" ("nayak" is typical for the area around Wamena).

The Ekari people who live around the Panias Lake always use "koya" to greet people, whether they are male or female. A few more phrases of Dani (which also apply to Wamena and the surrounding area):

huben ke	=	good morning
dikane	=	"good day" (The greeting used at midday)
hiam ke	=	good afternoon
hibako	=	good evening
noge	=	good night
nayak	=	thank you

The men of some highland tribes also hook fingers when they greet each other. One man grasps the index or middle finger of the man he has met, between his own index and middle fingers and then the hands are pulled away from each other. The sound produced in doing so is the desired effect.

amount of pigs one month before the wedding – just how generous the gift is depends upon the wealth of the groom's family. The wedding ceremony and its duration varies from clan to clan. In the event of incompatibility between marriage partners or among the wives, separation is the solution. After the birth of a child, sexual relations between husband and wife come to a halt for four to five years. After the second child, most Dani women take steps to induce an abortion because the necessity of feeding many mouths in times of bad harvests can place an entire tribe in jeopardy. In addition to the loving care and affection of their parents, Dani children enjoy freedoms which help them develop into self-confident and responsible members of the tribe. Every tribe-member is guaranteed protection, food and shelter. As a rule, when a married man dies, his brother or best friend will marry his widow.

The belief in spirits figures centrally in Dani life. Everyone is certain that he is governed by a spirit of life and a spirit of death and that the latter will ultimately triumph. Tribal feuds once occured very frequently among the Danis, due to the necessity to appease the spirit of a relative fallen in battle, by killing an enemy warrior. The never-ending cycle of victory followed by the renewed call for revenge gave rise to the notorious system of justice known as "payback". Until recently, the Danis knew nothing of expansionism or the total annihilation of an enemy. Visits to the cinema in Wamena, however, have done much to familiarize them with the principles of warfare as practised by the civilized peoples. Eyewitnesses have reported that Dani battles, which as a rule were called off in the event of extreme heat, rain, darkness, or for the noontime break, were often characterized by much gaiety and laughter. If someone was seriously injured or even died, the victor retreated. The counterattack sometimes did not follow until months or even years later. No one was forced to participate in these battles, which were more like sporting events than incidents of war, but a man who stayed away regularly could be sure of remaining a bachelor all his life. Warfare was an intrinsic part of the Danis' concept of life; since the Indonesian government and the missions placed a ban on it, Dani society has undergone fundamental changes. Their old battle spirit has taken on a new form, however – that of the spirit of independence.

The traditional dress of the Dani men is the koteka or holim; it is a penis sheath made out of a long, conical gourd which acquires that shape by being weighted down with stones during growth. These gourds do not only serve as protection, but also as an expression of the virility of its wearer. Without his koteka, a man feels naked and vulnerable; its damage or loss would arouse in him a sense of shame. The sheath is held in place by a string wrapped around the hips and is often decorated with orchid petals, feathers or bits of fur.

A woman's marital status can be recognized by the kind of skirt she wears. The pride of every married woman is the yokal or skirt woven of orchid fibres, that she receives from her husband as a wedding present. Unmarried women, on the other hand, wear a grass skirt or kam thalis. Noken, or nets woven out of bark, are worn by women on their backs, not only as a carrying-bag, but also as protection against the cold. Wrapped around the forehead and draping down the back, these net bags not only hold food and belongings, but piglets and babies as well. Dani women keep their infants with them in their noken while working in the fields. In the highlands, these meticulously woven bags are a coveted bartering object.

As protection against the inclemencies of the weather, the Danis wear a rain cap which is made of pandanus leaves and covers part of the back as well as the head. Their bodies can adjust most satisfactorily

The Creation of the Danis

From out of a rock God created the first parents of the Danis; male and female he created them and they were called Tabeh and Hesage. God created them with light skins, but it came to pass on the first day of their earthly existence that the sun darkened their skin for all eternity. They dwelled in a cave, where Hesage, in the process of time, bore many dark-skinned children, and when these children were of age, God transformed Hesage, their mother into burning grass, and Tabeh, their father, into wilted leaves. He cast the leaves onto the flaming grass and the souls of the first parents rose up to return to their home in the cave. There, in the stones which lay scattered about, they found eternal peace. Their children, who had gone out into the world, returned to the home of their parents and found nothing but the stones which were lying about. And they took these stones with them into their own dwellings which were built in the fashion of their parents' cave, i. e., circular and with an arched roof.

Even today, one comes across sacred stones which are the dwelling-places of the spirits of ancestors, and to which the Danis ascribe magical and curative powers. When the power of an ancestral spirit seems to have exhausted itself, a Dani may then sell the stone to a tourist as a souvenir. Once the buyer places money into the hands of the seller, the power of that particular ancestor is confirmed anew. By the way, the cave of Tabeh and Hesage is said to be located in the village of Abulakma in the Analaga region of the Baliem Valley.

to the extreme temperature variatons (from 0 °C to 35 °C/0–96 °F depending on elevation, time of day and season), that distinguish the climate in the highlands – even without clothes. The distribution of western-style clothing by the government and missions, without the necessary washing-powder and instructions on personal hygiene have had devastating effects on many tribes: chronic respiratory and skin ailments were the result. It is no wonder that the "birthday suit" is once again the height of fashion. Men beautify themselves by rubbing their bodies with soot and pork grease. They wear their curly hair in small, oiled strands, often fashioned in the form of a mushroom. Colourful seeds, pieces of weaving and strips of fur serve as adornment. Boar tusks, which used to be part of the once popular battle dress, are now worn through the nose on festive occasions. The Danis also like to adorn themselves when they go to market. Women who smear their bodies with mud or clay, do so to show that they are in mourning. Earlier, it was customary for women, children and old men to amputate a finger as a sign of personal grief over the death of a loved-one. The thumb was never touched, however, in order that one hand could still be used as a prehensile tool. This custom has been prohibited by the government, but is still practised in some remote areas.

Although some of the measures taken by the authorities and the missions may seem logical or necessary, they undermine the structure of a highly-developed social order. What then remains is usually an artificial system which moves further and further away from its origins and is thus required to be always open to change. Integrity and sincerity make way for cunning and deceit which, in turn, will become a problem for new institutions of power. Only the brazen would dare call this cultural change.

The Asmat Region

The home of the Asmat people lies to the south of the central highlands in an alluvial basin approximately the size of Belgium. Along its 200 kilometre/124 mi. coastline, a host of large and small rivers flow into the Arafura Sea.

Further inland, these rivers form a confusing, swampy labyrinth. Although this area of marsh land is about 100 km/62 miles from the coast, the effects of the tides are ever apparent there.

At high tide, large amounts of salt water pass into the rivers, changing their flow and turning the water brackish. Drinking water is therefore a valuable commodity and has to be brought from far away. In the brackish portion of the river network, the giants of the rainforest dominate the landscape along with the sago and nipa palms, and the mangrove. The latter is found all the way into the permanently flooded areas which form mud flats extending for several miles.

At low tide, many coastal villages cannot be reached in dugout canoes, and inland navigation is also impeded. For example, some small tributaries, which can save the traveller several hours, often dry up at low tide.

These rivers and the shallow sea which borders on the Asmat region have an abundance of fish. Large salt-water fish such as the thorn back, the sawfish and the dolphin, are also native to the brackish water of the rivers. Although the cowrie is not indigenous to these waters, the shells that can be found here serve as ideal objects for trading with the people of the hinterland – the Asmat people exchange them for stone which cannot be found in their region.

The seemingly endless rainforests of the Asmat (that for years now have been overrun by logging companies), are home to a multitude of bird species. Inert from the heat, all of the birds are silent during the day, and as in other lowland areas, only the metallic chirp of large cicadas can be heard. The Asmat region is beleaguered by two other armies of very bothersome insects – during the day the region is occupied by a

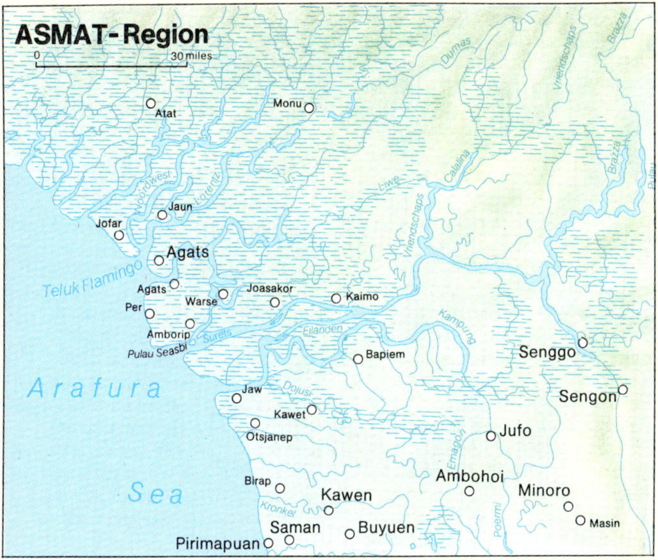

division of flies, which at dusk retreat to make way for a squadron of mosquitos.

The most common mammal in the Asmat region is the wild boar – this was, in fact, originally a domestic pig. The region is also the home of many species of marsupials: phalangers, bandicoots, bush and tree kangaroos. The egg-laying platypus is, however, very rare.

Should heavy rain and the high tide coincide with swollen rivers in the central highlands, then extensive flooding is often the result. When flooding occurs, animals which cannot swim well (or not at all) keep to the treetops – this is especially true of certain reptiles such as the monitor lizard and iguana. Among snakes, the small orange-brown adder, still to be found in the foothills, is the one most feared by the people of the region. Anyone wearing boots is generally well-protected, because these venemous reptiles can only reach up to the ankles. The taipan, which can grow to a length of 2.5 metres and which lives primarily in the dry savannahs around Merauke, is notorious for its aggressiveness and should therefore be avoided at all costs. The Asmat people, as well as the Jale in the highlands, believe that only evil people are bitten by snakes. Crocodiles, on the other hand, are considered to be a threat to one and all. The women who have to stand hip-deep in the water to fish, particularly fear the salt-water crocodile, of which specimens up to eight metres/26 feet in length have been caught. Since many riverbanks are shaded by the canopy of the rainforest, they do not provide the temperatures needed for the incubation of crocodile eggs. The Crocodilus novaguineae has developed the same method of safeguarding its offspring as the wallnister (which is also indigenous). Both lay their eggs in piles of rotting leaves which, on decomposing, produce the heat necessary for hatching.

Plants, animals and human beings have all found the most amazing ways of dealing with the obstacles which nature at times puts in their path – be it mud, heat, humiditiy, insects, or whatever. Although the Asmat region is not everybody's idea of an idyllic holiday retreat, much can be learned here about man's "oneness" with Nature.

How can the Asmat be reached? The region is not only geographically remote, but also lies well away from any main traffic routes. There is as yet no regular air service there, so planes must be chartered – as is the case in many areas of Irian. The occasional missionary plane that takes off can seldom transport tourists, because space on the five-seaters is needed for letters and parcels, food packages, fuel and employees. The small Ewer airstrip near the district post of Agats is probably the most frequented in the Asmat; the Basim and Yaosokor airstrips can only accommodate S.T.O.L. aircraft, however. Owing to the southern coast's high annual precipitation (approx. 5,200 mm/205 ins), the landing strips there are often soaked through; when this happens, air-traffic comes to a halt.

Another way to reach the Asmat is via Merauke, which can be reached daily from Jayapura. From this administrative centre which lies on the southernmost tip of Irian, a ship operated by the state-run Pelni Lines sails once a month for Sorong and calls at Agats, Kokonau, Kaimana, Fak Fak and Teluk Bintuni. The journey takes from ten to twelve days. Information about exact times of departure is generally hard to come by, but those who are interested could nevertheless try inquiring at the Pelni agencies in Sorong, Merauke or in Jayapura itself.

Anyone who has his eye on the Asmat as a possible destination, should bear in mind that it cannot be explored on foot. In this vast swamp even short distances usually have to be negotiated by boat. And the fact that fuel has to be flown in, should give you some idea of the cost of motorized transport here.

Another relatively convenient mode of transport is offered by the Crosier Mission in the form of diesel boats, which they rent out for about 95,000 rupiah per day – if the boats aren't damaged or already rented out, that is. Those who have less money and more time at their disposal, should use a dugout canoe for shorter distances. Because these canoes capsize easily, passengers would do well to remain seated while the Asmat men paddle – which they do standing up. Electronic and optical equipment should be packed in water-tight containers. The advantage of this mode of transport lies in the fact that there is no engine noise to disturb the tranquility of the swamp – animals can, therefore, be observed and their calls more clearly heard. the missions are often glad to be of service when it comes to bargaining for lower fares – in this way, they do their best to counter one by-product of tourism: inflationary prices.

Conventional forms of lodging are few and far between in the Asmat: apart from two "losmens" in Agats, the selection is quite limited. The visitor has the option of becoming the guest of a village or of spending the night in his own tent. Since such journeys are usually undertaken for the purpose of experiencing new cultures first hand, staying in a village would seem the ideal solution – all the more so when you consider that the people here are generally very hospitable towards foreign visitors. It is, however, only a viable option for the traveller who has no problems sleeping on a hard, wooden floor and who can accustom himself to eating sago and fish every day! (It would, of course, be ill-mannered and disrespectful to accept the hospitality of the village people and then eat tinned and vacuum-packed provisions.) A small token of appreciation to the host should be brought along. Try to avoid gifts which reflect the affluence of the West or, indeed, its preconceptions – radios, clocks, beads and mirrors are useless and inappropriate. Practical items such as fish-hooks, cords and axe blades are, on the other hand, indispensable to life in the Asmat. Money is usually unsuitable as a gift since it will probably be considered as payment for lodgings. Anyone who feels that money should not change hands at all (out of concern for the traditional values of the native people) should be sure to examine his real motives carefully.

The Asmat People

They call themselves "asmat ow", which means, "we, the real people". Just another example of the widespread tendency in humans to consider their own family, tribe or nation as superior to all others.

As far as the Asmat tribes are concerned their belief that they are the "real people" is founded upon their version of the creation: "Fumeripitsj", the Wind, carved them out of the wood of the yoa tree but formed the people of other tribes out of the flesh of a treacherous crocodile.

The Asmats, estimated to be about 46,000 in number, are divided into several linguistic groups, some of which comprise only a few villages. The classification of the Asmats according to language (not necessarily synonomous with a classification according to cultural traits), has resulted in their being divided into three distinct groups: the Asmats of the Casuarina Coast, those of the northwest coast and those of the upper courses of the rivers.

Owing to their woodcarvings, which take on some quite lively and fascinating forms, the Asmats were already well-known in Europe at the beginning of this century. The symbolic meaning behind their work, however, remained a mystery for a long time. Today, every reputable museum of ethnology should possess at least a few Asmat artefacts. Before the government finally placed restrictions on exportation, the creative powers of the Asmat people had provided a veritable treasure trove for the international art trade. Through the exemplary effort of the Crosier Mission in Agats, a museum has been established for the Asmats as a confirmation of their cultural identity.

Although their homeland is swampy, inhospitable and malaria-infested, the Asmats consider themselves and their land as one. These people live in the shadow of their ancestors. Drums form the link between the living and the dead, the spirits of whom constantly remind them of their duty to headhunt, a practise which has now, however, been outlawed. Headhunting was never based on arbitrary aggression against neighbouring villages, but on the mythical belief that new life can only spring from death. Although this may seem a dubious idea to us, the comprehensive ban on headhunting has robbed the Asmats of an important element of their lives. Death, the permanent separation of the body and the soul, which, according to the Asmats, are only loosely united, always stems from magic or violence. The Asmats go to great lengths to please the spirits and thus prevent their leaving the body. To prevent dreams, which are seen as an escape route for the spirit, the Asmats sleep with their heads resting on the skull of a relative or on a carved neck-rest. The fact that the unpredictable spirits of the ancestors roam around freely is perceived as a threat. For them, a new body is carved out of wood, symbolizing their re-animated self. In their honour, celebrations are also held in which "mbis" (ancestor poles), "kawe" (ancestor figures) and other carvings play a central role. These celebrations are regarded as vital to the continuing existence of the tribe and were, at one time, often an occasion for head-hunting. Villages that were once hostile towards one another have now curbed their antagonistic relations or ritualized them. In order to effectively eliminate the tensions between villages, a form of adoption is practised, whereby chosen inhabitants of one village are received into a family belonging to another village. Through the ritual simulation of birth, the former enemy is symbolically reborn into the community. Adopted males show their loyalty to the village by shooting an arrow into the air when their new name is called out. Women bang a pair of tongs against the house symbolizing their sense of solidarity and community spirit. The bond between the adoptee and his new family and community is thereby lasting and firm.

Asmat settlements can be quite large; the larger ones containing up to 2,000 inhabitants, can be found in the coastal areas. As protection against enemy attack, crawling animals and flood waters, the Asmat erect their houses on 2–3-metre/ 6½–10 ft high stilts. The men of the villages do not live with the women and children. "Yeu", the unadorned, rectangular men's houses, are the focal point of every village, and the place where the living and the dead commune with each other. Every beam, every wall, every corner of the house personifies an esteemed ancestor and thus carries a name. Under their auspices, drums, shields, "mbis" poles and statues are made and then serve to appease the fickle spirits. The distinctiveness of Asmat woodcarvings, the basic design of which varies from area to area, lies in their highly symbolic abstract form. Also serving as storage places for drums, weapons and shields, the men's houses are off-limits to women under normal circumstances. Only on special occasions (in the case of a funeral, for example) is an exception made. This does not mean that the women lack power, however – if the men of the village are shirking their duties, the women may air their displeasure by staging an attack on the men's house. The Asmats practise polygamy, usually marrying before the onset of puberty. The children's education is primarily the mother's duty, but when boys reach the age of ten, they are sent to live in the men's house under the care of their fathers; girls, however, remain under the supervision of their mothers. Children are included in all activities (excluding warfare) and, through play, they become acquainted with their everyday tasks at an early age. Children even go fishing with their parents: spear-fishing with their fathers and net-fishing with their mothers.

The Asmat people of the coastal regions are hunters and gatherers and are not accustomed to cultivating plots of land. The sago palm, which provides them with their main source of nourishment, grows profusely in this swampy terrain. Virtually the entire tree can be put to good use: in addition to the treasured sago meal, it yields fibre and leaves which are invaluable as raw materials. From them, nets, ornaments, skirts and thatch are made and the sheaths of the leaves are used as a means of rinsing during the preparation of the sago starch. In order to gather 140 kilogrammes/308 lbs. of sago, an entire family has to put in one long day of work. Even though the duties involved in the harvesting of sago are divided up according to sex, help is given and received on all sides when needed. In one day, enough meal can be gathered to last a family approximately six weeks – it is smoked immediately so it will keep longer. A sago palm will only yield an abundant crop if it has not yet borne flowers.

The felling of a palm tree is an act of a magical nature and is a symbol of human death as well. Most likely, the name "as asmat" (we, the tree-people) is derived from the notion of the tree as suggestive of the human body: the roots correspond to the feet, the trunk to the body, the branches to the arms and the fruit to the head. It follows that the sago palm has great ritual significance. An important social event in the Asmat region centres around the eating of the big, fat larvae that the weevil deposits in the decaying stumps of sago palms. While felling and chopping up sago palms, the men also provide for the safety of the women and children. In the 1960's, enemy attacks were still frequent in the Asmat, although the Dutch colonial administration had long before tried to put a stop to tribal warfare by prohibiting the construction of the 32 ft-high watch towers which served as strongholds. This structural form, which at one time was common in the entire region, can now only be found around certain tributaries upriver. Dwellings are not built along the rivers, but rather in the shelter of the forest.

Many battles were once waged on the rivers, enemy warriors attacking each other in their 46 ft-long dugout canoes. Today, they only serve as a means of transport which, in the river-maze of the Asmat, is only possible by water. Because of the strong currents upstream, smaller dugouts are used (up to 26 feet in length). Unlike those of the coastal inhabitants, they are still often made with the help of a stone ax and have no ornamentation.

Like the Dani people of the highlands, the Asmats do not wait for festive occasions in order to deck themselves out. Headbands made of cuscus skin, necklaces made of dogs' teeth, bracelets and earpegs are worn every day. The characteristic shell or bone worn through the nose is reserved for special occasions, however. Until only few years ago, clothing was unknown to Asmat men. The women, on the other hand, have always covered themselves with an apron made of sago fibres, which has yet to be totally supplanted by western clothing. The people of the remote interior cover themselves with only leaves or rushes; their relationship to their bodies has not yet been distorted by fear and shame. Even there, however, it is more than likely that clothes will soon come to "make the man". When that happens, it will mean that, for the first time, the Asmats will be using something they have not produced themselves – and it will also mark the first step towards dependence upon the outside world. Many more will follow. The presence of ready-made clothes of different colours and materials will no doubt stir up envy, jealously and hate – in addition, the Asmat will be confronted with the age-old problem of finding the right detergent.

Those who wish to experience the world of the Asmat – a world governed by magic and taboos – should try to avoid obvious and trite comparisons with their own world. How to greet the Asmat people in their own language:

tam kubitnakap – Good morning
yok fak – Hello
parainimnakap – Good evening

The Villages and Towns of Irian

There is hardly a tourist who would make the long journey to Irian solely to visit its cities. Besides having little to offer in the way of points of interest, their hotels are modest and few, and the prices are high for Indonesian standards. However, since they round off the many-sided portrait of life on the island, a stay of two to three days is a good idea. Those who are planning more extensive tours or even expeditions will probably have to spend more time in the cities than they care to, in order to make all necessary arrangements and take care of formalities.

Biak

Biak is an island located just outside the Geelvik Bay (Teluk Sarena). Long-distance domestic flights from Jakarta, Ujung Pandang and Ambon end here, while connections are offered to Jayapura, Manokwari, Sorong and Fak Fak, as well as to Enarotali, Moanemani and Hometo via Nabire. The government plans to open Biak to international air traffic in order to stimulate economic growth in this region.

Large portions of the island were originally coral growth: the town of Biak is popularly known as Kota Karang (Town of Coral) because of its foundation of coral limestone. There are many inviting beaches here, but most of them can be reached only by boat or after a long hike. At weekends, the islanders seek out the beaches at Korim (on the island's north side), because those near Biak are not exactly conducive to swimming, due to sharp coral and various kinds of flotsam. Those who love empty beaches, however, would do better to come to Korim on a weekday. A true bather's paradise can be found on the uninhabited coral islands south-east of Biak which are only occasionally visited by fishing boat. Day trips or longer visits to these islands can be arranged by Mr. Engels, the head of the Titwaka hotel chain on Biak. He is an expert on this region and is glad to be of service to its visitors.

In addition to two markets and a beautiful view of the coral sea and the nearby island of Japen, Biak also offers the historically-minded visitor war relics which bear witness to the use of heavy combat equipment by the Japanese and the Allies in World War II. Now it is nature which stages a unending battle aginst landing barges and tanks, causing them to rust in the ebb and flow of the tide. A special attraction for tourists is the Japanese cave which can be reached on foot in two hours or by four-wheel drive jeep. In the summer of 1944, several thousand Japanese took shelter here during an American air attack – most of them subsequently perished in the heat of battle and burning kerosene. Today, relatives still come to mourn their dead and pray in this limestone cave.

Jayapura

Those on their way to the Baliem Valley will most likely have to make a stop in this town of 40,000 inhabitants, west of the fantastically beautiful Humboldt Bay. Sentani Airport is situated about 45 kilometres/ 28 miles from Jayapura on the Sentani Lake and offers connections to Wamena, Bokondini, Merauke and Timika. The mission and charter airlines are based here as well. In addition, there is a flight once a week to Wewak in Papua New Guinea – relations between the two countries permitting.

Seen from the coast, this idyllically situated town seems to hug the hilly landscape. In addition to its beautiful location, Jayapura's attractions include a beach (called Base G) and a museum of ethnology which is part of the University of Abepura.

The debris left behind on Hamadi Beach shows that Jayapura was not left unscathed by World War II – and the settlements near the dockyards east of the city and around Sentani Lake show how this debris has been used: the houses made of corroded metal parts blemish the otherwise lovely countryside. The fascinating Sentani civilization, which once flourished around the lake, also fell victim to the war: only the older generation still produces wood carvings that carry traditional patterns. In the hills overlooking Jayapura and Humboldt Bay, General McArthur established temporary headquarters during the New Guinea phase of the war. A visit to the command post, however, is not quite as spectacular as the view this vantage point offers of the city, the bay, and the islands in the distance.

Being the administrative centre and seat of government of the province of Irian-Jaya, Jayapura has been included in a comprehensive development program. Life in this town remains tranquil and easy going, however. Between noon and 4 pm, the streets are deserted, and those looking for exciting nightlife will find themselves disappointed. After patronizing the Paradiso Bar and the other bar on the harbour, as well as the two cinemas, one has exhausted all the possibilities.

Manokwari

Manokwari lies in a rich and therefore relatively populous region. Since it is separated by mountains from the jungles of the interior, it profits fully from a balmy maritime climate. Along the coast, one finds idyllic fishing villages, which are, however, only approachable via very poor roads. The inhabitants are a mixture of Papuan, Melanesian, Buginese and Chinese peoples. The area's proximity to the Philippines is clear from its inhabitants as well.

Those who wish to hike from Manokwari into the interior should undertake the first leg of the trip without guides or carriers – the coastal people, who have a relatively high standard of living, are apt to stretch your funds with their charges. The Arfak region in the interior can only be reached with some difficulty; adventuresome tourists usually go there by chartered plane from Sorong. Owing to its natural harbours. Manokwari is important to regional navigation.

Sorong

This oil town in western Irian is the headquarters of Indonesia's state-run oil company, Pertamina. Besides Papuans and Indonesians from other provinces, specialists from Texas are employed here as well, to help get the black gold out of the ground. The above-average earnings of those employed in the oil branch have sent prices in the city spiralling. Sorong is also well aware of the fact that Texas oilmen need whisky and entertainment to keep them going. Those who do not know how to handle alcohol, however, are bound to take a tumble down the social ladder – unfortunately, the authorities don't seem too concerned that this problem effects mainly the local population.

Besides a lovely beach promenade and a many-faceted city scene, Sorong has a very little else to offer its visitors. Jefman Airport, which lies on an island thirty kilometres/ 18.5 miles off the coast, can be reached only by boat (two scheduled crossings a day) or, if one cannot stomach the waves, by helicopter (This costs Rp 19,500 one way!).

Hotels in Irian Jaya

Name/ Address	No. of Rooms	With WC/Bath	Km to Airport	Km to Bus
Biak				
Irian Jl. Moh. Yamin Biak P.O.Box 546 Tel. 21139, 21839	50	50	0.2	2
Titawaka Jl. Selat Makasar Biak P.O.Box 536 Tel. 21835, 21885, 21685	53	53	2	1
Mapia Jl. Jend. A. Yani Biak P.O.Box 541 Tel. 21383, 21961	44	44	3	2
Maju Jl. Imam Ronjol 45 Biak Tel. 21218	11	–	2	0.1
Jayapura				
GKI Jl. Sam Ratulanoi 6 Jayapura Tel. 21574	14	–	35	0.4
Dafonsoro Jl. Percetakan 20 Jayapura Tel. 21870, 21285	27	20	34	0.5
Asia Jl. Pasar Sentral 18 Tel. 41277	18	9	30	5
Lawu Jl. Sulawesi 22 Jayapura Tel. 21937	11	–	35	1.5
Irian indah Jl. A. Yani Jayapura	18	14	35	0.5

Name/ Address	No. of Rooms	With WC/Bath	Km to Airport	Km to Bus
Numbay Jl. Trikora	44	12	40	3
Sederhana Jl. Halmahera Nr. 2 Jayapura Tel. 21297, 41157	15	15	35	0.35
Manokwari				
Arfak Jl. Brawijaya Manokwari Tel. 11	18	–	6	–
Merauke				
Praja Jl. Sabang Merauke Tel. 190	24	–	3.5	2
Nabire				
Titawaka Jl. Siliwangi Nabire P.O.Box 61	10	–	2.5	–
Serui				
Bonsera Jl. Yos Sudarso Serui	10	–	–	–
Sorong				
Batanta Jl. Barito 1 P.O.Box 451 Sorong Tel. 93 S	18	18	–	–
Cendrawasih Jl. Sam Ratulangi 28 Sorong Tel. 21740, 21966	21	21	5	2
Mamberano Jl. Sam Ratulangi Sorong Tel. 300	21	–	5	2

Pilihan Jl. Jend. A. Yani P.O. 425 Sorong Tel. 210 R	18	18	–	–
Wamena				
Baliem Cottage P.O.Box 3 Wamena	18	18	1.5	–
Nayak Jl. Angkasa 1 Wamena	12	–	0.2	–

From Sorong, many airstrips in West Irian (the so-called Bird's Head) can be reached. Merpati-Nusantara Airlines also offers scheduled flight to Fak Fak in the southern part of the island.

Merauke

Merauke is the southernmost city in Indonesia and lies near the border the Republic shares with Papua New Guinea. Owing to its proximity to Australia, this part of New Guinea is often characterized by arid landscapes. The vicinity of Merauke, with its savannahs and eucalyptus trees, not to mention its kangaroos, is very reminiscent of the sixth continent. Sago palms, which are the people's main source of nourishment, grow along rivers and in swamps. Merauke itself is dusty and hot – it is easy to feel that one is on forgotten territory here. Tourists who nevertheless venture this far usually do so in order to catch a boat or a plane into the Asmat region or to arrange a trip up the Bian or Maro Rivers. When its water level allows, the Maro River provides a 300 km/186 mile-long link with Tanah Merah, where the Dutch once detained political prisoners, Sukarno among them. This climatically oppressive place allegedly serves the same purpose today.

Applying for Permission to visit a Nature Reserve

Nature and everything connected with nature has become popular again. So it's more than likely that visitors to Indonesia will also wish to experience the country's unspoilt nature at first hand. For all those people, with a love of nature, Indonesia has an enviable variety of fauna and flora: large rain and monsoon forests, areas of savannah and bush land, mountain scenery and volcanic landscape, not forgetting the marine life with its corals and the dense evergreen forests. Most people will want to see something of everything. And then there are the animals, of course. Who wouldn't like to be able to observe elephants, tigers, rhinoceros, leopards, monitor lizards, parrots, wild buffalo, cassowries, cuscus and many more animals, all in their natural environment?

If you stop to consider the size of the land, however, you will realise that it would be impossible to attempt to see every animal in each of Indonesia's reserves. So it's worth

taking the time to pinpoint your own particular area of interest.

The **Direktorat Perlindungan dan Pengawatan Alam** – Directorate of Nature Conservation and Wildlife Management – (**P. P. A.** for short) is responsible for the management and administration of over 55 Nature Reserves and National Parks within Indonesia. Their main office is situated in Bogor, 60 km/37 miles south of Jakarta – Jl. Juanda 9, opposite the main entrance to Bogor's Botanical Gardens. They will be happy to answer any queries you might have regarding travel, accommodation, or the general organization of your trip. This is also the place where you apply for permission to visit the reserves. Only on rare occasions will this permission be granted by one of the 27 regional offices. Their staff can, however, be of assistance in other matters.

Should there be no P. P. A. office nearby, it is possible to apply instead to an official from the Forestry Administration. This body is answerable to the P. P. A.

To visit more isolated areas, such as Kalimantan, some areas of Nusa Tenggara, the Moluccas and Irian Jaya, you also need a letter of permission, surat jalan, containing information about yourself, the names of the places you wish to travel to, and your reason for going. Though the

completion of these formalities takes a lot of time, it is important to comply with regulations. Experience has shown that a letter from the regional governor can be very useful, too. Forestry officials are responsible for the safety of all visitors to their reservations; they share this responsibility with the police, and often arrange for visitors to see the police authorities.

If a village lies within a reservation, then it is a good idea to pay a courtesy visit to the village chief. Not only will he be able to tell you a multitude of tales about the people, the animals, and the area itself, but he is also the man generally responsible for providing porters, guides, and accommodation. If it is at all possible, try to visit the Camat (district head), too. Roads, or tracks suitable for vehicles, are few and far between here, so that you must be prepared for a lot of walking. Sometimes it is possible to find air-services that operate in the area of a particular Nature Reserve. In Nusa Tenggara horses are available for hire.

If you require porters, please note that the present rate of pay lies between 2,000 and 3,000 Rp. a day depending on the area concerned. You will also be expected to provide your porters with supplies – e.g. rice, vegetables, dried-fish or corned beef, tea and sugar. It goes without saying that the food should be of the quality you would expect yourself. In many places the porters also act as guides.

Visitors touring rainforests are constantly plagued by mosquitoes, leeches, and heavy rain, though with time they become accustomed to these discomforts. Plastic sheeting, which can be bought off the roll, provides a quick-drying, practical alternative to the usual tent covers. Food and clothing must also be protected from the rain.

Many people who toy with the idea of tracking down animals in the rainforest, more often than not decide not to go after all, worried about the unpredictability of "untamed nature". In reality the dangers are minimal, and those people who comply with the recommendations made by the P. P. A., and follow the exemplary behaviour of the porters, should encounter few problems. Roll on safari – and for once not in Africa!

Please note:
In accordance with the "Convention on International Trade in Endangered Species of Wild Fauna and Flora in Commerce" (**Cites**), you should make a point of not buying any souvenirs, the production of which involves the use of wild animals or wild flowers.

Please do refrain from buying souvenirs of this nature. In doing so, you will be making an important contribution to the preservation of endangered animals and plants.

Appendix – Indonesia from A to Z

Aceh/N. Sumatra (A5, 6) – northwesternmost Indonesian province, capital: Banda Aceh, attractions: Lake Tawar in the Gayo Highlands. Tobacco farming around Bireuen, rigidly Islamic population.

Adat – Traditional system of values and rules of behaviour rooted in religion and which serves to regulate the social life of the people within a certain community.

Agats/W. Irian (E6) – Village on the southern coast, centre of the Asmat people. Woodcarving, point of departure for interesting boat-trips.

Agung Gg./Bali (J6) – highest and holiest mountain (volcano) on Bali, elevation: 3,142 m/10,308′. The ascent takes 1–2 days.

Alang alang – also called elephant grass, grows up to 2 m/about 78″ high, usually as secondary growth.

Alfuro people – Aboriginal people of the Moluccas and some of the Lesser Sunda Islands.

Ambarita/N. Sumatra (B6) – Toba Batak village on Samosir Island; megalithic civilization; royal palace and place of execution.

Ambon/Moluccas (E5) – administrative capital of the Moluccas on island of the same name. Attractions: Fort Rotterdam, Fort Amsterdam (taking photos is not allowed!), old Portuguese church and fort in Hila. Cultivation of cloves.

Ancol/Jakarta (G2) – amusement park near Jakarta, also called Bina Ria: golf, swimming, boats for hire, souvenirs, drive-in cinema, casino, jai alai, and much more.

Ampenan/Lombok (F3) – port city in western Lombok, ferry connections to Bali, lovely beach.

Angklung – bamboo instrument which produces four harmonious tones. Sound is produced by shaking the bamboo pipes. See also "Sudanese".

Arjuna, Gg./Java (H7) – 3,344-m/10,970'-high volcano east of Surabaya near Tretes; takes 1–2 days.

Arjuna Temple/C. Java (H5) – oldest temple complex in Indonesia, located on the Dieng Plateau; cool high-altitude climate, beautiful countryside, worth seeing!

Arjuna – Hindu hero; often sold as wayang figure in souvenir shops.

Asmat/W. Irian – Papua tribe of the southern coastal region, famous for their wood carvings, fascinating culture.

Atoni – Aboriginal population of Timor; an austronesian people who still hunt with blow-pipes.

Babi Guling – Balinese sucking pig; should only be eaten well-done.

Badui - tribe in western Java; scorn the use of the wheel and other mechanical aids; prefer to live in isolation from the outside world; approx. 4,000 tribespeople.

Bahasa – Indonesian word for "language".

Bahau – Dayak people of East Kalimantan; interesting war dances.

Bajai – small, three-wheeled motorized taxi.

Bajang Ratu/E. Java (H7) – Hindu temple near Trowulan; terraced bathing-place; very well preserved ruins.

Bajau – nomadic, seafaring people inhabit the area from Southeast Sulawesi to the Philippines; strict Moslems.

Bali/Lesser Sundas (F3) – about 2.8 million inhabitants, mostly Hindus. Touristic centre of Indonesia. Aboriginal people called the Bali Aga. Area: 5,600 sq. km/2,162 sq. miles.

Bali Aga – live in Trunyan, on the banks of the lake in Mt. Batur and in Tenganan/E. Bali.

Baliem/W. Irian (E6) – river that flows through a beautiful mountain valley; home of the Danis; limestone caves; extraction of salt by traditional methods.

Balikpapan/E. Kalimantan (F3) – port and centre of Kalimantan's oil industry. Approx. 100,000 inhabitants, first class hotel "Benakutai".

Baluran/E. Java (H9) – nature reserve 20 km/12½ miles from Wonorejo; dry savannahs, volcanoes, leopards, wild boars, bantengs, deer and much more.

Banda Aceh/N. Sumatra (A5) – provincial capital with 2.3 million inhabitants. Traditional football called bohawe played here. Museum with relics from the period of uprisings against Holland; Baturahman Mosque built during the reign of the sultan Iskander Muda; graves of the sultans.

Banda/C. Moluccas (E5) – small archipelago, old Portuguese fortifications; main port is Bandaneira; population of mixed descent (Portuguese and other).

Bandung/W. Java (H3) – Indonesia's third-largest city; elevation: 1,500 m/4,921′, pleasant highland climate; internationally-known Institute of Technology; centre of modern painting; Afro-Asian Conference in 1955 made the city world-famous; Geological Museum, Army Museum.

Bangka/S. Sumatra Ig. (D9) – island group north of S. Sumatra known for its rich tin deposits; beautiful white beaches here and at Belitung.

Bangli/C. Bali (K5) – friendly place, beautiful view from the Gunung Agung, interesting temple; inexpensive accommodation.

Banjarmasin/S. Kalimantan (F3) – provincial capital on the Barito River surrounded by mangrove swamps. Islamic centre, many canals, Lampung Mangkurat Museum. Point of departure for boat trips upriver.

Bantanghari/Sumatra (D8) – Sumatra's longest river; originates from the Kerinci volcano.

Banten/W. Java (G2) – settlement on the northern coast of Java; site of the landing of the first Dutch ships under Cornelius Houtman in 1596. Attractions: Fort Spelwijk, 200-year-old Chinese temple, remains of the Suwosawan Palace, Mesjid Agung.

Banyuniba/C. Java – 9th-century Buddhist temple; double makara motif.

Banyuwangi/E. Java (H9) – ferryboats to Bali, beautiful mosque, good beaches nearby.

Barito/S. Kalimantan F4) – river in southern Borneo that extends deep into the interior, navigable up to 750 km/466 miles, regular boat service.

Baris – Balinese war dance with a solo performance for a male dancer; well-known for its expressiveness.

Baron Beach/C. Java (H6) – 50 km/31 miles south-east of Yogyakarta. A safe beach as it is protected by a bay.

Barong dance – wild Balinese dance that portrays the battle between the sacred mythical figure Barong and the witch Rangda.

Batak – a people indigenous to Lake Toba and Samosir Island, divided into several groups: Karo, Simalungan, Pak Pak, Gayo and Toba Batak. Various architectural forms, interesting customs, largely Christianized.

Batavia – Dutch East India Company's stronghold founded in 1618 by Jan Pieterszoon Coen; now called Jakarta after the village of Jayakarta originally on that site; once the capital of the Dutch East Indies, now the capital of the Indonesian Republic.

Batik – material decorated with patterns using a negative dying process. Wax covers areas which are already coloured or are to remain white.

Batuan/Bali (K4) – centre of naive painting, carvings of dance masks.

Batubulan/Bali (K4) – centre of stone sculpture. From here, life-size statues of gods and demons are shipped all over the world.

Batukau/Bali (K4) – next to a lake in a jungle on the slope of this 2,276-metre/7,467'-high mountain, lies the temple of Pura Lahur.

Batur Gg./Bali (J5) – huge volcanic crater with lake and the newly emerged Batur volcano near Kintamani; Bali Aga village of Trunyan near the lake, hot springs, one of Bali's most beautiful countrysides.

Batusangkar/W. Sumatra (C7) – 56 km/35 miles south-east of Bukittinggi; breathtaking scenery, ancient inscriptions in stone, bullfights.

Batu Tulis/W. Java (G2) – 3 km/about 1¾ miles south of Bogor; stone inscription dating from the 5th century, footprints of King Purnawarman and one of his elephants.

Bawamataluo/S. Nias (C6) – typical South Niah village situated on a hill. Megalithic culture, war dances and stone-jumping, ornamental obelisks and reliefs.

Becak – traditional bicycle-taxi found all over the archipelago.

Bedugul/Bali (K5) – lovely village on the Bratan crater lake, Uludanu temple.

Bedulu/Bali (K5) – ruins of Yeh Pulu near the national temple; frieze, 14 metres high and 24 metres long.

Belahan/E. Java – 11th-century bathing-place, hermitage of King Airlangga.

Bemo – small motorized taxi which seats 8–12 people.

Bengkulu/SW. Sumatra (E8) – lovely old town; beautiful beaches in the vicinity, ruins of an English fort, Fort York.

Besakih/Bali – oldest and holiest of Bali's temples, situated at an elevation of 1,000 metres/3280' on the slopes of Gg. Agung, 60 km/37 miles from Denpasar.

Betel – widely used narcotic, chewed together with lime, pepper leaves and/or tobacco; stains the mouth and teeth red.

Biak/Irian – island to the north of Irian, battlefield from World War II, wreckage in the forests and on the beaches; attraction: Korim Beach and Japanese cave.

Bima/Sumbawa (F4) – port in the eastern part of the island, boats to Komodo, rigidly Islamic population.

Bima – war-loving hero of the Ramayana epic, a dark-haired villain.

Bogor/W. Java (G2) – botanical gardens with over 15,000 different species of plants; laid out in 1817 by the German professor Caspar G. Reinwardt at the request of the British Governor-General Sir Stamford Raffles; museum of natural history, former residence of the Dutch governor-generals; pleasant mountain climate.

Bohorok/N. Sumatra (B6) – orang-utan rehabilitation centre 80 km/50 miles from Medan.

Bondowoso/E. Java (H9) – known for its bullfights (bull against bull); Ijen Plateau and Kawah Lake especially scenic.

Borneo – known in Indonesian as Kalimantan.

Borobudur/C. Java (H5) – largest Buddhist shrine in the world; dates from the 8th century; over 1,500 reliefs on four circular galleries recount events from the life of the enlightened Buddha.

Brahma – Hindu god of creation portrayed with four heads, a sceptre, and other symbols.

Brastagi/N. Sumatra (B6) – village at the foot of the Sibayak volcano 78 km/about 48 miles south of Medan; pleasant high-altitude climate; colourful market on Tuesdays and Saturdays.

Bratan, lake/Bali (J4) – see Bedugul.

Bromo/E. Java (H8) – caldera with several small volcanos within it; accommodation on the edge of the crater; can be approached from Probolinggo and Ngadisari; seeing the sun rise over the rim of the crater is a unique experience.

Buddhism – teachings of Buddha.

Bugis – a seafaring people found throughout the entire archipelago. Buginese schooners in the small port of Sunda Kelapa near Jakarta.

Burkit Barisan/Sumatra – mountain ridge which extends lengthwise across the entire island.

Bukittinggi/W. Sumatra (C7) – lovely village with a pleasant climate at an elevation of 920 metres/3,018′; university, Fort de Kock (1825), beautiful scenery, the rare animals of Sumatra are exhibited in the zoo here.

Celebes – known in Indonesian as Sulawesi.

Celuk/Bali (K4) – centre of silver-working on Bali.

Ceram/Moluccas (E6) – Moluccan island with a limited infrastructure.

Many Alfuro tribes, mountainous interior, most colourful birds in the Moluccas.

Ceta, C. Java – 15th-century temple dedicated to Bima.

Cipanas/W. Java (G2) – President's Victorian-style country residence.

Dalang – shadow-play puppeteer, familiar with the roles and texts of over 200 characters of numerous epics; a dying art.

Dani – These tribespeople, estimated at 80,000, live in West Irian's Baliem Valley and other neighbouring valleys. They practise a very efficient method of farming. As opposed to other highland tribes, Danis do not live in open villages, but rather in fenced-in hamlets.

Dayak – a collective term for the tribes of Borneo, the Dayak tribes include the Bahau, the Kayan, the Kenyah, the Iban and many more. They live in longhouses; some practise dry-rice farming.

Demak/C. Java (G6) – 20 km/about 12½ miles east of Semarang; first Islamic kingdom, dates from the 15th century.

Denpasar/Bali (K4) – capital of Bali; over 100,000 inhabitants. Attractions: Bali Museum, evening market, shopping district; not suitable for extended stays.

Dewi Sri – goddess of rice; many ceremonies held in her honour on Java and Bali during harvest-time.

Dieng/C. Java (H5) – plateau 26 km/16 miles north-west of Wonosobo; Indonesia's oldest temple – dates from the early Mataram period.

Dokar, Benhur or andong – two-wheeled, horse-drawn chariots.

Dongson – North Vietnamese Bronze-Age culture characterized by drums cast in bronze; brought to Indonesia by the deutero-Malayan peoples.

Durga – Shiva's wife.

Ekagi – Papua tribe west of the Paniai Lakes; interesting culture.

Enarotali/Irian (E7, 3) – missionary post west of the Paniai Lakes;

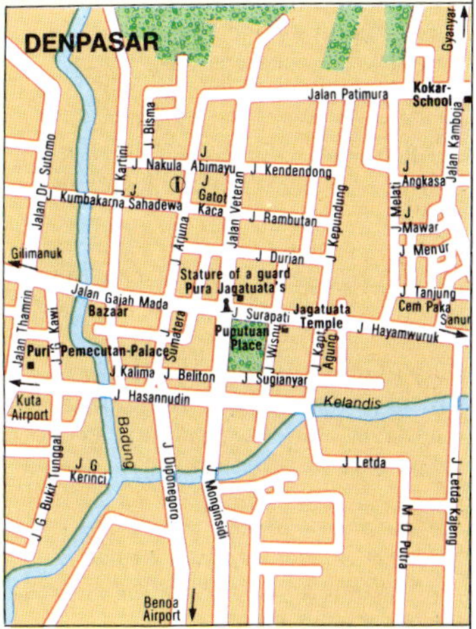

pleasant climate, magnificent countryside; flights to Nabire and Biak.

Ende/Flores (F5) – small coastal town in the centre of Flores; tours to Mt. Kelimutu.

Enggano/SW. Sumatra (F8) – island south-west of Sumatra; Engganese culture has virtually died out; cattle-breeding.

Galumpang/C. Sulawesi (A2) – centre of the Toalan population of Sulawesi.

Gamelan – traditional Javanese or Balinese orchestra made up of gongs and bronze xylophones, flutes and stringed instruments – up to 70 in total.

Ganesha – Hindu deity with the head of an elephant; Shiva's son.

Garuda – divine eagle, symbol of the sky, usually carries the Hindu god Vishnu.

Gilimanuk/Bali (I1) – Bali's westernmost port; ferries to Banyuwangi on Java.

Glodok/Jakarta (G2) – Chinatown in the northwestern part of the city.

Goa Gajah/Bali (K5) – 11th-century Buddhist monastery; grotto with statue of Ganesha; bathing-place dates from a later time.

Halmahera/Moluccas (E5, 6) – largest of the Moluccan islands; mountains and volcanoes with elevations of up to 1,500 metres/4,921′. 30 tribes, 17 languages including Papuan dialects; pearl divers.

Hari Raya, also known as Lebaran – 3-day celebration marking the end of the Islamic month of fasting and the first day of the 10th month of the Muhammedan calendar. Visits to family and friends are made on the 3rd day.

Hila/Ambon (E6) – on the island's northern coast; Fort Amsterdam, old Portuguese church.

Hilisimaetano/S. Nias (C6) – typical South Niah village with 140 traditional houses 16 km/9 miles from Teluk Dalam; megalithic culture.

Hitu/Ambon (E6) – oldest Moslem village on Ambon; Alfuro language spoken.

Helicak – small exotic-looking taxi with a streamlined passenger area.

Iban – Seedayan tribe in northern Kalimantan and Sarawak.

Ikat – traditional art of weaving practised by the Batak, Toraja and some Dayak tribes, as well as on Flores, Timor and Roti.

Imogiri/C. Java (H6) – royal cemetery of the sultanates of Yogya and Solo.

Irian – Indonesian portion of New Guinea, annexed by the republic in 1969; over 5,000-metre/16,404′-high glaciated mountains covered with perpetual snow; vast, swampy coastal lowlands; very little infrastructure.

Islam – the teachings of the prophet Mohammed professed to by 90% of the Indonesian population. Interpreted more liberally than in other Islamic countries, especially with respect to the position of women.

Istana Negara/Jakarta (G2) – presidential palace.

Istiglal/Jakarta (G2) – largest mosque in Southeast Asia; can seat 20,000.

Jagaraga/Bali (I4) – temple in Sawan south-east of Singaraja with modern-looking reliefs showing Europeans in model-T cars, airplanes and ships. A caricature of the colonial life-style and its destruction by the Hindu powers.

Jago (H8) – belongs to a temple complex in Malang/East Java which dates from different centuries.

Jakarta (G2) – capital of the republic; about 6 million inhabitants (see page).

Jayapura/Irian (E7, 4) – regional capital of Irian.

Jayawijaya/Irian (E7, 5) – Indonesia's highest mountain: 5,030 metres/16,502′.

Jepara/Java (G6) – centre of Javanese woodcarving.

Jiwika/Irian (E7, 6) – place where the people of the Baliem extract salt by traditional methods.

Kalasan temple/Java (H6) – Buddhist mausoleum dating from the year 800 and situated between Yogya and Solo.

Kalimantan (E4) – third-largest island in the world; the northern part (with the exception of Brunei) belongs to Malaysia; aboriginal people are the Dayaks; oil and timber industries.

Kaliurang/C. Java (H6) – mountain resort on the slopes of Mt. Merapi 20 km/12½ miles from Yogya; elevation: 900 m/2,952′, swimming pool.

Kapuas (F3) – Indonesia's longest river, located in western Kalimantan, navigable up to 300–400 km/186–250 miles.

Karo – Batak tribe which lives around Lake Toba consisting of 5 groups and 83 sub-groups. The centre of Karo population is Kaban Yahe.

Kartini – Raden Kartini fought for the Indonesian woman's right to education; died during childbirth at age of 24. Kartini Day is observed in her honour.

Kawah, Lake/E. Java (H9) – crater lake with a diameter of 1.3 km/ 4,625′ near the Ijen Plateau.

Kayan/Kalimantan (E3) – river as well as the name of a Dayak tribe known for their bone carvings.

Kayu putih – eucalyptus tree grown mainly on the Moluccas and in Irian, for pharmaceutical purposes.

Kebayoran – elegant residential suburb of Jakarta.

Kecak – Balinese dance, the so-called "Monkey Dance"; accompanied by a choir of seated men; very expressive.

Keli Mutu/Flores (F5) – volcano containing three lakes, each of a different colour; magnificent scenery.

Kelud Gg./E. Java (H7) – 1,700 m/5,577′-high volcano with a hot crater lake. After an eruption in 1919, thousands of people died in the hot mud flows.

Kendari/S. Sulawesi (B3) – capital, high-quality silverwork, e.g. figures and ornaments.

Kenyan/Kalimantan (D7) – Dayak tribe in the northwestern part of the island; impressive war dances.

Kerinci/C. Sumatra (D7) – highest mountain (volcano) on Sumatra: elevation: 3,100 metres/10,170′; source of many rivers.

Kete Kesu/S. Sulawesi (B2) – characteristic Toraja village in a fascinatingly beautiful region 4 km/about 2½ miles south of Rantepao. Traditional burial site 100 metres from the village; Tau Taus.

Kidal temple/E. Java (H8) – grave of the second Singarasi king located 7 km/about 4½ miles west of Tumpang.

Kintamani/Bali (J5) – village located on the edge of the Batur volcano; pleasant climate, aromatic oranges and passionfruit.

Koran – the holy book of the Moslems.

Kota Gadang/W. Sumatra (C7) – centre of silverworking.

Kota Gede (H6) – centre of Javanese silverworking, south of Yogyakarta.

Krakatoa (F9) – volcano in the Sunda Strait between Sumatra and Java. Greatest eruption known to mankind in 1883. On the site of the volcanic ruin, a new volcano, the Anak Krakatoa, has emerged.

Kraton – sultan's palaces in Central Java, Yogyakarta and Solo.

Kris – double-edged dagger often forged out of meteorite iron. Magical powers are attributed to them; they have more symbolic value than value as a weapon.

Kubu – tribe of hunters and gatherers who live on Sumatra between Bengkulu, Palembang and Jambi.

Kudus/C. Java (G6) – 50 km east of Semarang; centre of clove cigarette industry and Javanese clove production.

Kupang/W. Timor (F5) – 55,000 inhabitants; largest city in the Lesser Sundas; interesting variety of languages and ethnic groups; boat connections to the neighbouring islands.

Kusambe/Bali (K5) – coastal village east of Klungkung; Goalawah (Bat Cave) and temple; highly recommended.

Kuta/Bali (L4) – busy tourist resort in south-west Bali; inexpensive lodgings, performances of traditional dances, good surfing, restaurants of all kinds; overrun in July and August.

Kutai/E. Kalimantan (E4) – Tengarong was the centre of this former sultanate; Kutai Nature Reserve; regular boat connections into the interior.

Ladang – shifting cultivation; arable land acquired by the slash-and-burn method; land remains arable for 3–4 years.

Lawu/C. Java (H6) – 3,265-m-high volcano with interesting temple complex.

Legian/Bali (L4) – small tourist centre north of Kuta; quiet and relaxing.

Legong – one of the most famous classic Balinese dances; performed by three pre-adolescent girls; the theme of the dance is based on the legend of King Lasem and his longing for Princess Langkasari; splendid costumes.

Lembang/W. Java (H3) – suburb of Bandung; mountain village with a planetarium and an SOS Children's Village which does fine relief work; tours to the Tangkuban Prahu volcano.

Lemo/S. Sulawesi (B2) – burial places hewn out of cliffs; characteristic villages in the vicinity, beautiful scenery (see picture section).

Lingga/N. Sumatra (B6) – lovely Karo village 5 km/about 3 miles west of Kabanjahe; 400-year-old houses built without the use of nails; inhabited by extended families, with up to one hundred members.

Lombok/Lesser Sunda Islands (F4) – island east of Bali; Balinese culture predominates on its western coast; east of the Wallace Line, area of transition between Asian and Australian plant and animal kingdoms; Islamic Sasak people in the interior and eastern part of island; 3,375 m/12,385′ high Rincani volcano with large crater lake, second-highest mountain in Indonesia.

Londa/S. Sulawesi – Toraja burial sites in limestone caves with tau tau figures (ancestor images).

Lontar – palm which yields a sweet juice used to make alcoholic beverages; grows in dry zones of the Lesser Sundas; the leaves are used to make an array of everyday articles, e. g. baskets.

Madura (G8) – island east of Java known for its bull races; very dry from April to August; can be reached from Kalimas near Surabaya; hot springs, salt production, cattle-breeding.

Mahabharata – Hindu epic, tells the tale of a battle in ancient India; greatly influenced the modern Indonesian theatre.

Mahakam/E. Kalimantan (E4) – Borneo's second-longest river; ethnically varied population along its banks; Tanjung Issuy is the centre of Dayak culture on the lower course of the river; timber industry.

Majapahit – East Javanese empire which flourished from 1290–1400 A.D.

Makale/S. Sulawesi B– along with Rantepao, this village is a centre of Torajaland; regular bus service to Ujung Pandang.

Makassar – see Ujung Pandang.

Manado/ N. Sulawesi – district capital; centre of Sulawesi's clove production; located in the Minahasa region, population largely Christian, Portuguese descendents; underwater nature reserve near Bunaken.

Mandailing – Batak tribe, best wet-rice farmers; south-west of Lake Toba.

Maninjau/W. Sumatra – picturesque lake in an ancient volcanic crater; inexpensive lodgings, fishing, a favourite with the local people.

Manokwari/Irian – province and capital city on Bird's Head Peninsula; mountainous hinterland, pleasant climate.

Mas/Bali – centre of Balinese woodcarving.

Medan/N. Sumatra – provincial capital with about 1 million inhabitants; several flights daily to Singapore; plantations, palm oil, rubber, international port of Belawan; colourful ethnic mixture: Arabs, Indians, Chinese; palace of the sultan of Deli dates from 1888, colonial buildings around Merdeka Square, Raya Mosque, Gang Bengkok Mosque (17th century), old Dutch forts, Medan Garnison.

Mendut/C. Java – 9th-century temple 3 km/about 1¾ miles east of Borobudur, discovered in 1836! Inside the temple there is a statue of Buddha and two other statues of unknown origin. Over the years, its stupa fell to ruin (see also Candi Pawon).

Mengwi/Bali – centre of the Gelgel Dynasty; temple complex of Pura Taman Ajun, the second-largest and among the most beautiful on Bali.

Mentawai Islands – south-west of Sumatra, includes the islands of Siberut, Sipora and Pagai; tribes of hunters and gatherers with an interesting culture, main source of nutrition is sago, live in longhouses; malaria zone.

Merak/W. Java (G1) – ferryboats to Telukbetung in South Sumatra.

Merapi/C. Java (H6) – 2,991 m/ 9,813′ high active volcano; 1931 eruption caused 1,000 deaths; can be climbed from Boyolali; depending on the weather, there is a danger of noxious gases.

Merapi/E. Java (H9) – 2,800 m/ 9,186′ high volcano northwest of Banyuwangi.

Merauke/Irian – Indonesia's southeasternmost city; dry climate, savannahs, kangaroos, cattle-breeding main source of livelihood.

Minahasa/N. Sulawesi – territory of the Minahasa tribe; interesting grave stones (so-calld warugas).

Minangkabau (C/D7) – West Sumatran tribe centered around Bukit Tinggi; matriarchal society – family business, such as weddings, inheritance, money, is handled by the mother; most beautiful architecture in the archipelago.

Moluccas – island group with a predominantly Melanesian population; spices, kajuh puti oil, fishing; many Portuguese and Dutch fortifications; surat jalan (travel permit) required for the outer islands.

Negritos – original inhabitants of the Indonesian archipelago – were there before the arrival of the proto-Malayans; traces of these people can be found on the Moluccas and in Irian.

Nias/island west of Sumatra (C6) – roundhouses in the north, fortified villages with stilted houses in the south; megalithic culture; stone-jumping and war dances.

Nusa Dua/Bali (L4) – peninsula in the southern part of the island; Ulu Watu sea temple on a cliff, good surfing; plans for a large tourist centre are being made.

Nusa Tenggara – Lesser Sunda Islands.

Padang/W. Sumatra (D7) – provincial capital and main port on Sumatra's west coast; many points of interest in the area, lovely coastal villages and beaches.

Padang Bay/Bali (K6) – small port in southeastern part of the island; boats to Lombok, Nusa Penida and Sumbawa.

Palembang/S. Sumatra (E9) – city of 650,000 inhabitants on the Musi River; Chinatown, Pasa Illir, teeming with activity; centre of the oil-industry on Sumatra; Limas House Museum, relics of the Srivijaja Empire; touristically uninteresting.

Panataren/E. Java (H8) – 80 km/50 miles south-east of Malang; East Java's largest temple complex; dates from the 13th-century Singosari Dynasty.

Panca Sila – the Five Principles (the philosophical foundation of the republic): 1. Belief in God, 2. Humanitarianism, 3. National unity, 4. Democracy guided by consensus, 5. Social justice. In 1945, the Panca Sila was incorporated into the constitution.

Pandaan/E. Java (H8) – 60 km/37 miles south of Surabaya; large open-air amphitheatre. May–October four performances of classic East Javanese dances each month during the full moon period.

Paniai/Irian (E7) – large, flat region covered with lakes discovered by the pilot, Wissel, in 1936; breathtaking lake scenery, territory of the Ekagi and Moni tribes; can be reached by plane from Biak via Nabire.

Papua – dark-skinned inhabitants of New Guinea and neighbouring islands; 800,000 – 1 million in West Irian, 250 different languages spoken.

Parangtritis/C. Java (H6) – beach south of Yogyakarta; beautiful beach but dangerous currents.

Pasir Putih/E. Java (G9) – beautiful white beach west of Panarukan; sea gardens, palm trees, reasonably priced hotels.

Pawon Temple/C. Java (H5) – 9th-century temple located 1 km east of Borobudur; well-preserved, small stupa, lovely statues.

Pekalongan/C. Java (G5) – 90 km – west of Semarang; batik industry, characteristic motifs.

Pekanbaru/C. Sumatra (C7) – oil town on the Siah River; many foreigners; tigers, elephants and other animals still inhabit the surrounding jungles.

Pematang Purba/N. Sumatra (B6) – royal palace of the Simalungun Batak; houses with ornamental carvings.

Pematangsiantar/N. Sumatra (B6) – near Medan; North Sumatra's second-largest town; Simalungan Museum, Pasarbesar (large market), good bargains on handicrafts.

Pencak sila – the Indonesian art of self-defense, similar to Chinese shadow boxing.

Penelokan/Bali (J5) – elevation: 1,400 m/4,953′; on the southern edge of Mt. Batur; do not miss the oranges when they are ripe! Inhabitants rough but friendly.

Plaosan/C. Java (H6) – 9th-century Buddhist temple dedicated to Princess Shailendra; complex divided into several sections; in the middle there are two large, identical temples surrounded by walls and separated from each other by still another wall; 2 km/1¼ miles northeast of Prambanan.

Pontianak/W. Kalimantan (F3) – provincial capital; timber trade and processing; situated directly on the Equator at the mouth of the Kapuas River; regular boat service into the interior.

Prahu – term used for a boat hollowed out of a log (dugout).

Parambanan/C. Java (H6) – temple complex 17 km/10½ miles east of Yogyakarta on the road to Solo; 11th-century Hindu temple; former mausoleum; main temple dedicated to Shiva; temple to the south dedicated to Brahma and the one to the north dedicated to Vishnu; over 30 temples scattered around the immediate vicinity.

Prapat/N. Sumatra (B6) – tourist centre on Lake Toba; boats to Samosir Island in the middle of the lake; wide selection of hotels and losmens; pleasant climate.

Punan – a tribe of hunters and gatherers of the jungles of Kalimantan.

It is said they can follow the tracks of an ant.

Puncak/W. Java (GH2) – mountain pass between Bogor and Bandung (4,921′); cool and misty. Tea producing centre of W. Java; botanical gardens near Cibodas with specimens of mountain flora. Hotels and restaurants.

Pulau Seribu (G2) – Thousand Islands in the Java Sea north of Jakarta. The main island of Pulau Putri is a favourite weekend retreat; hotel, diving, swimming, reservations recommended.

Pulau Mata Hari/Java Sea (G2) – small island paradise in the Pulau Seribu; bamboo huts provide clean lodgings but there is no electricity! The motto here is: "Back to nature". Diving, coconut palms (lacking on Pulau Putri). Reservations at: Tamborah Parawisata, Inc. Jl. Prapanca Raya 24, Jakarta.

Ramayana – Hindu epic consisting of 500 songs and 2,500 verses; tells the story of Rama's wife who was abducted by the Ceylonese king, Rawana. This epic poem which is over 2,000 years old, is known throughout Southeast Asia.

Rantepao/S. Sulawesi (B2) – centre of tourism in Torajaland; its surroundings offer unique scenery and a fascinating culture which features ancestor worship; interesting market.

Ratubarka/C. Java (H6) – remains of a former kraton (9th century) a few miles south of the Prabanan; lies on a slope of Gunung Sewu.

Riau/S. Sumatra (C8) – about 1,000 islands make up this province; oilfields, big game animals in the jungles, malaria zone.

Rinjani/Lombok (F4) – Indonesia's second-highest mountain (11,072′); it is best to approach it from either the north or the south-east; the climb should only be attempted in the dry season.

Ruteng/Flores (F5) – small village in the western part of the island; flights to Ende (Central Flores); a road leading to Reo on the north coast; mountain hikes to typical West Florenese villages can be made from Ruteng; characteristic architecture.

Sago – starch obtained from the pulp of the sago palm; staple diet in coastal lowlands, particularly on the Moluccas and in Irian.

Sadan/S. Sulawesi – centre of weaving in Torajaland.

Samarinda/E. Kalimantan (E4) – provincial capital located at the mouth of the Mahakam River; centre of East Borneo's timber and oil industry.

Samosir/N. Sumatra (B6) – island in the middle of Lake Toba; 600 sq. km/232 sq. miles; inhabited by the Toba Batak; old graves and tombs; the villages of Tomok and Ambarita; Simanindo is especially interesting.

Sangeh/Bali (K4) – Monkey Forest 20 km/12½ miles north of Denpasar near the Bukir Sari Temple.

Sangiran/C. Java (H6) – site of the discovery of the remains of Pithecanthropus erectus; 16 km/10 miles north of Solo; small museum with prehistoric objects.

Sangsit/Bali – typical northern Balinese temple without a merus (see photograph).

Sanskrit – classic language of culture and learning in India; existed as early as 300 B.C.; Indian traders brought it to the archipelago.

Sanur/Bali (L4) – centre of tourism on the southeastern coast 9 km/about 5½ miles east of Denpasar; large international hotels; its beach is protected by a coral reef, making it suitable for children.

Sarangan/C. Java (H6) – lovely village on the banks of a crater lake located between Solo and Madiun; pleasant climate.

Sarong – traditional wrap-around garment whose patterns and form vary from region to region; woven, or printed with batik designs.

Sawah – Indonesian term for wet-rice fields.

Seketan – Yogyakartan celebration in honour of Mohammed's birthday featuring performances on the alun alun (open square) north of the Kraton.

Semarang/C. Java (G5) – administrative centre of Central Java, located on the northern coast; Chinese temple, Klinteng Sam Poo; Tengalwareng Zoo with many species of Indonesian snakes; Baiturahan, the largest and most beautiful mosque in Central Java.

Semeru/E. Java (H8) – 3,677 m/12,063′ high; Java's highest and Indonesia's most beautiful volcano due to its almost perfectly symmetrical cone; a typical composite cone-volcano; ascent takes at least two days.

Sentani/Irian (E7, 8) – chain of lakes connected by a river to the Humboldt Bay. Before World War II, the Sentani villages housed a fascinating culture. Now all that can be seen are houses made of scrap metal collected from wreckage lying about. Jayapura's Sentani Airport is located near these lakes.

Serangan/Bali (L4) – island north-east of the port of Benoa; can be reached by sailboat from Sanur; an annual turtle festival takes place here which ends with the slaughtering of hundreds of sea turtles. This controversial event has been the object of protests from international animal protection societies.

Serimpi – slow dance performed in Central Java; performances can be attended at the Susono Mulyo Dance Academy on Fridays.

Sewu/C. Java (H6) – "The 1,000 Temples" located 1 km/⅝ mile north of the Prambanan; laid out in the shape of a mandala. Largely in ruins; it consisted earlier of one large temple surrounded by 250 smaller ones.

Shiva – the main Hindu god; personifies the original force. Destroyer of the World; source of human fertility.

Sibayak/N. Sumatra (B6) – volcano near Brastagi with a cracked crater; ascent takes 4–5 hours; beautiful scenery.

Siberut/Mantawai (D6) – largest of the Mentawai Islands; very swampy. Afther the island was cleared by woodcutters, a nature reserve was established. Here, there is a species of black monkey unique to this island; interesting native culture. Not recommended for those without some knowledge of Indonesian.

Sibolga/N. Sumatra (B6) – small port on Sumatra's west coast; boats to Telukdalam/S. Nias.

Simalungun – Batak tribe centred around Pematang Purba; former chief's house, architectural style differs from that of the other Batak groups.

Simanindo/Samosir/N. Sumatra (B6) – village in the western part of the island; former king's house; performances of tor tor dances.

Singarak/W. Sumatra (D7) – lake nestled in beautiful surroundings; also known as Lake Maninjau. Accommodation available.

Singaraja/Bali (I4) – district capital on the north coast; harbour and museum.

Singosari/E. Java (H8) – temple in the town of Singosari near Malang, erected by Kertanegara, the last Singosari monarch (1268–1292). Contains some of the ashes of the king, who was murdered by rebels. This temple complex, dedicated to Shiva, is the largest in East Java.

Sipisopiso/N. Sumatra (B6) – waterfall at the northern end of Lake Toba; magnificent scenery, sweeping view of the lake and Samosir Island. Can be reached via Kabanjahe or Seribudolok.

Solo/C. Java (H6) – formerly called **Surakarta;** 66 km/41 miles from Yogyakarta; pop: 650,000. Java's oldest cultural centre and largest batik centre. Information about differences in quality can be obtained at the following factories: Batik Kris, Danar Hadi, Batik Semar. The kratons of Susu hunan and Mangkunegaran are open mornings; Solo Museum has a collection of objects from the early Mataram period as well as a collection of old kris daggers.

Sorong/Irian (E6) – large oil town in the western part of New Guinea. Expensive, lovely location, but little to see.

Spies, Walter – German painter who was influenced by the art, land and life of Bali. His techniques and style, in turn, influenced Balinese painters. Along with the Belgian, Bonnet, whose home is now a museum, and others, he belonged to the European artist's colony on Bali which flourished from 1933–1939.

Sriwiyaya – Buddhist kingdom whose centre was at Palembang/Sumatra; was at the height of its power in the 12th and 13th centuries. Hardly any traces left today.

Stupa – bell-shaped cult symbol or temple construction; burial-place for Buddha relics.

Suharto – born on Java of humble parents in 1921; military career. Led the retaliatory attack during the Communist putsch of 1965. Elected president of the republic by the People's Congress in 1968 and re-elected three times. Only responsible to the People's Congress.

Sukarno – became first president of the republic in 1945; established the Partei Nasional Indonesia; repeatedly imprisoned by the Dutch. His power faded after the Communist putsch of 1965. Died in 1970.

Sukuh/C. Java (H6) – temple complex on the slopes of Mt. Lawu east of Solo; at an elevation of 900 m/ 2,952′. View of the Central Javanese plains. This temple shows great similarities to the Mayan temples of Central America. Dedicated to the god Bima and dates from the 15th century. Explicitly erotic images.

Sulawesi/Greater Sunda Islands (formerly Celebes) – great ethnic diversity, mountainous, dry zones. Tourism in Torajaland; 9.3 million people; main cities are Ujung Pandang, Kendari, Manado. Northern portion of the island covered by tropical rainforest.

Sulukang/S. Sulawesi (B2) – remote village 3 km/about 1¾ miles from Kete Kusu; gravesite with tau tau figures.

Sultan Agung – 1613–1645; Javanese ruler and enemy of the Dutch East India Co.; unsuccessfully beseiged Batavia with an army of 30,000 men.

Sumatra/Greater Sunda Islands – 1,750 km/1,087 miles long, 400 km/248 miles at its widest point. More than 20 million inhabitants. Bukit Barisan Mountain Range divides the island lengthwise; lowland plains overgrown with mangroves, vast, continuous jungle lands. Wide variety of animals, ethnic diversity. Oil and timber industries; main cities are Medan, Palembang, Banda Aceh and Padang.

Sumba/Lesser Sunda Islands (F4, 5) – dry, eucalyptus forests and savannahs. Horse-breeding, sandalwood and cinnamon. Main city is Waingappu. Boats to Flores and Sumbawa; known for ikat, a method of decorating cloth.

Sumbawa/Lesser Sunda Islands (F4) – north-west of Sumba; dry climate, bushlands and savannahs, volcanic ridge in the south; 360,000 mostly Moslem inhabitants. Towns: Bima, Sumbawa Besar.

Sumberawan/E. Java (H8) – one of the two stupas in East Java; near Singosari.

Sundanese – ethnic group of West Java; lively dances; kecapi-suling orchestra with violin-like instruments. Best-known Sundanese instrument is the angklung which consists of bamboo pipes of different lengths suspended in a frame.

Surabaya/E. Java (G8) – Indonesia's second-largest city; 3.5 million inhabitants. International port, centre of industry. Zoo and sea aquarium; amusement park with traditional dance and theatre performances. Tunjungan Shopping Centre for good buys.

Tamansari/Yogyakarta (H6) – former pleasure park of the Yogya Kraton; today centre of independent batik artists.

Tambora/Sumbawa (F4) – 2,755 m/9,039′ high volcano; the eruption of 1815 cost over 10,000 people their lives.

Tanah Lot/Bali (K4) – Bali's most beautiful sea temple; located on a black volcanic rock. A shrine – dedicated to the gods of the sea – can be approached via Kedira.

Tondano/N. Sulawesi (E5) – beautiful lake in the Minahasa region. Inexpensive accommodation; friendly people; clove production.

Tanimbar/S. Moluccas (F6) – island group consisting of more than 50 islands. Colourful mixture of peoples: Papuans, Negritos, Melanesians with diverse customs. Saumlaki Airport on Jamdena.

Tanjung Issuy/E. Kalimantan (E4) – first village with Dayak longhouses on the Mahakam River. Interesting market frequented by people of many different tribes.

Telaga Warna/W. Java (GH2) – lake which changes colour. Here, around the Puncak Pass, the best tea is grown.

Teluk Dalam/S. Nias (C6) – small port in southern part of the island. Connections to Sibolga on Sumatra and Gunungsitoli/Nias from where there are flights to Medan. Bawamataluo, Hilisimaetano and La Gundi in the vicinity. The latter is a surfer's paradise, and offers better accommodation.

Tenganan/Bali (K6) – located between Klungkung and Amlapura. One of the few villages on Bali still inhabited by the aboriginal Bali Aga; these people live by their own rules.

Tengger/E. Java (H8) – area around Mt. Bromo. Traces of a Hindu-Buddhist culture with a caste system similar to that on Bali. Inhabitants preserved this culture which originated during the Majapahit Empire, by retreating to this mountain region.

Ternate/N. Moluccas (E5) – circular island with three volcanoes; known in the 17th century thanks to its cloves. First in the possession of the Portuguese and the Spanish, later taken over by the Dutch; many forts and ruins from colonial times. The following forts are worth seeing: Benteng Oranje in Ternate, Toloko in Dufa Dufa, Kaju Merah in Kalumata, Kastella in Kastela.

Tidore/N. Moluccas (E5) – former sultanate south of Ternate; 1,730 m/ 5,676′ high volcano. Rum is a lovely old town in the northern part of the island with thick walls and an old fort; interesting market.

Timor/Lesser Sunda Islands (F5) – once divided into West Timor (Indonesia) and Portuguese East Timor. As of 1975, the latter belongs to Indonesia as well. Towns: Dilli and Kupang; dry and mountainous countryside, savannahs; cattle-breeding, sandalwood; Atoni (Austronesian aboriginal people) live in the island's mountainous interior.

Tirtha Empul/Bali (J5) – bathing-place near Tampaksiring fed from a holy well, which is thought to have curative powers. Lovely temple nearby.

Toba, Lake/N. Sumatra (B6) – covers area of about 1,300 sq. km/ 502 sq. miles. Lies in a magnificent volcanic crater. In the middle of the lake lies Samosir Island (about 293 sq. miles). Lake reaches depths of 450 m/1,476′.

Tomok/Samosir (B6) – village with burial grounds, stone sarcophagus of King Sidabutar, mausoleums. Traces of megalithic Batak culture; typical Toba Batak houses.

Toraja/S. Sulawesi (B2) – a proto-Malayan people numbering 350,000. Former headhunters. Now 45% Christians. Ancestor worship, fascinating cult of the dead. Unique way of life. Impressive architecture. Torajaland is an area of beautiful scenery.

Trowulan/E. Java (H7) – former centre of the Majapahit Empire located 60 km/37 miles south of Singosari. Attractions: museum, remains of the palace of Gajah Mada (influential prime minister to King Hajam who increased the standing of the kingdom in the 14th century).

Trunyan/Bali (J5) – Bali Aga village on the eastern bank of Lake Batur. They do not burn their dead, here, but rather, leave them out to decompose. A small contribution is asked of people wishing to visit the cemetery.

Tuk Tuk/N. Sumatra (B6) – peaceful village on Samosir. Batak houses can be rented by tourists; there are also hotels, swimming.

Ubud/Bali (K4) – centre of Balinese culture (dance, music and painting); palaces; Puri Lukisan Art Museum contains the best collection of modern Balinese painting.

Ujung Kulon/W. Java (H1) – wildlife reserve with the last of the Javanese one-horned rhinos. Waterfalls, rainforests and swamps, provide an ideal retreat for many animal species; gibbons, crocodiles, hornbills, deer, panthers, some tigers, buffalos, etc. Agaphos, Jl. Gajah mada 16, Jakarta, specializes in tours through the nature reserves. Best time to visit Ujung Kulon is from April to October.

Ujung Pandang/S. Sulawesi (C2) – former name: Makassar; provincial capital; Paotere Harbour with Buginese schooners; Fort Rotterdam,

Shell Museum and other museums. Small coral islands 2–3 hours from the city; Boletambu (reachable by motorboat) is a miniature paradise.

Uludanu Temple/Bali (J4) – see Bedugul.

Ulu Watu/Bali (L4) – sea temple on 295′ high cliff, on the peninsula of Nusa Dua; according to legend, it is a ship turned to stone; good surfing conditions.

Vishnu – all-encompassing Hindu divinity, the guardian of the world.

Waicak – celebration to commemorate Buddha's enlightenment which originated in 5th-century India. During the full moon in May, Buddhists from Indonesia, Thailand and Sri Lanka come to the Borobudur for this celebration.

Wamena/Irian (E7, 9) – main community in the Baliem Valley; interesting market; beautiful surroundings; point of departure for camping tours. Hotel Nayak and Hotel Baliem are the only accommodation – very modest. Inhabited by Papuans and transmigrants from other parts of Indonesia.

Wayang – means "shadow". The different forms of wayang include:
Wayang orang – plays performed by actors (Java).
Wayang kulit – shadow plays (Java and Bali).
Wayang golek – puppet plays (West Java).
Wayang kulit is over 2,000 years old. Approximately 300 different figures are manipulated by one man alone, the dalang.

Yogyakarta/C. Java (H6) – centre of the Sultanate of Yogyakarta which still exists today. Local point of tourism on Java; university, batik industry; Sultan's Palace open daily until noon. Sono Budoyo Museum exhibits Javanese and Balinese art; performances of the Ramayana epic in the Lorojonggrang open-air theatre near Prambanan on evenings with a full moon from June through October. Traditional dance academies. Yogyakarta offers every form of accommodation from a four-star hotel to an inexpensive losmen.

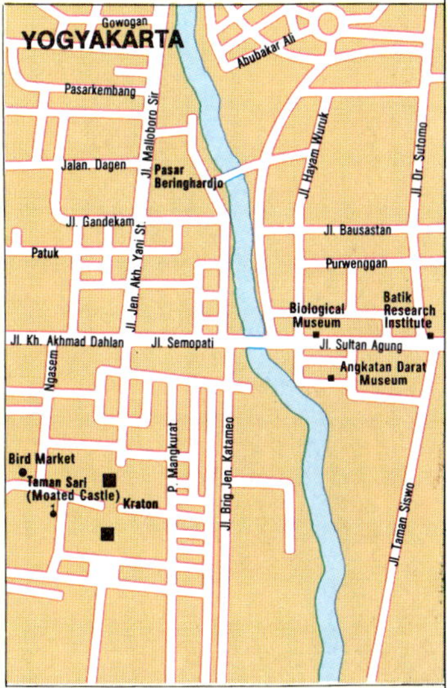

BURMA
Rangoon
THAILAND
LAOS
VIETNAM
Bangkok
KAMPUTSCHEA
Phnom Penh
Ho-Chi-Minh-Town
(Saigon)
Manila
PHILIPPINES
Banda Aceh
MALAYSIA
Medan
Pemantangsiantar
Toba-See
Prapat
Sibolga
Nias
Telukdalam
Pekanbaru
Riau
Singapur
City
Bengkulu
Padang
Batusangkar
Siberut
Kerinci
Sumatra
Bangka
Palembang
Kuching
Pontianak
Kalimantan
(Borneo)
Samarinda
INDONESIA
Bajarmasin
Greater Sunda Islands
Ujung Pandang
Makassar
Sulawesi
(Celebes)
Rantepao
Toraja
Makale
Kendari
Tondano
Ternate
Tidore
Halmahera
Biak
Sorong
Irian
Ceram
Ambon
Tanimbar
Enggano
Pulau
Seribu
Banten
Jakarta
Ujung Kulon
Bogor
Bandung
Java
Yogyakarta
Semarang
Kudus
Surakarta/Solo
Madura
Surabaya
Banyuwangi
Bali
Denpasar
Lombok
Sumbawa
Bima
Flores
Ende
Lesser Sunda Islands
Timor
Kupang
AUSTRALIA
INDONESIA
0 500 miles

Useful Information

Currency

The currency of Indonesia is the rupiah (Rp). 1 Rp = 100 sen. Because of their slight value, however, sen are no longer in circulation. The import and export of Indonesian currency exceeding a value of Rp 50,000 is prohibited; there are no restrictions on foreign currency and traveller's cheques, however. While in the cities the exchange rate for traveller's cheques is often better than that for cash, the opposite can hold true in the remote parts of the country. As the value of the rupiah is based on the U. S. dollar, a better rate of exchange can often be obtained for that currency.

Passports, Visas

Nationals of the following countries need only a valid passport for visits of up to two months: Australia, Canada, New Zealand, United Kingdom, United States of America and 21 other countries. The passport must be valid for at least six months after the date of arrival (the period of validity is entered in the passport upon arrival). Special visas are required for business trips and for longer stays.

Vaccinations

International certificates of valid smallpox and cholera vaccinations no longer required, but a cholera vaccination is recommended. A preventive treatment against malaria is strongly recommended for those visiting elevations of less than 1,200 metres/3,937′ (including cities). Up-to-date information on recommended forms of prevention should be obtained as there are plasmodia strains in Indonesia which are resistant to the usual Malaria prophylaxis.

Medicine Kit

Besides personally-required medicines in ample amounts, one should also include something for stomach upsets and intestinal disorders. Other important remedies include: disinfectants or penicillin powder for sores, a cream to protect you from the sun and allergy pills should you be sensitive to insect bites, etc.

Hints on Health

It is advisable to heed the following: Drink only boiled water. Fruit should be washed before peeling, as bacteria on the peel can be passed on via the hands. Except on the beach, do not go barefoot (danger of picking up hookworms). Drink plenty of fluids and eat well-salted foods to prevent dehydration and desalination (caused by heavy perspiring). In the case of faintnes, salt tablets also help. Shower 2–3 times daily, but avoid the use of soap. Avoid drinking alcoholic beverages before sundown. Exaggerated health precautions should be avoided as well. In areas where malaria and filariasis are endemic (Irian), the use of a mosquito net is recommended despite any malaria tablets you may be taking.

Medical care
Doctors and hospital care are available in the tourist centres. In most areas of the country, however, there is a shortage of physicians and hospital beds. The large international hotels have their own house physicians. In the case of an emergency, the embassy or cunsulate of one's country can advise and assist.

Clothing
Light clothing, of cotton or linen is best; a sweater or pullover is needed in mountain areas. In addition to summer shoes (sandals), sturdy footwear and rainwear should also be brought along. In Indonesia itself, you can buy reasonably priced batik dresses and shirts, which certainly are best suited to the country and the climate. Hats of all shapes and sizes are also available on the spot. Suits and evening wear are only required when making official calls or for formal occasions.

Customs Regulations
Items brought in for one's personal use are duty-free provided they are taken out again upon departure. Every visitor over the age of 16 may import up to 400 cigarettes, 150 cigars, or 300 g of tobacco, as well as up to two litres of alcoholic beverages. The importation of drugs and pornographic material is prohibited. Written permission must be obtained before importing animals and firearms. There are no restrictions on the exportation of souvenirs which have no museum value.

Transport
Taxis from the airport to the hotels of downtown Jakarta cost between 2,000 and 3,000 rupiahs. The meters in the blue Blue Bird Taxis are always in working order – always insist that the meter be turned on. There are also buses into the city, but they are slow and overcrowded. Many of the large hotels provide a bus service for their guests.

Hours of Business
Government offices:
Mon–Thurs, 8:00 am–3:00 pm
Fri, 8:00–11:30 am
Sat, 8:00 am–2:00 pm
Business offices:
Mon–Fri, 8:00 am–4:00 or 5:00 pm
Saturdays, half-day
Banks:
Mon–Fri, 8:00 or 8:30 am–12:00 or 1:00 pm; Sat, 9:00 am–12:00 noon
Moneychangers stay open well into the evening.

In the terminal at **Jakarta's Halim Airport** there are branches of Bank Bumi Daya and Bank Negara (it pays to compare rates!), as well as a post-office counter and a tourist information desk which is rarely manned!

The **Ngurah Airport** on Bali has a bank and a post-office counter. Taxis must be booked and paid for at a special stand (simple and fast, but not exactly cheap). The large hotels have reservation counters here as well.

Shops are open from 8:00 am–8:00 pm and longer, but some of them close at noontime. It must be taken into consideration that Moslems go to the mosque on Fridays and that offices may therefore close earlier. Large department stores such as the Sarinah Department

Store stay open all week, long into the evening hours. In remote provinces, business hours can vary from these norms.

Post and telephone services

Post offices are open:
Mon–Thurs, 8:00 am–2:00 pm
Fri, 7:00–11:30 am
Sat, 7:00 am–1:00 pm
Large hotels have their own postal counters. Telegrammes can be sent from all post offices as well as from large hotels. Telephone calls to many countries can be made through International Direct Dialing.

Time

There are three time zones in Indonesia. West Indonesian Standard Time (Sumatra, Java, Bali) is 7 hours ahead of Greenwich Mean Time; Central Indonesian Standard Time (Kalimantan, Sulawesi, Nusa Tenggara) is 8 hours ahead of GMT; and East Indonesian Standard Time (Moluccas and Irian) is 9 hours ahead of GMT.

Mains Voltage

In most hotels the voltage is 220 AC; in some areas, 110 volts is still used. Large hotels provide plug adapters when necessary. Black-outs may occur during the rainy season.

Taxis, Car Hire

Taxis are available in most cities. Insist on the use of the taxi meter or have the hotel negotiate the price in advance. The following guidelines may be of service to those who negotiate fares themselves:
In the cities: about Rp 4,000 per hour (minimum: 2 hours);
Rp 25,000–35,000 per day (8–10 hours).
In the country: about Rp 2,500 per hour (minimum: 2 hours);
Rp 15,000–25,000 per day (8–10 hours).
When a taxi is hired for an entire day, the driver should be given a tip of Rp 500–1,000.

One should drive a hired car oneself only after having carefully studied the traffic conditions in Indonesia (driving is on the left). Traffic regulations are rather freely interpreted. In the event of an accident, Indonesian motorists are often not in a position to cover the damage – a general system of insurance protection is only just being developed. On Bali and in Central Java, bicycles and motorcycles can be hired. For the latter, an international driving licence valid for class A is required. Chickens, dogs and water buffalos can make riding a motorcycle a very stressful undertaking. High accident rate among tourists!

Entrance fees

Entrance is charged for must cultural attractions – a permit to take pictures most often be purchased in addition. Visitors to Torajaland (Sulawesi) must pay a tourist tax of Rp 1,000. In villages which are frequently visited by tourists, one is often asked to sign a guestbook and to make a contribution toward the upkeep of that village's attractions.

Guides

Authorized, multi-lingual guides can be obtained by applying to the offices of tourist information. Large hotels and travel agencies can also be of assistance. Specialized guides

are available in museums, palaces, temples and the like.

Reading material
Foreign newspapers and periodicals usually appear on the newsstands of international hotels two to four days late.

Laundry service
The laundry service provided by the large hotels is, as a rule, fast and reliable. There are only a few dry cleaners in the cities. The dry cleaners in Hotel President, Jl. Thamrin 59, Jakarta is also open to the general public.

Tipping
In large hotels and restaurants, a service charge is added to the bill. If not, 10 per cent is usual. Porters, pages and taxi drivers customarily receive Rp 200 for their services. A 500-rupiah note would brighten up the day of someone who has rendered you a special service.

Departure
Individual travellers must have their return flight confirmed three days before departure. Airline counters open two hours before the scheduled departure of the flight. An exit permit is required only of those who have been in the country for more than six months.

Airport tax
An airport tax of Rp 1,200 for domestic flights and Rp 3,000 for inter-

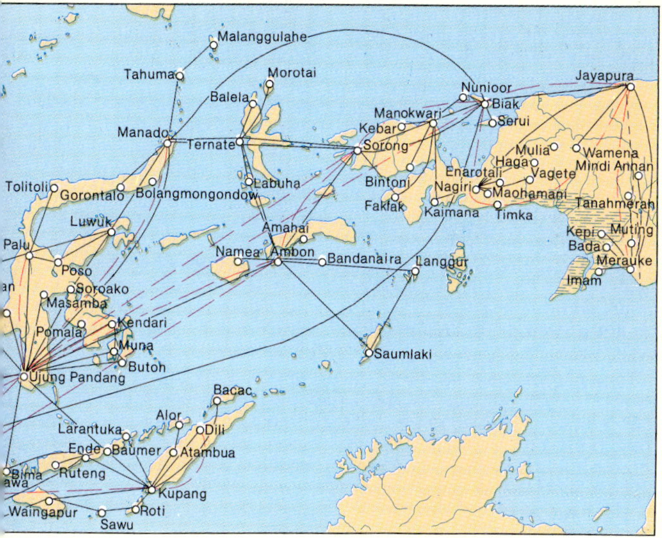

national flights is levied at Jakarta's Halim and Kemayoran Airports, as well as at Bali's Ngurah Rai Airport. The tax charged at other airports varies from Rp 700 to 1100 for domestic flights and Rp 1,800 and 2,550 for international flights. Transit passengers are exempt from paying the airport tax; they must remain in the transit terminal, however.

Shopping

Those looking for souvenirs and gifts can choose from a wide selection of items displaying excellent craftsmanship and artistic flair. One should take one's time shopping, however, in order to compare prices and quality. Through adept bargaining, one can obtain discounts of up to 30 per cent on the asking price. It should be kept in mind, however, that these low prices are made possible by the low wages paid in Indonesia. In shops and department-stores, prices are fixed. The most popular souvenirs – batik products, silverware, woodcarvings, leatherwork. Bronze and stone replicas of old Buddhas and Hindu deities are also sought after. Objects characteristic of Indonesian culture, such as wavang puppets, kris daggers and dance masks, are also firm favourites. Some tourists even go to the length of transporting life-size wooden statues, or a complete set of rattan living-room furniture. Many art shops can help with export formalities and arrange transport.

Those who buy direct from the producer can be sure of getting high quality at a low price. If the price is quoted in dollars, you can be sure it is higher than average. The following is a list of crafts and the centres where they are produced:

Silverwork: Kendari/Sulawesi, Celuk/Bali, Kota Gede/Central Java, Kota Gadang/West Sumatra.

Woodcarving: Mas/Bali, Asmat/Irian, Jepara/Central Java.

Batik: Solo/Central Java, Yogyakarta/Central Java.

Basket-weaving: Tasikmalaya/West Java.

When purchasing batik, one should know that stamped or cap batik is less expensive than the prized printed batik or batik tulis. Those who shop in established batik factories avoid the danger of ending up with mass-produced goods from Singapore or Hong Kong.

Some addresses:
Silver: M.D. Silver
Jl. Kebon, Kota Gede,
Nr. Yogyakarta/Java
Batik: Koesnadi
Jl. Kadipaten Kidul 16
Yogyakarta/Java
Woodcarving: Sjadja
Mas, Gianjar/Bali.
Panjang
Jl. Pemuda 25
Jepara/C. Java
Paintings: Wayan Gerendeng
Jl. Hutan Kera
Ubud/Bali

Bandung and Ubud are the centres of Indonesian painting. The work of Ubud's artists, in particular, has acquired a certain amount of fame beyond Indonesia's borders. In Jakarta. Their paintings command two to three times the price asked in the village itself.

At the flea market on Jalan Surabay, the varied assortment of Indonesian crafts can be taken in at a glance. Often, one can find skilfully made copies side-by-side with genuine antiques; when in doubt, one should obtain a confirmation from the merchant to the effect that the object is not one of national importance. This applies, in particular, to stone figures, which are often very difficult to distinguish from originals. It is advisable to avoid purchasing silver coins, as most of the ones offered for sale are counterfeit; precious and semi-precious stones, as well, are, in most cases, only good imitations. The Sarinah Department Store on Jl. Thamrin has a vast selection of typical Indonesian souvenirs.

Please note:
In accordance with the "**C**onvention on **I**nternational **T**rade in **E**ndangered **S**pecies of Wild Fauna and Flora in Commerce" (**CITES**), you should make a point of not buying any souvenirs, the production of which involves the use of wild animals or wild flowers.

In Indonesia's case this applies to ivory (trading in ivory from Asian elephants, including tame elephants, is forbidden), tortoiseshell, rhinoceros horns, butterflies, products from reptiles (lizard skins!) and various types of birds. Don't let yourself be pursuaded to buy one of the young monkeys so often on offer – licenses for private ownership do not exist!

Prices

It's as well to remember how unstable the value of money is nowadays. Many Third World countries are struggling with a high inflation rate and prices change from day to day.

Prices vary greatly from province to province – for example, the Moluccas and Irian are considerably more expensive than Java or Bali. First rule of world travel: Ask the price first!

Hotels

Of all the Indonesian islands, Java and Bali offer the largest selection of accommodation. In addition to Jakarta, which has several five-star hotels, the other large cities of the two islands offer accommodation which fall into the remaining categories, which, however, are equipped, for the most part, with air-conditioning. In small hotels, losmens and cottages, on the other hand, it is much easier to get in touch with the local population because of the atmosphere that often prevails. Accommodation can sometimes pose a problem on the small outer islands of the archipelago. Often, one must resort to using private lodgings. In remote areas, the teacher, pastor, policeman or missionary, is often prepared to put up travellers for a small fee. In any event, a tent should be brought along on hikes in uninhabited or sparsely inhabited areas.

Information concerning accommodation can be obtained from the Directorate General of Tourism or from Garuda Indonesian Airways.

Sports

Jakarta offers many opportunities for sports lovers, be they participants or spectators. Besides football matches in Senajan Stadium, tennis, gold and horse-racing, dog-races are held three times weekly in the Canidrome. Those who enjoy swimming should head for Bina Ria Amusement Park which is located on the coast. There, the hottest hours of the day can be whiled away at the modern swimming pool complete with waterfall, waves and currents and gigantic slides. The nearby sea, on the other hand, is far less enticing. Every evening, the ball game of jai alai attracts hundreds of spectators to Bina Ria, who have succumbed to the sport of betting.

Aquatic sports obviously have special status here on the Indonesian islands. Windsurfing is gaining great popularity alongside ordinary surfing – some hotels, such as the Hotel Krakatau at Charita Beach near Labuan, are keeping up with the trend by renting out complete sets of windsurfing equipment. This hotel also offers diving equipment and expertise together with the opportunity to engage in many other types of sports. On Bali and in North Sulawesi, as well, divers can get in touch with reliable instructors, who have the necessary experience and technical know-how at their command:

Nusantara Diving Club,
Malalayang 1, P.O. Box 15,
Manado/N. Sulawesi.
P.T. Baruna Watersports,
Jl. Seruni 21, Denpasar/Bali.

Entertainment

Those seeking entertainment in Indonesia will not be disappointed either. Follow the loud posters to one of the countless cinemas where European and American films (often censored) can be seen in addition to Indonesian, Indian and Chinese films (usually with English subtitles). Those who prefer the traditional forms of entertainment can attend one of the many dance, theatre and shadow play performances that take place on Java and Bali, and usually continue on until sunrise (though tourist versions only last about two hours). Nightlife in the big cities of Jakarta, Surabaya and Semarang is no longer the monopoly of the big hotels, but is spreading more and more to other areas of the cities. In these cities, which virtually never close down, the novice should avoid spending a night on the town alone. For information on what's going on in Jakarta, consult the English-language dailies, "Indonesian Observer" and "Indonesian Times". Information can also be obtained from local tourist offices or from hotel reception clerks.

Official Holidays (with fixed dates):
1st January – New Years Day;
30th January – Birth of Mohammed (Maulid Nabi Muhammed);
17th August – Independence Day;
19th October – Islamic Pilgrims Day (Idul Adak); 25th December – Christmas Day.

Official Holidays (dates vary from year to year):
Good Friday, Easter Sunday, Ascension, Islamic New Year (Muharam), White Sunday, Ascension of the Prophet Mohammed (Mi'raj Nabi Mohammed), Idul Fitri (see Ramadan).

Semi-official Holidays:
21st April – Kartini Day (A day on which women attend parades etc. and which is devoted to them. In her writings, Kartini first drew attention to the plight of women in Javanese society); 10th November – Heroes Day; 31st December – New Year's Eve.

Chinese Holiday:
End of January/Beginning of February: Chinese New Year.

Ramadan

Ramadan, the period of fasting, takes place in the ninth month of the Muslim year. Strict fasting is observed by Muslims during all daylight hours of Ramadan (during this time they will eat 2–3 times at night). The end of the period of fasting is marked by the celebration of Idul Fitri. Since the Islamic calendar is based upon special astronomical rules, Ramadan and Idul Fitri fall at different times each year.

Celebrations and Ceremonies

Indonesia is a state which is made up of many different peoples so it's not really feasible to draw up a comprehensive list of all celebrations. Dates are also a problem. The Balinese calendar, for example, consists of 210 days and this means that the Odalan celebrations (anniversary of a temple) take place at different times each year – from our point of view. The calendar of the Bataker people (North Sumatra) is different again.

To find out about the celebrations and events which will take place during a visit to Indonesia, it's a good idea to get hold of the "Calendar of Events" which the Ministry of Communication and Tourism publishes every year.
Apply to
Directorate General of Tourism (DGT)
Jl. Kramat Raya 81/P. O. Box 409
Tel.: 34 90 01–6
Jakarta
or ask at an Indonesian Tourist Office.

Foreign Embassies and Consulates

Any tourist information office or your travel agent should be able to give you the address of your embassy or consulate.

We would advise you to keep the address and telephone number handy in case of loss or damage to personal property, or should you require re-patriation.

Indonesia Tourist Promotion Offices Overseas

Europe

Indonesia Tourist Promotion Office
Wiesenhüttenplatz 26
D 6000 Frankfurt am Main 1
Phone: (069)23 56 81
Telex: 04 18 91 86 ITPBD
Cable: INDOTOUR, West Germany

North America

Indonesia Tourist Promotion Office
323 Geary Street, Suite 305
San Francisco, CA 94102
Phone: (4 15)9 81–35 85
Telex: 34 05 54
Cable: INDOTOUR, San Francisco, USA

Japan

Indonesia Tourist Promotion Office
Asia Trans Co.
2nd Floor Sankaido Building
1–9–13 Akasaka, Minato-ku, Tokyo
Phone: 5 85 35 88, 5 82 13 31
ext. 15–16
Telex: J. 2 29 90
Cable: ASTRAJUG TOKYO, Japan

Asia
Indonesia Tourist Promotion Office
c/o Indonesian Embassy
"Wisma Indonesia"
435, Orchard Road, Singapore
Phone: 2 35 12 68
Telex: INDO S. P. R S. 3 57 31
INTOUR
Cable: INDOTOUR – Singapore

Australia
Public Relations Agencies
Garuda Indonesian Airways Office
4, Bligh Street, P. O. Box 3836
Sydney N. S. W. 2000
Phone: 2 32–60 44
Telex: 2 25 76
Welbeck International Public Relations
6th Floor, Westfield Towers
100 William Street, King Cross: 2011
Pitts Point, 2011,
Sydney N. S. W. 2000
Phone: (02)3 57 18 44
Telex: 2 12 72

Tourist Information
Directorate General of Tourism (DGT)
Jl. Kramat Raya 81 – PO Box: 409, Jakarta
with further branch offices in:

Bali, Jl. Raya Puputan, Kompleks Nitimandala, Renon-Denpasar;

Central Java, Jl. Veteran 65, Semarang, Tel.: 31 46 69;

East Java, Jl. Ayani 242–244 Surubaja, Tel.: 81 53 12, 81 22 91;

West Java, Jl. K.H. Pengh, M. Mustafa, Bandung, Tel.: 7 23 55;

Jakarta, DK1 Jl. Gatot Subrato, Tel.: 51 17 42 (for Jakarta and vicinity);

Yogyakarta, Jl. Adisucipto (near the airport) PO Box 64, Tel.: 51 50;

North-Sulawesi, Jl. Diponegoro 111, Manado, Tel. 5 17 23;

South Sulawesi, Jl. A. Pangeran Peta Ani, Ujung Pandang, Tel.: 2 11 42;

North Sumatra, Jl. Alfalah 29, Medan, Tel.: 2 20 99;

West Sumatra, Jl. Khatib Sularman Padang (baru), Tel.: 2 32 31, 22 18

Information on other provinces or regions can be obtained from the offices of regional tourism which are identifiable by the abbreviations DIPARDA or BAPPARDA. In some cases they are housed in the Kantor Gubernur of the respective provincial capital.

Literature
Quite a lot has been written about different aspects of Indonesia. As a general guide, Bill Dalton's Indonesia Handbook, can be recommended. This informative book is published by Moon Publications, Chico, USA.

International Direct Dialling

	Telephone Code		Telephone Code
Algeria	00213	New Zealand	0064
Australia	0061	Norway	0047
Austria	0043	Nigeria	00234
Argentina	0054	Netherlands	0031
Antilen (Netherlands)	00599	Papua New Guinea	00675
Bahrain	00973	Philippines	0063
Belgium	0032	Poland	0048
Brazil	0055	Portugal	00351
Chili	0056	Samoa (USA)	00624
Columbia	0057	Singapore	0065
Czechoslovakia	0046	Roumania	0040
Denmark	0045	South Korea	0082
Egypt	0020	Sri Lanka	0094
East Germany	0037	Sweden	0046
France	0033	Saudi Arabia	00966
Greece	0030	Switzerland	0041
Gabon	00241	Spain	0034
Hawaii (USA)	001808	Taiwan	00886
Hong Kong	00852	Thailand	0066
India	0091	Turkey	0090
Indonesia	0062	Unite Arab Emirate	00971
Iceland	00354	United Kingdom	0044
Iraq	00964	U.S.A. (Mainland)	001
Japan	0081	West Germany	0049
Kuwait	00695	Yugoslavia	0038
Luxemburg	0352		
Malaysia	0067		
Malawi	00265		
Mexico	00052		

Emergency Calls

Telephone	:	108
Long Distance Overseas	:	101/102
Long Distance	:	100
Ambulance	:	118–119
Time	:	103
City Hall (Jakarta)	:	370909

Intercity Telephone Code (Long Distance Direct Dialling)			
City	**Telephone Code**	**City**	**Telephone Code**
Ambon	0311	Mataram	0364
Balikpapan	0542	Medan	061
Banda Aceh	0651	Merauke	0971
Bandung	022	Mojokerto	0321
Banjarmasin	0511	Padang	0751
Banyuwangi	0333	Pekanbaru	0761
Bekasi	0219	Palembang	0711
Bengkulu	0736	Palangkaraya	0541
Biak	0961	Pamekasan	0324
Binjai	0619	Parapat	0622
Blitar	0342	Pasuruan	0343
Bogor	0251	Pare-Pare	0421
Bojonegoro	0353	Pati	0295
Bondowoso	0332	Pekalongan	0285
Bukittinggi	0752	Pematang Sianta	0622
Cianjur	0263	Ponorogo	0351
Cibinong	0219	Pontianak	0561
Cimahi	0229	Prigen	0343
Cipanas	0255	Probolinggo	0335
Cirebon	0231	Purwakarta	0281
Denpasar	0361	Purwokerto	0281
Gadog/Cisarua	0251	Sabang	0652
Garut	0262	Salatiga	0298
Gresik	0319	Samarinda	0541
Jakarta	021	Semarang	024
Jambi	0741	Serang	0254
Jayapura	0967	Sidoarjo	0319
Jember	0311	Situbondo	0332
Jombang	0331	Solo	0271
Kebumen	0287	Sorong	0951
Kediri	0354	Sukabumi	0266
Kendal	0294	Sumbawa Besar	0371
Kisaran	0623	Sumedang	0261
Karawang	0264	Surabaya	031
Klaten	0272	Tangerang	0219
Kudus	0291	Tanjungkarang	0721
Kupang	0391	Tasikmalaya	0265
Lahat	0731	Tebingtinggi	0621
Lumajang	0334	Tegal	0283
Madiun	0351	Ternate	0921
Magelang	0293	Tulungagung	0355
Malang	0341	Ujungpandang	0411
Manado	0431	Yogyakarta	0274
Manokwari	0962		

Long distance direct dialling can be achieved by firstly dialling the code number followed by the local number desired.

Indonesia
Currency in circulation:

Notes:	Coins:
Rupiah 100, 500, 1,000, 5,000, 10,000	Rupiah 10, 25, 50, 100

When travelling in remote areas bring along plenty of change, as 10,000 rupiah notes are frequently not accepted.

Attention!

All prices and currency indications were accurate at the time of printing. As it is not possible for any travel guide to keep up with the constantly changing rates of exchange, you are advised to contact your bank regarding the current rates.

The publishers would be pleased to have your opinion regarding any omissions or alterations.

Contents

Photographs

Impressions

Information

Regional Section

Personal Notes

Personal Notes